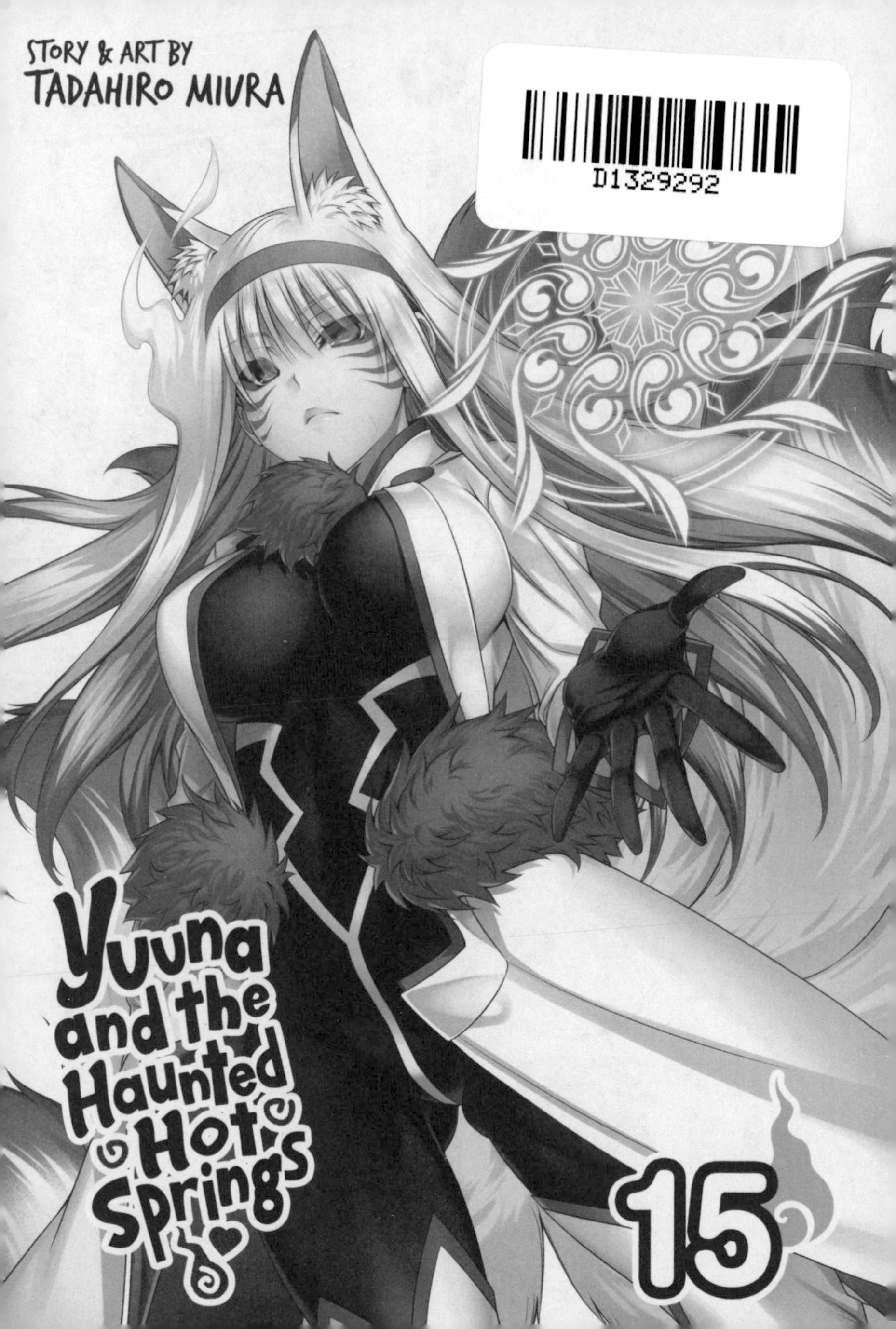
STORY & ART BY
TADAHIRO MIURA
Yuuna and the Haunted Hot Springs
15

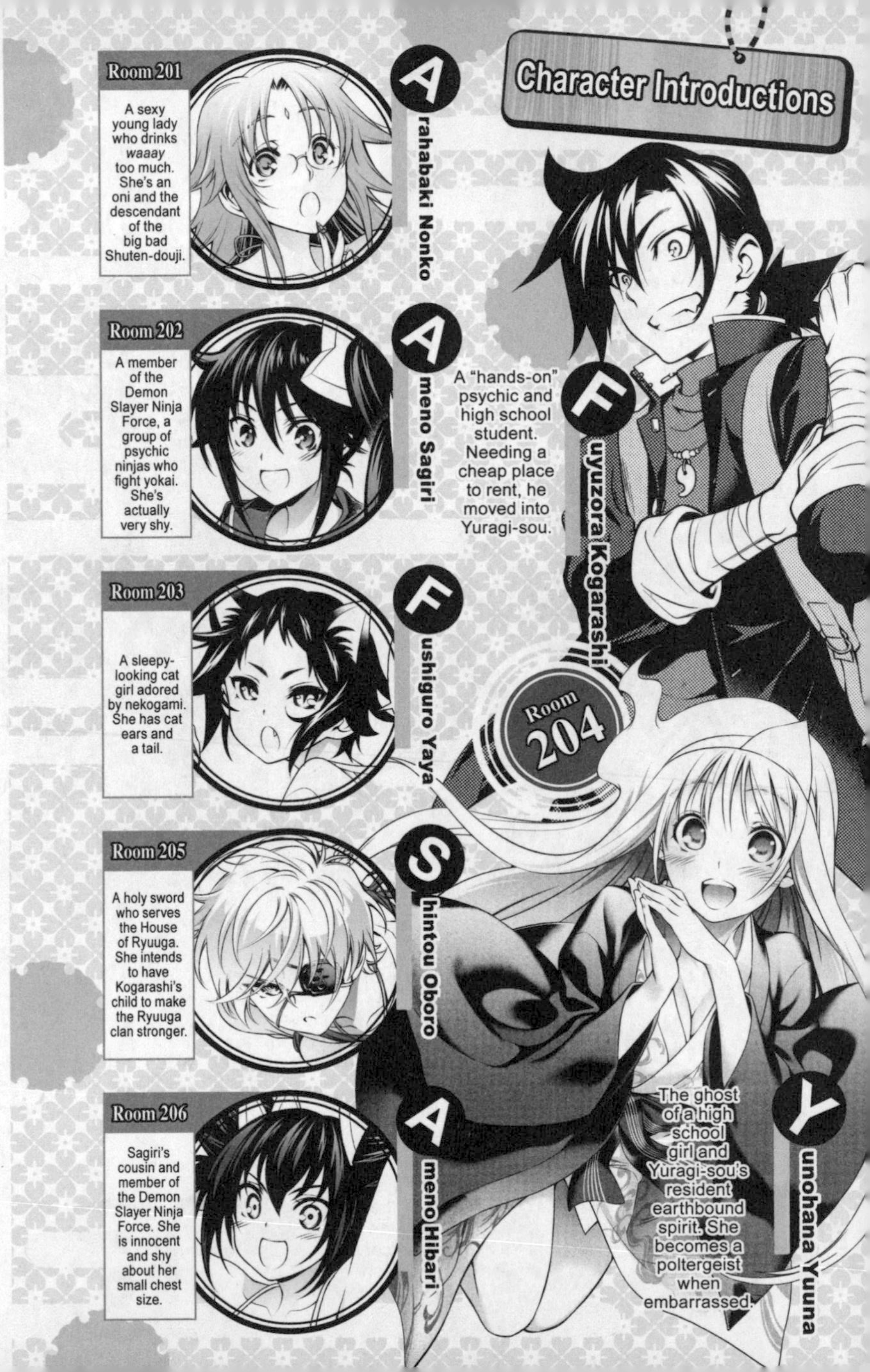
Character Introductions
Fuyuzora Kogarashi
A "hands-on" psychic and high school student. Needing a cheap place to rent, he moved into Yuragi-sou.
Room 204
Yunohana Yuuna
The ghost of a high school girl and Yuragi-sou's resident earthbound spirit. She becomes a poltergeist when embarrassed.
Room 201
Arahabaki Nonko
A sexy young lady who drinks waaay too much. She's an oni and the descendant of the big bad Shuten-douji.
Room 202
Ameno Sagiri
A member of the Demon Slayer Ninja Force, a group of psychic ninjas who fight yokai. She's actually very shy.
Room 203
Fushiguro Yaya
A sleepy-looking cat girl adored by nekogami. She has cat ears and a tail.
Room 205
Shintou Oboro
A holy sword who serves the House of Ryuuga. She intends to have Kogarashi's child to make the Ryuuga clan stronger.
Room 206
Ameno Hibari
Sagiri's cousin and member of the Demon Slayer Ninja Force. She is innocent and shy about her small chest size.

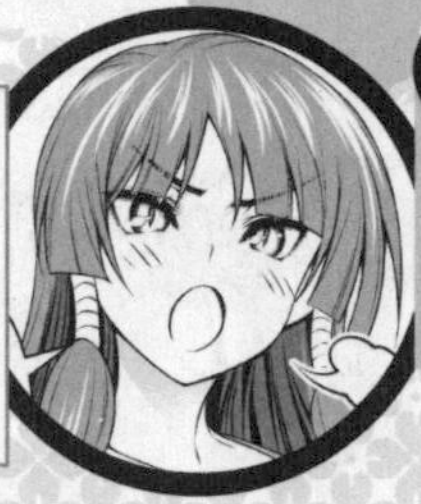

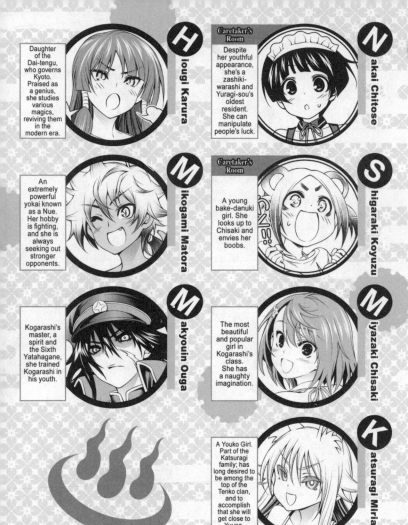

Hiougi Karura

Daughter of the Dai-tengu, who governs Kyoto. Praised as a genius, she studies various magics, reviving them in the modern era.

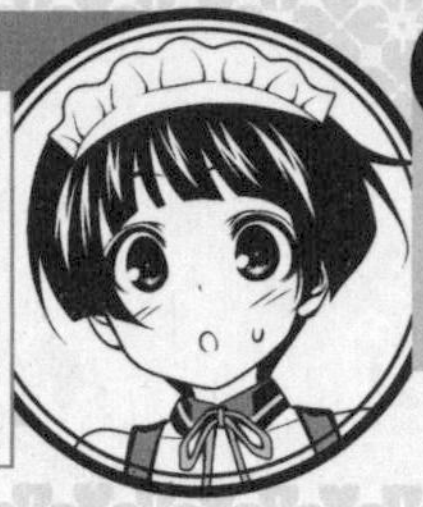

Nakai Chitose

Caretaker's Room

Despite her youthful appearance, she's a zashiki-warashi and Yuragi-sou's oldest resident. She can manipulate people's luck.

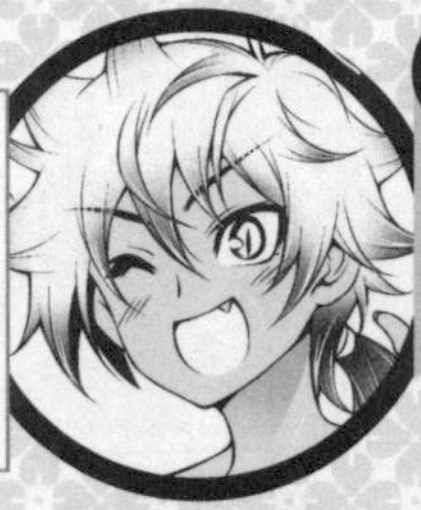

Mikogami Matora

An extremely powerful yokai known as a Nue. Her hobby is fighting, and she is always seeking out stronger opponents.

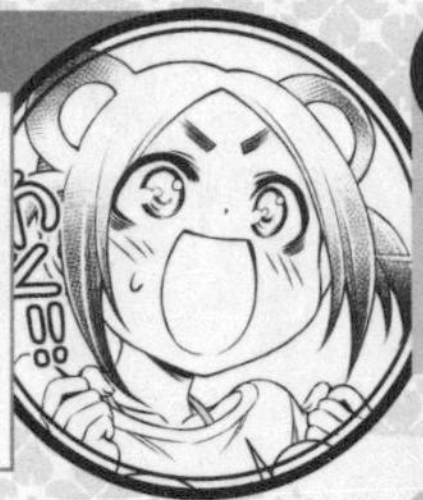

Shigaraki Koyuzu

Caretaker's Room

A young bake-danuki girl. She looks up to Chisaki and envies her boobs.

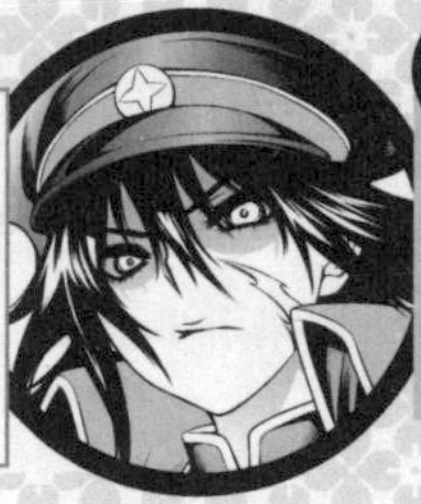

Makyouin Ouga

Kogarashi's master, a spirit and the Sixth Yatahagane, she trained Kogarashi in his youth.

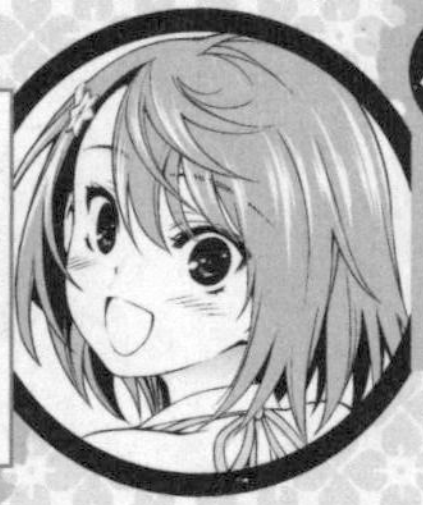

Miyazaki Chisaki

The most beautiful and popular girl in Kogarashi's class. She has a naughty imagination.

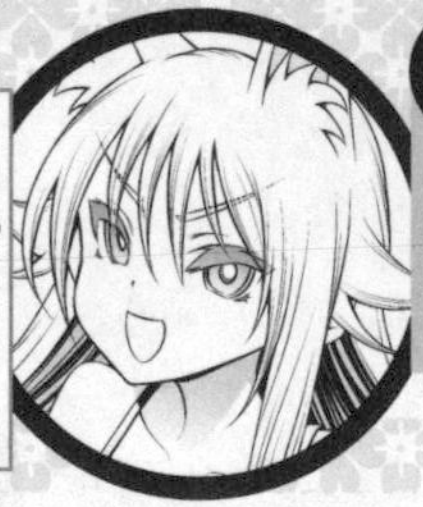

Katsuragi Miria

A Youko Girl. Part of the Katsuragi family; has long desired to be among the top of the Tenko clan, and to accomplish that she will get close to Yuuna.

Summary

While living in Yuragi-sou, a hot-spring inn-turned-boardinghouse with an unusual history, "hands-on" psychic Fuyuzora Kogarashi promised Yuuna, the earthbound spirit of a high school girl, that he would make her happy and help her pass on. Kogarashi's master and the sixth Yatahagane, Makyouin Ouga appears, claiming that Yuuna is being controlled by the world destroying Evil Spirit, Garandou, which leaves Kogarashi quite dismayed. On the run from Kogarashi's master, Yuuna flees to Tenko's world where she finally discovers she is none other than Tenko Genryusai!

125 Tenko Genryusai is...Yuuna?

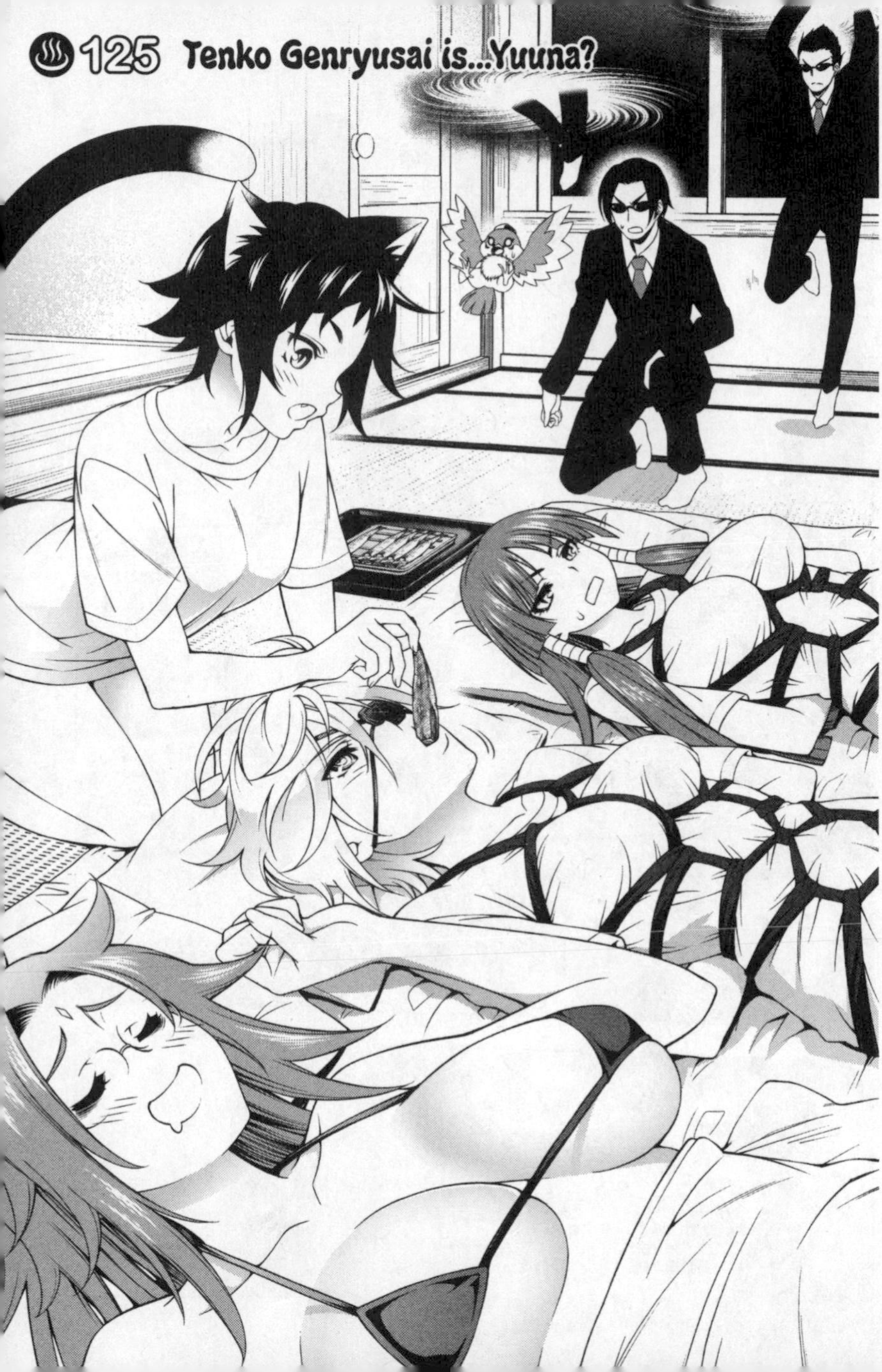

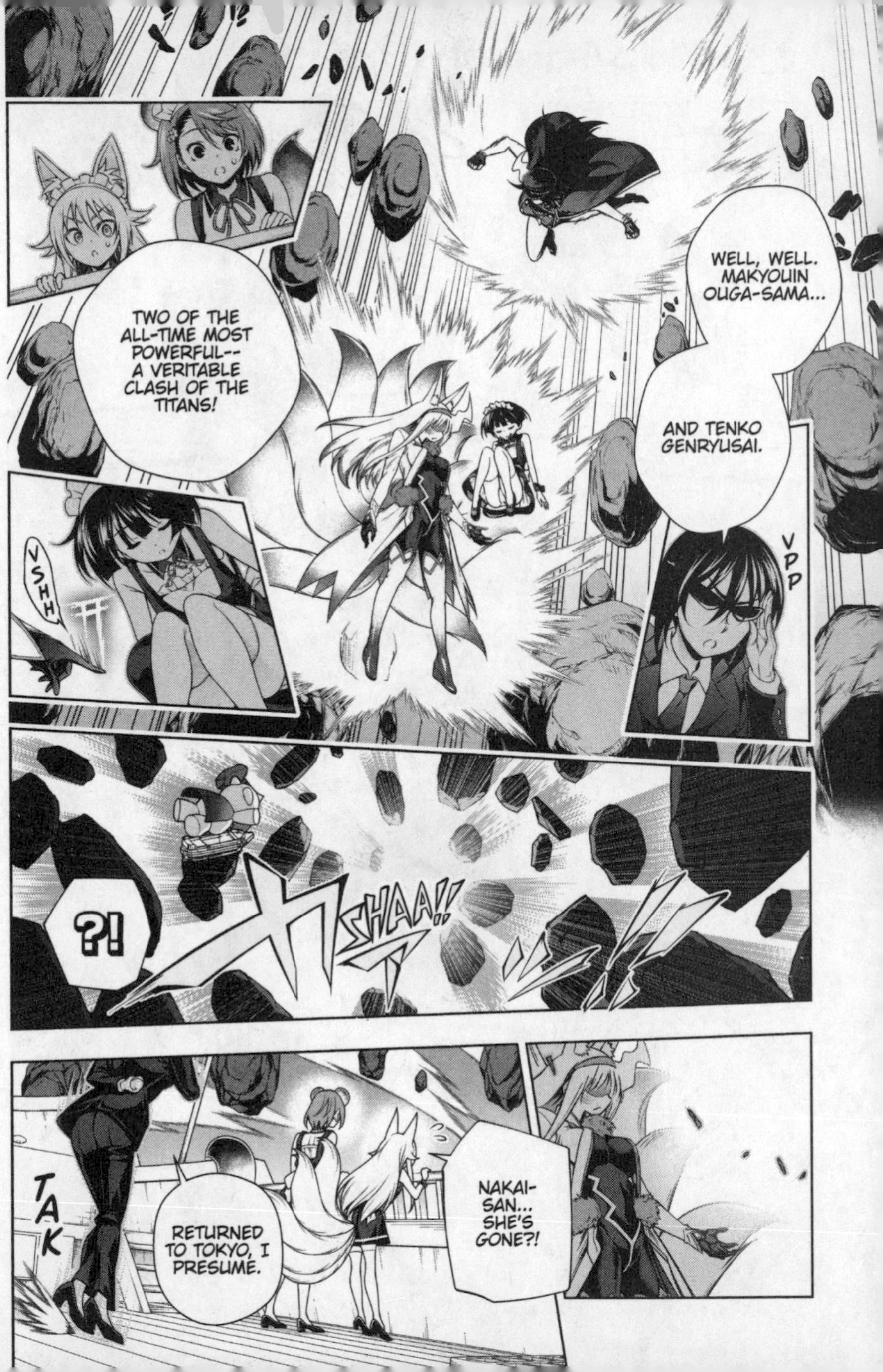
WELL, WELL. MAKYOUIN OUGA-SAMA...
AND TENKO GENRYUSAI.
VPP
TWO OF THE ALL-TIME MOST POWERFUL-- A VERITABLE CLASH OF THE TITANS!
VSHH
SHAA!!
?!
NAKAI-SAN... SHE'S GONE?!
RETURNED TO TOKYO, I PRESUME.
TAK

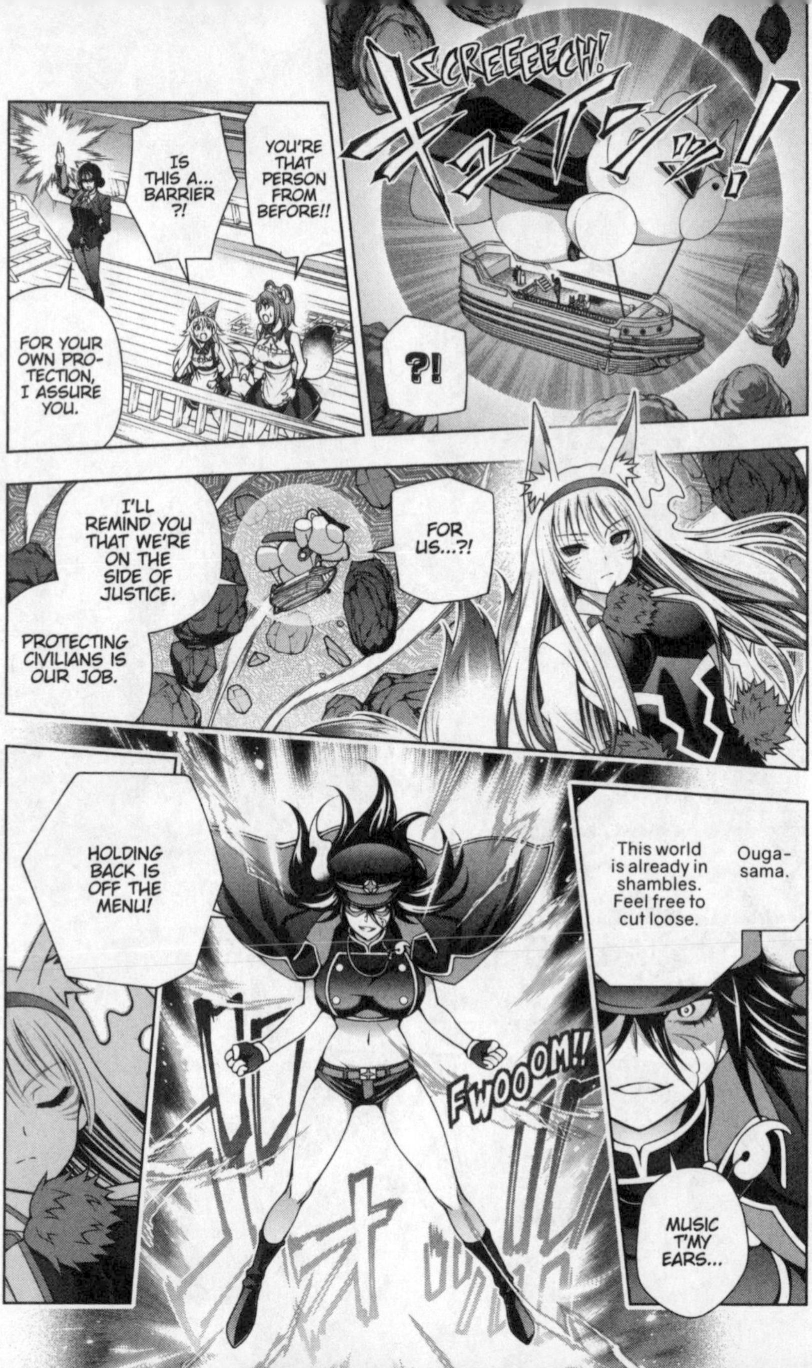
SCREEEEECH!
?!
YOU'RE THAT PERSON FROM BEFORE!!
IS THIS A... BARRIER ?!
FOR YOUR OWN PROTECTION, I ASSURE YOU.
FOR US...?!
I'LL REMIND YOU THAT WE'RE ON THE SIDE OF JUSTICE.
PROTECTING CIVILIANS IS OUR JOB.
Ouga-sama.
This world is already in shambles. Feel free to cut loose.
MUSIC T'MY EARS...
HOLDING BACK IS OFF THE MENU!
FWOOOM!!

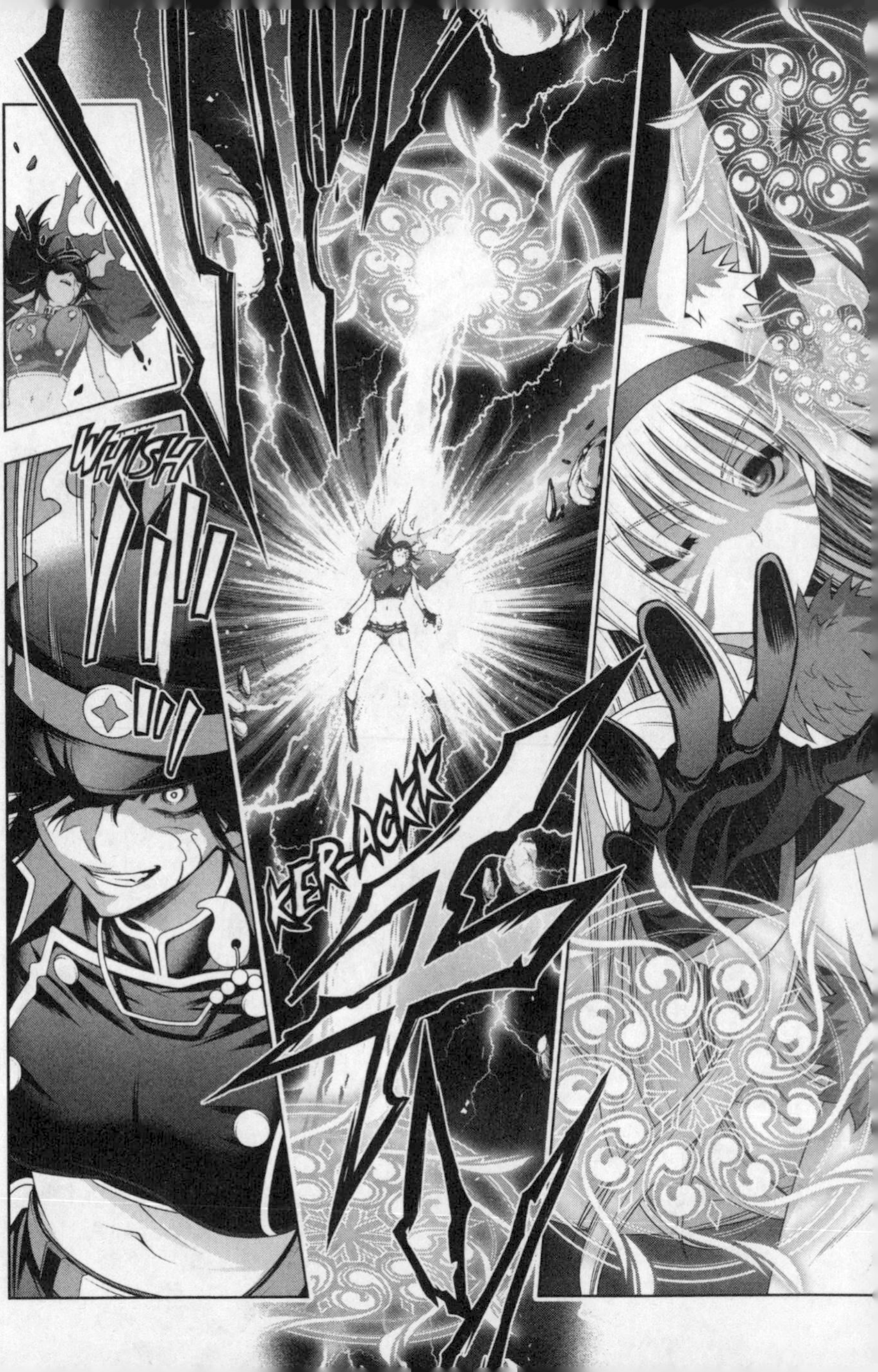
KER-ACKK
WHISH

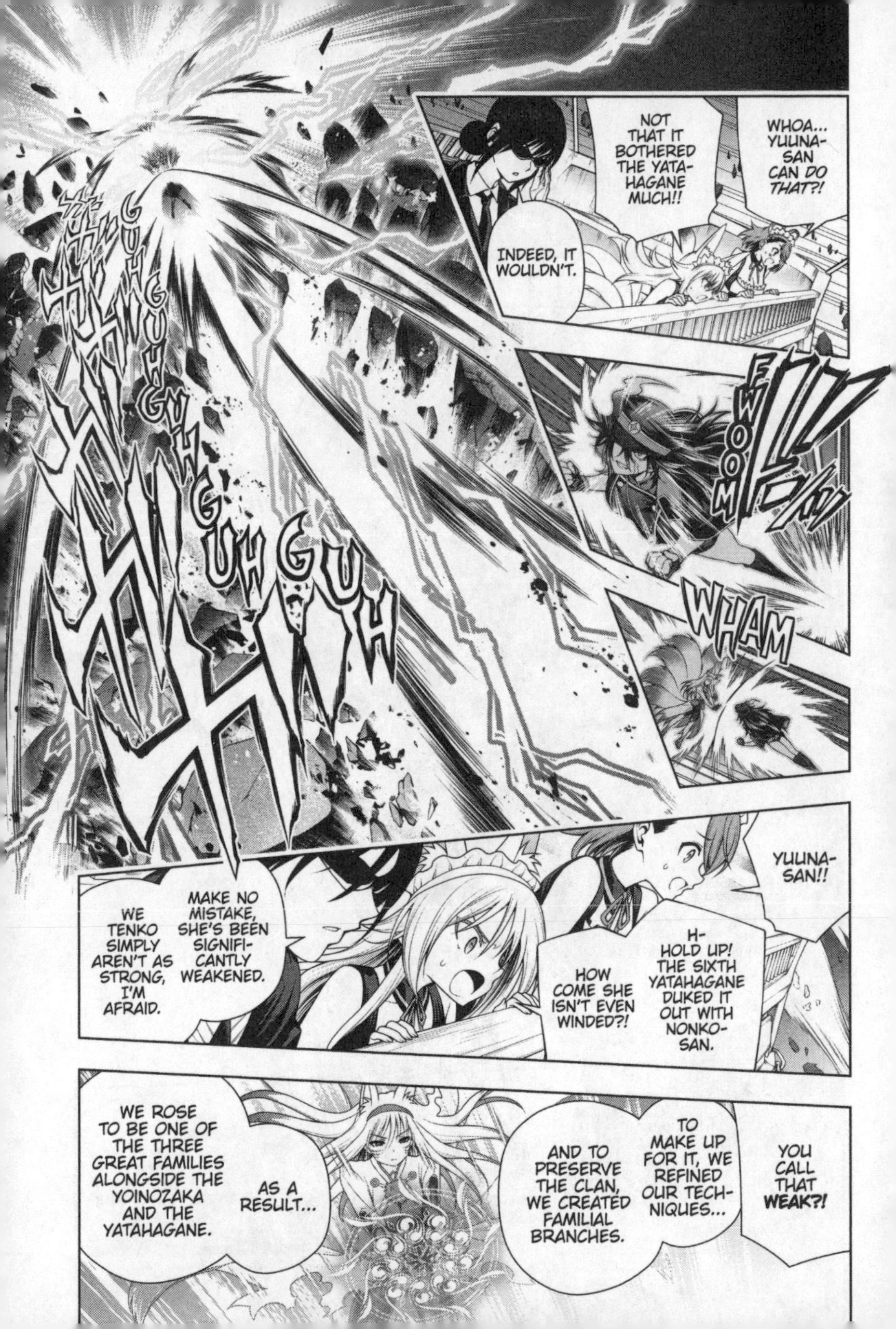

WHOA... YUUNA-SAN CAN DO THAT?!
NOT THAT IT BOTHERED THE YATAHAGANE MUCH!!
INDEED, IT WOULDN'T.
FWOOM
WHAM
YUUNA-SAN!!
H- HOLD UP! THE SIXTH YATAHAGANE DUKED IT OUT WITH NONKO-SAN.
HOW COME SHE ISN'T EVEN WINDED?!
MAKE NO MISTAKE, SHE'S BEEN SIGNIFI-CANTLY WEAKENED.
WE TENKO SIMPLY AREN'T AS STRONG, I'M AFRAID.
YOU CALL THAT **WEAK?!**
TO MAKE UP FOR IT, WE REFINED OUR TECH-NIQUES...
AND TO PRESERVE THE CLAN, WE CREATED FAMILIAL BRANCHES.
AS A RESULT...
WE ROSE TO BE ONE OF THE THREE GREAT FAMILIES ALONGSIDE THE YOINOZAKA AND THE YATAHAGANE.

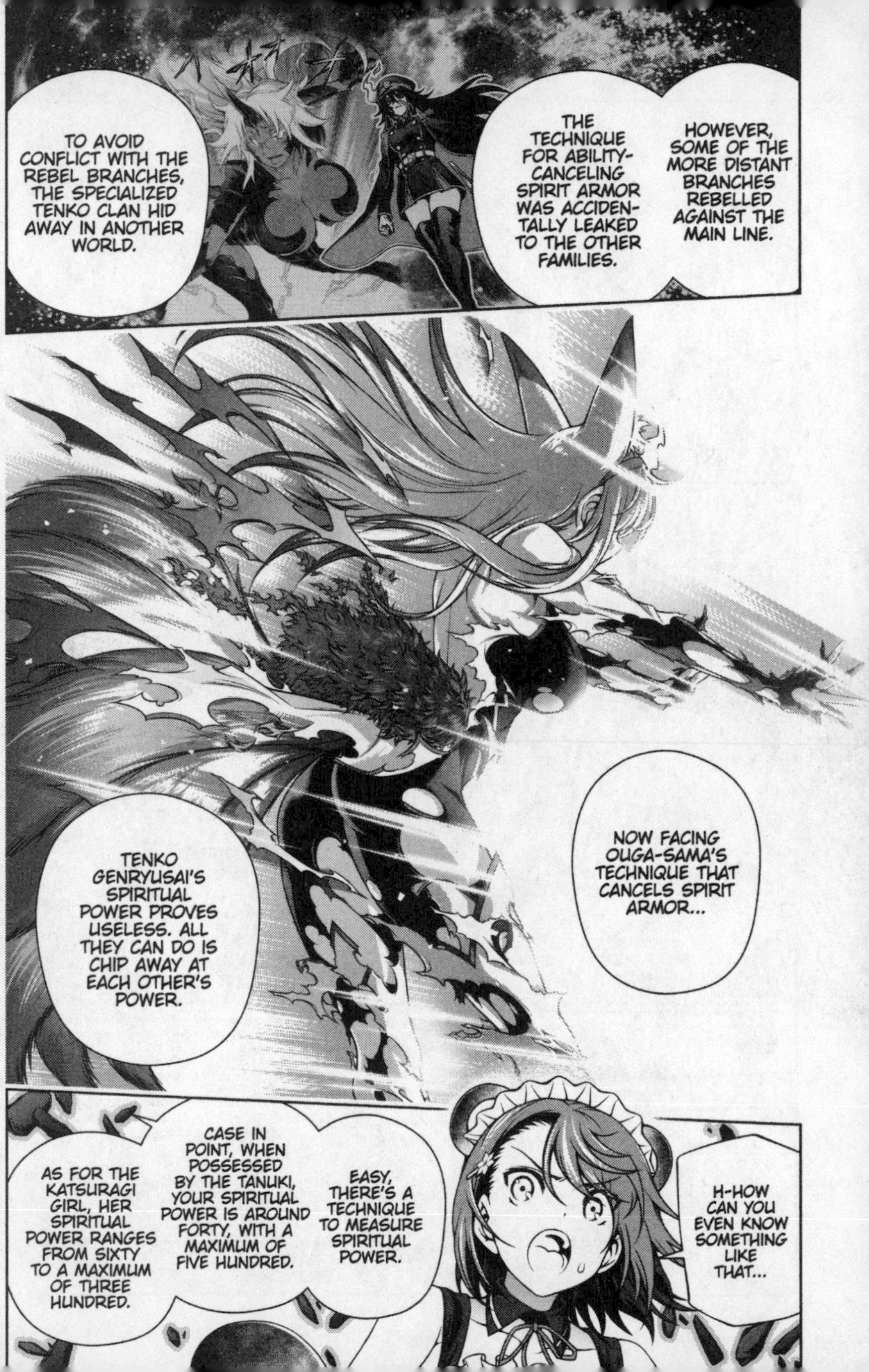

HOWEVER, SOME OF THE MORE DISTANT BRANCHES REBELLED AGAINST THE MAIN LINE.
THE TECHNIQUE FOR ABILITY-CANCELING SPIRIT ARMOR WAS ACCIDENTALLY LEAKED TO THE OTHER FAMILIES.
TO AVOID CONFLICT WITH THE REBEL BRANCHES, THE SPECIALIZED TENKO CLAN HID AWAY IN ANOTHER WORLD.
NOW FACING OUGA-SAMA'S TECHNIQUE THAT CANCELS SPIRIT ARMOR...
TENKO GENRYUSAI'S SPIRITUAL POWER PROVES USELESS. ALL THEY CAN DO IS CHIP AWAY AT EACH OTHER'S POWER.
H-HOW CAN YOU EVEN KNOW SOMETHING LIKE THAT...
EASY, THERE'S A TECHNIQUE TO MEASURE SPIRITUAL POWER.
CASE IN POINT, WHEN POSSESSED BY THE TANUKI, YOUR SPIRITUAL POWER IS AROUND FORTY, WITH A MAXIMUM OF FIVE HUNDRED.
AS FOR THE KATSURAGI GIRL, HER SPIRITUAL POWER RANGES FROM SIXTY TO A MAXIMUM OF THREE HUNDRED.

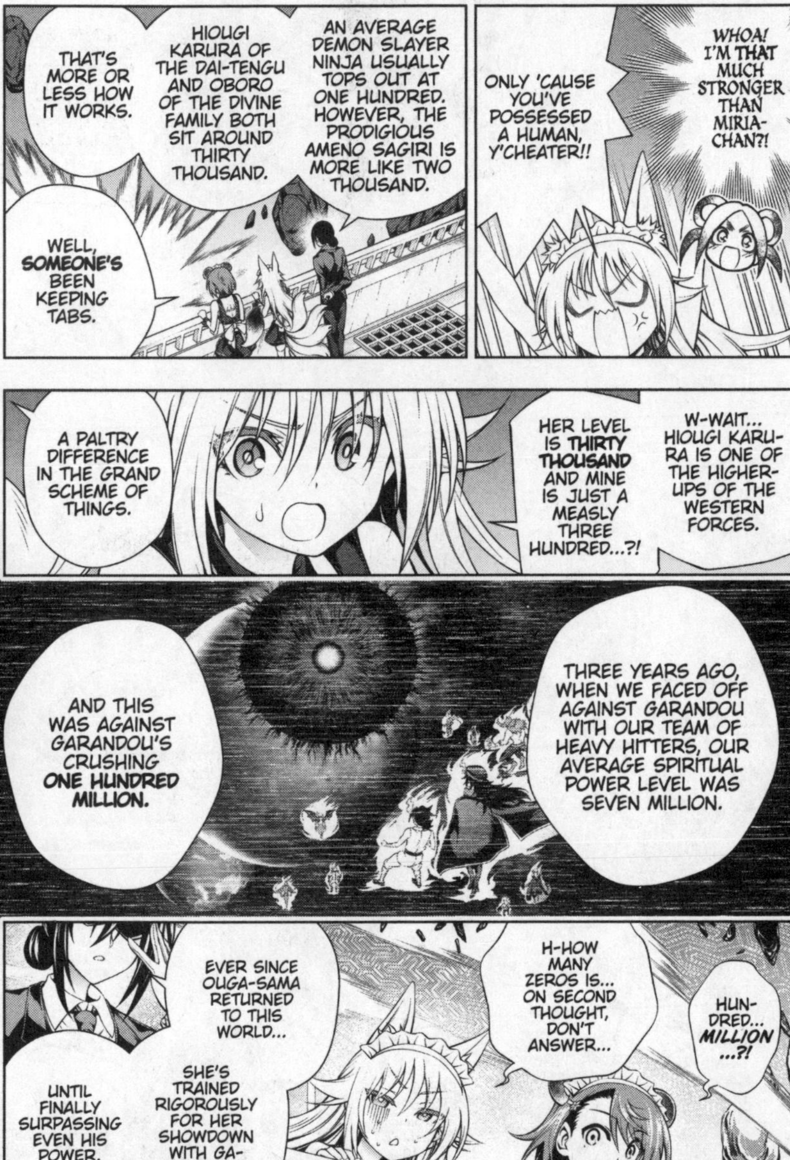
WHOA! I'M THAT MUCH STRONGER THAN MIRIA-CHAN?!
ONLY 'CAUSE YOU'VE POSSESSED A HUMAN, Y'CHEATER!!
AN AVERAGE DEMON SLAYER NINJA USUALLY TOPS OUT AT ONE HUNDRED. HOWEVER, THE PRODIGIOUS AMENO SAGIRI IS MORE LIKE TWO THOUSAND.
HIOUGI KARURA OF THE DAI-TENGU AND OBORO OF THE DIVINE FAMILY BOTH SIT AROUND THIRTY THOUSAND.
THAT'S MORE OR LESS HOW IT WORKS.
WELL, SOMEONE'S BEEN KEEPING TABS.
W-WAIT... HIOUGI KARURA IS ONE OF THE HIGHER-UPS OF THE WESTERN FORCES.
HER LEVEL IS THIRTY THOUSAND AND MINE IS JUST A MEASLY THREE HUNDRED...?!
A PALTRY DIFFERENCE IN THE GRAND SCHEME OF THINGS.
THREE YEARS AGO, WHEN WE FACED OFF AGAINST GARANDOU WITH OUR TEAM OF HEAVY HITTERS, OUR AVERAGE SPIRITUAL POWER LEVEL WAS SEVEN MILLION.
AND THIS WAS AGAINST GARANDOU'S CRUSHING ONE HUNDRED MILLION.
HUNDRED... MILLION ...?!
H-HOW MANY ZEROS IS... ON SECOND THOUGHT, DON'T ANSWER...
EVER SINCE OUGA-SAMA RETURNED TO THIS WORLD...
SHE'S TRAINED RIGOROUSLY FOR HER SHOWDOWN WITH GA-RANDOU...
UNTIL FINALLY SURPASSING EVEN HIS POWER.

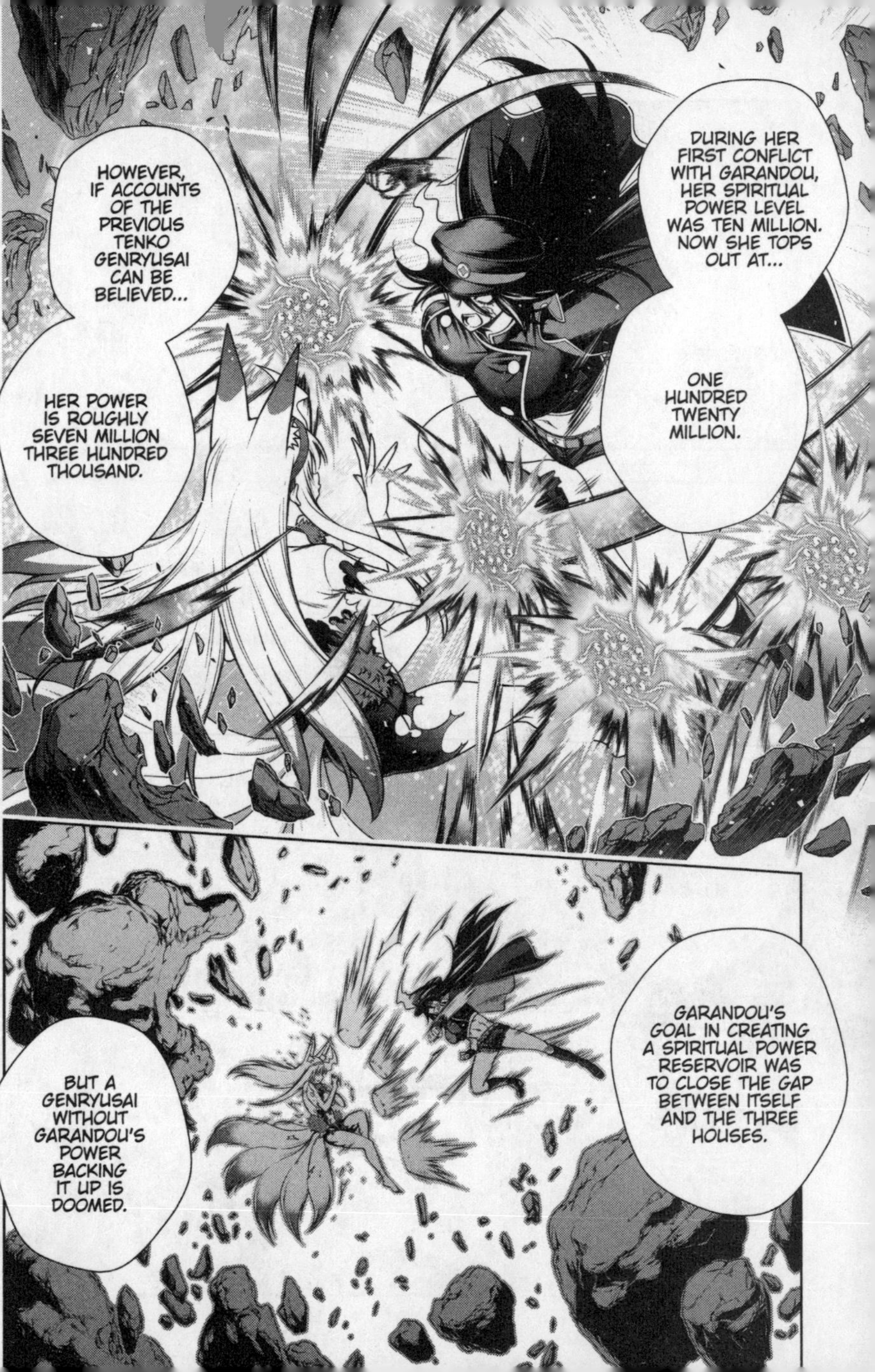
DURING HER FIRST CONFLICT WITH GARANDOU, HER SPIRITUAL POWER LEVEL WAS TEN MILLION. NOW SHE TOPS OUT AT...
ONE HUNDRED TWENTY MILLION.
HOWEVER, IF ACCOUNTS OF THE PREVIOUS TENKO GENRYUSAI CAN BE BELIEVED...
HER POWER IS ROUGHLY SEVEN MILLION THREE HUNDRED THOUSAND.
GARANDOU'S GOAL IN CREATING A SPIRITUAL POWER RESERVOIR WAS TO CLOSE THE GAP BETWEEN ITSELF AND THE THREE HOUSES.
BUT A GENRYUSAI WITHOUT GARANDOU'S POWER BACKING IT UP IS DOOMED.

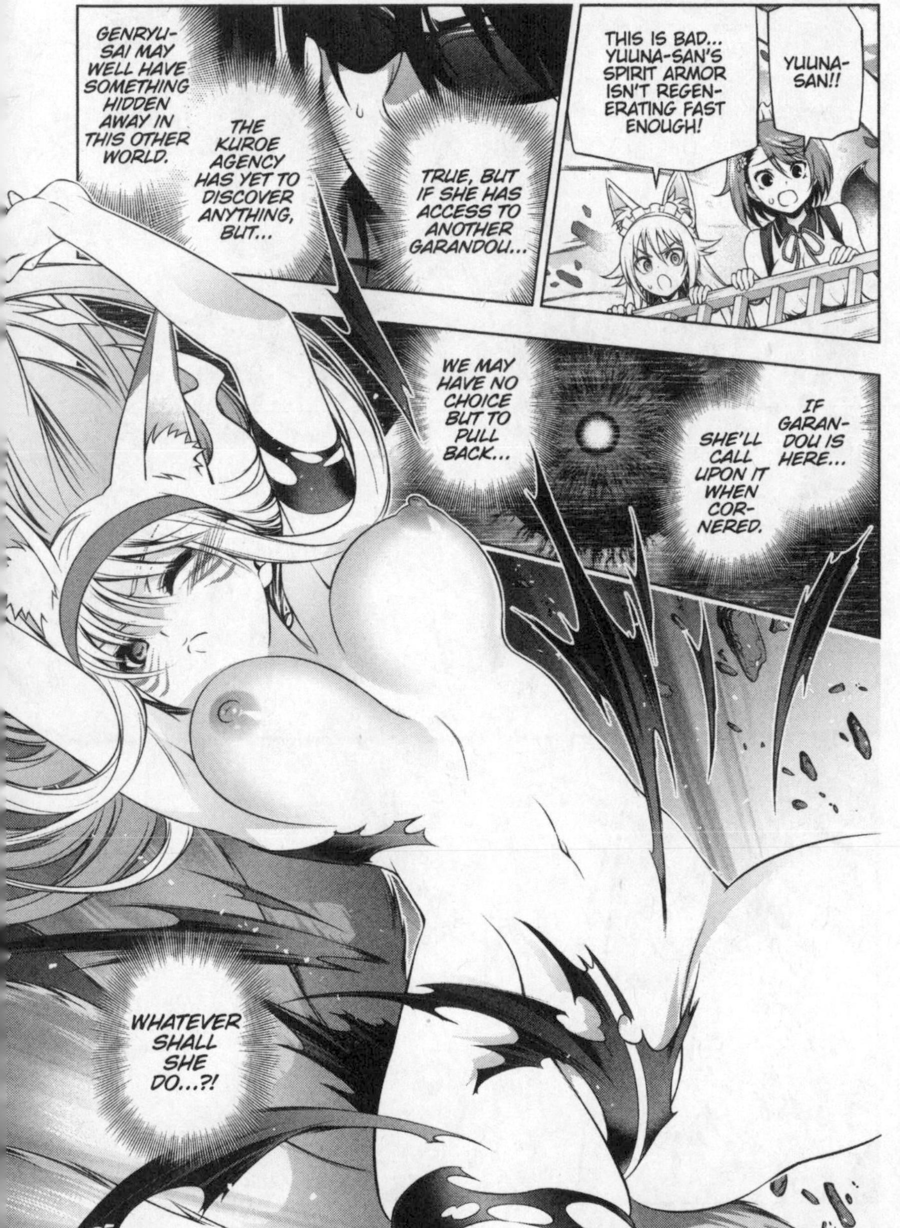
YUUNA-SAN!!
THIS IS BAD... YUUNA-SAN'S SPIRIT ARMOR ISN'T REGEN-ERATING FAST ENOUGH!
GENRYU-SAI MAY WELL HAVE SOMETHING HIDDEN AWAY IN THIS OTHER WORLD.
THE KUROE AGENCY HAS YET TO DISCOVER ANYTHING, BUT...
TRUE, BUT IF SHE HAS ACCESS TO ANOTHER GARANDOU...
IF GARAN-DOU IS HERE...
SHE'LL CALL UPON IT WHEN COR-NERED.
WE MAY HAVE NO CHOICE BUT TO PULL BACK...
WHATEVER SHALL SHE DO...?!

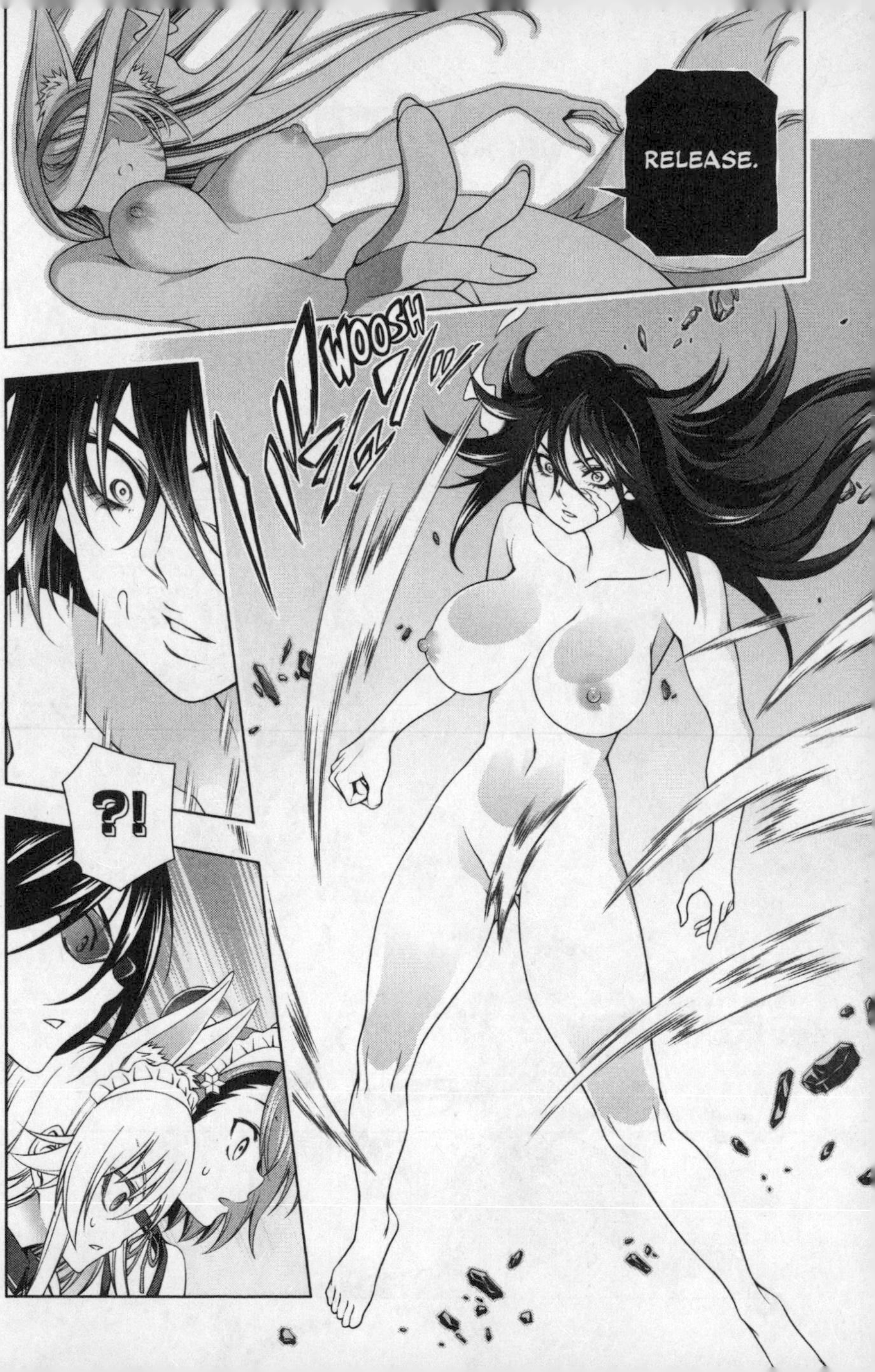
RELEASE.
WOOSH
?!

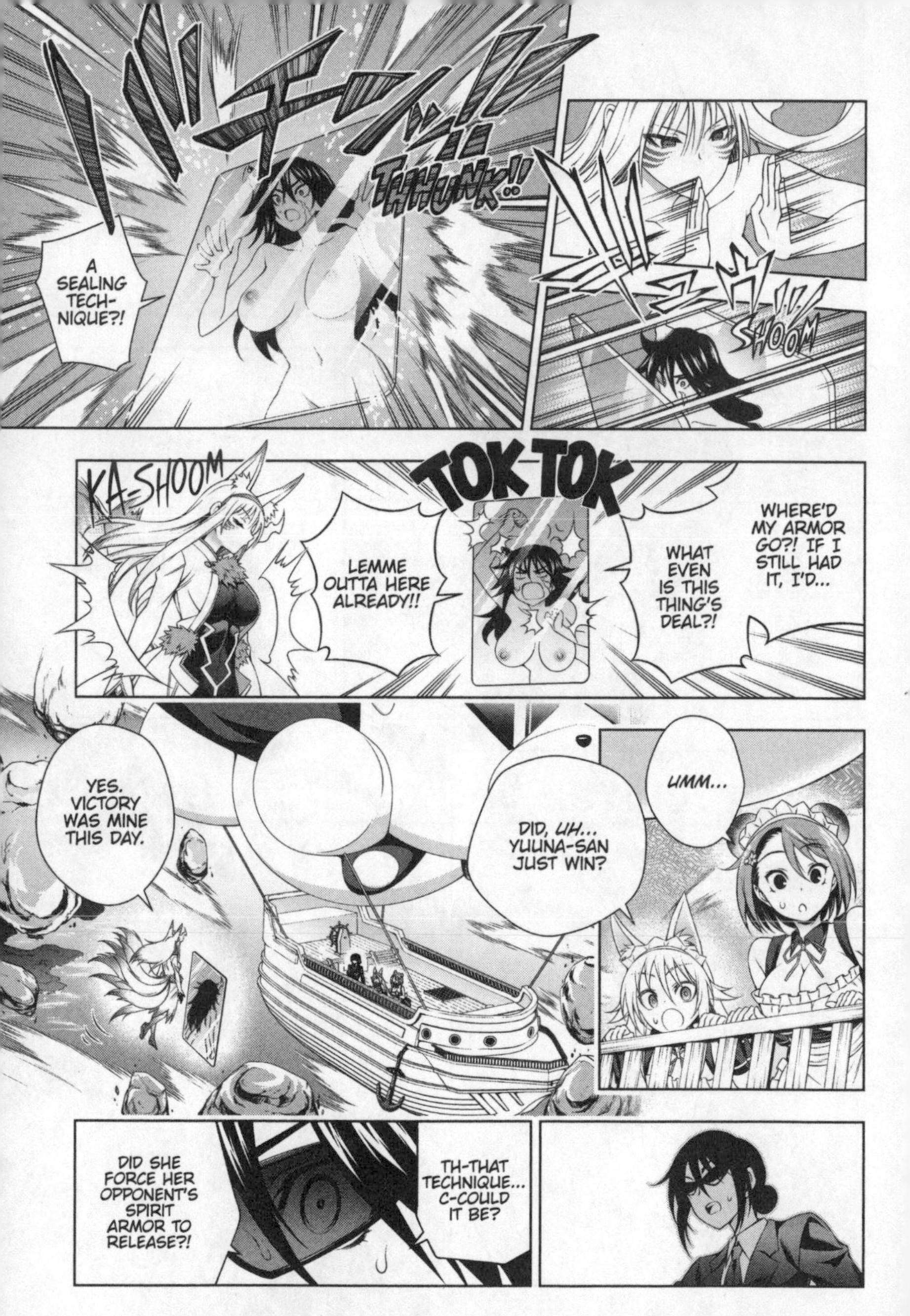
SHOOM
THUNK!!
A SEALING TECH-NIQUE?!
WHERE'D MY ARMOR GO?! IF I STILL HAD IT, I'D...
WHAT EVEN IS THIS THING'S DEAL?!
TOK TOK
LEMME OUTTA HERE ALREADY!!
KA-SHOOM
UMM...
DID, UH... YUUNA-SAN JUST WIN?
YES. VICTORY WAS MINE THIS DAY.
TH-THAT TECHNIQUE... C-COULD IT BE?
DID SHE FORCE HER OPPONENT'S SPIRIT ARMOR TO RELEASE?!

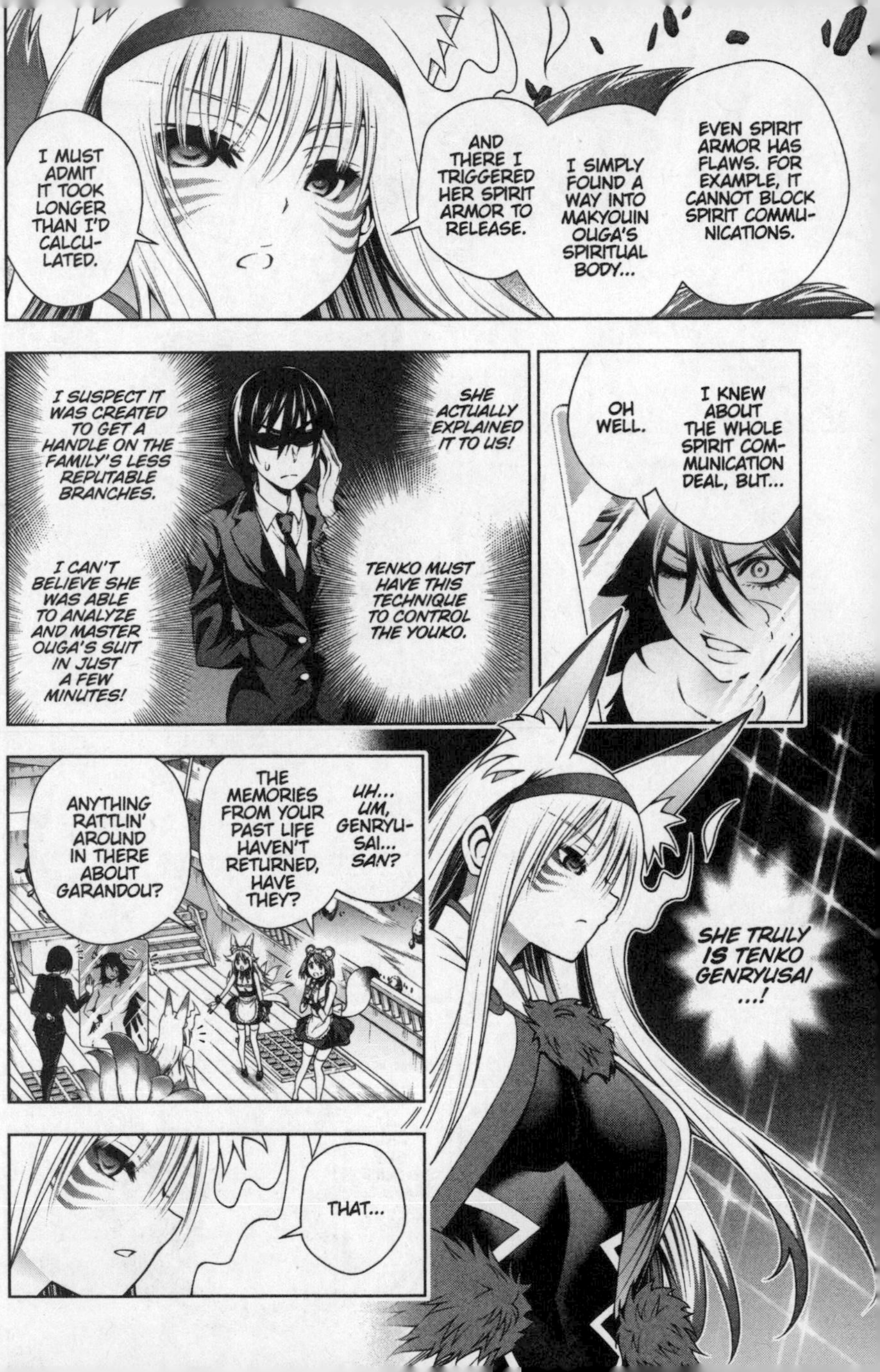

EVEN SPIRIT ARMOR HAS FLAWS. FOR EXAMPLE, IT CANNOT BLOCK SPIRIT COMMUNICATIONS.
I SIMPLY FOUND A WAY INTO MAKYOUIN OUGA'S SPIRITUAL BODY...
AND THERE I TRIGGERED HER SPIRIT ARMOR TO RELEASE.
I MUST ADMIT IT TOOK LONGER THAN I'D CALCULATED.
I KNEW ABOUT THE WHOLE SPIRIT COMMUNICATION DEAL, BUT...
OH WELL.
SHE ACTUALLY EXPLAINED IT TO US!
I SUSPECT IT WAS CREATED TO GET A HANDLE ON THE FAMILY'S LESS REPUTABLE BRANCHES.
TENKO MUST HAVE THIS TECHNIQUE TO CONTROL THE YOUKO.
I CAN'T BELIEVE SHE WAS ABLE TO ANALYZE AND MASTER OUGA'S SUIT IN JUST A FEW MINUTES!
SHE TRULY IS TENKO GENRYUSAI ...!
UH... UM, GENRYUSAI... SAN?
THE MEMORIES FROM YOUR PAST LIFE HAVEN'T RETURNED, HAVE THEY?
ANYTHING RATTLIN' AROUND IN THERE ABOUT GARANDOU?
THAT...

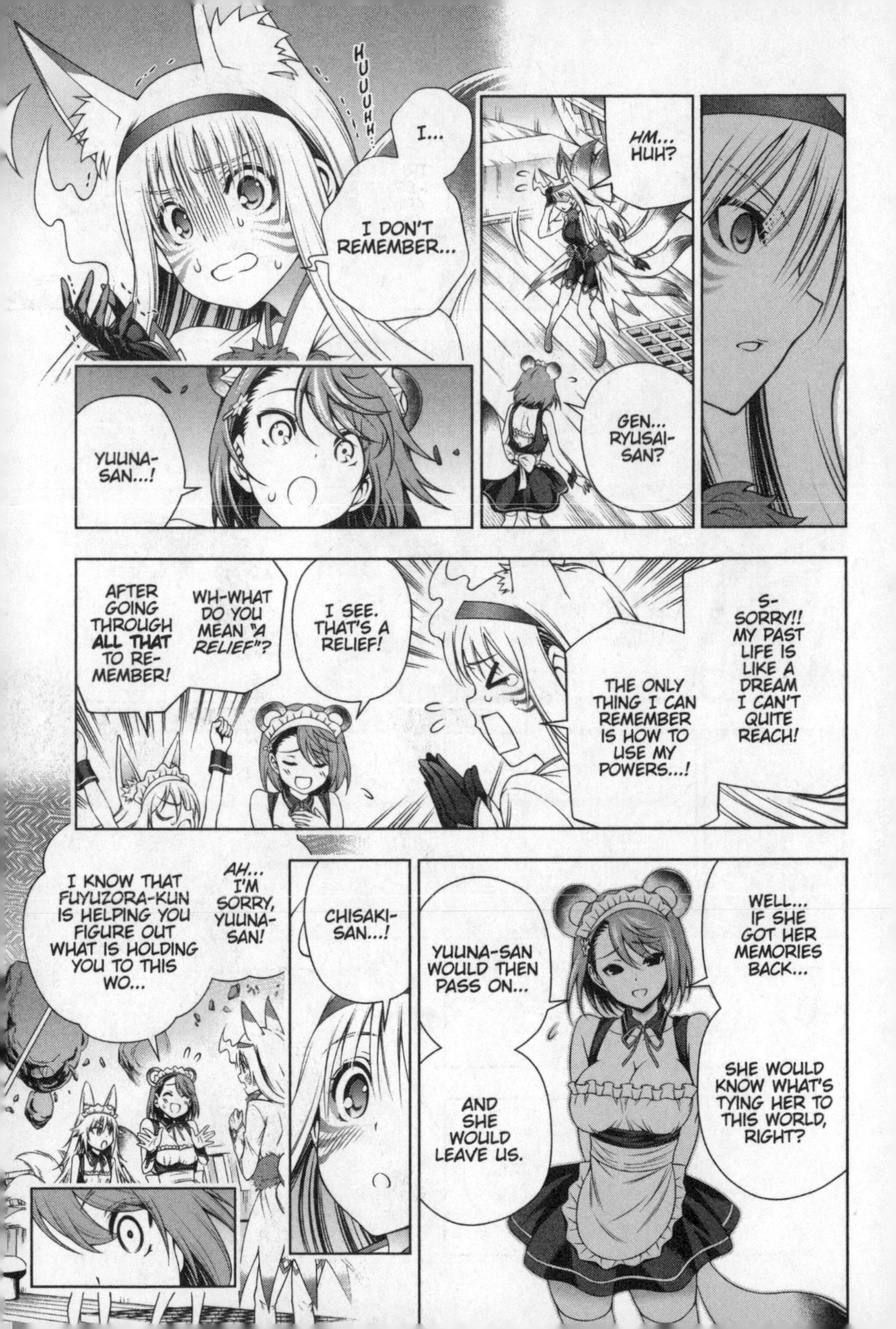
HM... HUH?
GEN... RYUSAI-SAN?
HUUUHH...
I...
I DON'T REMEMBER...
YUUNA-SAN...!
S-SORRY!! MY PAST LIFE IS LIKE A DREAM I CAN'T QUITE REACH!
THE ONLY THING I CAN REMEMBER IS HOW TO USE MY POWERS...!
I SEE. THAT'S A RELIEF!
WH-WHAT DO YOU MEAN "A RELIEF"?
AFTER GOING THROUGH ALL THAT TO REMEMBER!
WELL... IF SHE GOT HER MEMORIES BACK...
SHE WOULD KNOW WHAT'S TYING HER TO THIS WORLD, RIGHT?
YUUNA-SAN WOULD THEN PASS ON...
AND SHE WOULD LEAVE US.
CHISAKI-SAN...!
AH... I'M SORRY, YUUNA-SAN!
I KNOW THAT FUYUZORA-KUN IS HELPING YOU FIGURE OUT WHAT IS HOLDING YOU TO THIS WO...

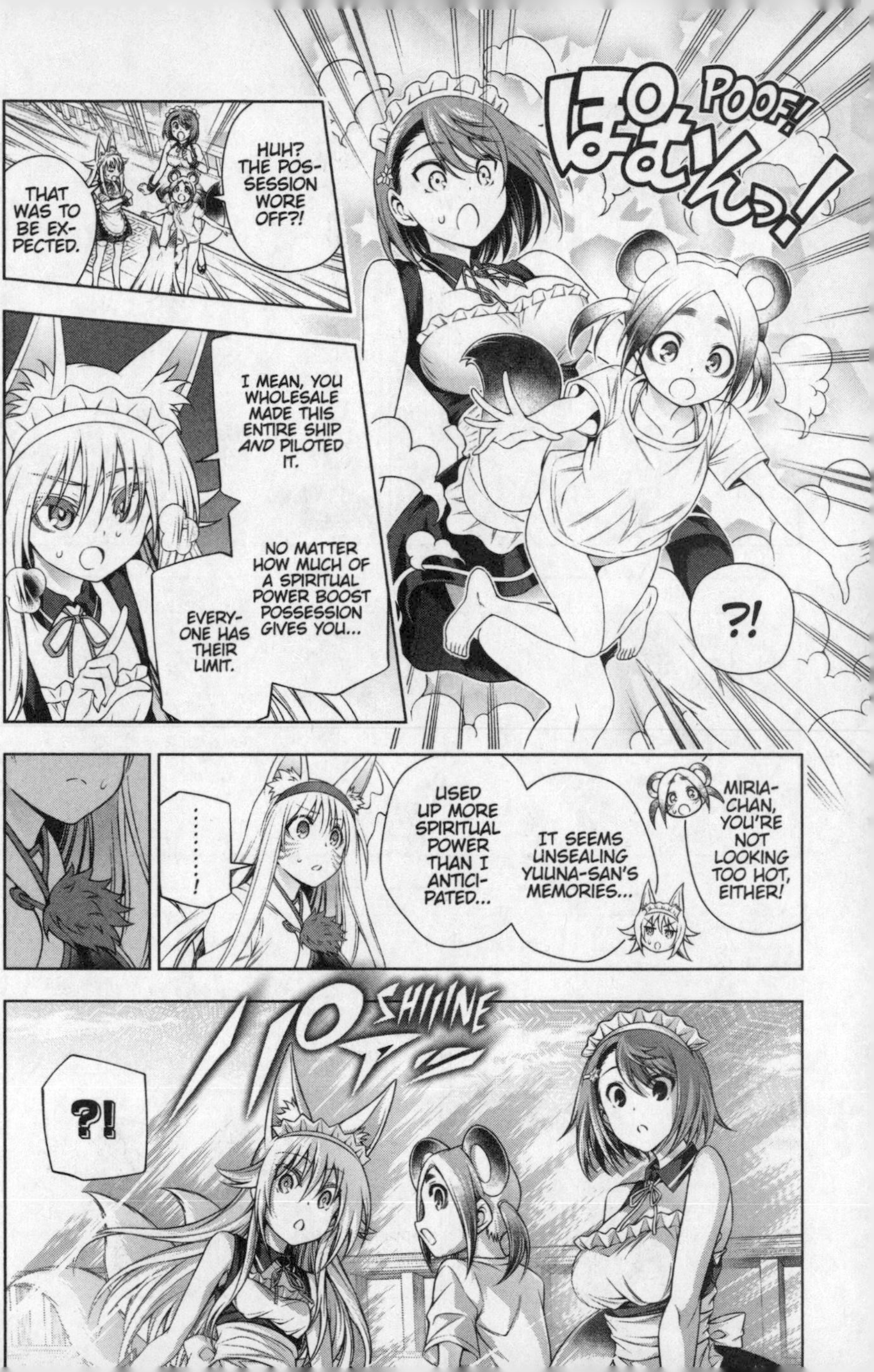
ほわんっ!
POOF!
?!
HUH? THE POS-SESSION WORE OFF?!
THAT WAS TO BE EX-PECTED.
I MEAN, YOU WHOLESALE MADE THIS ENTIRE SHIP AND PILOTED IT.
NO MATTER HOW MUCH OF A SPIRITUAL POWER BOOST POSSESSION GIVES YOU...
EVERY-ONE HAS THEIR LIMIT.
MIRIA-CHAN, YOU'RE NOT LOOKING TOO HOT, EITHER!
IT SEEMS UNSEALING YUUNA-SAN'S MEMORIES...
USED UP MORE SPIRITUAL POWER THAN I ANTICI-PATED...
.........!
パァ〜
SHIIINE
?!

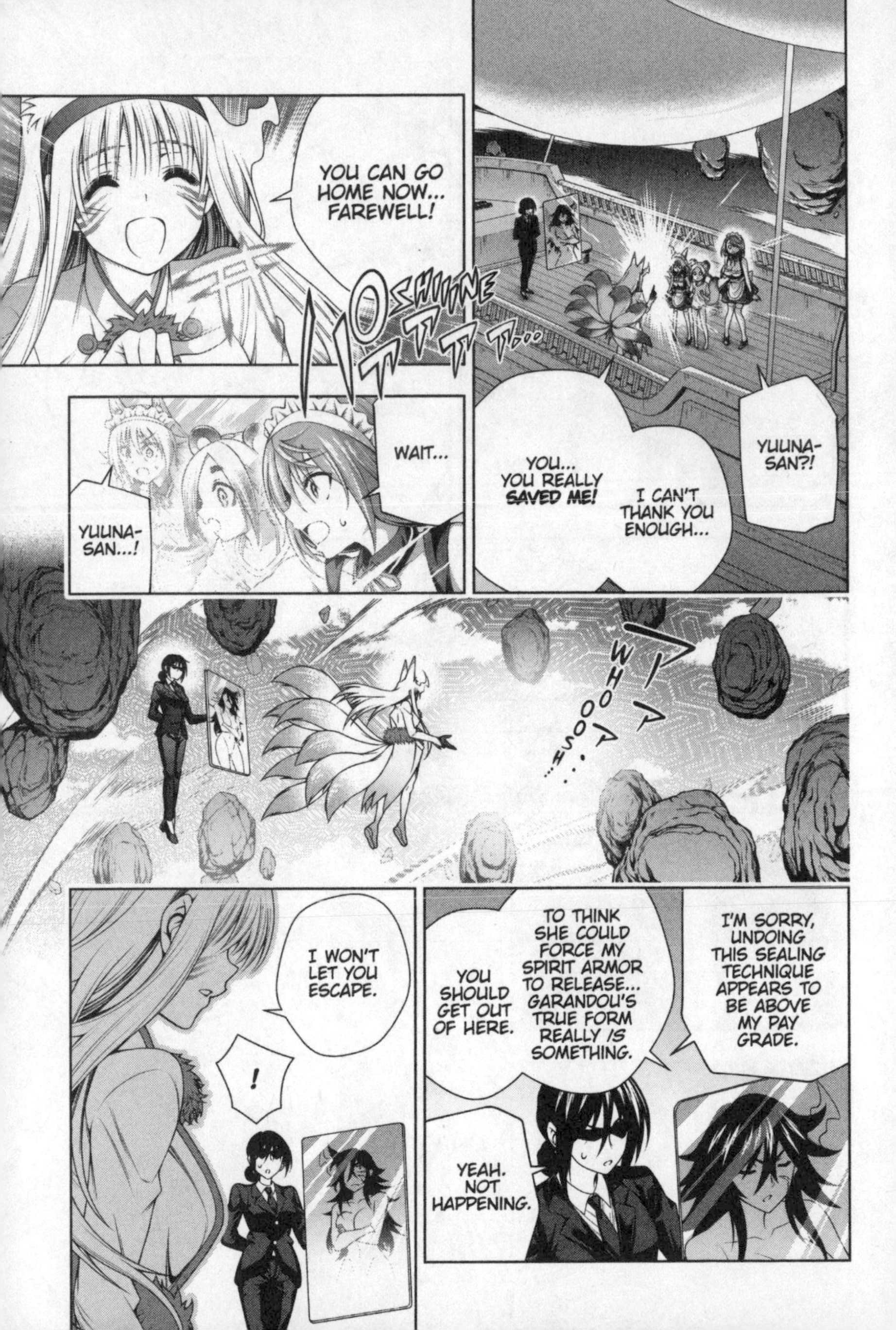
YUUNA-SAN?!
I CAN'T THANK YOU ENOUGH...
YOU... YOU REALLY SAVED ME!
YOU CAN GO HOME NOW... FAREWELL!
OSHIIINE
TTTT...
WAIT...
YUUNA-SAN...!
WHOOOSH...
I'M SORRY, UNDOING THIS SEALING TECHNIQUE APPEARS TO BE ABOVE MY PAY GRADE.
TO THINK SHE COULD FORCE MY SPIRIT ARMOR TO RELEASE... GARANDOU'S TRUE FORM REALLY IS SOMETHING.
YOU SHOULD GET OUT OF HERE.
YEAH. NOT HAPPENING.
I WON'T LET YOU ESCAPE.
!

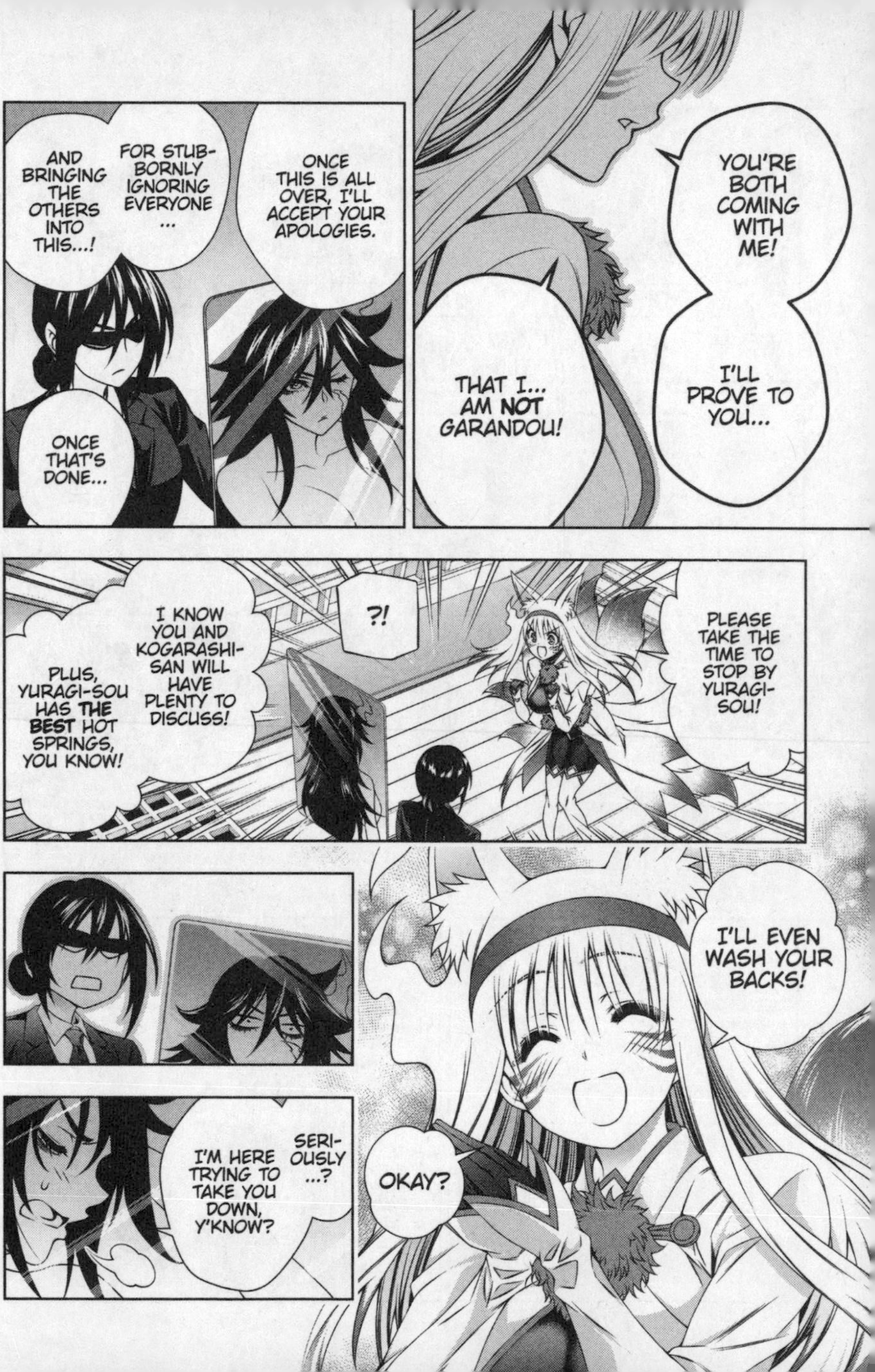
YOU'RE BOTH COMING WITH ME!
I'LL PROVE TO YOU...
THAT I... AM **NOT** GARANDOU!
ONCE THIS IS ALL OVER, I'LL ACCEPT YOUR APOLOGIES.
FOR STUBBORNLY IGNORING EVERYONE ...
AND BRINGING THE OTHERS INTO THIS...!
ONCE THAT'S DONE...
PLEASE TAKE THE TIME TO STOP BY YURAGI-SOU!
?!
I KNOW YOU AND KOGARASHI-SAN WILL HAVE PLENTY TO DISCUSS!
PLUS, YURAGI-SOU HAS **THE BEST** HOT SPRINGS, YOU KNOW!
I'LL EVEN WASH YOUR BACKS!
OKAY?
SERIOUSLY ...?
I'M HERE TRYING TO TAKE YOU DOWN, Y'KNOW?

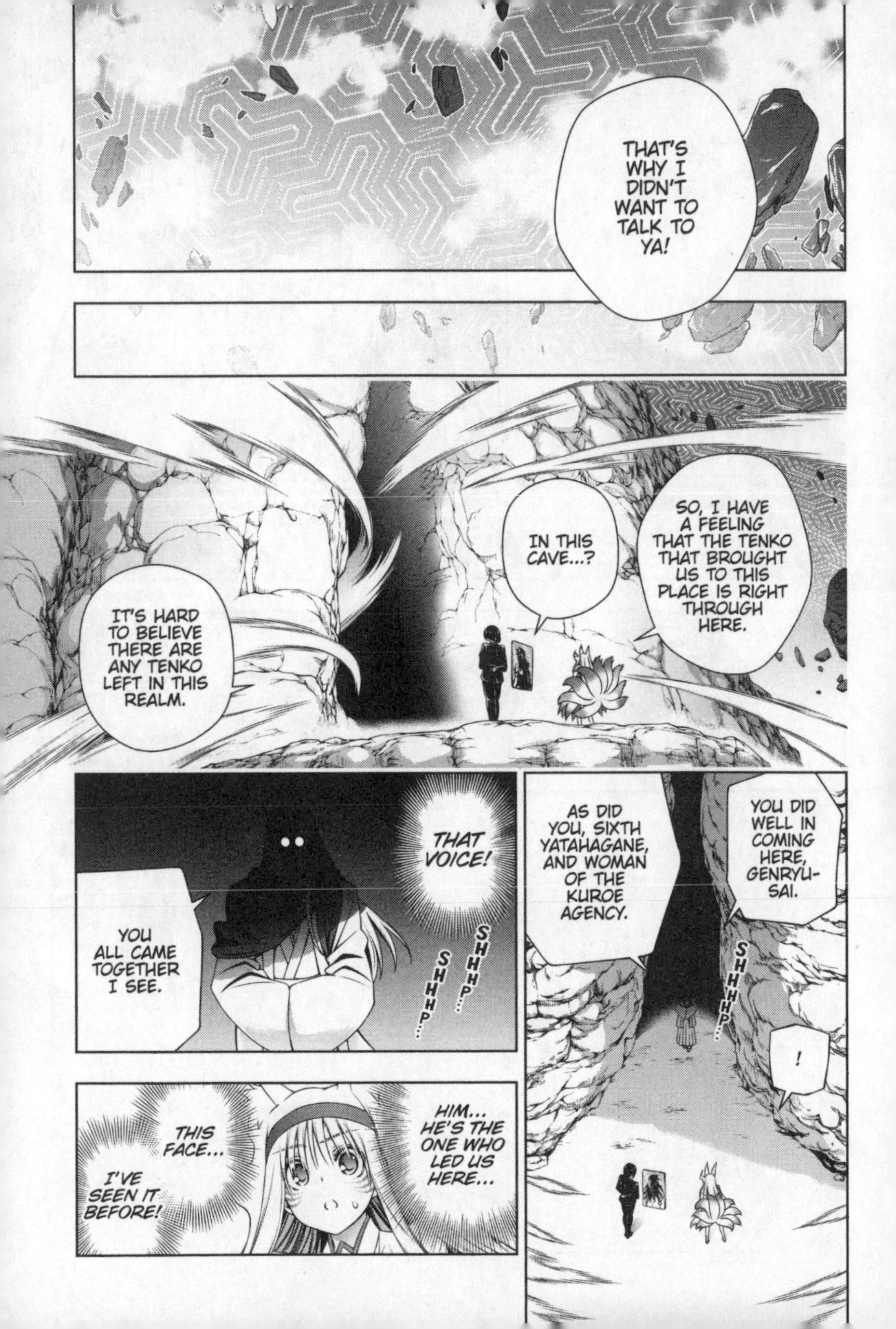
THAT'S WHY I DIDN'T WANT TO TALK TO YA!
SO, I HAVE A FEELING THAT THE TENKO THAT BROUGHT US TO THIS PLACE IS RIGHT THROUGH HERE.
IN THIS CAVE...?
IT'S HARD TO BELIEVE THERE ARE ANY TENKO LEFT IN THIS REALM.
YOU DID WELL IN COMING HERE, GENRYU-SAI.
AS DID YOU, SIXTH YATAHAGANE, AND WOMAN OF THE KUROE AGENCY.
SHHHHP...
!
THAT VOICE!
SHHHP...
SHHHP...
YOU ALL CAME TOGETHER I SEE.
HIM... HE'S THE ONE WHO LED US HERE...
THIS FACE... I'VE SEEN IT BEFORE!

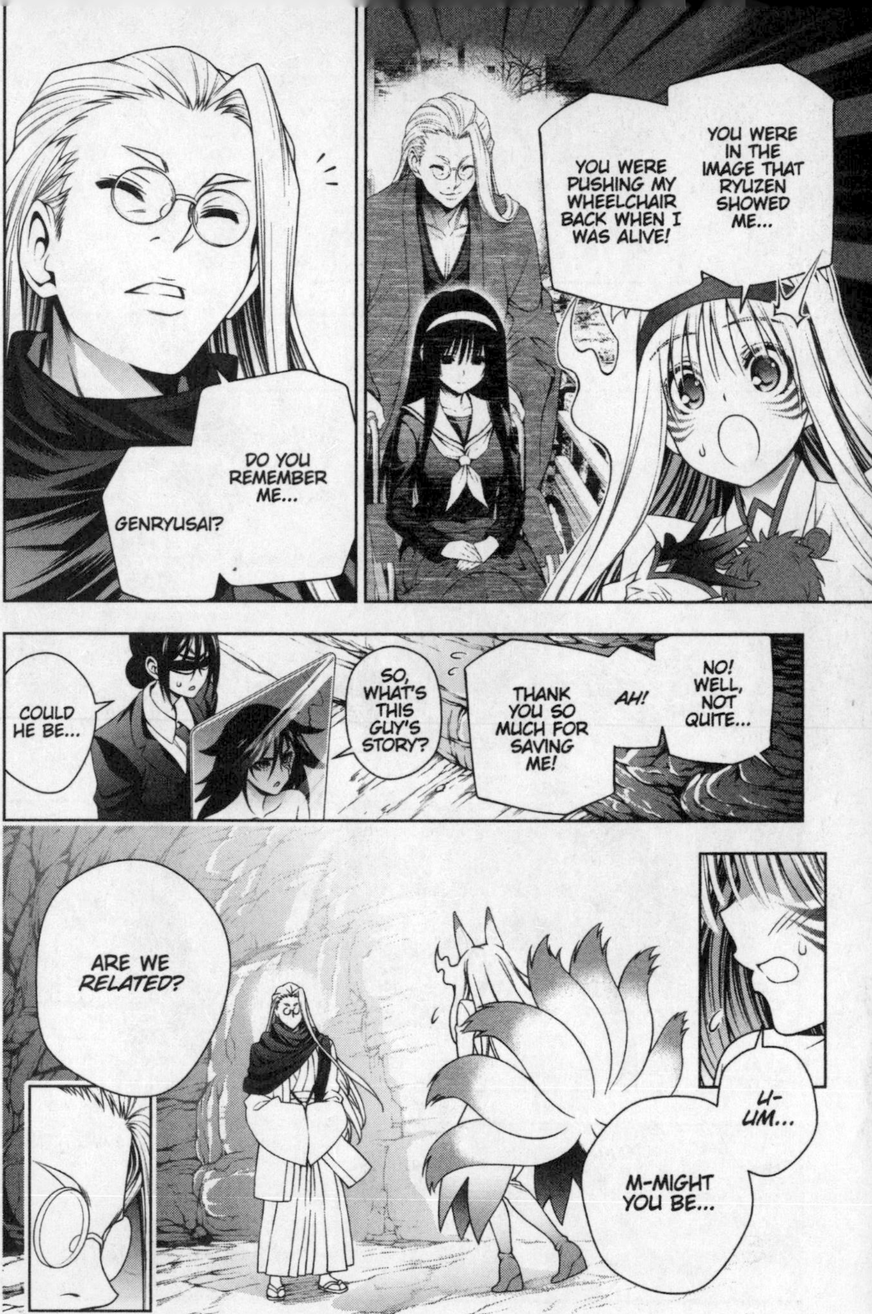
YOU WERE IN THE IMAGE THAT RYUZEN SHOWED ME...
YOU WERE PUSHING MY WHEELCHAIR BACK WHEN I WAS ALIVE!
DO YOU REMEMBER ME...
GENRYUSAI?
NO! WELL, NOT QUITE...
AH!
THANK YOU SO MUCH FOR SAVING ME!
SO, WHAT'S THIS GUY'S STORY?
COULD HE BE...
U-UM...
M-MIGHT YOU BE...
ARE WE RELATED?

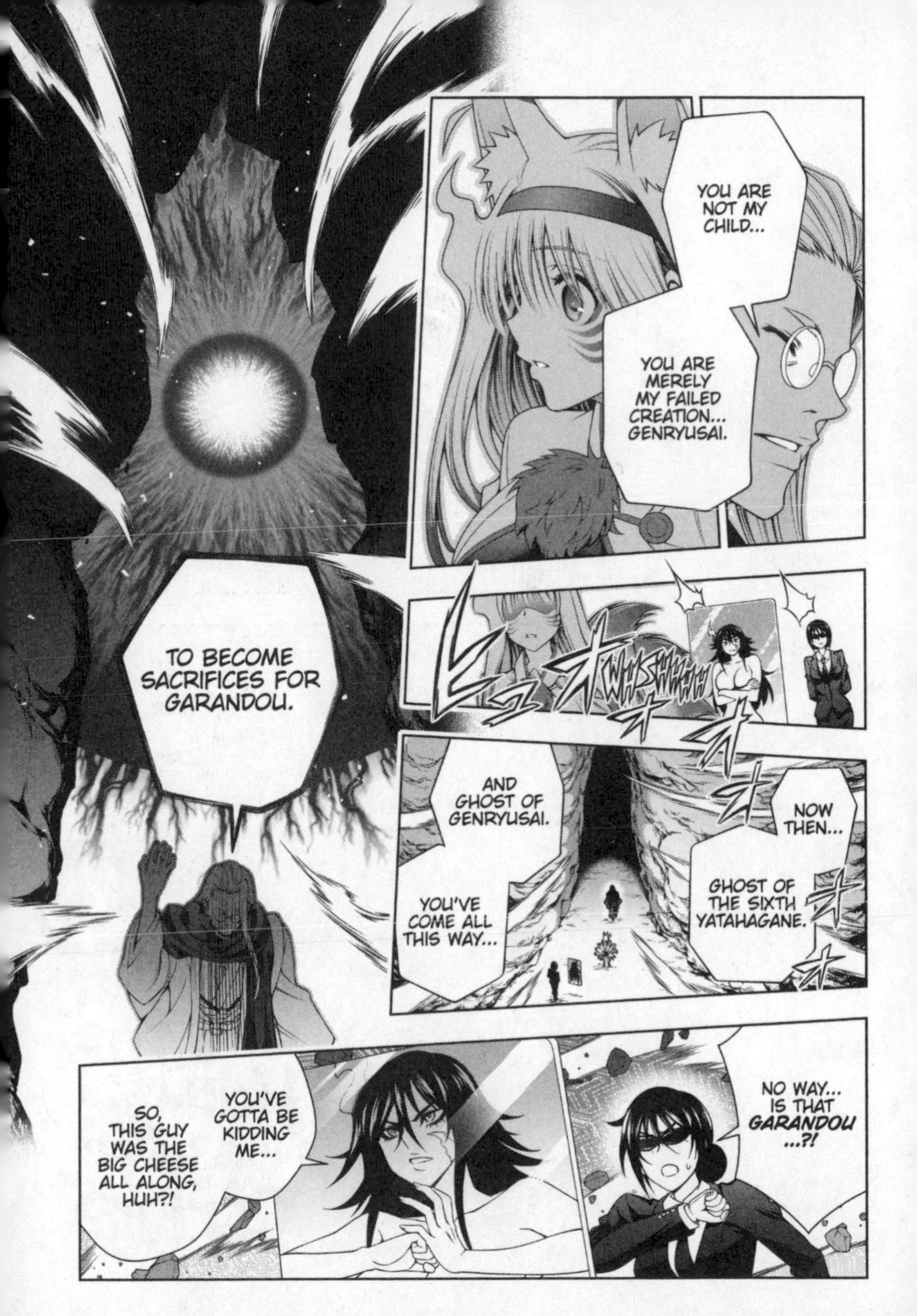
YOU ARE NOT MY CHILD...
YOU ARE MERELY MY FAILED CREATION... GENRYUSAI.
NOW THEN...
GHOST OF THE SIXTH YATAHAGANE.
AND GHOST OF GENRYUSAI.
YOU'VE COME ALL THIS WAY...
TO BECOME SACRIFICES FOR GARANDOU.
NO WAY... IS THAT GARANDOU...?!
YOU'VE GOTTA BE KIDDING ME...
SO, THIS GUY WAS THE BIG CHEESE ALL ALONG, HUH?!

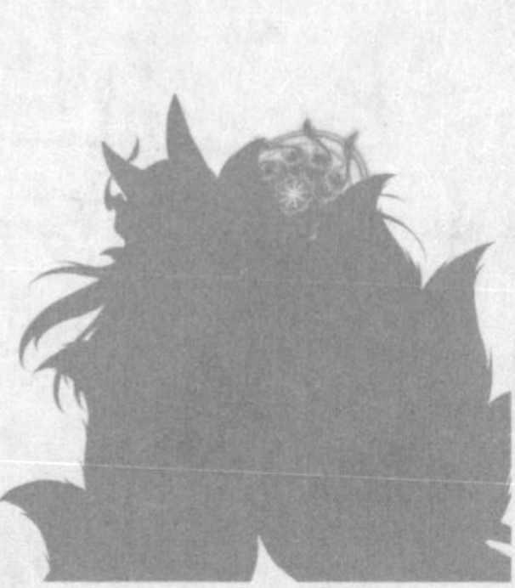

Yuuna and the Haunted Hot Springs

126 The Mastermind Revealed?!

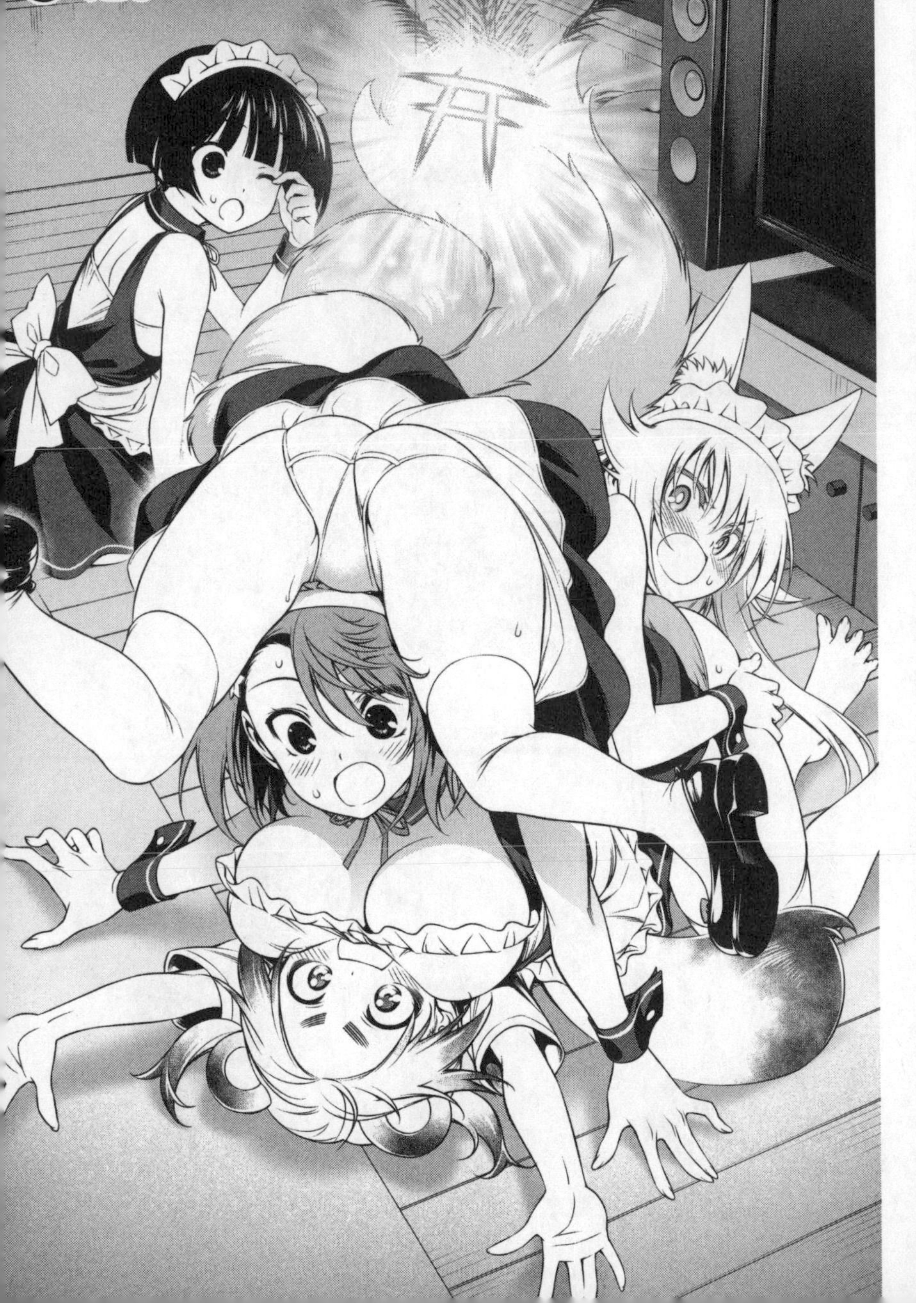

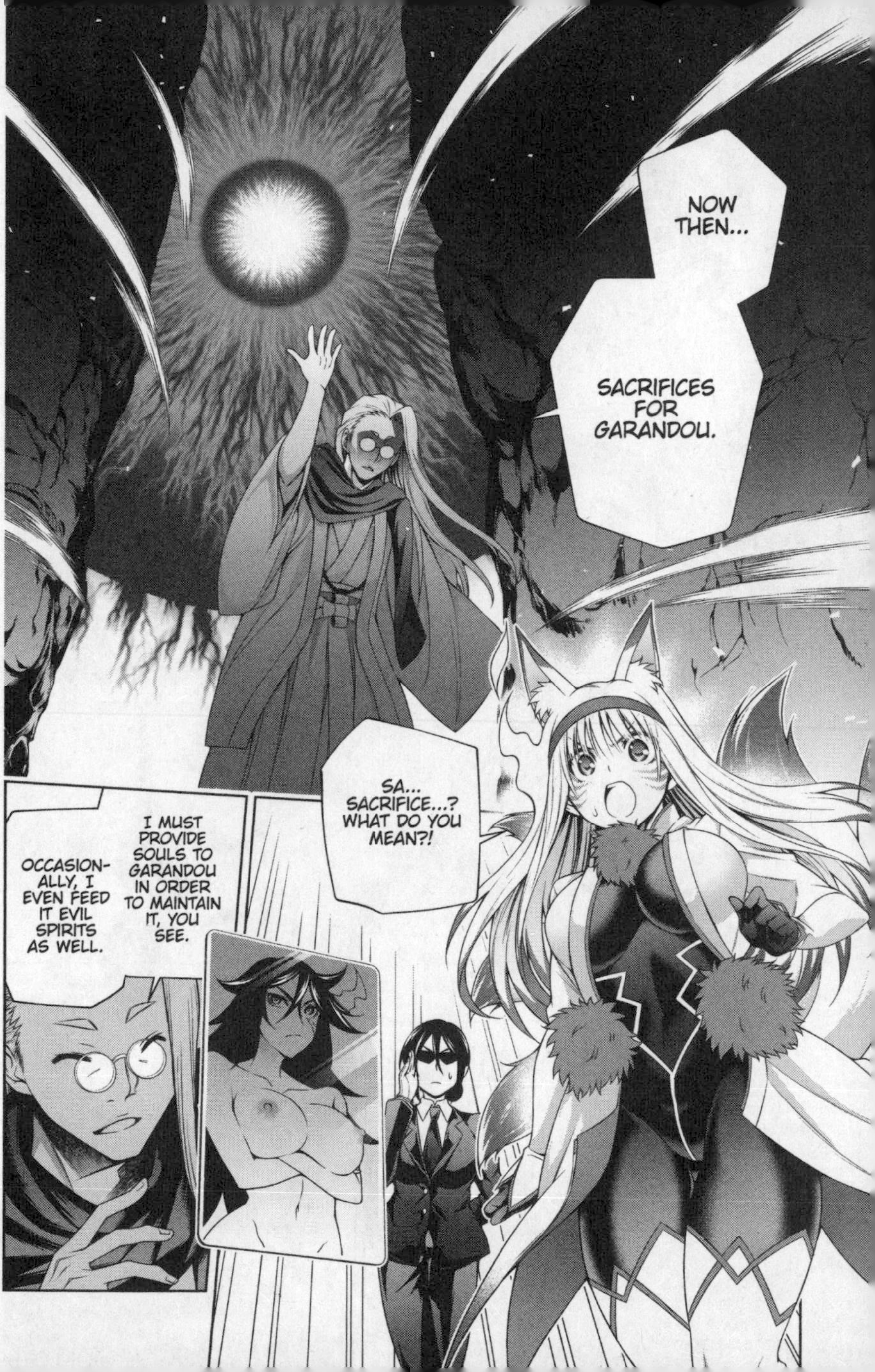
NOW THEN...
SACRIFICES FOR GARANDOU.
SA... SACRIFICE...? WHAT DO YOU MEAN?!
I MUST PROVIDE SOULS TO GARANDOU IN ORDER TO MAINTAIN IT, YOU SEE.
OCCASION-ALLY, I EVEN FEED IT EVIL SPIRITS AS WELL.

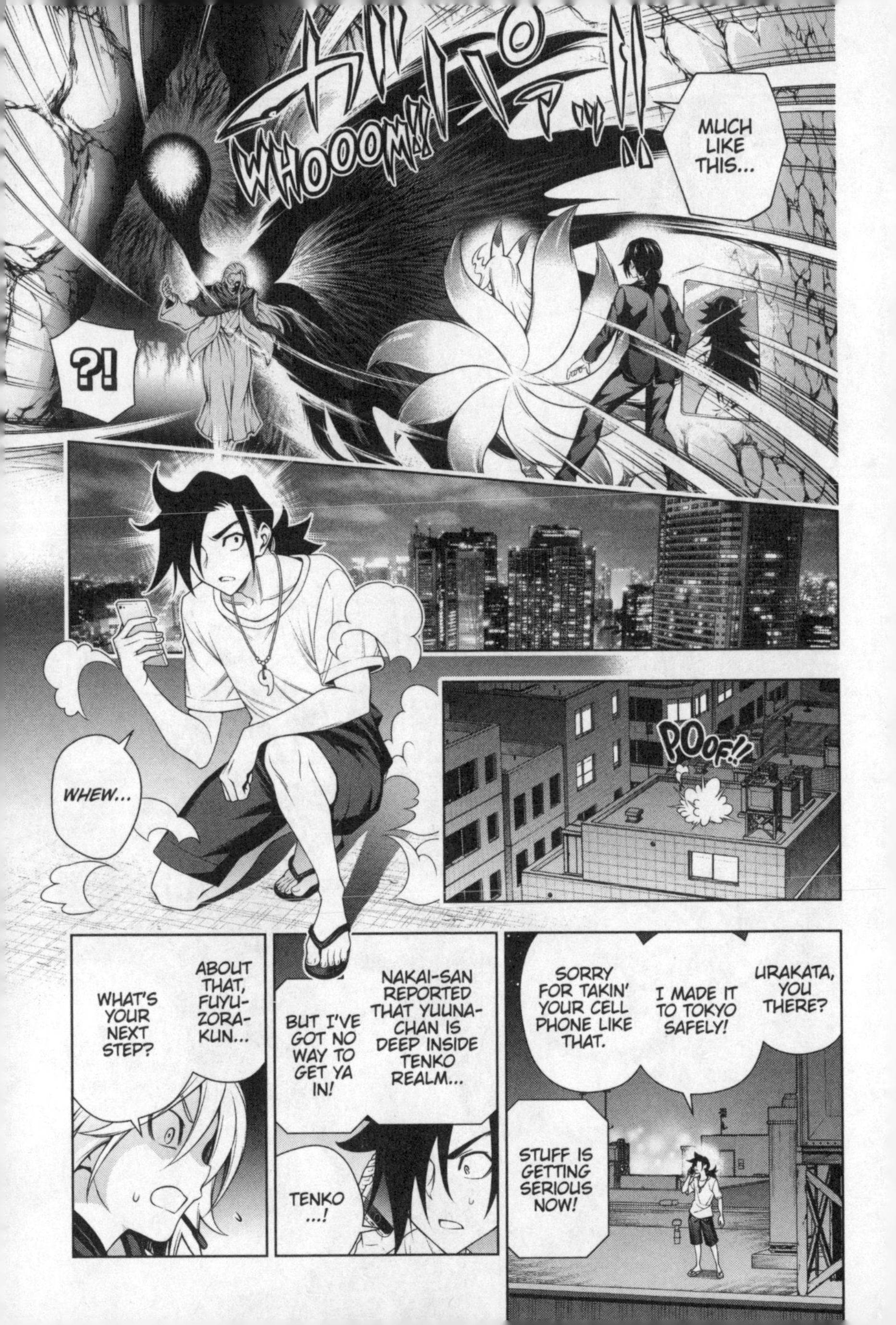
MUCH LIKE THIS...
WHOOOM!!
?!
POOF!!
WHEW...
URAKATA, YOU THERE?
I MADE IT TO TOKYO SAFELY!
SORRY FOR TAKIN' YOUR CELL PHONE LIKE THAT.
STUFF IS GETTING SERIOUS NOW!
NAKAI-SAN REPORTED THAT YUUNA-CHAN IS DEEP INSIDE TENKO REALM...
BUT I'VE GOT NO WAY TO GET YA IN!
TENKO ...!
ABOUT THAT, FUYU-ZORA-KUN...
WHAT'S YOUR NEXT STEP?

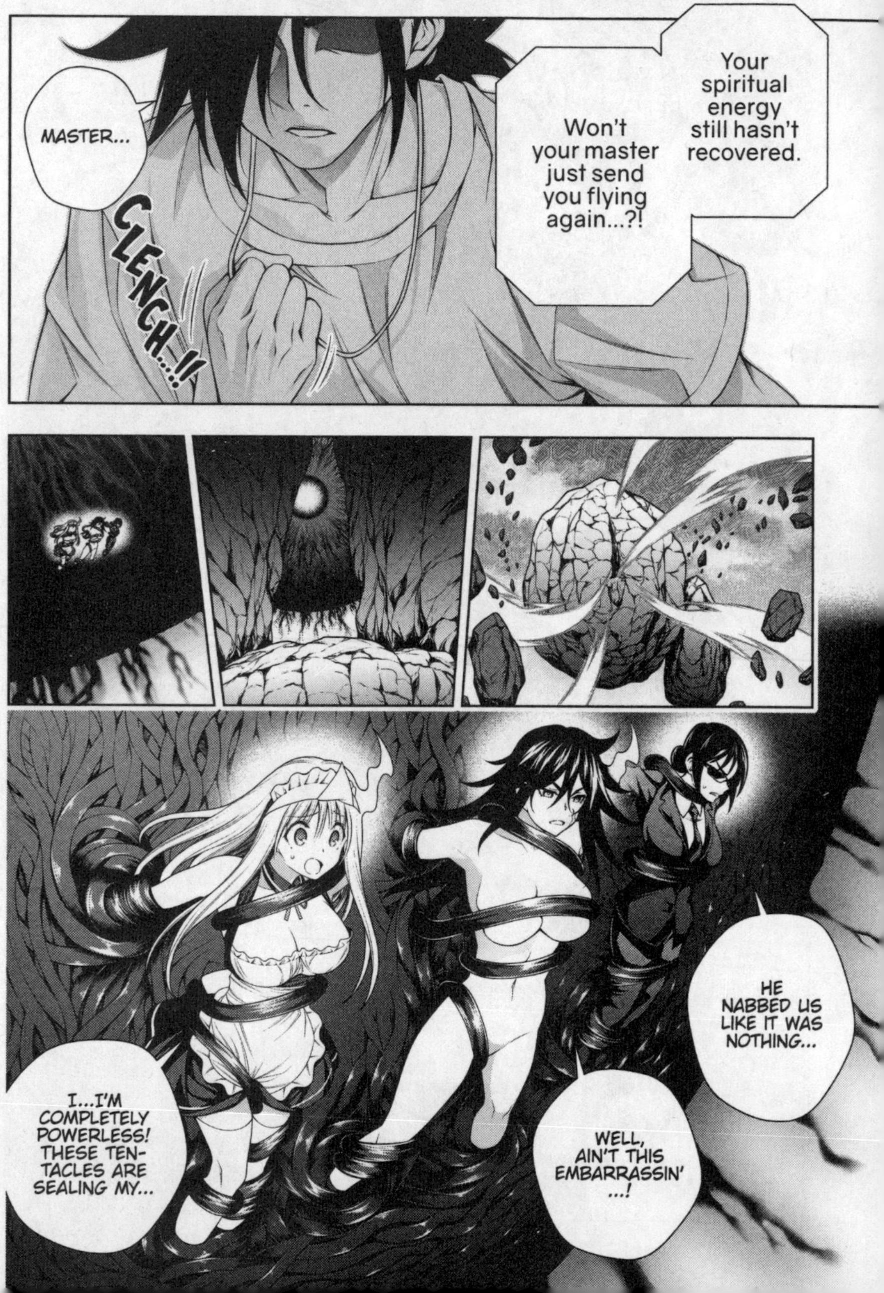
Your spiritual energy still hasn't recovered.
Won't your master just send you flying again...?!
MASTER...
CLENCH...!!
HE NABBED US LIKE IT WAS NOTHING...
WELL, AIN'T THIS EMBARRASSIN'...!
I...I'M COMPLETELY POWERLESS! THESE TEN-TACLES ARE SEALING MY...

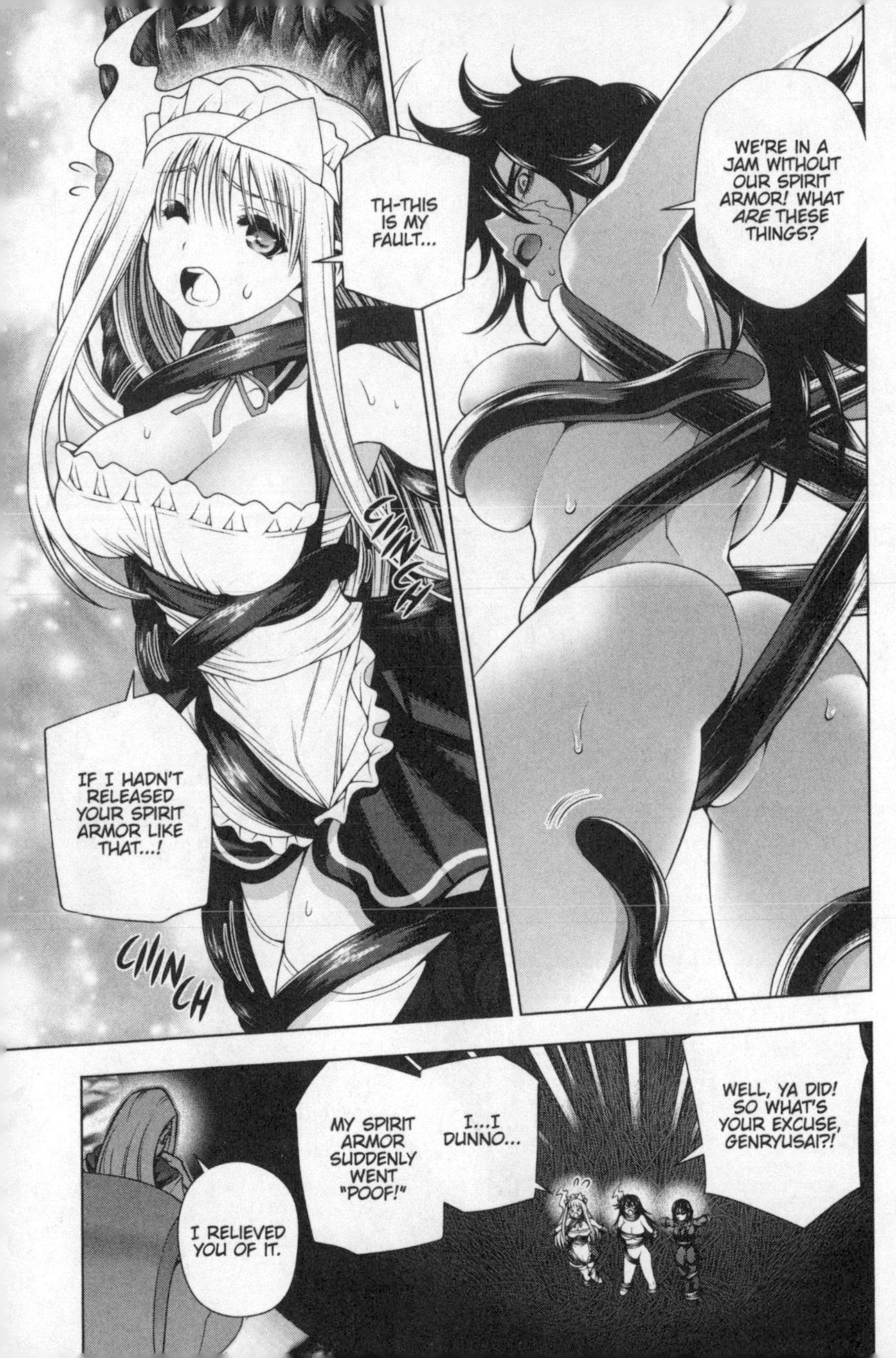
WE'RE IN A JAM WITHOUT OUR SPIRIT ARMOR! WHAT *ARE* THESE THINGS?
TH-THIS IS MY FAULT...
CIIINCH
IF I HADN'T RELEASED YOUR SPIRIT ARMOR LIKE THAT...!
CIIINCH
WELL, YA DID! SO WHAT'S YOUR EXCUSE, GENRYUSAI?!
I...I DUNNO...
MY SPIRIT ARMOR SUDDENLY WENT "POOF!"
I RELIEVED YOU OF IT.

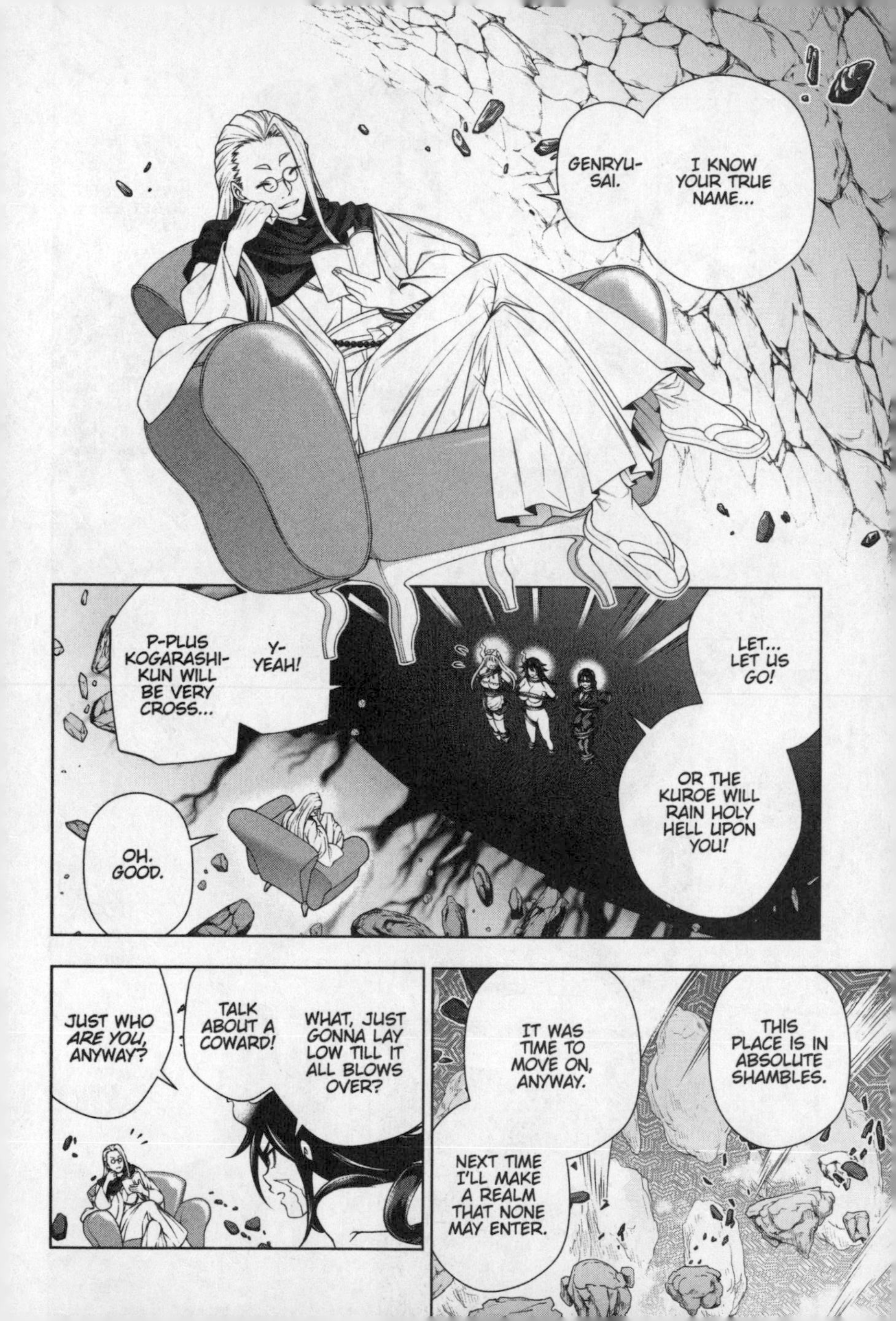

I KNOW YOUR TRUE NAME...
GENRYU-SAI.
LET... LET US GO!
OR THE KUROE WILL RAIN HOLY HELL UPON YOU!
Y-YEAH!
P-PLUS KOGARASHI-KUN WILL BE VERY CROSS...
OH. GOOD.
THIS PLACE IS IN ABSOLUTE SHAMBLES.
IT WAS TIME TO MOVE ON, ANYWAY.
NEXT TIME I'LL MAKE A REALM THAT NONE MAY ENTER.
WHAT, JUST GONNA LAY LOW TILL IT ALL BLOWS OVER?
TALK ABOUT A COWARD!
JUST WHO *ARE YOU,* ANYWAY?

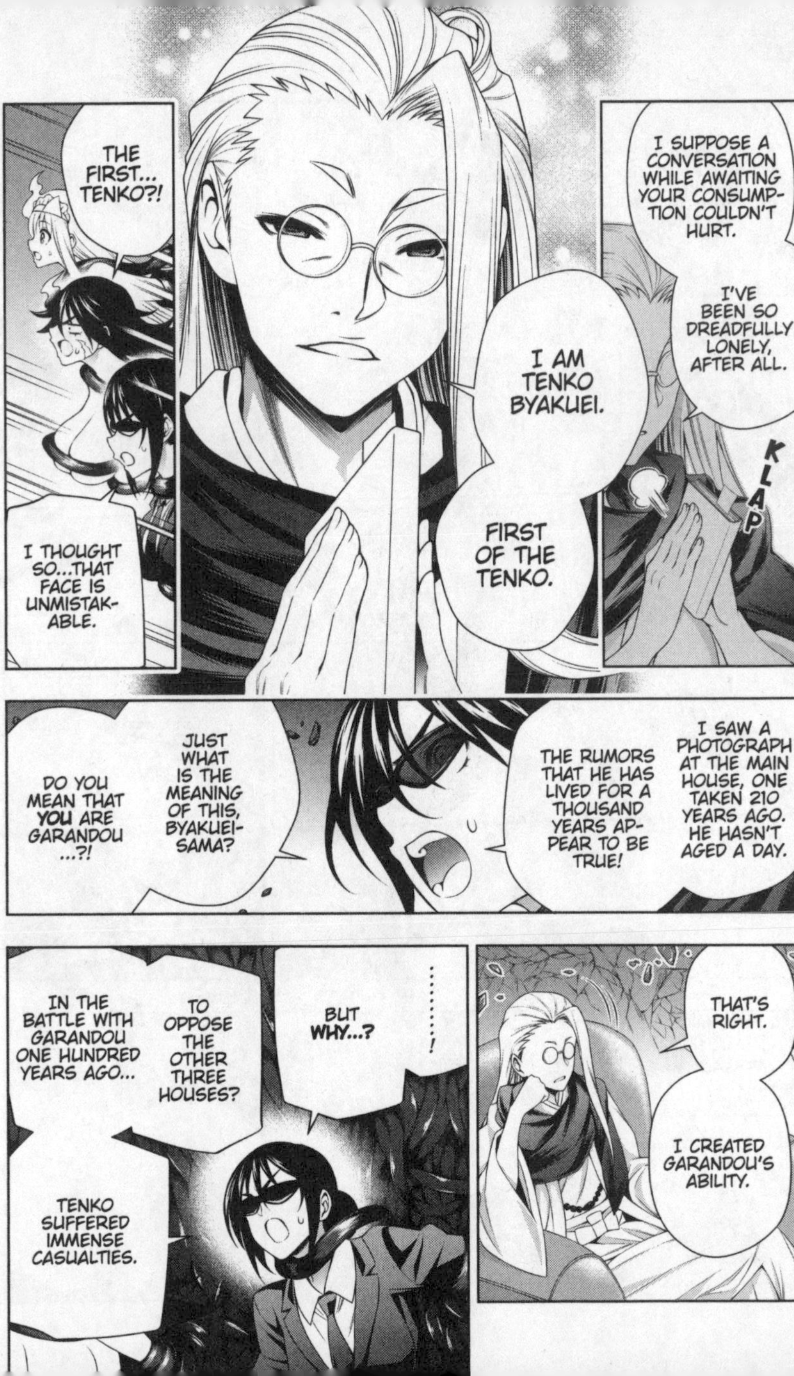
I SUPPOSE A CONVERSATION WHILE AWAITING YOUR CONSUMPTION COULDN'T HURT.
I'VE BEEN SO DREADFULLY LONELY, AFTER ALL.
KLAP
I AM TENKO BYAKUEI.
FIRST OF THE TENKO.
THE FIRST... TENKO?!
I THOUGHT SO...THAT FACE IS UNMISTAKABLE.
I SAW A PHOTOGRAPH AT THE MAIN HOUSE, ONE TAKEN 210 YEARS AGO. HE HASN'T AGED A DAY.
THE RUMORS THAT HE HAS LIVED FOR A THOUSAND YEARS APPEAR TO BE TRUE!
JUST WHAT IS THE MEANING OF THIS, BYAKUEI-SAMA?
DO YOU MEAN THAT YOU ARE GARANDOU...?!
THAT'S RIGHT.
I CREATED GARANDOU'S ABILITY.
......!
BUT WHY...?
TO OPPOSE THE OTHER THREE HOUSES?
IN THE BATTLE WITH GARANDOU ONE HUNDRED YEARS AGO...
TENKO SUFFERED IMMENSE CASUALTIES.

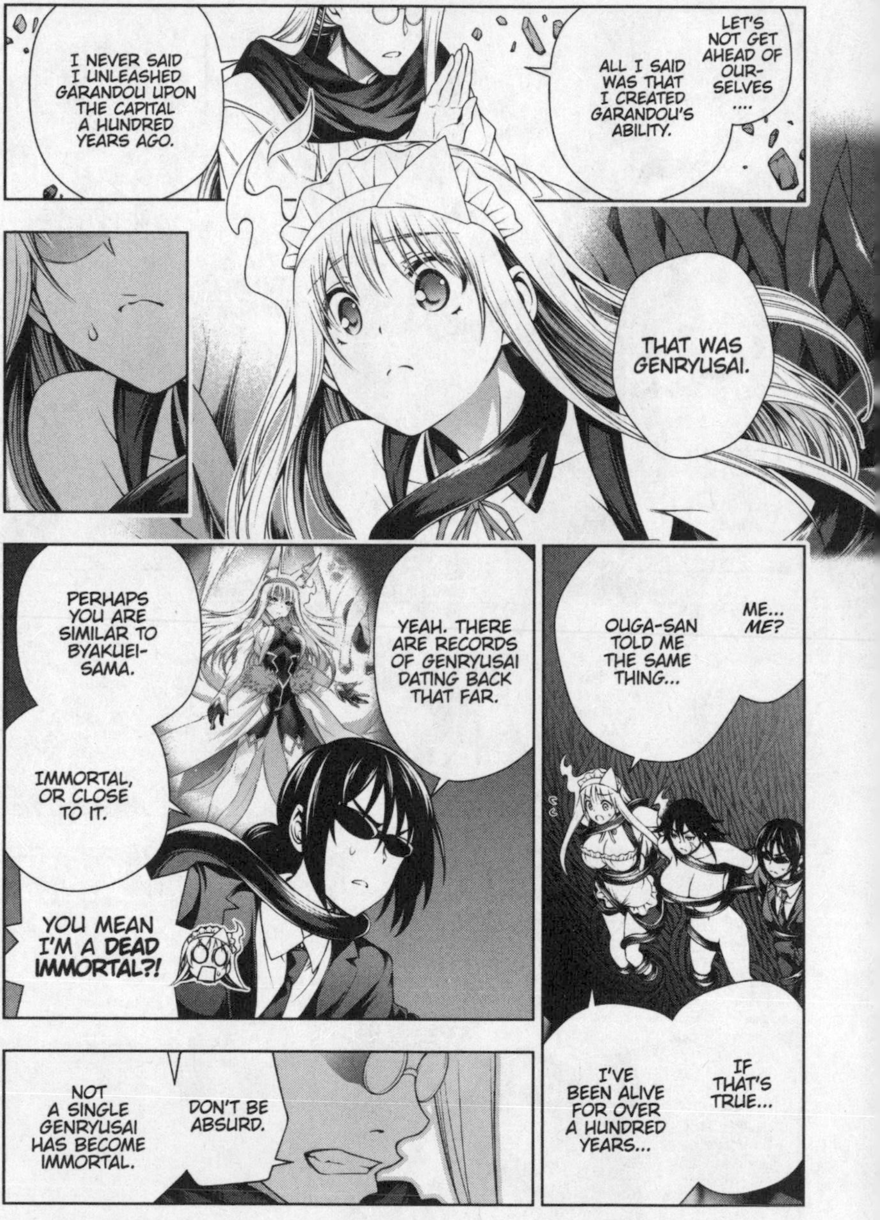
LET'S NOT GET AHEAD OF OUR-SELVES ....
ALL I SAID WAS THAT I CREATED GARANDOU'S ABILITY.
I NEVER SAID I UNLEASHED GARANDOU UPON THE CAPITAL A HUNDRED YEARS AGO.
THAT WAS GENRYUSAI.
ME... ME?
OUGA-SAN TOLD ME THE SAME THING...
YEAH. THERE ARE RECORDS OF GENRYUSAI DATING BACK THAT FAR.
PERHAPS YOU ARE SIMILAR TO BYAKUEI-SAMA.
IMMORTAL, OR CLOSE TO IT.
YOU MEAN I'M A DEAD IMMORTAL?!
IF THAT'S TRUE...
I'VE BEEN ALIVE FOR OVER A HUNDRED YEARS...
DON'T BE ABSURD.
NOT A SINGLE GENRYUSAI HAS BECOME IMMORTAL.

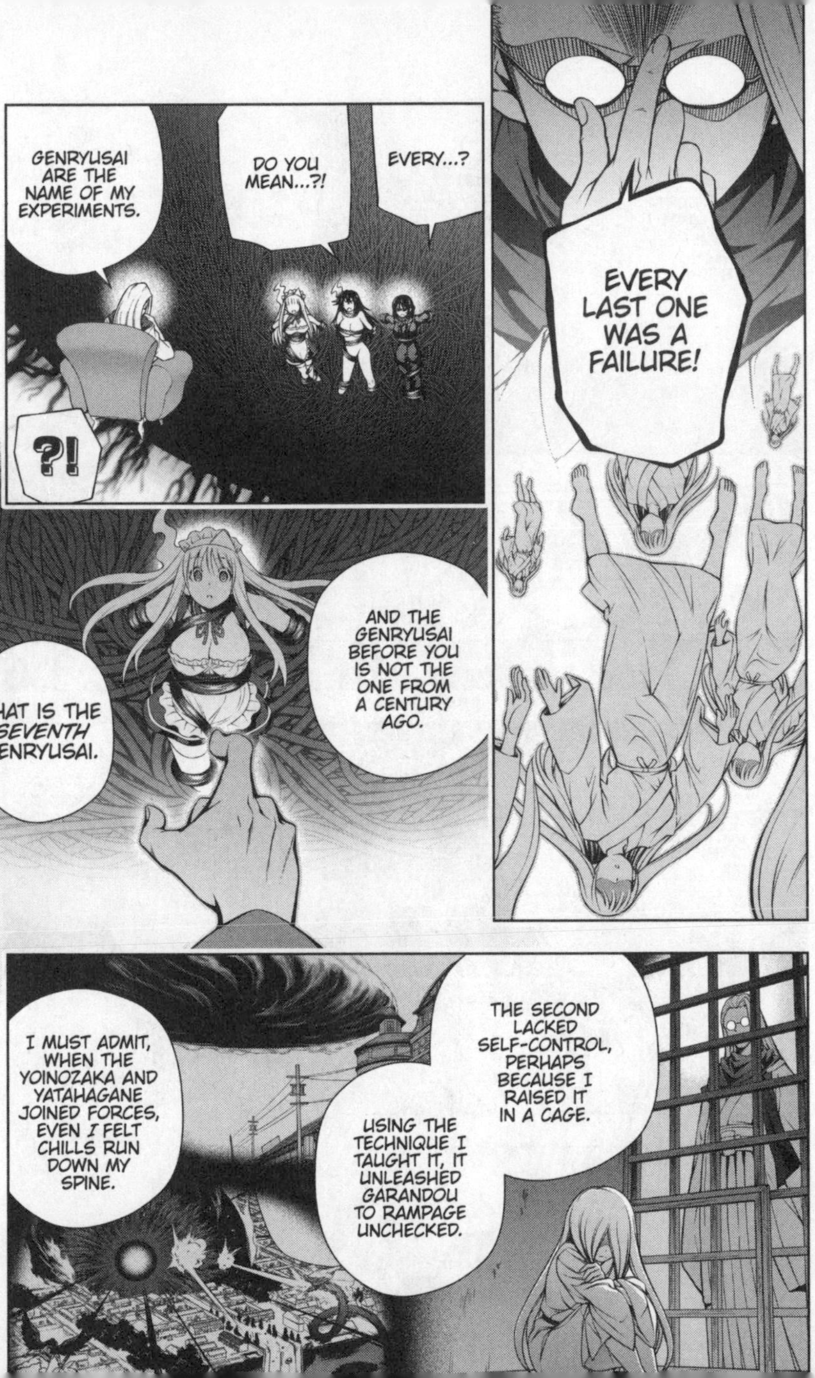
EVERY LAST ONE WAS A FAILURE!
EVERY...?
DO YOU MEAN...?!
GENRYUSAI ARE THE NAME OF MY EXPERIMENTS.
?!
AND THE GENRYUSAI BEFORE YOU IS NOT THE ONE FROM A CENTURY AGO.
THAT IS THE *SEVENTH* GENRYUSAI.
THE SECOND LACKED SELF-CONTROL, PERHAPS BECAUSE I RAISED IT IN A CAGE.
USING THE TECHNIQUE I TAUGHT IT, IT UNLEASHED GARANDOU TO RAMPAGE UNCHECKED.
I MUST ADMIT, WHEN THE YOINOZAKA AND YATAHAGANE JOINED FORCES, EVEN *I* FELT CHILLS RUN DOWN MY SPINE.

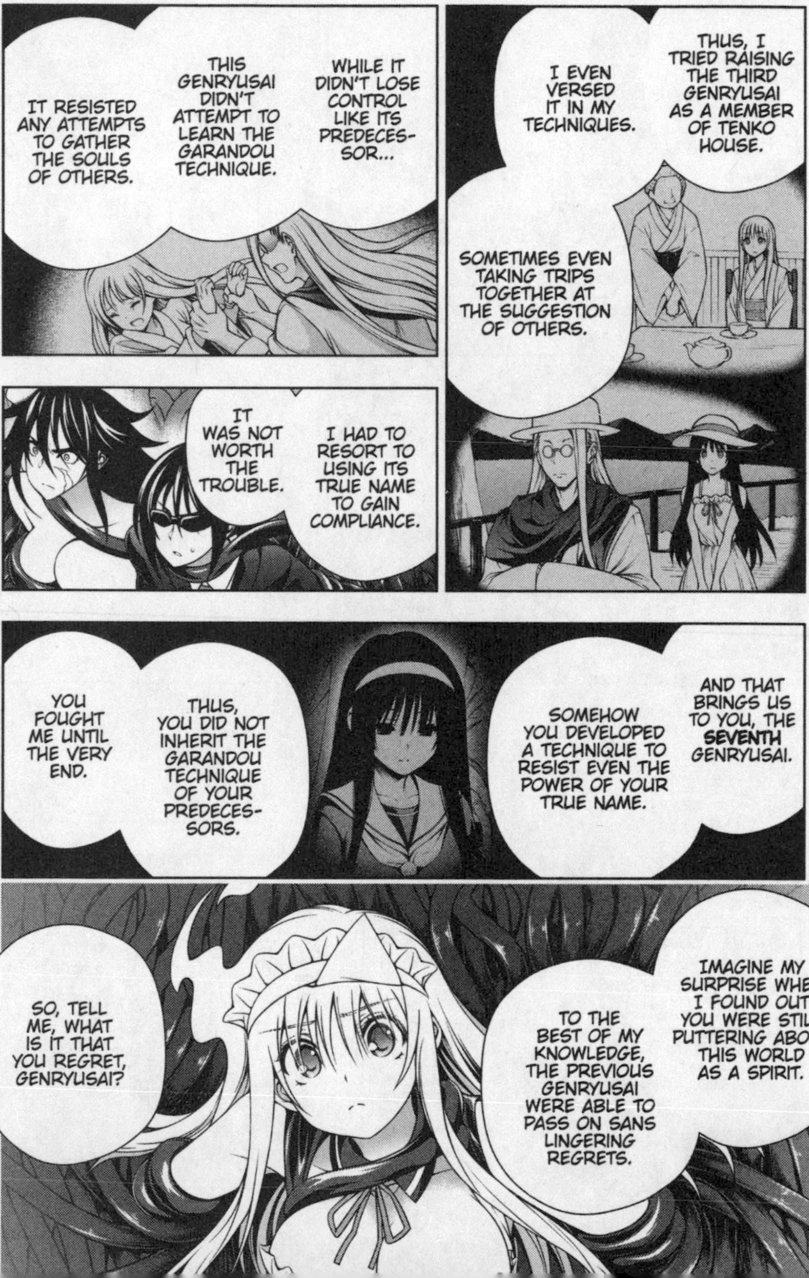
THUS, I TRIED RAISING THE THIRD GENRYUSAI AS A MEMBER OF TENKO HOUSE.
I EVEN VERSED IT IN MY TECHNIQUES.
SOMETIMES EVEN TAKING TRIPS TOGETHER AT THE SUGGESTION OF OTHERS.
WHILE IT DIDN'T LOSE CONTROL LIKE ITS PREDECES-SOR...
THIS GENRYUSAI DIDN'T ATTEMPT TO LEARN THE GARANDOU TECHNIQUE.
IT RESISTED ANY ATTEMPTS TO GATHER THE SOULS OF OTHERS.
I HAD TO RESORT TO USING ITS TRUE NAME TO GAIN COMPLIANCE.
IT WAS NOT WORTH THE TROUBLE.
AND THAT BRINGS US TO YOU, THE **SEVENTH** GENRYUSAI.
SOMEHOW YOU DEVELOPED A TECHNIQUE TO RESIST EVEN THE POWER OF YOUR TRUE NAME.
THUS, YOU DID NOT INHERIT THE GARANDOU TECHNIQUE OF YOUR PREDECES-SORS.
YOU FOUGHT ME UNTIL THE VERY END.
IMAGINE MY SURPRISE WHEN I FOUND OUT YOU WERE STILL PUTTERING ABOUT THIS WORLD AS A SPIRIT.
TO THE BEST OF MY KNOWLEDGE, THE PREVIOUS GENRYUSAI WERE ABLE TO PASS ON SANS LINGERING REGRETS.
SO, TELL ME, WHAT IS IT THAT YOU REGRET, GENRYUSAI?

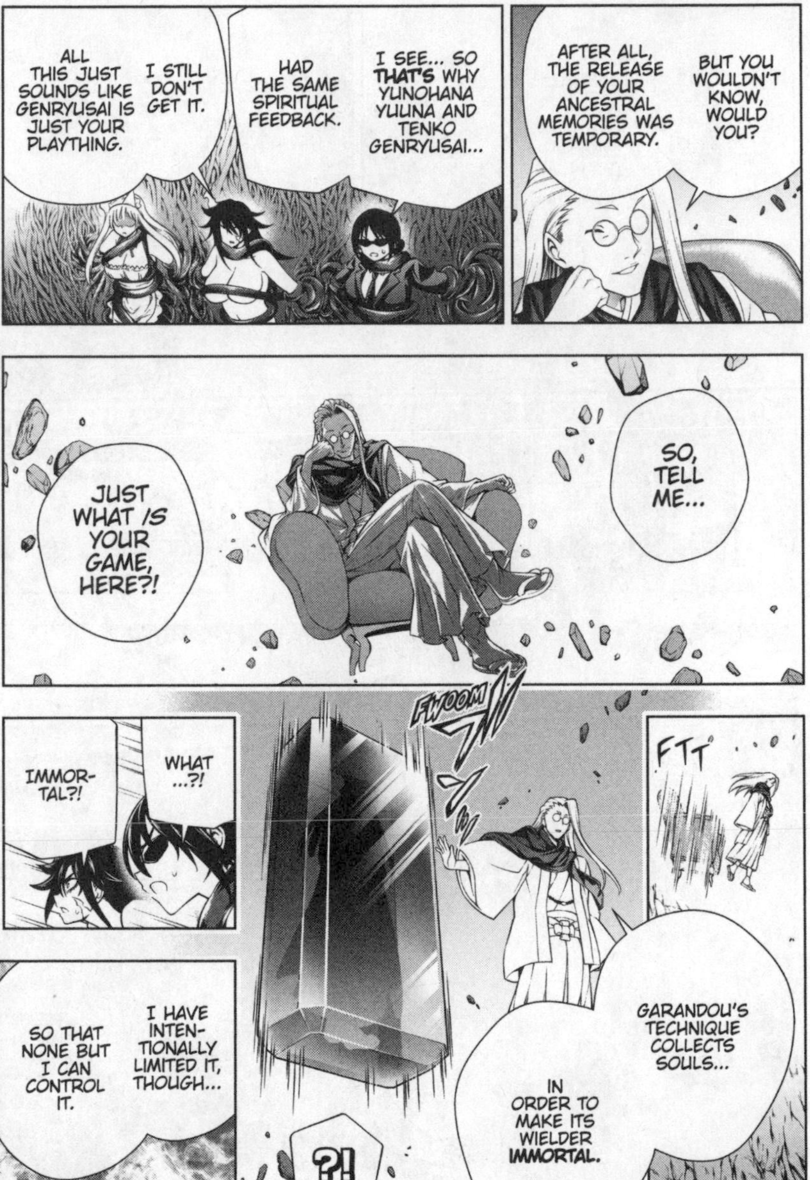
BUT YOU WOULDN'T KNOW, WOULD YOU?
AFTER ALL, THE RELEASE OF YOUR ANCESTRAL MEMORIES WAS TEMPORARY.
I SEE... SO THAT'S WHY YUNOHANA YUUNA AND TENKO GENRYUSAI...
HAD THE SAME SPIRITUAL FEEDBACK.
I STILL DON'T GET IT.
ALL THIS JUST SOUNDS LIKE GENRYUSAI IS JUST YOUR PLAYTHING.
SO, TELL ME...
JUST WHAT IS YOUR GAME, HERE?!
FTT
FWOOM
GARANDOU'S TECHNIQUE COLLECTS SOULS...
IN ORDER TO MAKE ITS WIELDER IMMORTAL.
?!
WHAT ...?!
IMMOR-TAL?!
I HAVE INTENTIONALLY LIMITED IT, THOUGH...
SO THAT NONE BUT I CAN CONTROL IT.

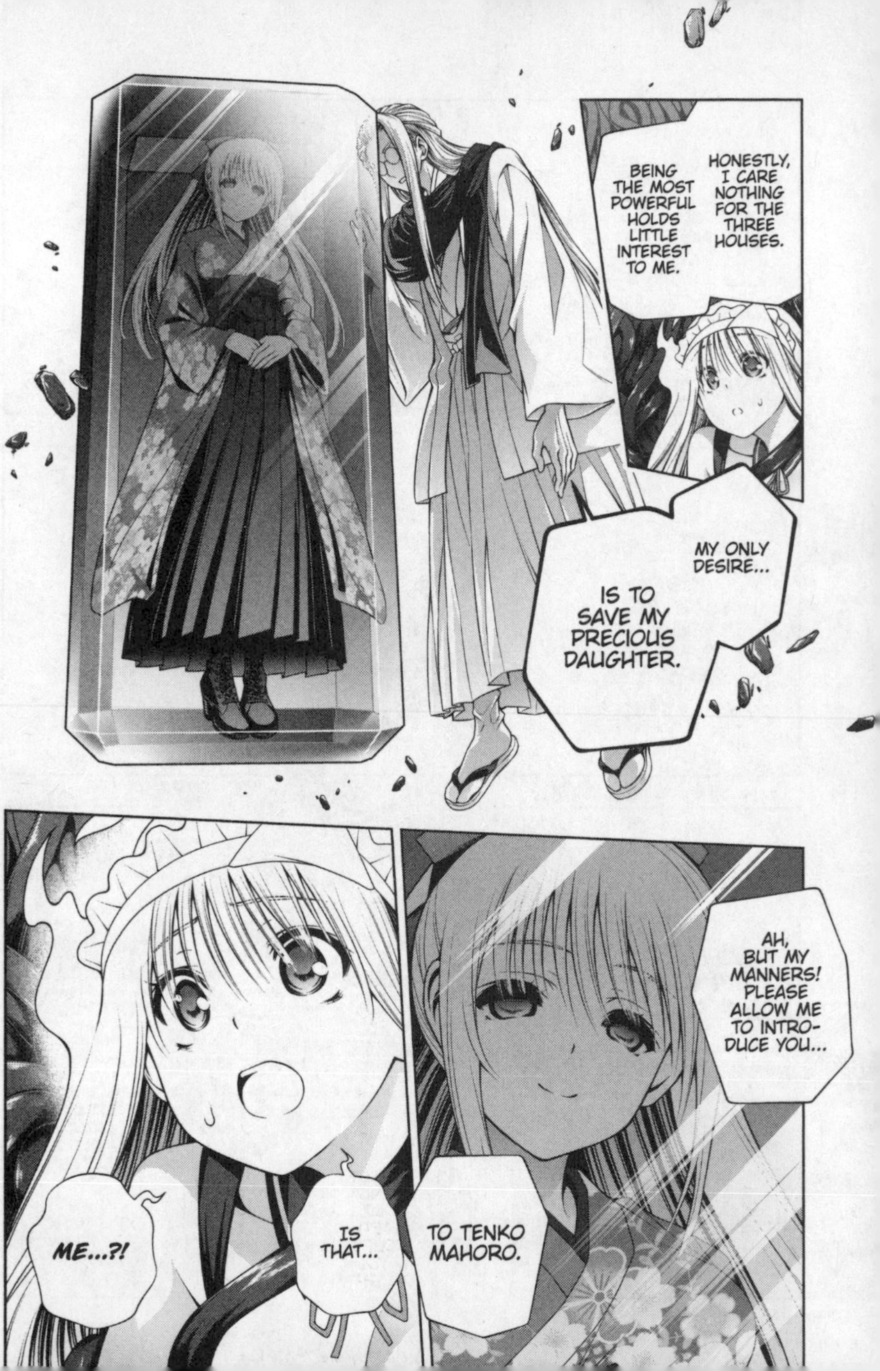
HONESTLY, I CARE NOTHING FOR THE THREE HOUSES.
BEING THE MOST POWERFUL HOLDS LITTLE INTEREST TO ME.
MY ONLY DESIRE...
IS TO SAVE MY PRECIOUS DAUGHTER.
AH, BUT MY MANNERS! PLEASE ALLOW ME TO INTRO-DUCE YOU...
TO TENKO MAHORO.
IS THAT...
ME...?!

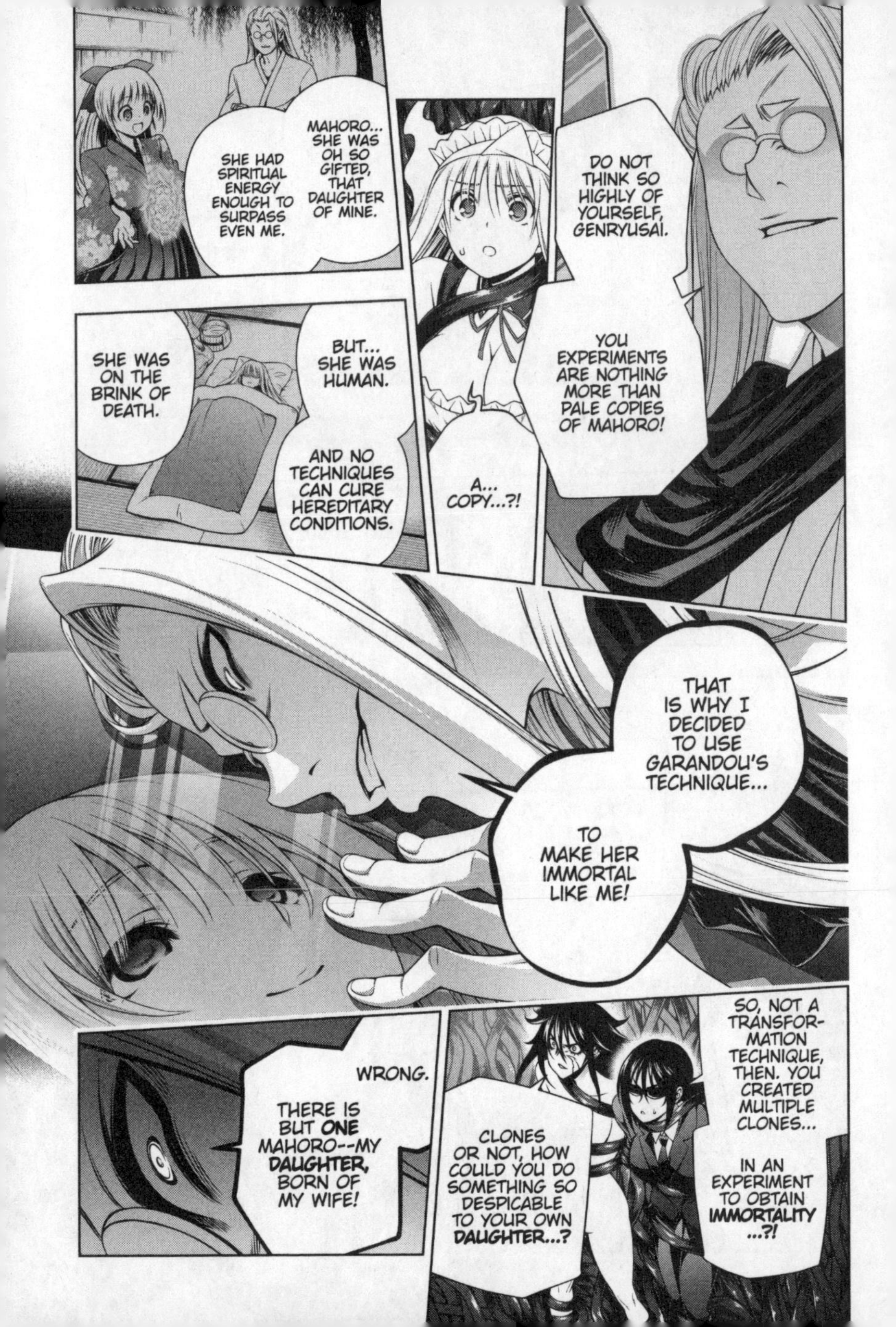
DO NOT THINK SO HIGHLY OF YOURSELF, GENRYUSAI.
YOU EXPERIMENTS ARE NOTHING MORE THAN PALE COPIES OF MAHORO!
A... COPY...?!
MAHORO... SHE WAS OH SO GIFTED, THAT DAUGHTER OF MINE.
SHE HAD SPIRITUAL ENERGY ENOUGH TO SURPASS EVEN ME.
BUT... SHE WAS HUMAN.
SHE WAS ON THE BRINK OF DEATH.
AND NO TECHNIQUES CAN CURE HEREDITARY CONDITIONS.
THAT IS WHY I DECIDED TO USE GARANDOU'S TECHNIQUE...
TO MAKE HER IMMORTAL LIKE ME!
SO, NOT A TRANSFORMATION TECHNIQUE, THEN. YOU CREATED MULTIPLE CLONES...
IN AN EXPERIMENT TO OBTAIN **IMMORTALITY**...?!
CLONES OR NOT, HOW COULD YOU DO SOMETHING SO DESPICABLE TO YOUR OWN **DAUGHTER**...?
WRONG.
THERE IS BUT **ONE** MAHORO--MY **DAUGHTER**, BORN OF MY WIFE!

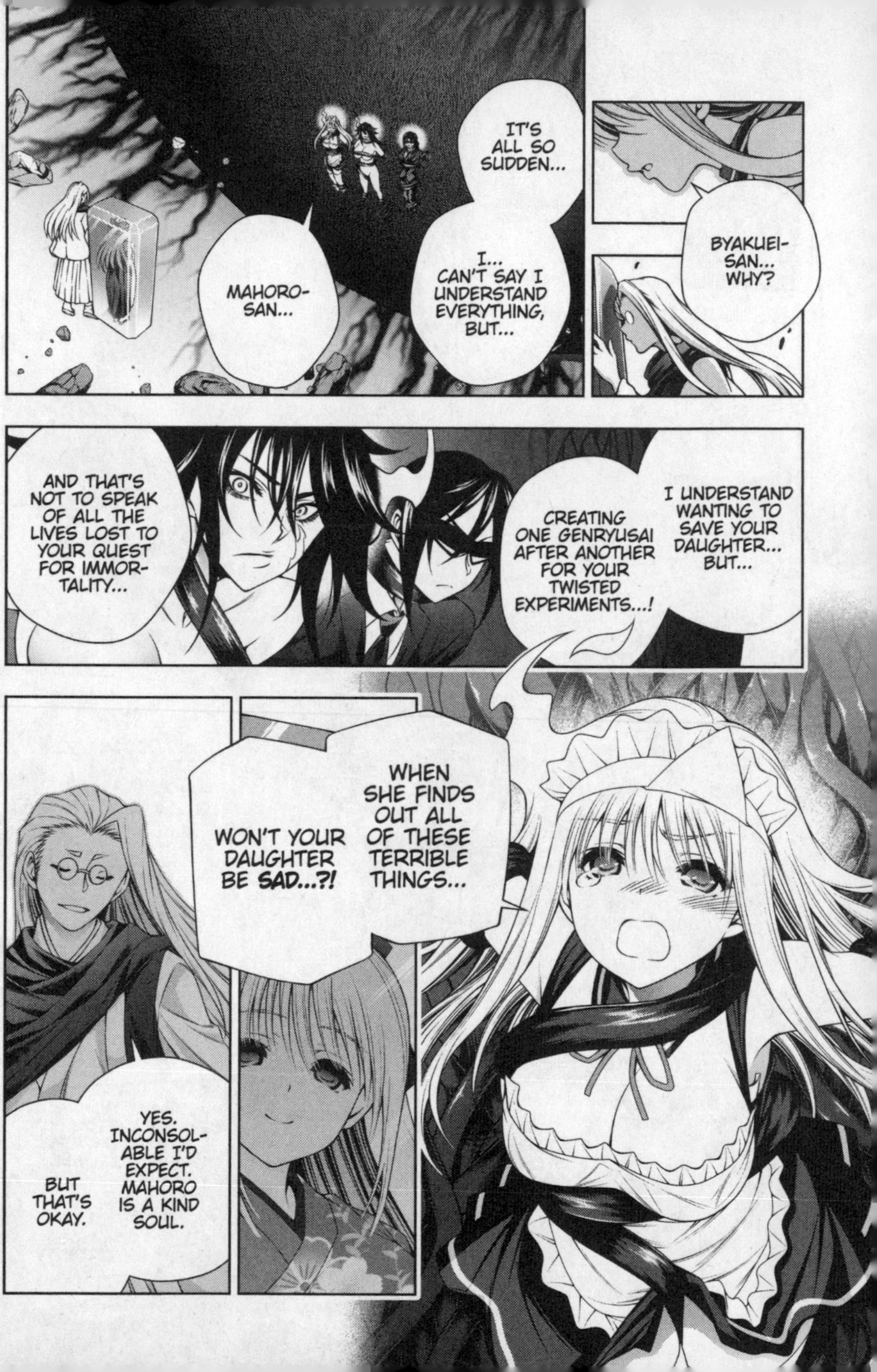
BYAKUEI-SAN... WHY?
IT'S ALL SO SUDDEN...
I... CAN'T SAY I UNDERSTAND EVERYTHING, BUT...
MAHORO-SAN...
I UNDERSTAND WANTING TO SAVE YOUR DAUGHTER... BUT...
CREATING ONE GENRYUSAI AFTER ANOTHER FOR YOUR TWISTED EXPERIMENTS...!
AND THAT'S NOT TO SPEAK OF ALL THE LIVES LOST TO YOUR QUEST FOR IMMOR-TALITY...
WHEN SHE FINDS OUT ALL OF THESE TERRIBLE THINGS...
WON'T YOUR DAUGHTER BE **SAD**...?!
YES. INCONSOL-ABLE I'D EXPECT. MAHORO IS A KIND SOUL.
BUT THAT'S OKAY.

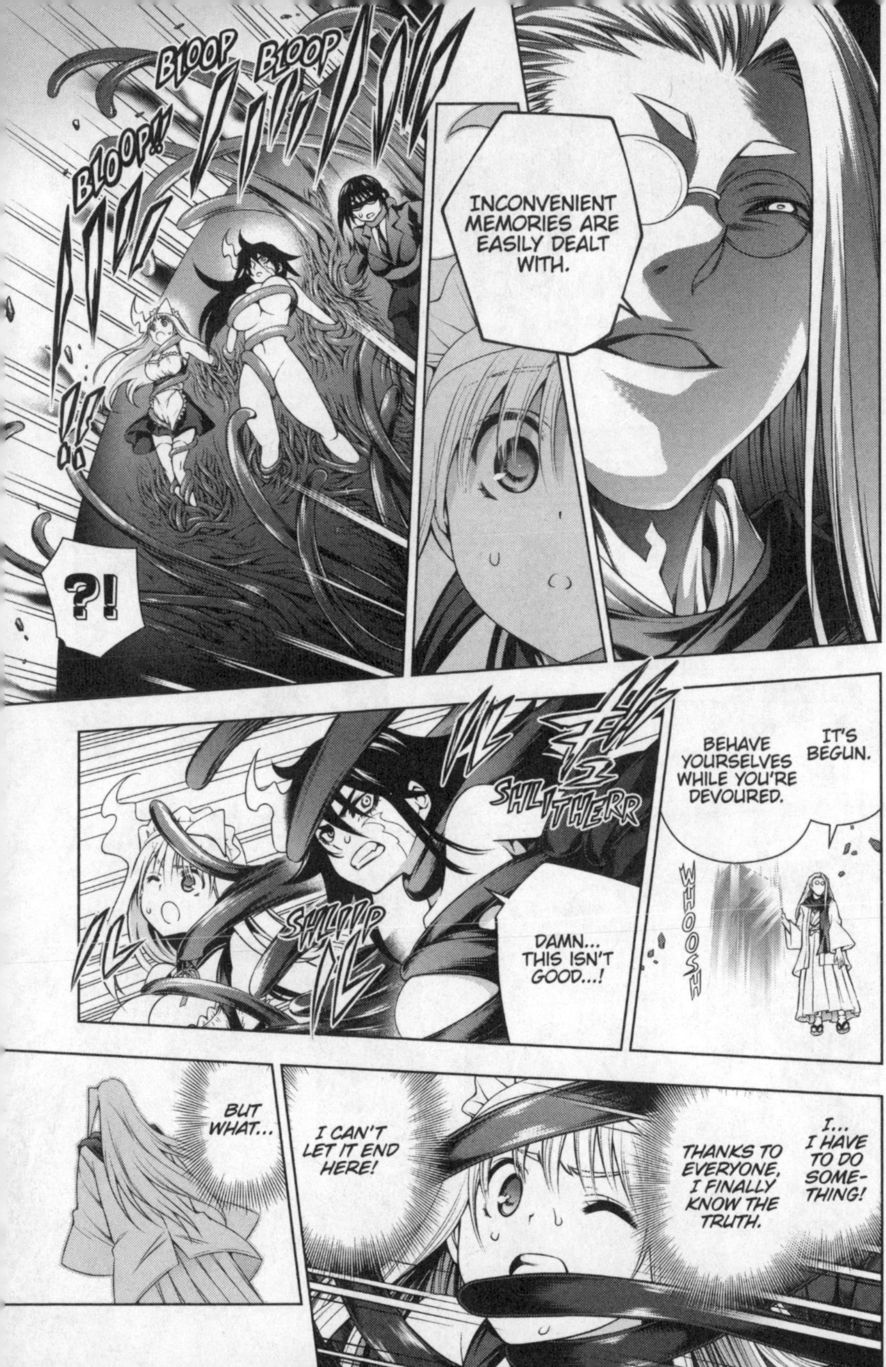
INCONVENIENT MEMORIES ARE EASILY DEALT WITH.
BLOOP
BLOOP
BLOOP!!
?!
IT'S BEGUN.
BEHAVE YOURSELVES WHILE YOU'RE DEVOURED.
WHOOSH
SHLITHERR
DAMN... THIS ISN'T GOOD...!
I... I HAVE TO DO SOME-THING!
THANKS TO EVERYONE, I FINALLY KNOW THE TRUTH.
I CAN'T LET IT END HERE!
BUT WHAT...

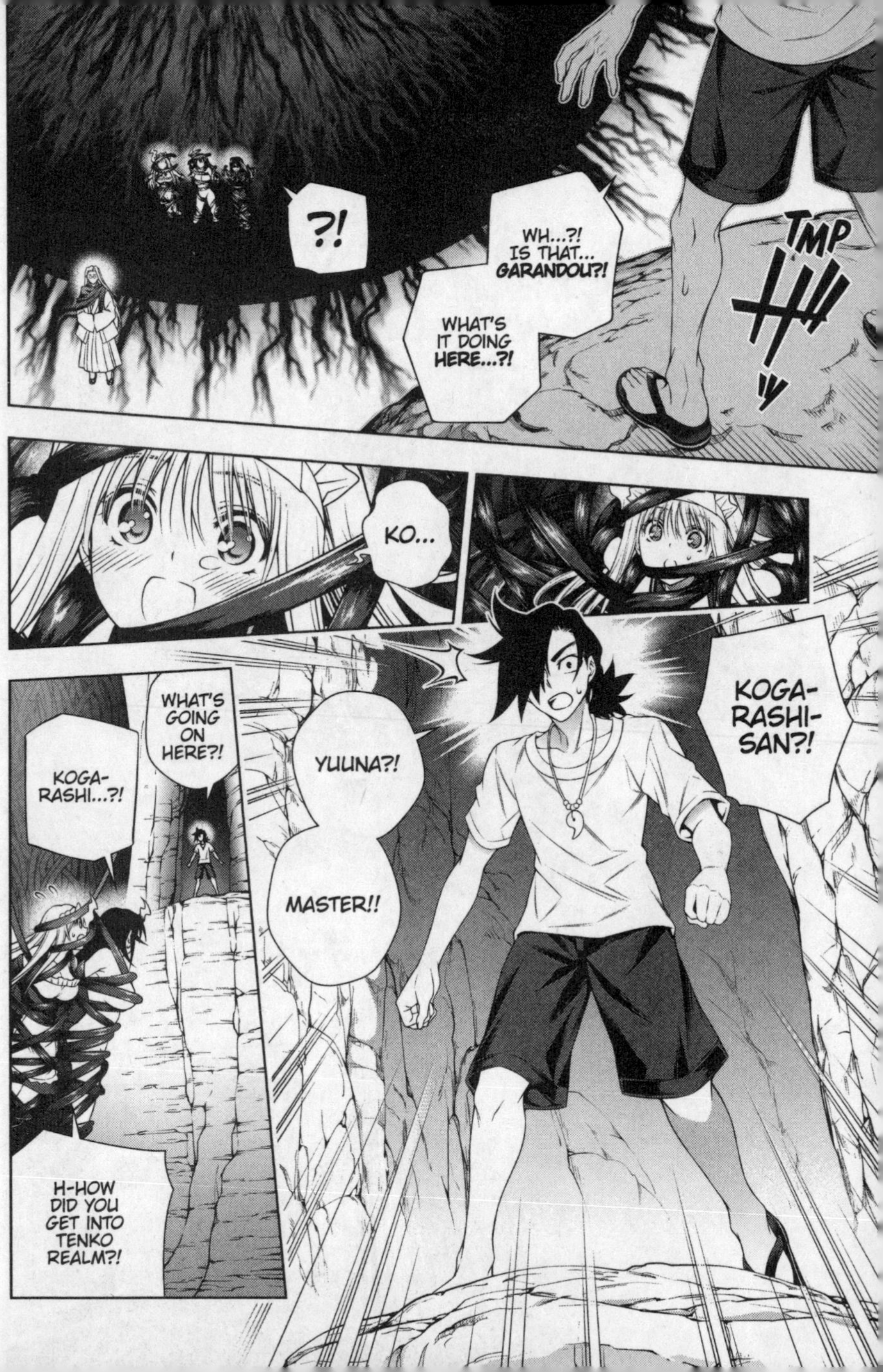
TMP
WH...?! IS THAT... GARANDOU?!
WHAT'S IT DOING HERE...?!
?!
KO...
KOGA-RASHI-SAN?!
YUUNA?!
MASTER!!
WHAT'S GOING ON HERE?!
KOGA-RASHI...?!
H-HOW DID YOU GET INTO TENKO REALM?!

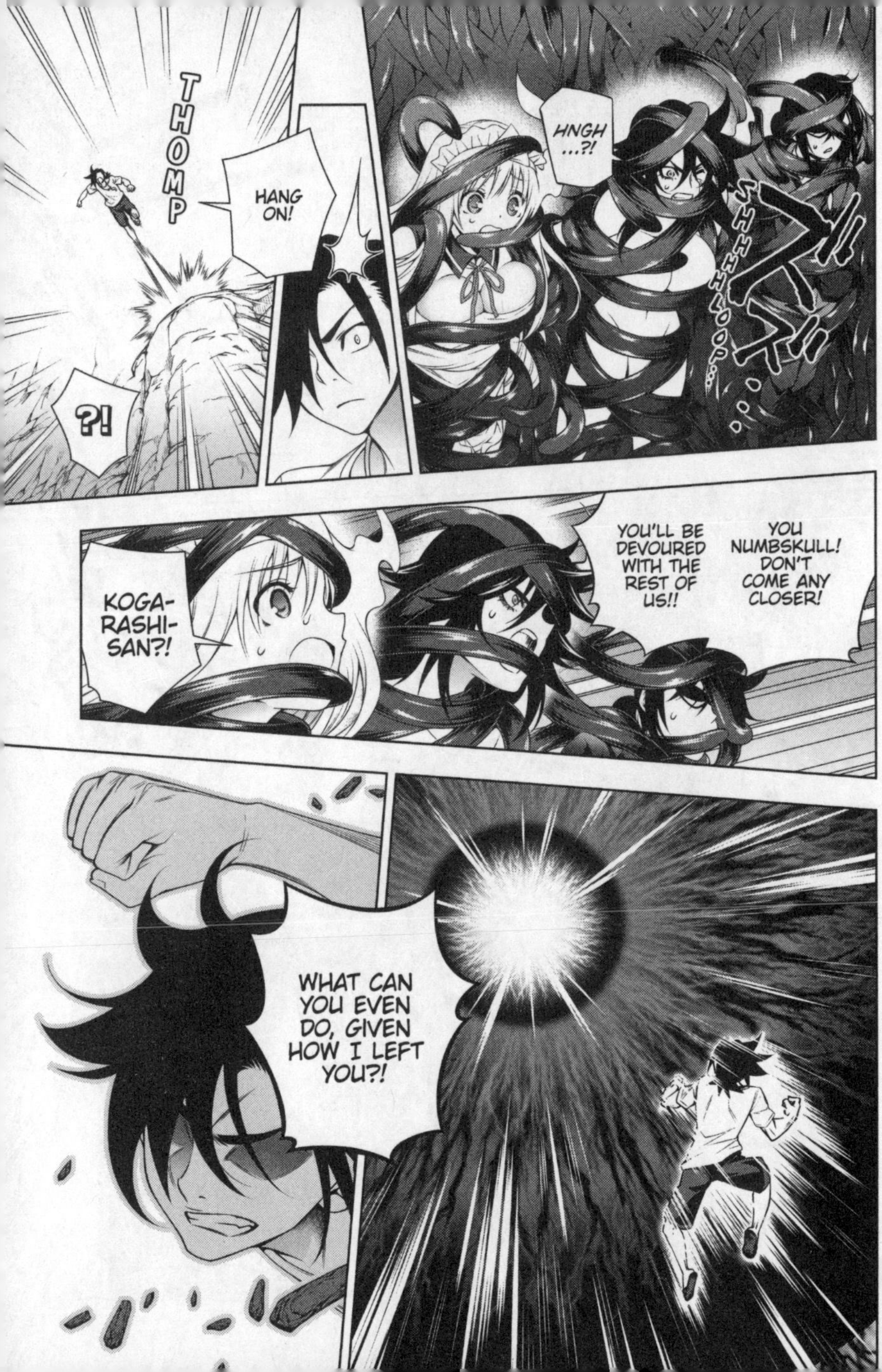
HNGH ...?!
SHHHHLOOP...
HANG ON!
THOMP
?!
YOU NUMBSKULL! DON'T COME ANY CLOSER!
YOU'LL BE DEVOURED WITH THE REST OF US!!
KOGA-RASHI-SAN?!
WHAT CAN YOU EVEN DO, GIVEN HOW I LEFT YOU?!

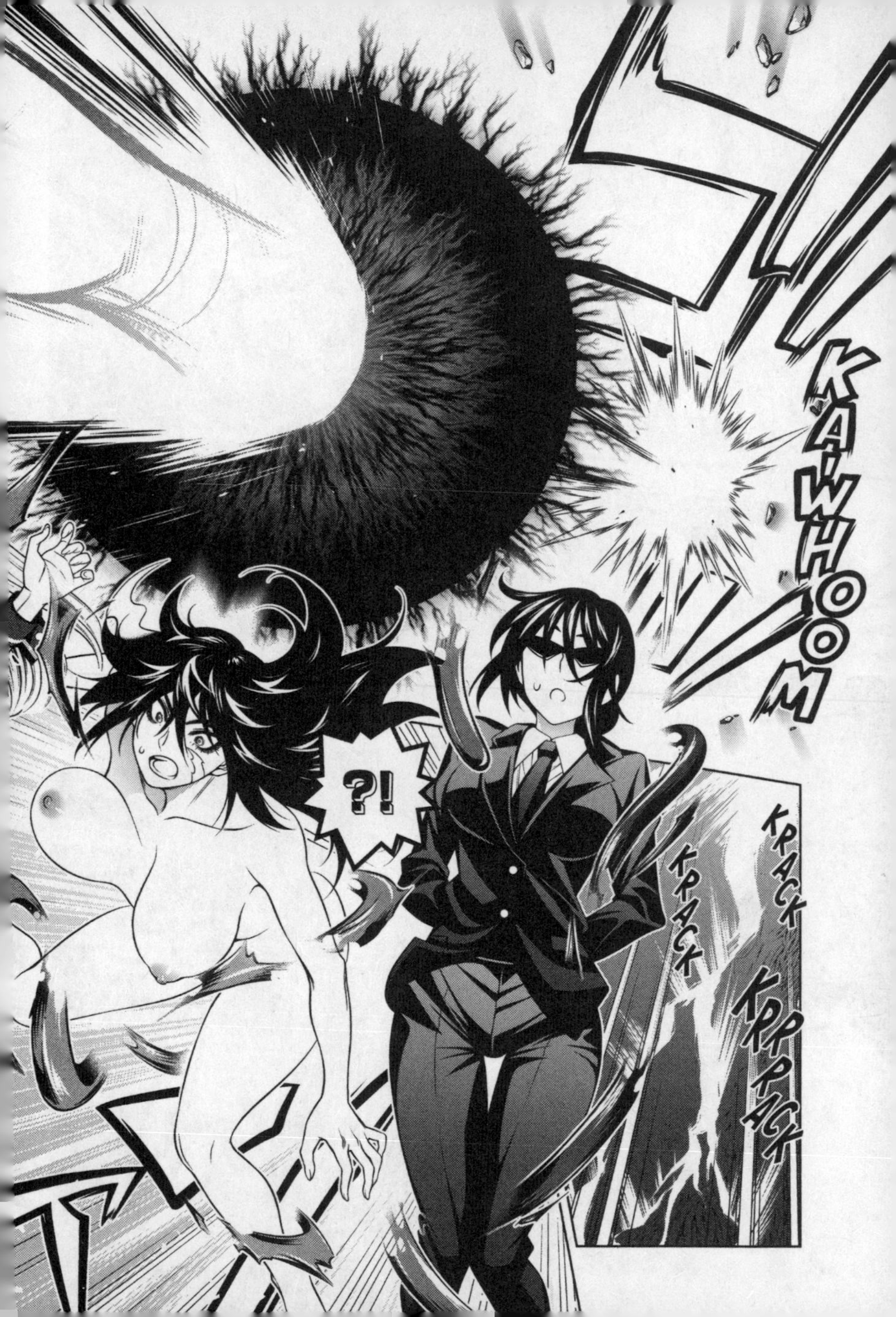
KA-WHOOOM
KRACK
KRACK
KRRRACK
?!

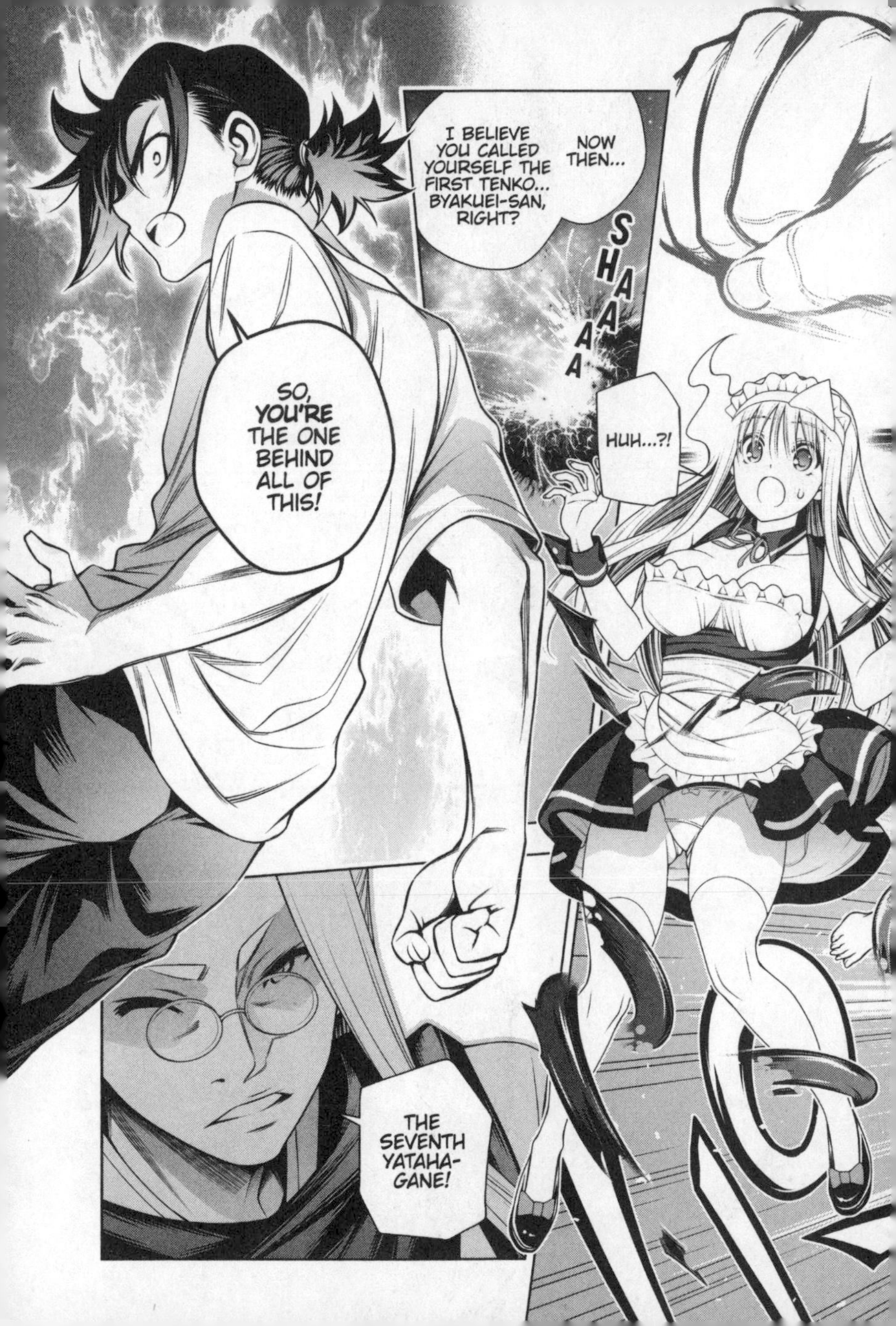
NOW THEN...
I BELIEVE YOU CALLED YOURSELF THE FIRST TENKO... BYAKUEI-SAN, RIGHT?
SHAAAAA
HUH...?!
SO, YOU'RE THE ONE BEHIND ALL OF THIS!
THE SEVENTH YATAHA-GANE!

Yuuna and the Haunted Hot Springs

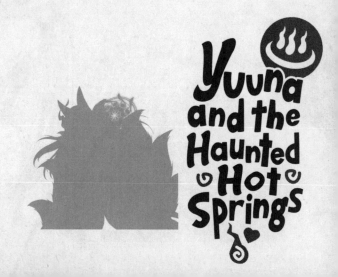

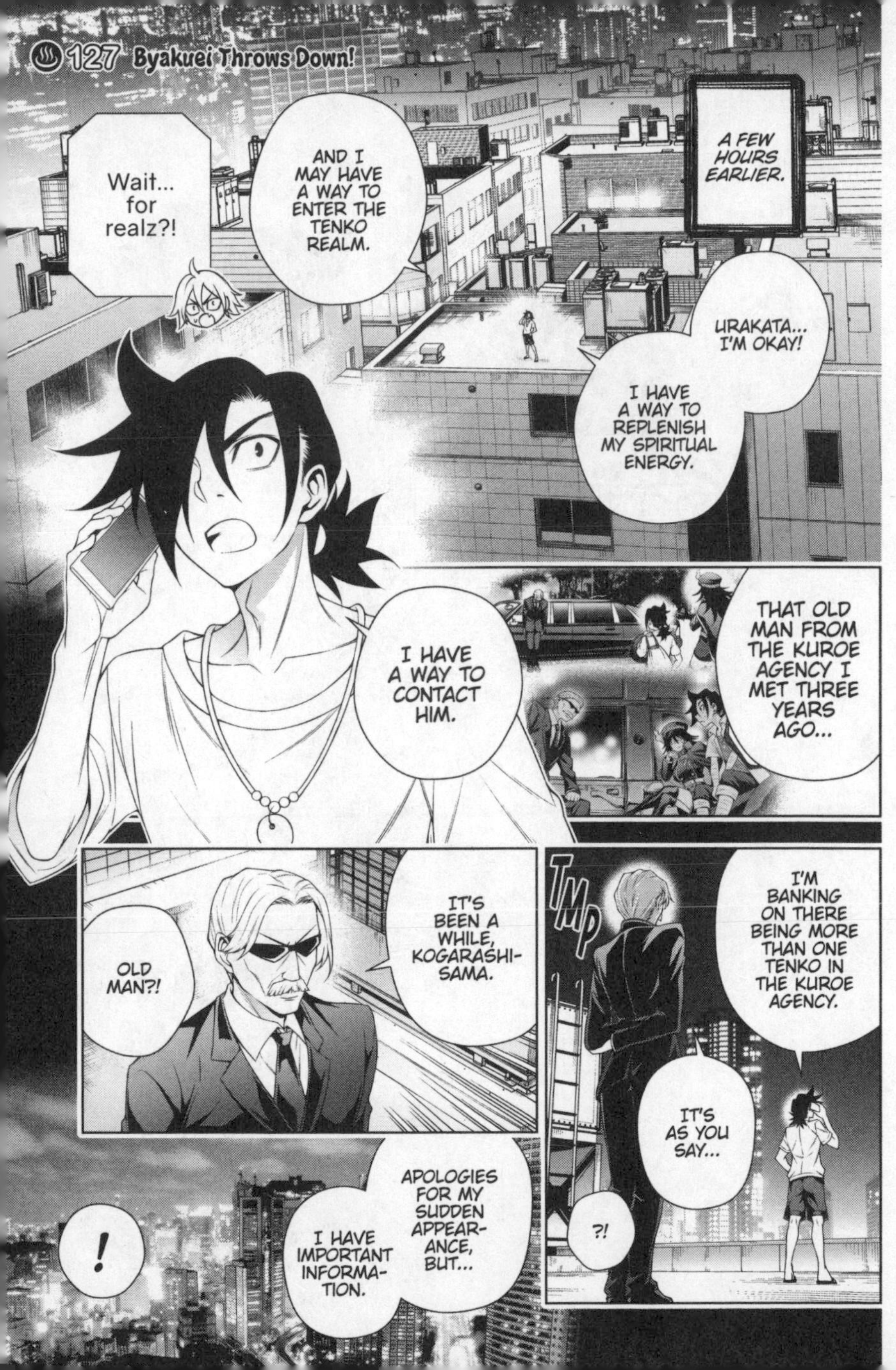
127 Byakuei Throws Down!
A FEW HOURS EARLIER.
URAKATA... I'M OKAY!
I HAVE A WAY TO REPLENISH MY SPIRITUAL ENERGY.
AND I MAY HAVE A WAY TO ENTER THE TENKO REALM.
Wait... for realz?!
THAT OLD MAN FROM THE KUROE AGENCY I MET THREE YEARS AGO...
I HAVE A WAY TO CONTACT HIM.
I'M BANKING ON THERE BEING MORE THAN ONE TENKO IN THE KUROE AGENCY.
TMP
IT'S AS YOU SAY...
?!
IT'S BEEN A WHILE, KOGARASHI-SAMA.
OLD MAN?!
APOLOGIES FOR MY SUDDEN APPEAR-ANCE, BUT...
I HAVE IMPORTANT INFORMA-TION.
!

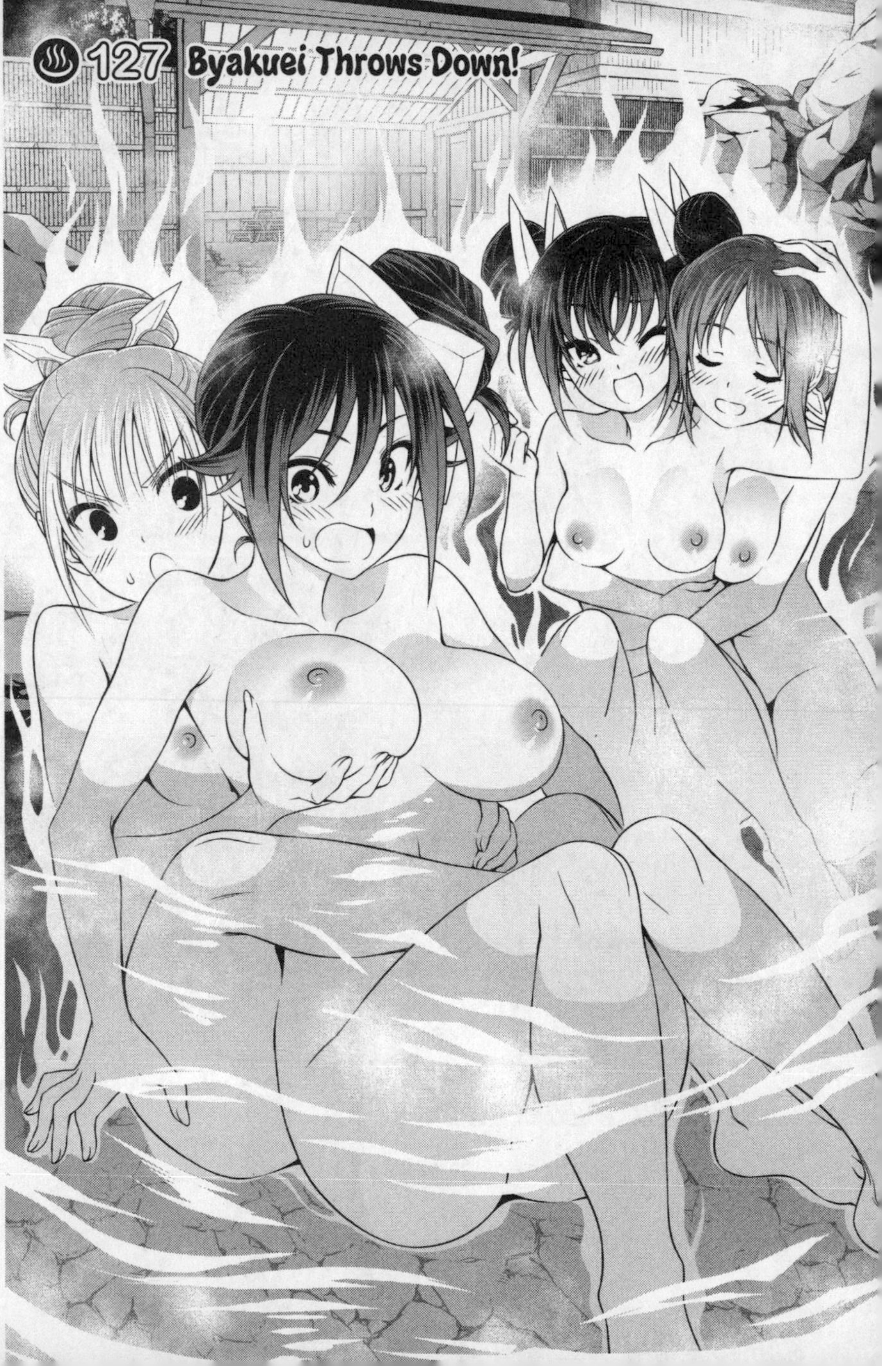
127 Byakuei Throws Down!

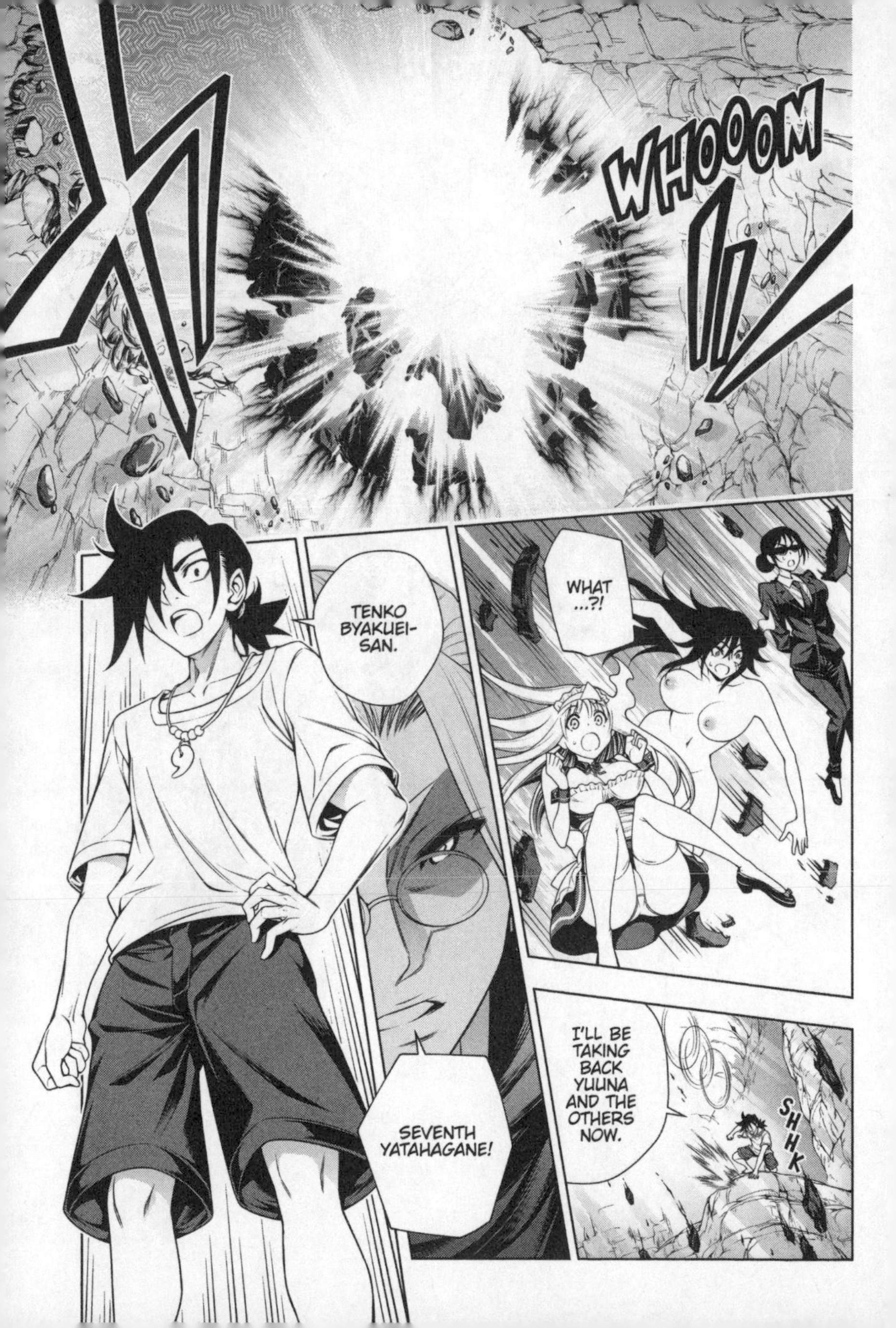
WHOOOM
WHAT ...?!
I'LL BE TAKING BACK YUUNA AND THE OTHERS NOW.
SHHK
TENKO BYAKUEI-SAN.
SEVENTH YATAHAGANE!

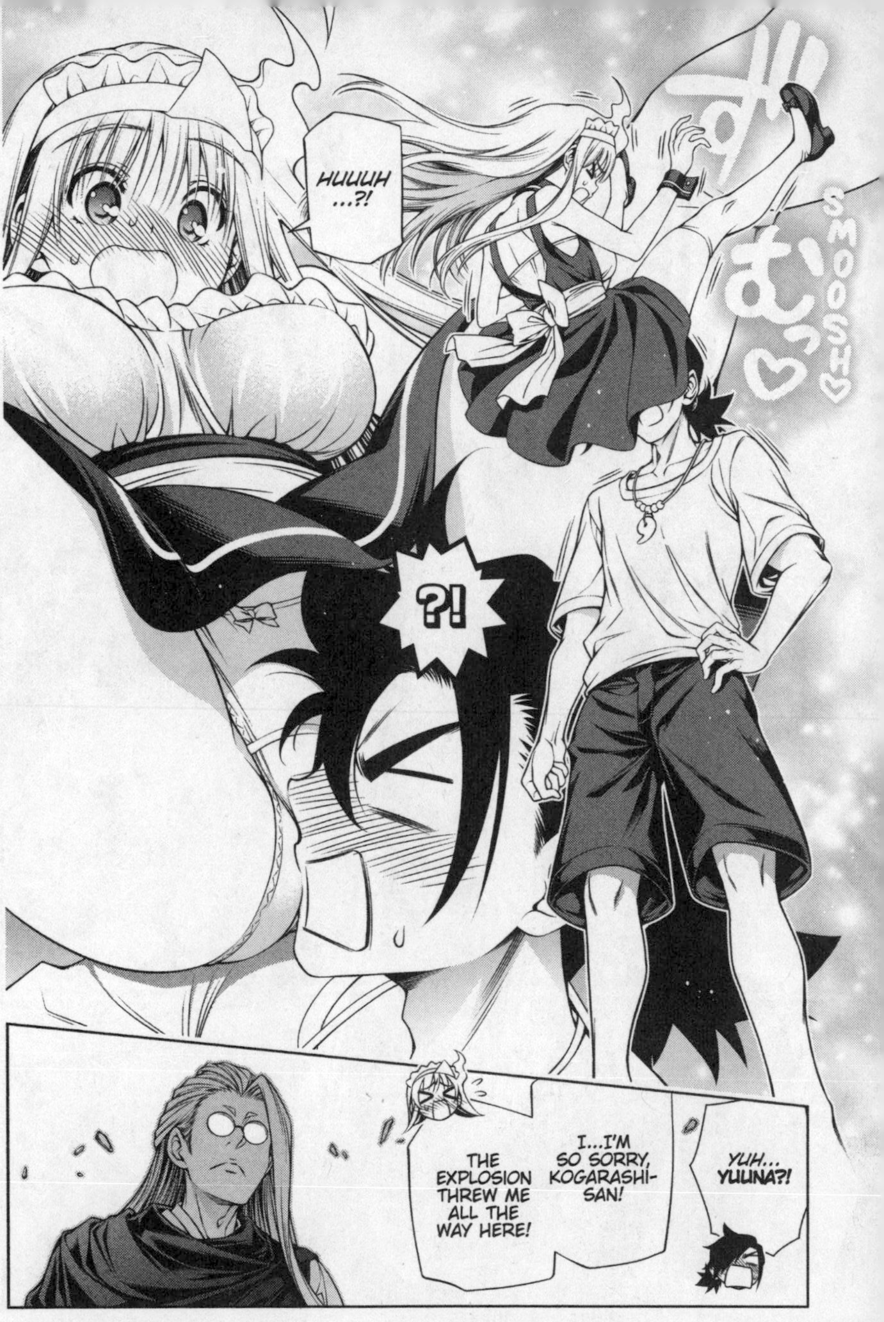
ずむっ♡
SMOOSH♡
HUUUH ...?!
?!
YUH... YUUNA?!
I...I'M SO SORRY, KOGARASHI-SAN!
THE EXPLOSION THREW ME ALL THE WAY HERE!

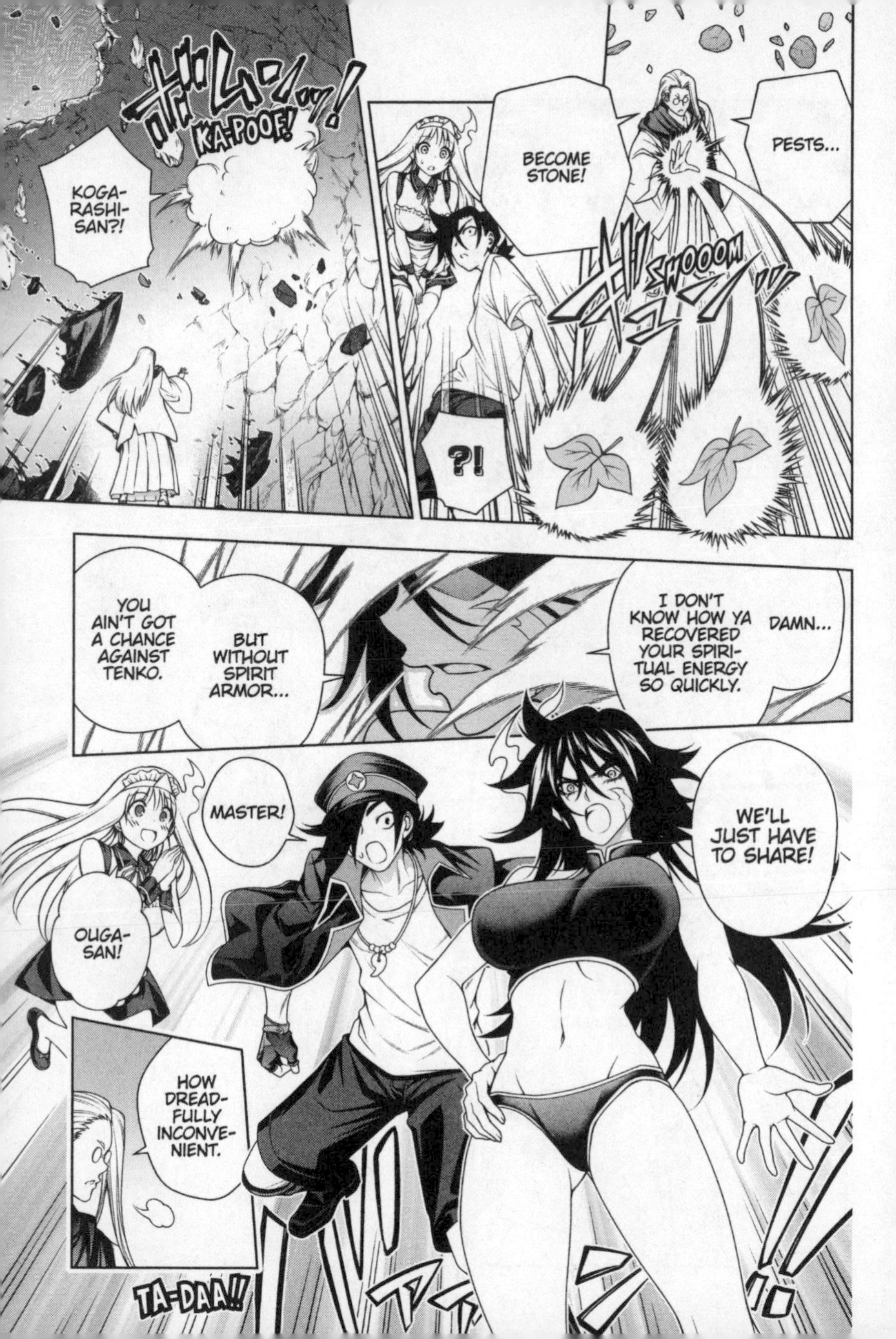
PESTS...
BECOME STONE!
SHOOOM
?!
KA-POOF!
KOGA-RASHI-SAN?!
DAMN...
I DON'T KNOW HOW YA RECOVERED YOUR SPIRI-TUAL ENERGY SO QUICKLY.
BUT WITHOUT SPIRIT ARMOR...
YOU AIN'T GOT A CHANCE AGAINST TENKO.
WE'LL JUST HAVE TO SHARE!
MASTER!
OUGA-SAN!
HOW DREAD-FULLY INCONVE-NIENT.
TA-DAA!!

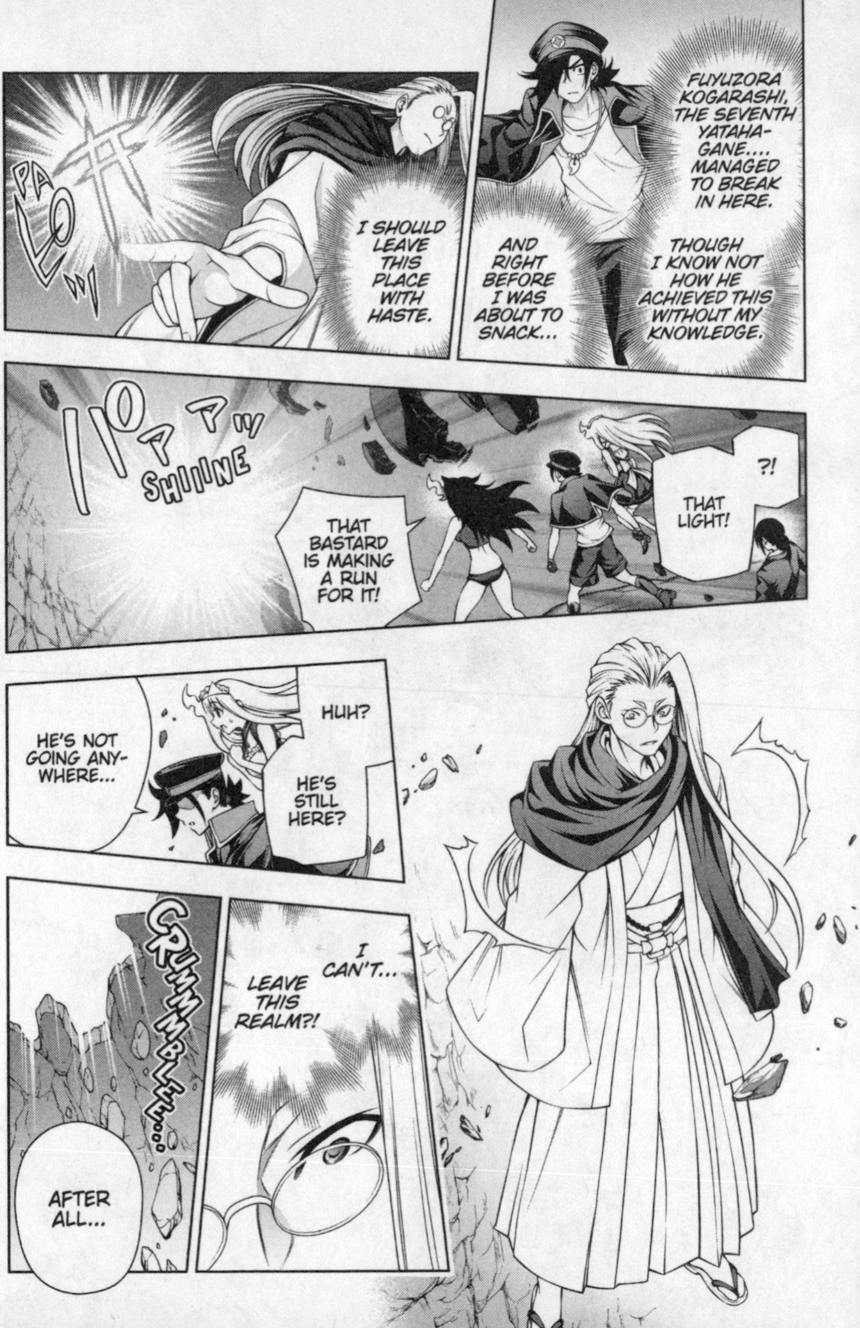
FUYUZORA KOGARASHI, THE SEVENTH YATAHA-GANE.... MANAGED TO BREAK IN HERE.
THOUGH I KNOW NOT HOW HE ACHIEVED THIS WITHOUT MY KNOWLEDGE.
AND RIGHT BEFORE I WAS ABOUT TO SNACK...
I SHOULD LEAVE THIS PLACE WITH HASTE.
PAO
?!
THAT LIGHT!
THAT BASTARD IS MAKING A RUN FOR IT!
SHIIINE
HUH?
HE'S STILL HERE?
HE'S NOT GOING ANY-WHERE...
I CAN'T...
LEAVE THIS REALM?!
CRUMMBLEE...
AFTER ALL...

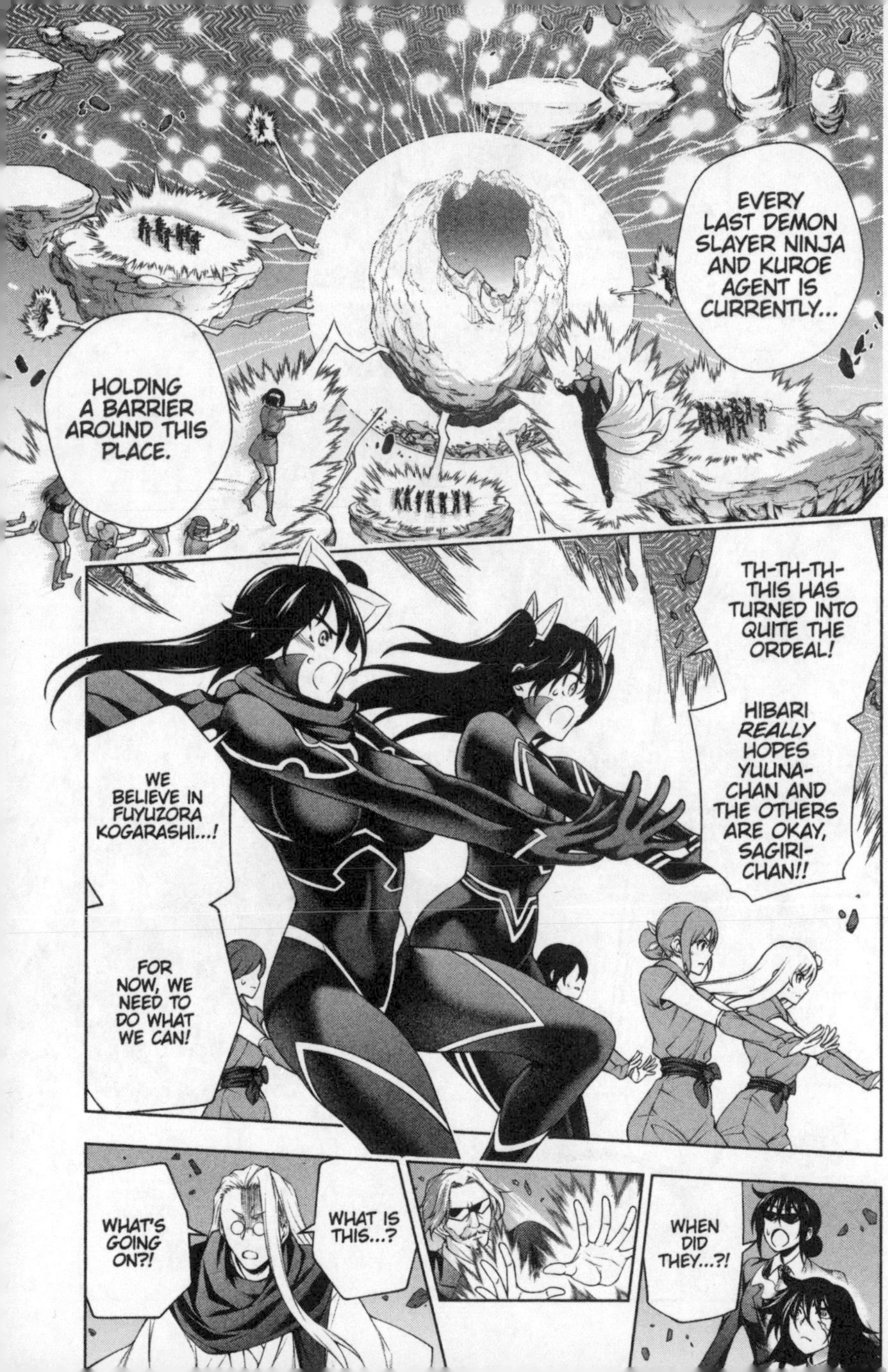
EVERY LAST DEMON SLAYER NINJA AND KUROE AGENT IS CURRENTLY...
HOLDING A BARRIER AROUND THIS PLACE.
TH-TH-TH-THIS HAS TURNED INTO QUITE THE ORDEAL!
HIBARI *REALLY* HOPES YUUNA-CHAN AND THE OTHERS ARE OKAY, SAGIRI-CHAN!!
WE BELIEVE IN FUYUZORA KOGARASHI...!
FOR NOW, WE NEED TO DO WHAT WE CAN!
WHEN DID THEY...?!
WHAT IS THIS...?
WHAT'S GOING ON?!

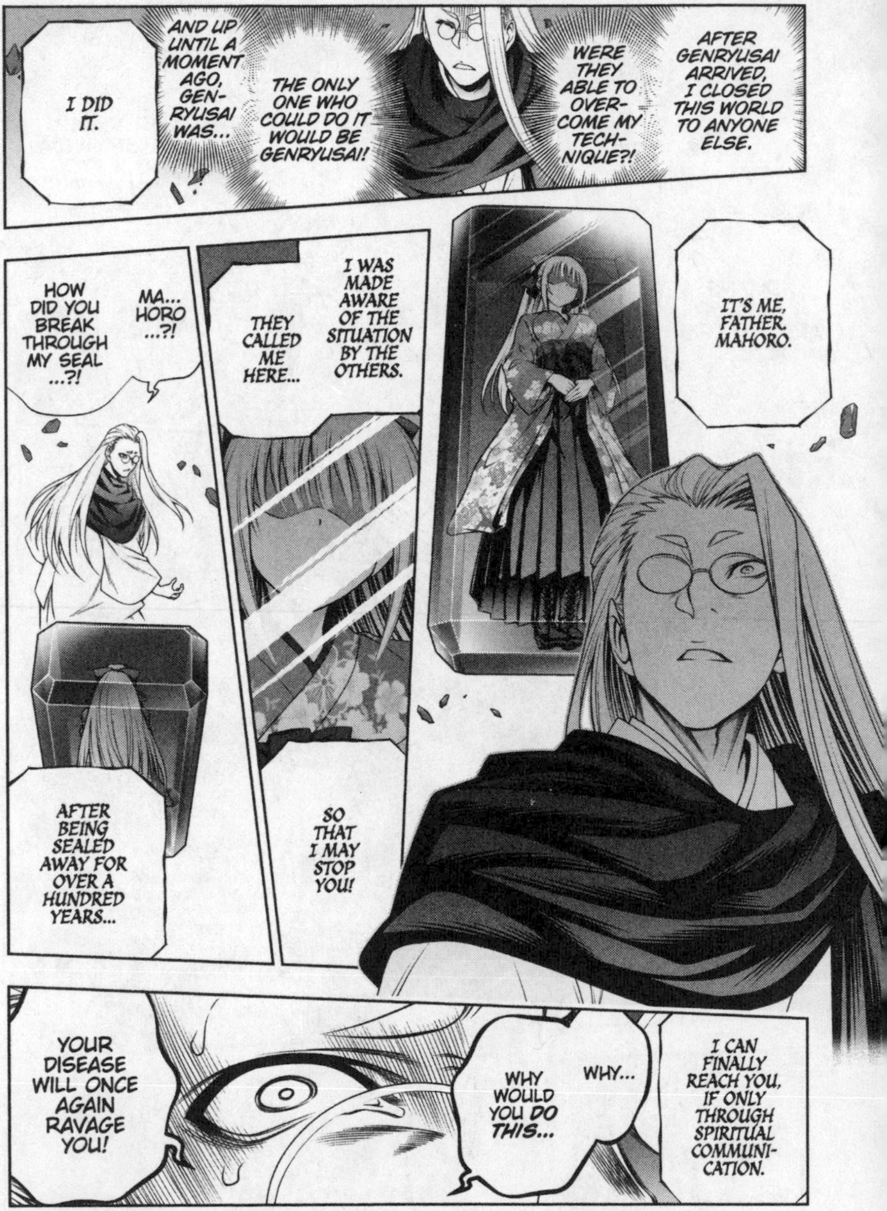
AFTER GENRYUSAI ARRIVED, I CLOSED THIS WORLD TO ANYONE ELSE.
WERE THEY ABLE TO OVER-COME MY TECH-NIQUE?!
THE ONLY ONE WHO COULD DO IT WOULD BE GENRYUSAI!
AND UP UNTIL A MOMENT AGO, GEN-RYUSAI WAS...
I DID IT.
IT'S ME, FATHER. MAHORO.
I WAS MADE AWARE OF THE SITUATION BY THE OTHERS.
THEY CALLED ME HERE...
SO THAT I MAY STOP YOU!
MA... HORO ...?!
HOW DID YOU BREAK THROUGH MY SEAL ...?!
AFTER BEING SEALED AWAY FOR OVER A HUNDRED YEARS...
I CAN FINALLY REACH YOU, IF ONLY THROUGH SPIRITUAL COMMUNI-CATION.
WHY...
WHY WOULD YOU DO *THIS*...
YOUR DISEASE WILL ONCE AGAIN RAVAGE YOU!

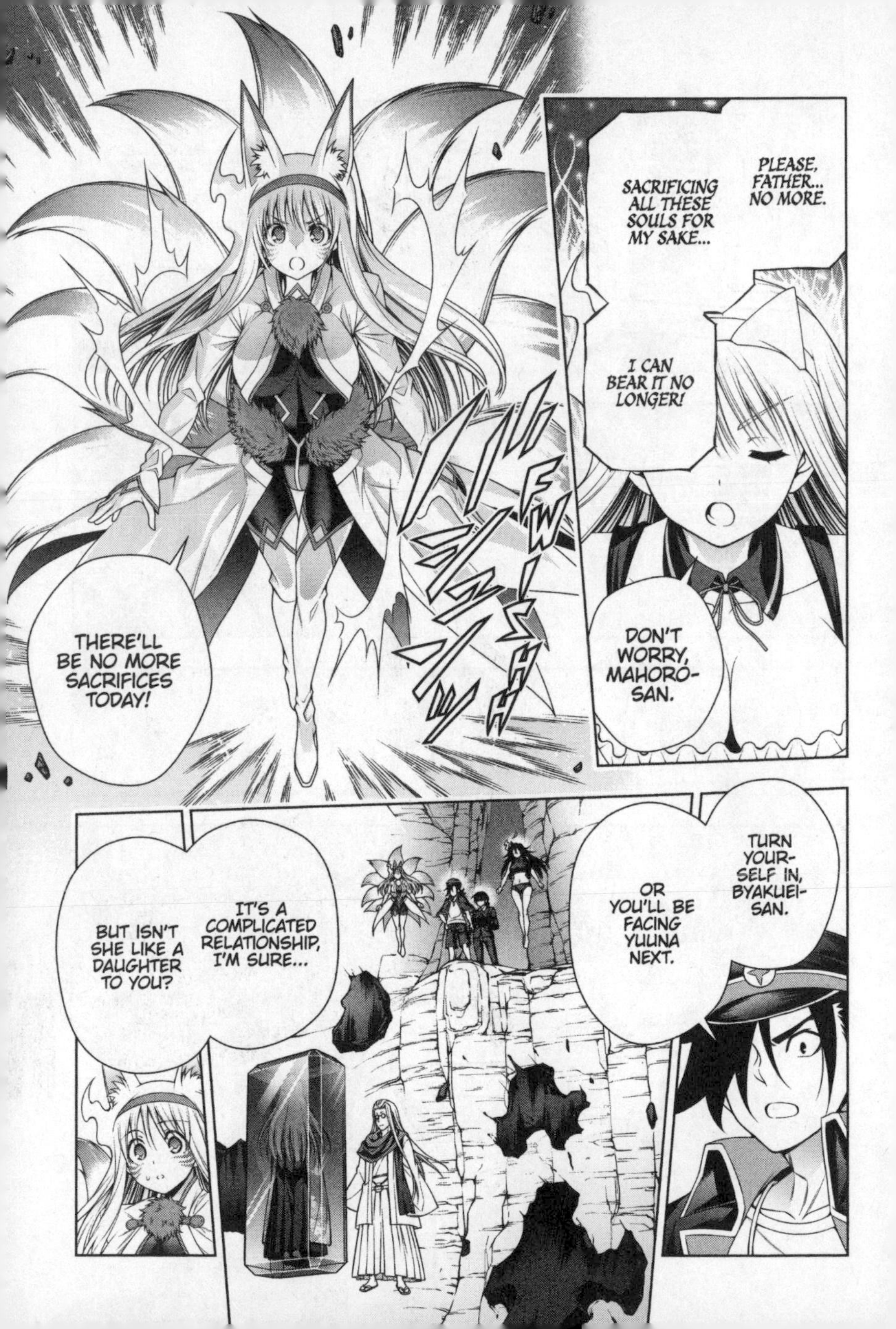
PLEASE, FATHER... NO MORE.
SACRIFICING ALL THESE SOULS FOR MY SAKE...
I CAN BEAR IT NO LONGER!
DON'T WORRY, MAHORO-SAN.
THERE'LL BE NO MORE SACRIFICES TODAY!
TURN YOUR-SELF IN, BYAKUEI-SAN.
OR YOU'LL BE FACING YUUNA NEXT.
IT'S A COMPLICATED RELATIONSHIP, I'M SURE...
BUT ISN'T SHE LIKE A DAUGHTER TO YOU?

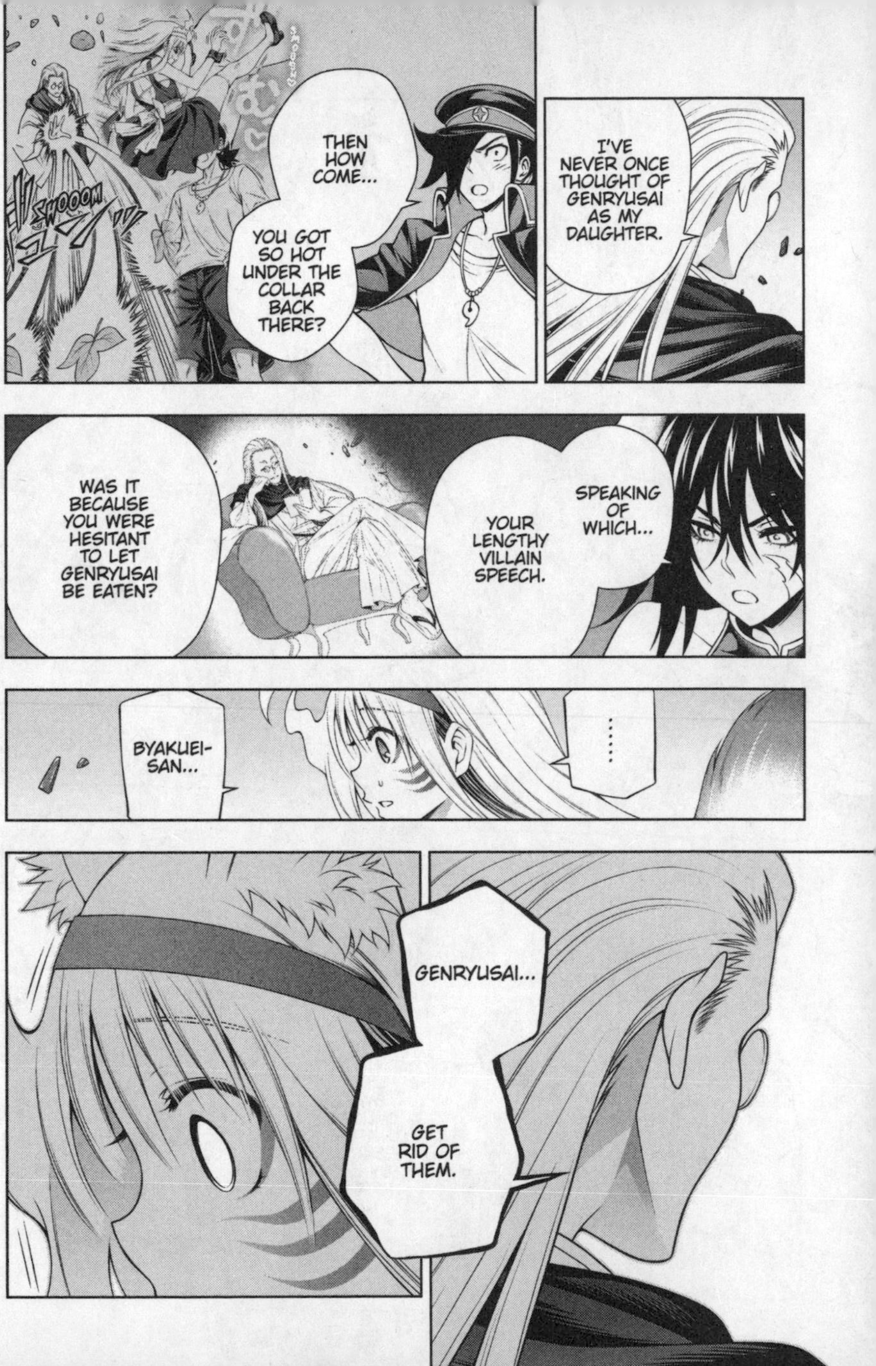

I'VE NEVER ONCE THOUGHT OF GENRYUSAI AS MY DAUGHTER.
THEN HOW COME...
YOU GOT SO HOT UNDER THE COLLAR BACK THERE?
SHOOOM
SPEAKING OF WHICH...
YOUR LENGTHY VILLAIN SPEECH.
WAS IT BECAUSE YOU WERE HESITANT TO LET GENRYUSAI BE EATEN?
......
BYAKUEI-SAN...
GENRYUSAI...
GET RID OF THEM.

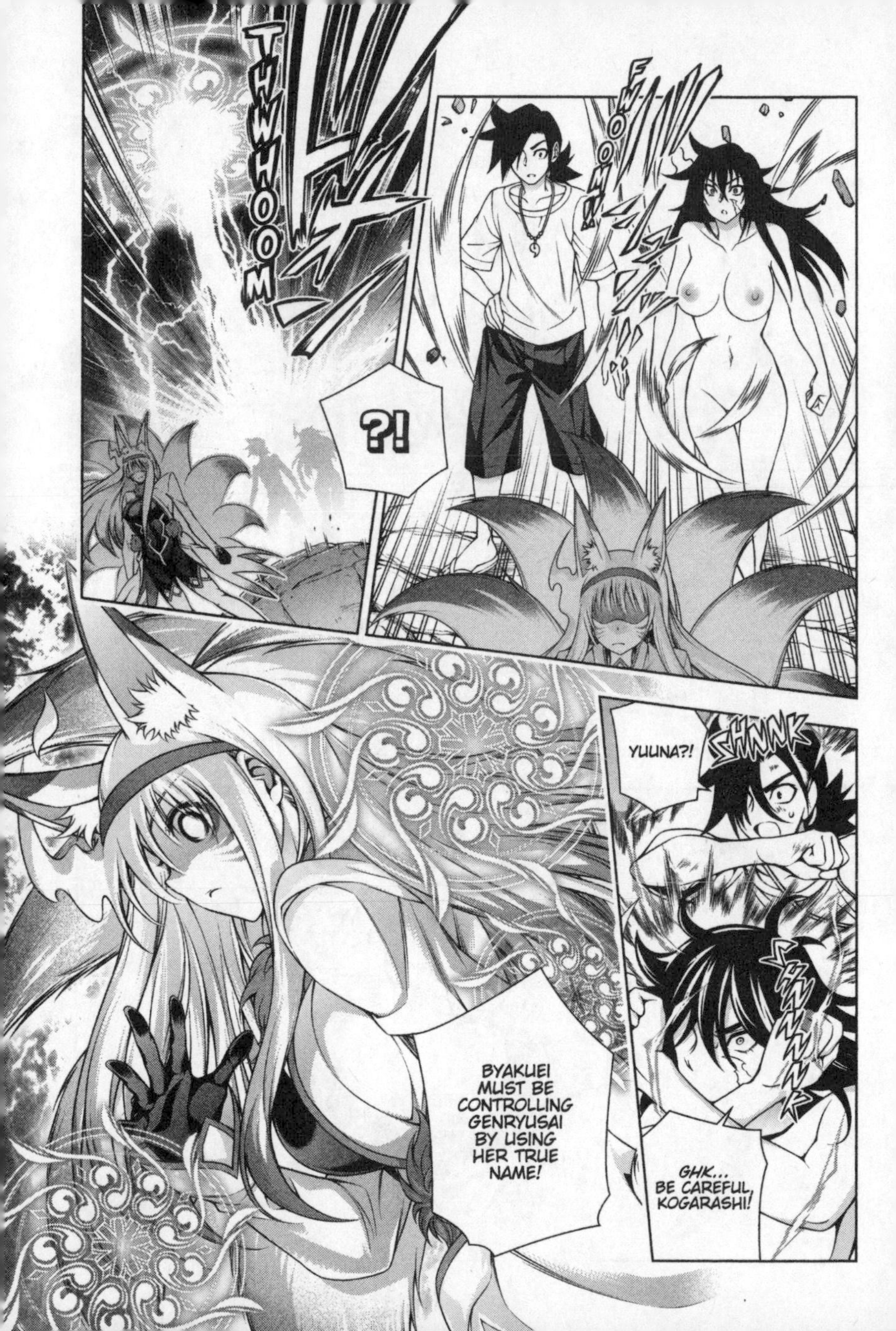
FWOOM
?!
THWHOOM
YUUNA?!
SHNNK
SHNNNNNK
GHK... BE CAREFUL, KOGARASHI!
BYAKUEI MUST BE CONTROLLING GENRYUSAI BY USING HER TRUE NAME!

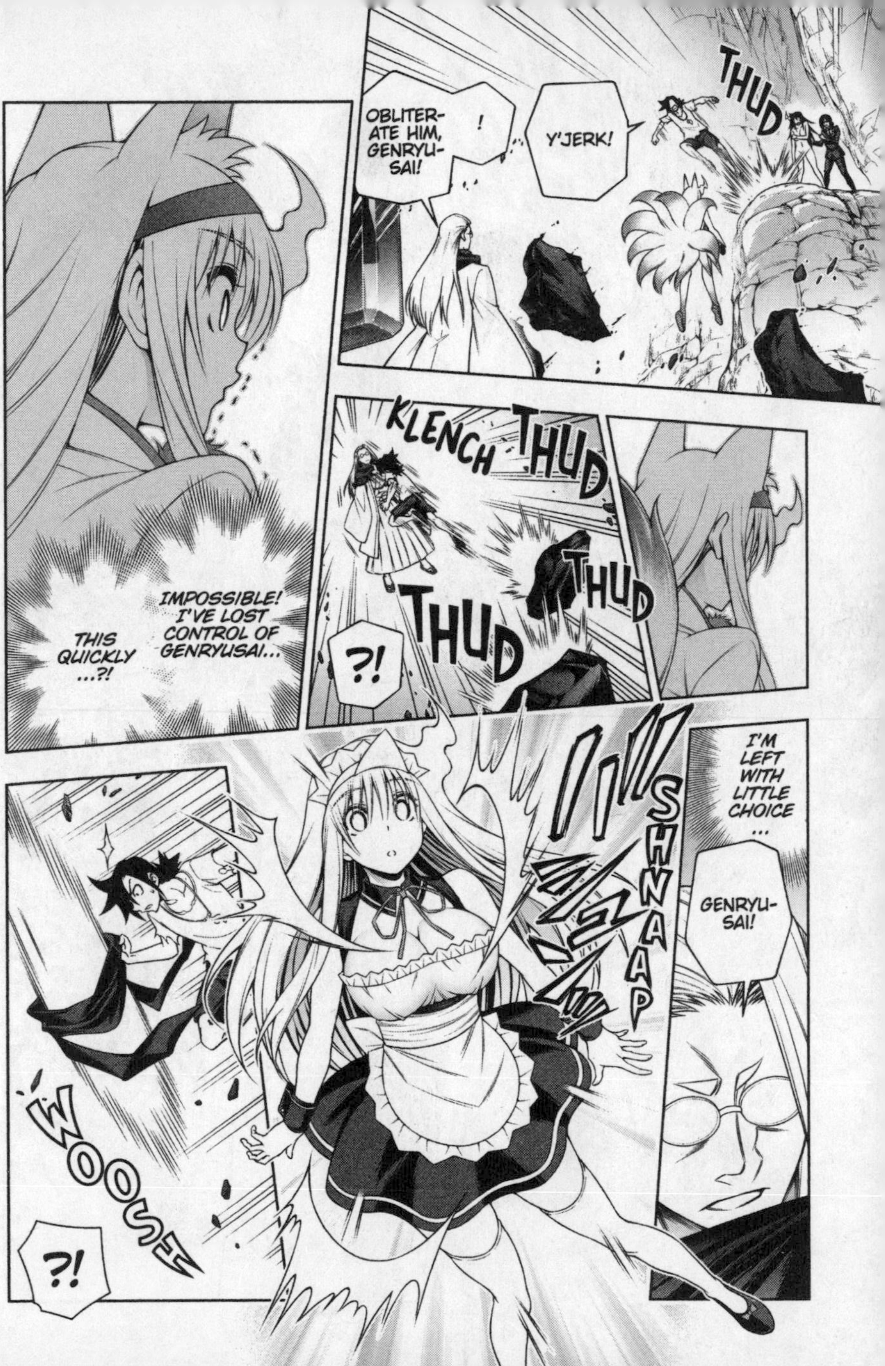
THUD
Y'JERK!
!
OBLITERATE HIM, GENRYUSAI!
KLENCH
THUD
THUD
THUD
?!
IMPOSSIBLE! I'VE LOST CONTROL OF GENRYUSAI...
THIS QUICKLY ...?!
I'M LEFT WITH LITTLE CHOICE ...
GENRYUSAI!
SHNAAP
WOOSH
?!

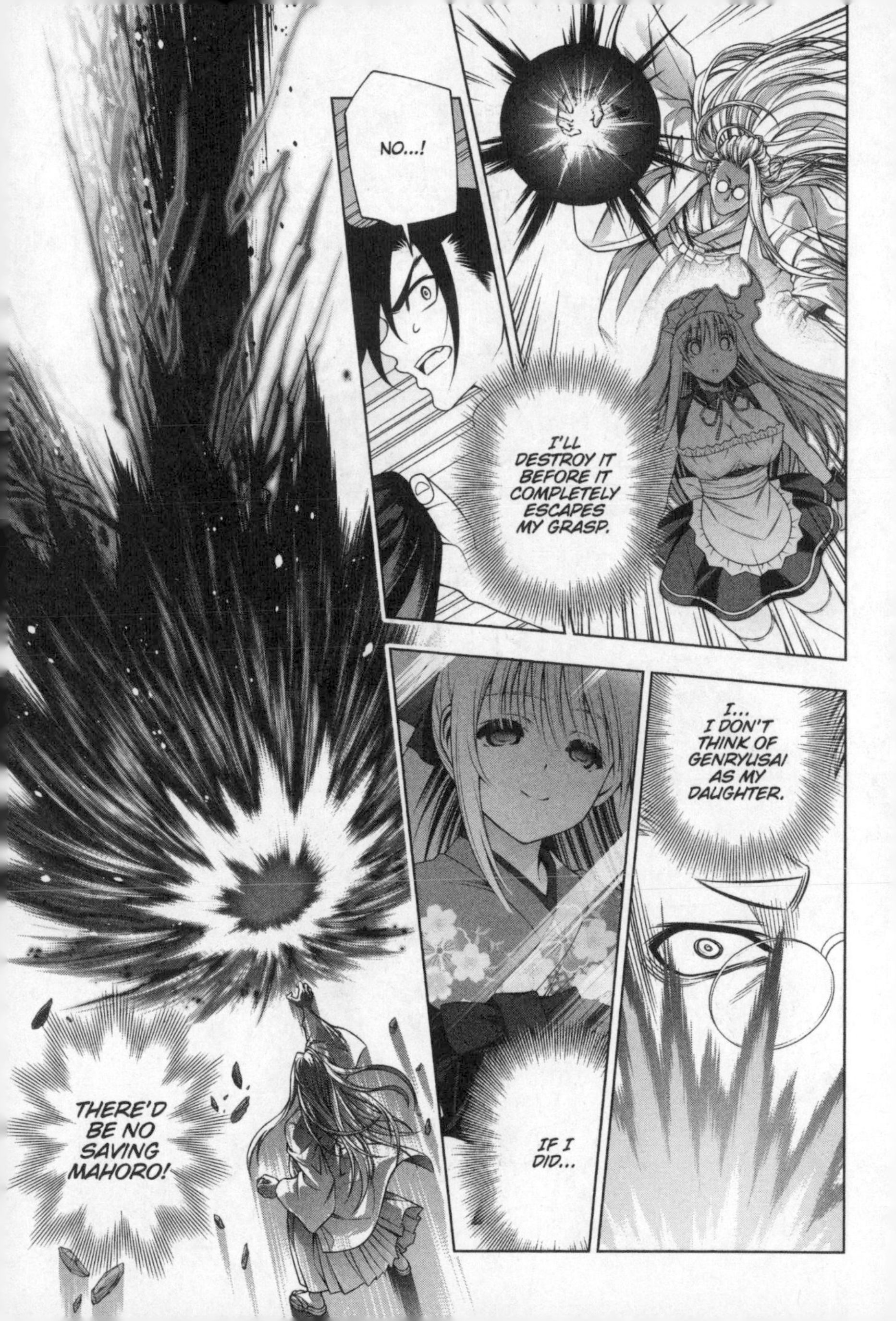
NO...!
I'LL DESTROY IT BEFORE IT COMPLETELY ESCAPES MY GRASP.
I... I DON'T THINK OF GENRYUSAI AS MY DAUGHTER.
IF I DID...
THERE'D BE NO SAVING MAHORO!

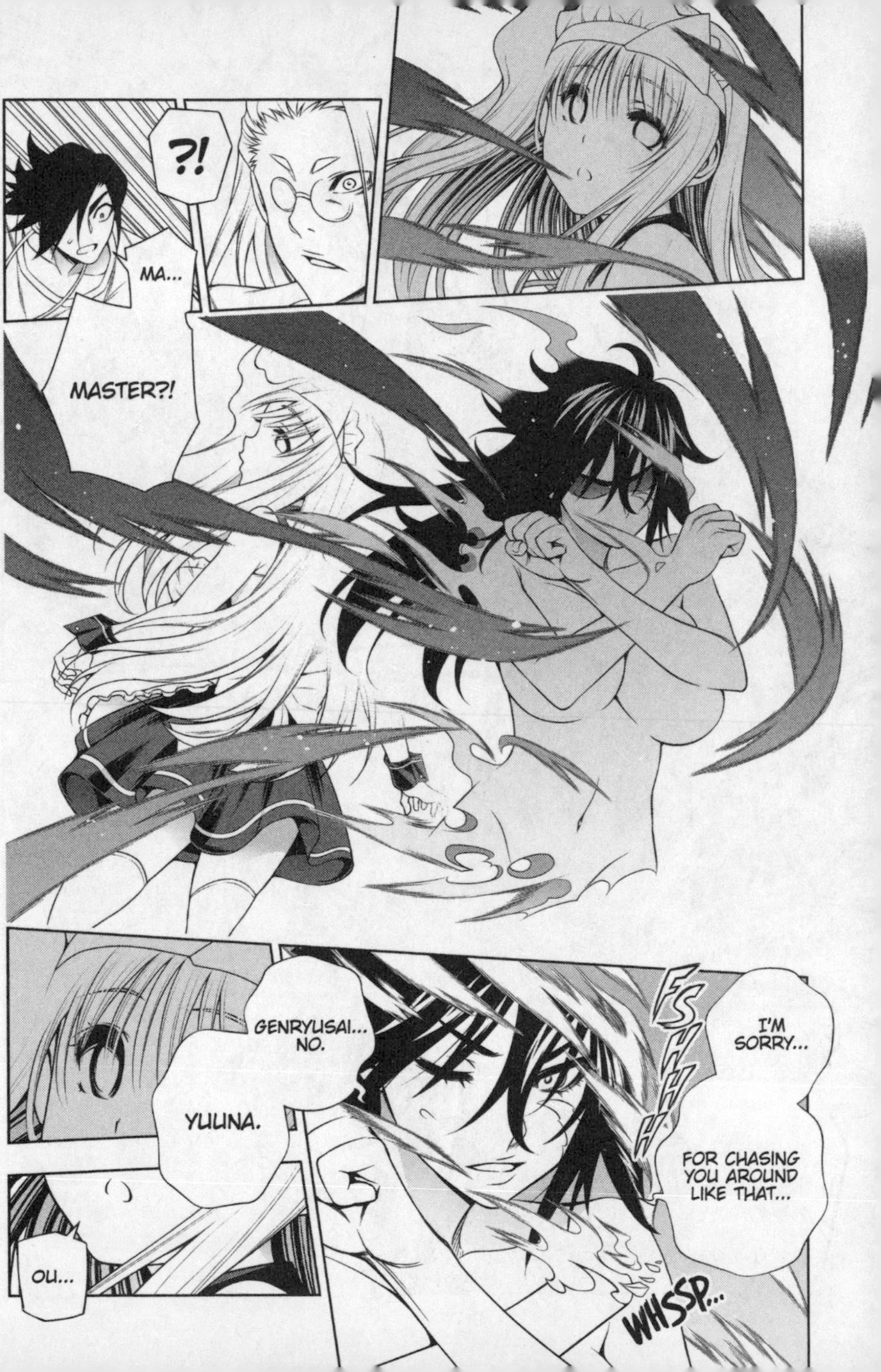
?!
MA...
MASTER?!
I'M SORRY...
FSHHHH
FOR CHASING YOU AROUND LIKE THAT...
WHSSP...
GENRYUSAI... NO.
YUUNA.
OU...

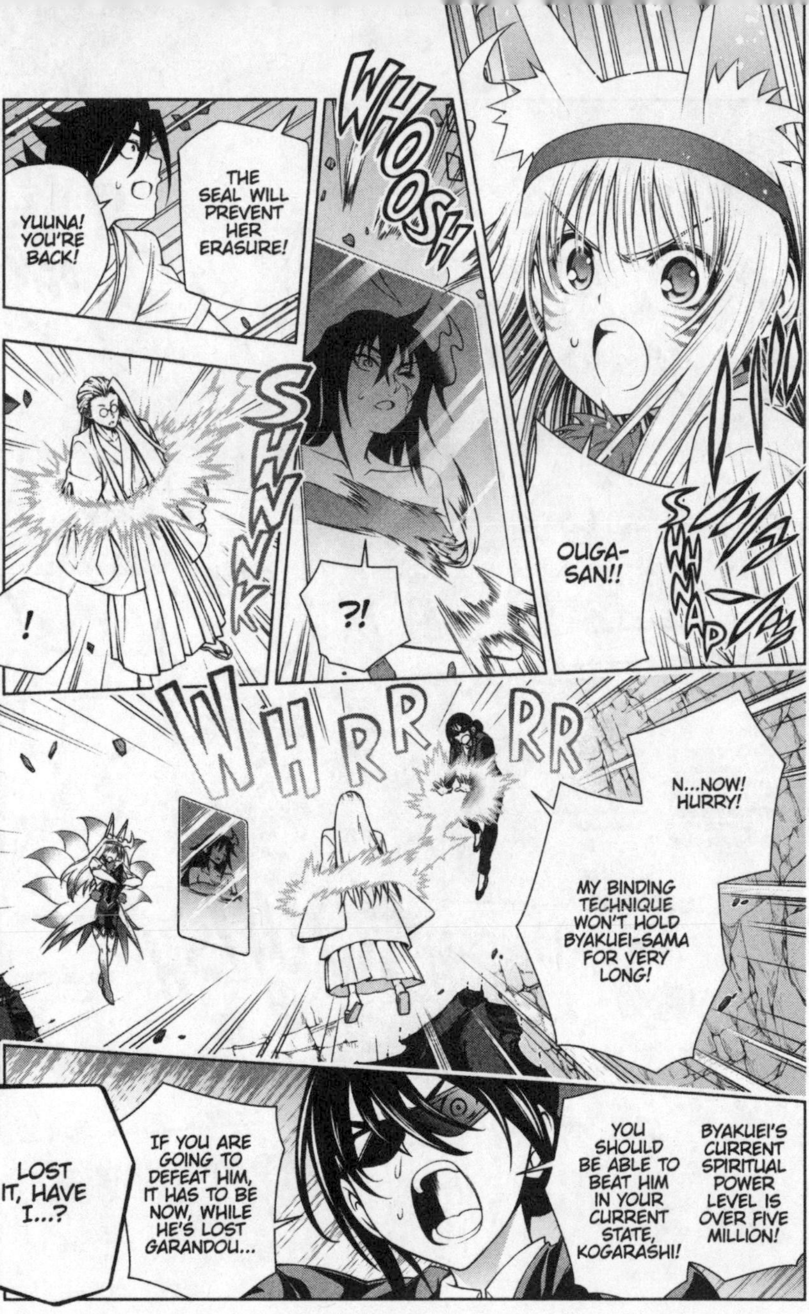
OUGA-SAN!!
SHWAP
WHOOSH
?!
SHWNK
THE SEAL WILL PREVENT HER ERASURE!
YUUNA! YOU'RE BACK!
!
WHRRRR
N...NOW! HURRY!
MY BINDING TECHNIQUE WON'T HOLD BYAKUEI-SAMA FOR VERY LONG!
BYAKUEI'S CURRENT SPIRITUAL POWER LEVEL IS OVER FIVE MILLION!
YOU SHOULD BE ABLE TO BEAT HIM IN YOUR CURRENT STATE, KOGARASHI!
IF YOU ARE GOING TO DEFEAT HIM, IT HAS TO BE NOW, WHILE HE'S LOST GARANDOU...
LOST IT, HAVE I...?

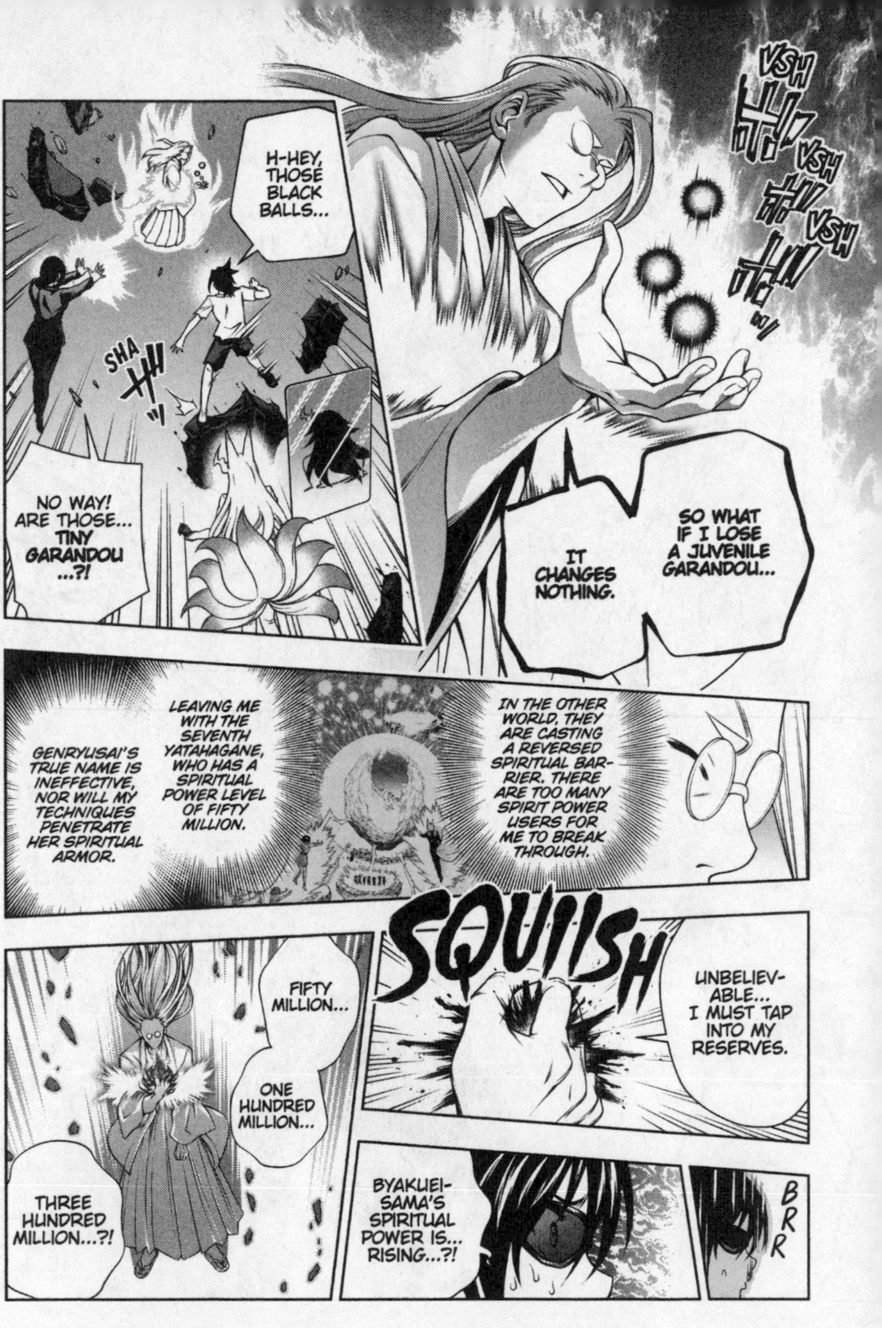
VSH
VSH
VSH
SO WHAT IF I LOSE A JUVENILE GARANDOU...
IT CHANGES NOTHING.
H-HEY, THOSE BLACK BALLS...
SHA
NO WAY! ARE THOSE... TINY GARANDOU ...?!
IN THE OTHER WORLD, THEY ARE CASTING A REVERSED SPIRITUAL BARRIER. THERE ARE TOO MANY SPIRIT POWER USERS FOR ME TO BREAK THROUGH.
LEAVING ME WITH THE SEVENTH YATAHAGANE, WHO HAS A SPIRITUAL POWER LEVEL OF FIFTY MILLION.
GENRYUSAI'S TRUE NAME IS INEFFECTIVE, NOR WILL MY TECHNIQUES PENETRATE HER SPIRITUAL ARMOR.
SQUISH
UNBELIEVABLE... I MUST TAP INTO MY RESERVES.
BRR
BYAKUEI-SAMA'S SPIRITUAL POWER IS... RISING...?!
FIFTY MILLION...
ONE HUNDRED MILLION...
THREE HUNDRED MILLION...?!

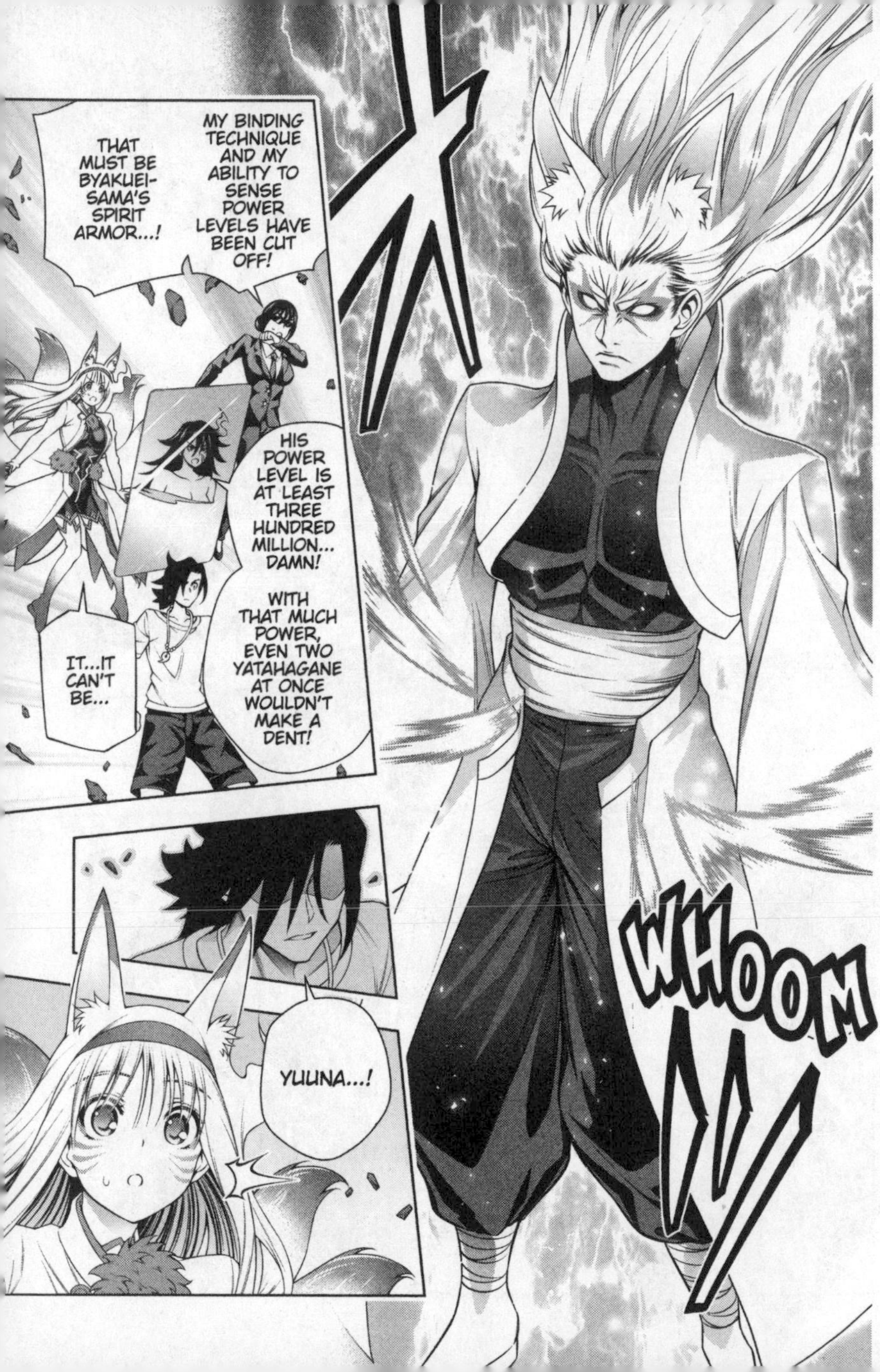
WHOOM
MY BINDING TECHNIQUE AND MY ABILITY TO SENSE POWER LEVELS HAVE BEEN CUT OFF!
THAT MUST BE BYAKUEI-SAMA'S SPIRIT ARMOR...!
HIS POWER LEVEL IS AT LEAST THREE HUNDRED MILLION... DAMN!
WITH THAT MUCH POWER, EVEN TWO YATAHAGANE AT ONCE WOULDN'T MAKE A DENT!
IT...IT CAN'T BE...
YUUNA...!

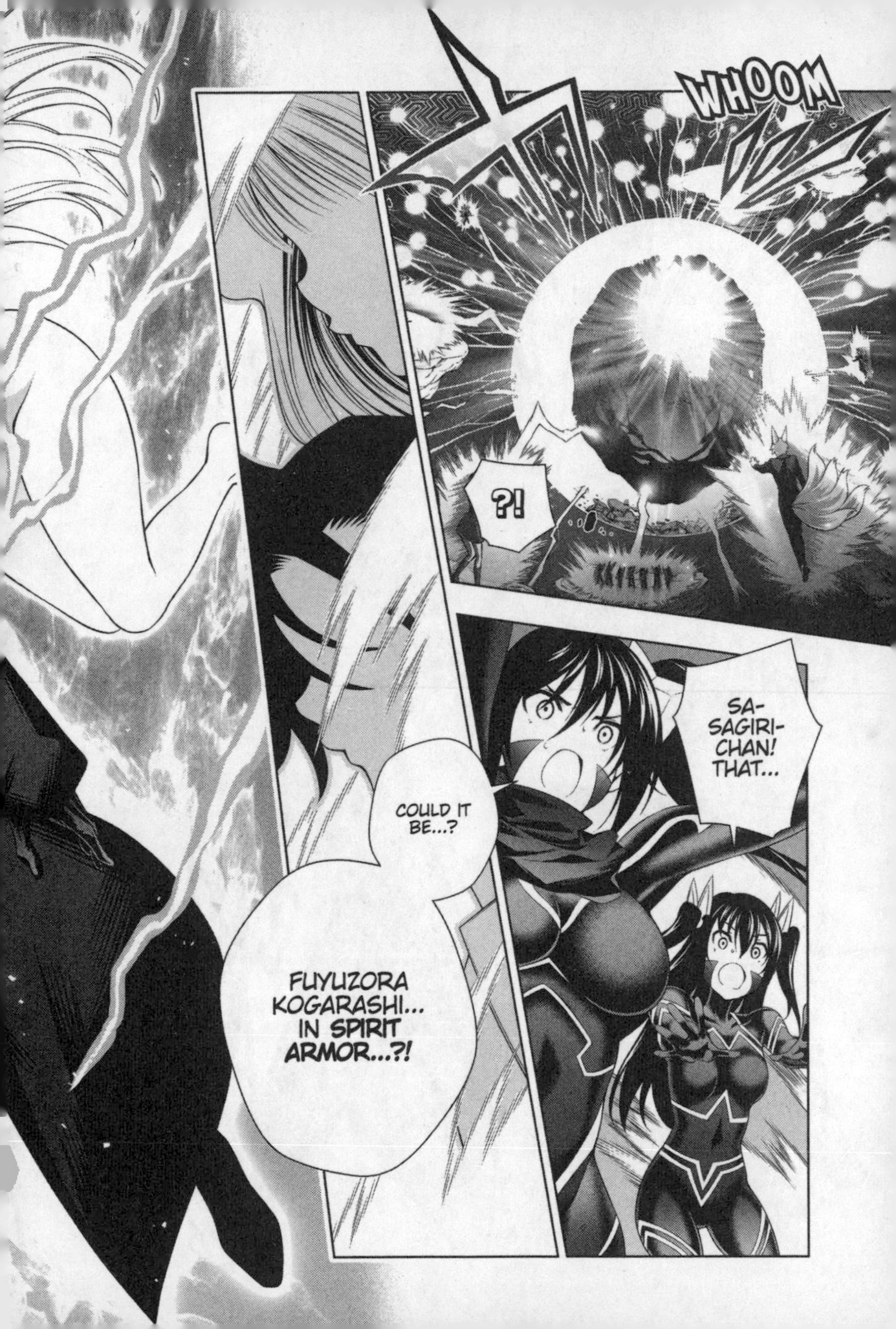

WHOOM
?!
SA-SAGIRI-CHAN! THAT...
COULD IT BE...?
FUYUZORA KOGARASHI... IN SPIRIT ARMOR...?!

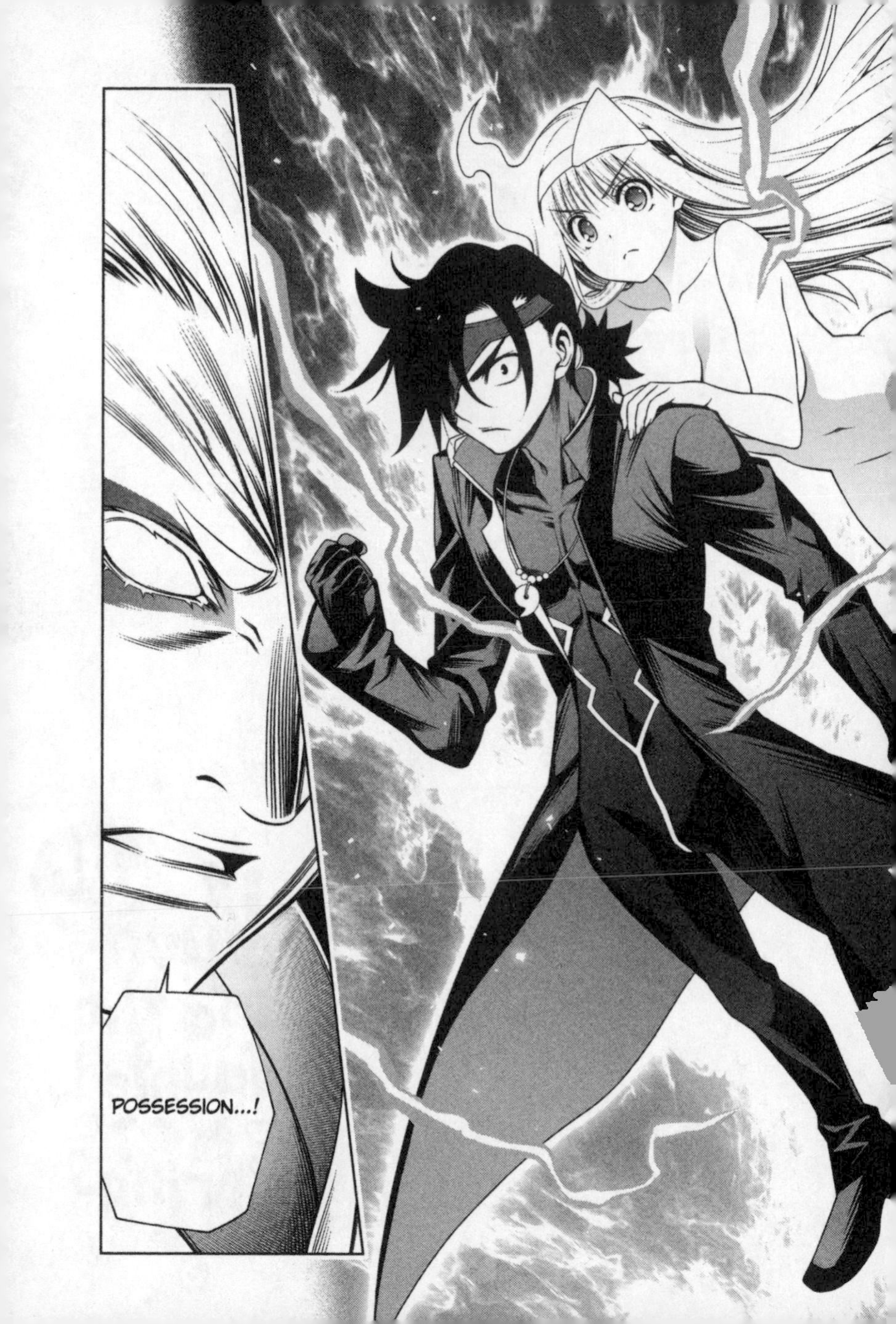
POSSESSION...!

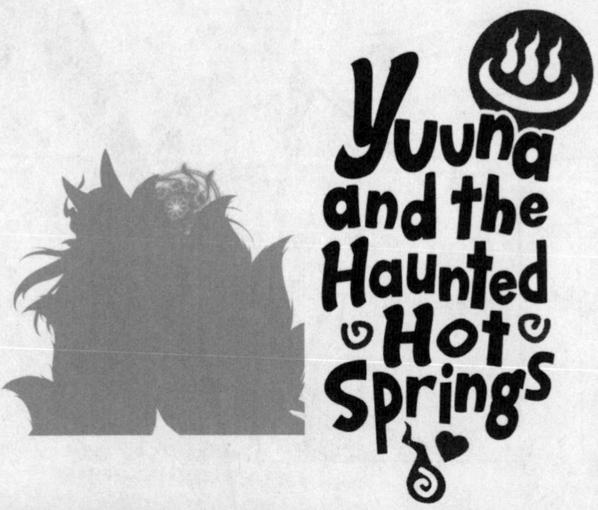

Yuuna and the Haunted Hot Springs

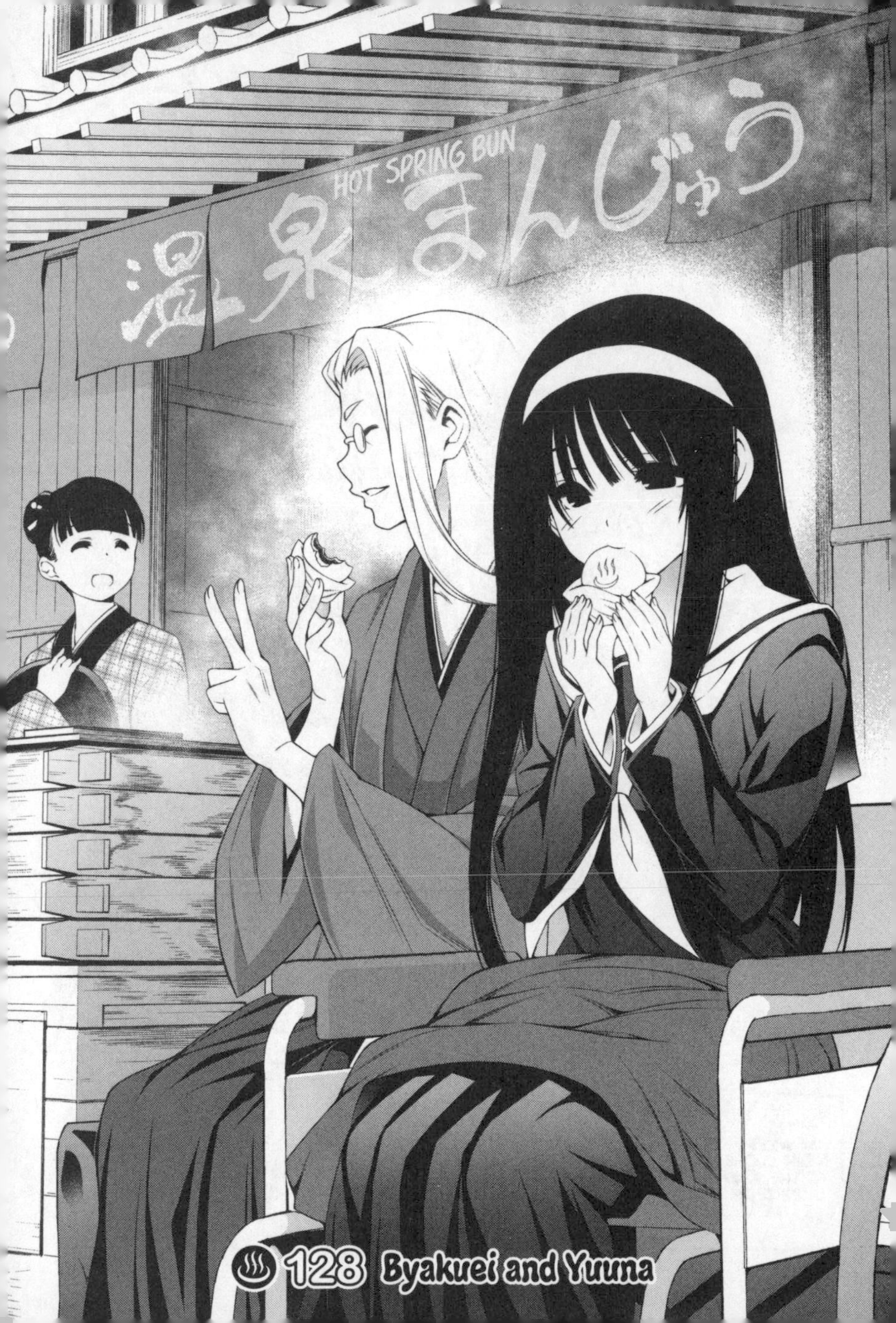
HOT SPRING BUN
温泉まんじゅう

128 Byakuei and Yuuna

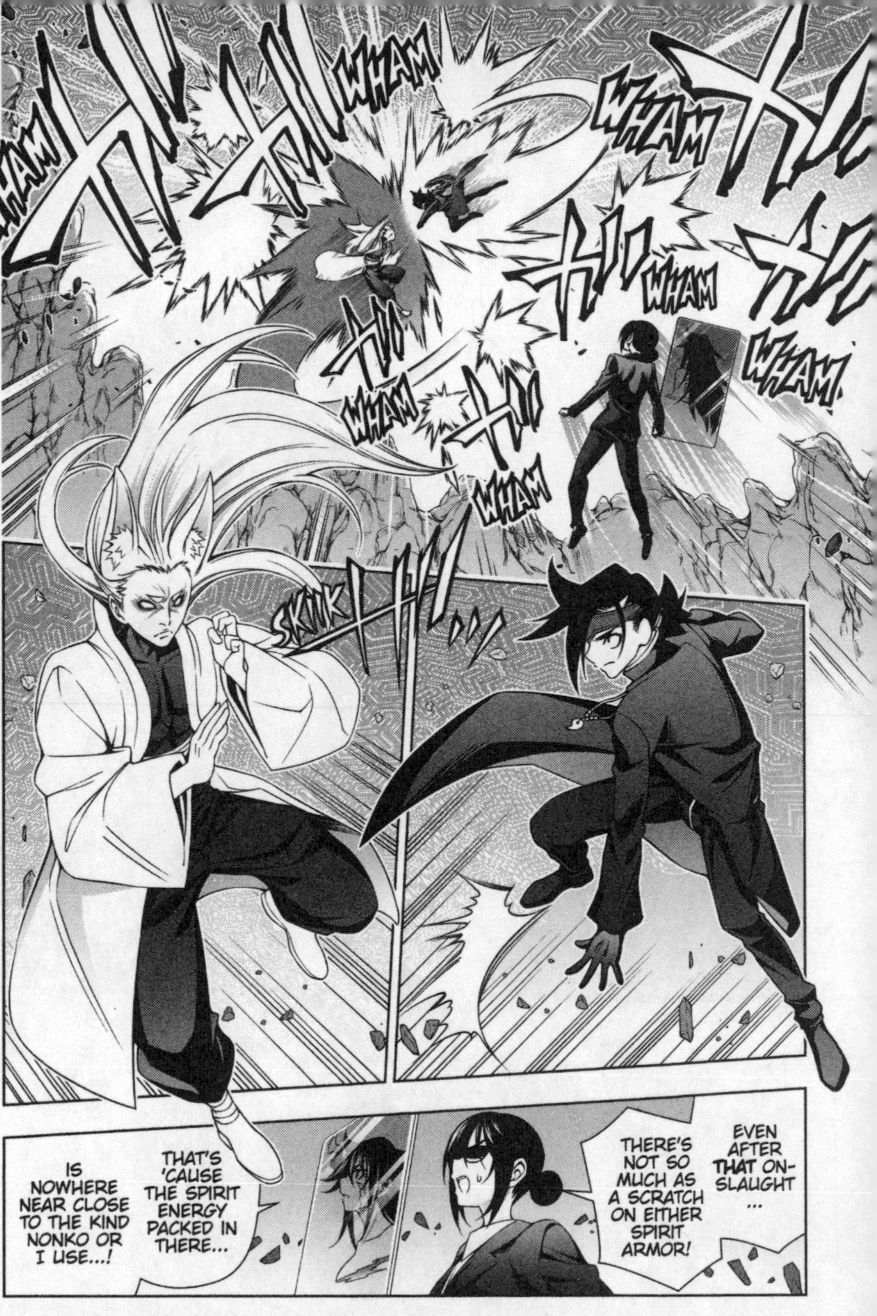
WHAM
WHAM
WHAM
WHAM
WHAM.
WHAM
WHAM
WHAM
SKTIK
EVEN AFTER THAT ON-SLAUGHT ...
THERE'S NOT SO MUCH AS A SCRATCH ON EITHER SPIRIT ARMOR!
THAT'S 'CAUSE THE SPIRIT ENERGY PACKED IN THERE...
IS NOWHERE NEAR CLOSE TO THE KIND NONKO OR I USE...!

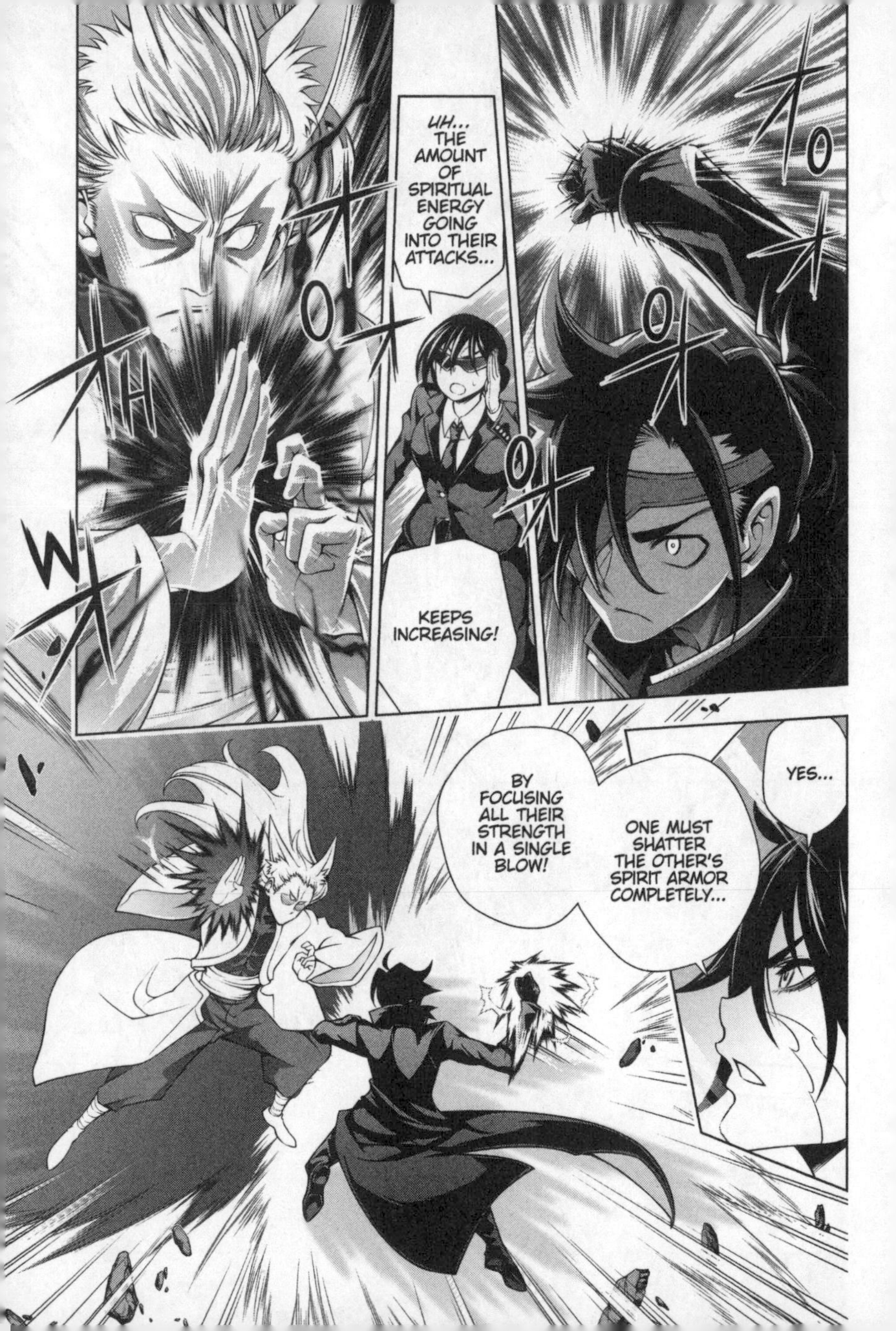
UH... THE AMOUNT OF SPIRITUAL ENERGY GOING INTO THEIR ATTACKS...
KEEPS INCREASING!
YES...
ONE MUST SHATTER THE OTHER'S SPIRIT ARMOR COMPLETELY...
BY FOCUSING ALL THEIR STRENGTH IN A SINGLE BLOW!

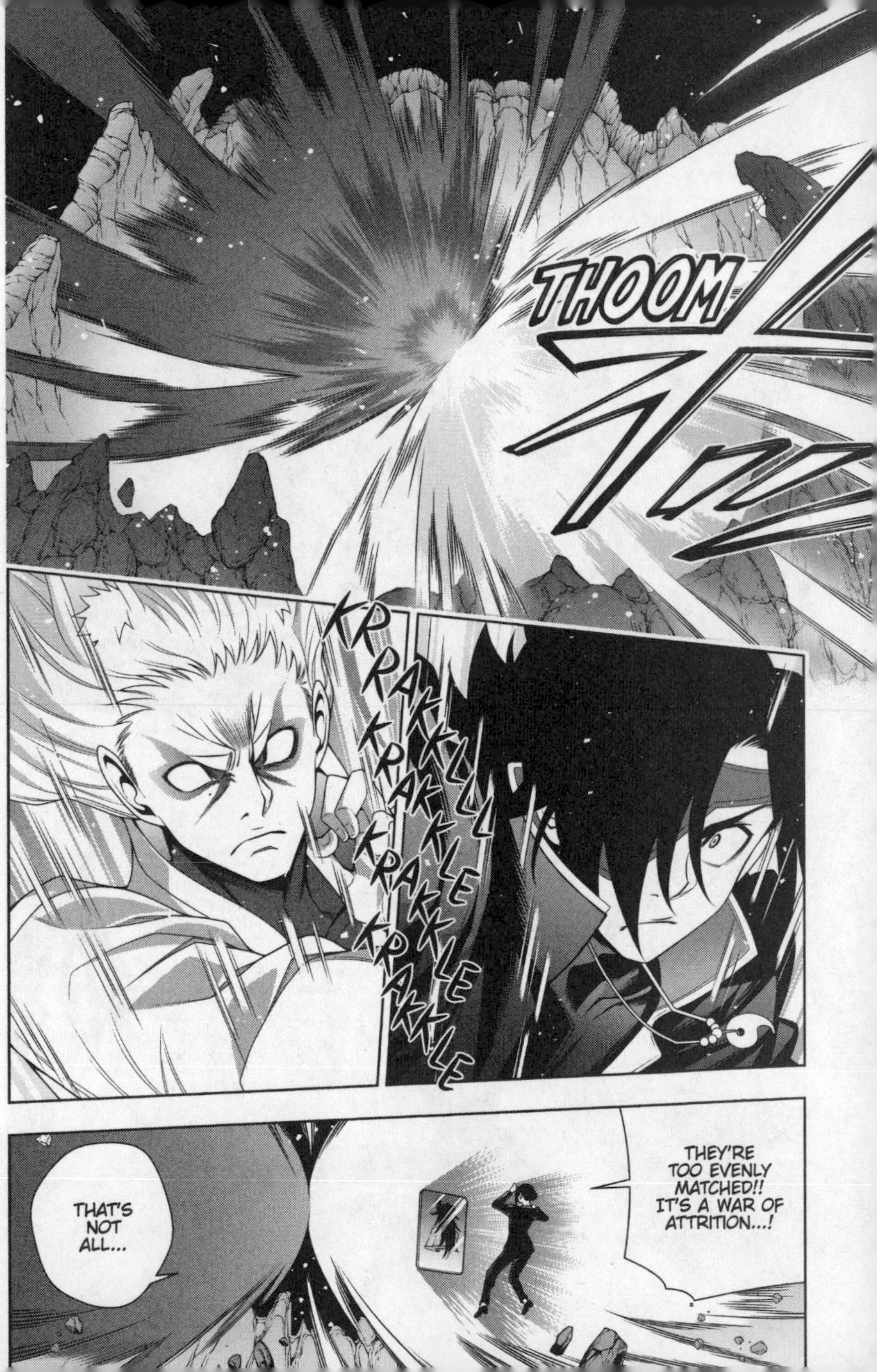
THOOM
KRAKKLLLL
KRAKKLE
KRAKKLE
KRAKKLE
KRAKKLE
THEY'RE TOO EVENLY MATCHED!! IT'S A WAR OF ATTRITION...!
THAT'S NOT ALL...

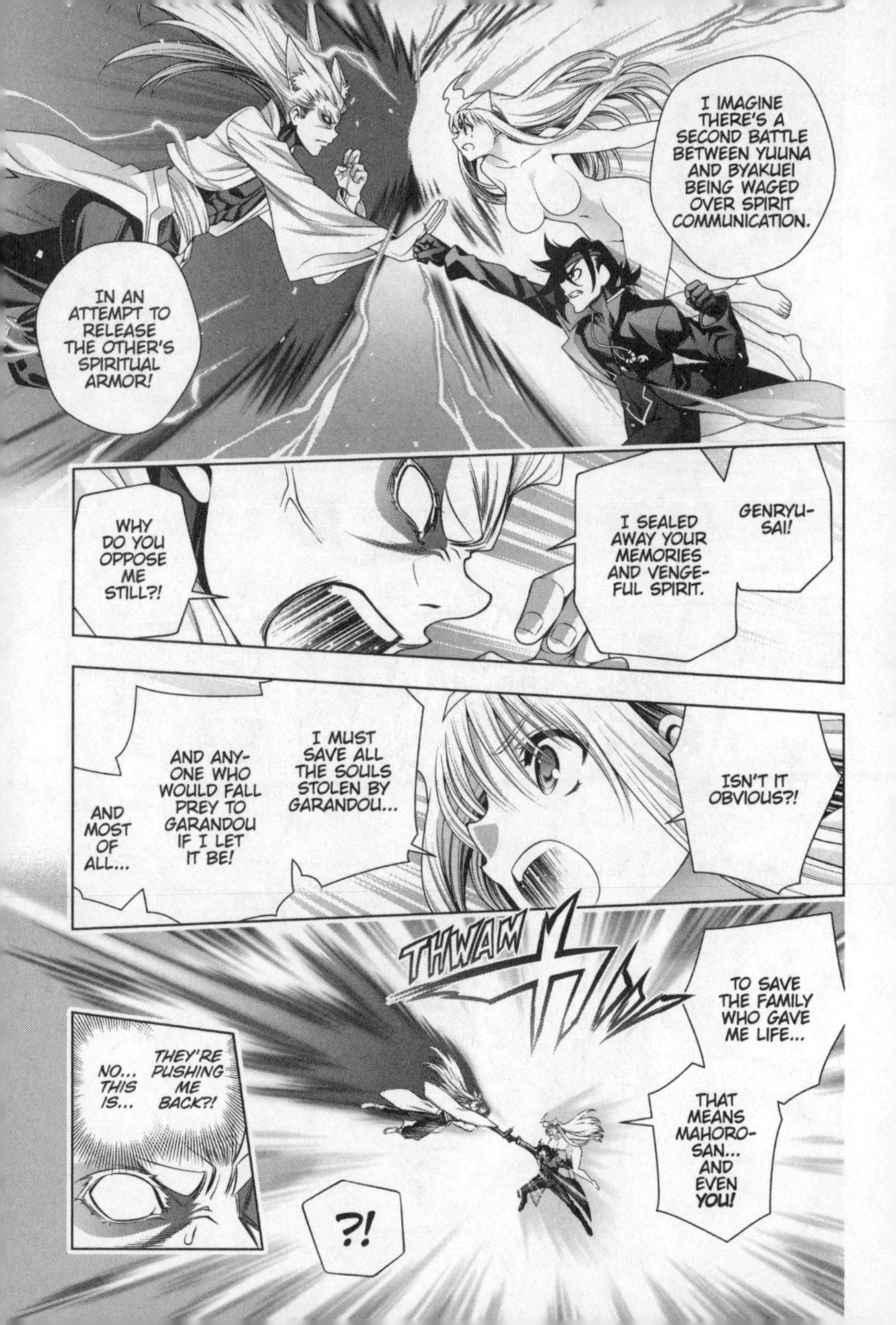
I IMAGINE THERE'S A SECOND BATTLE BETWEEN YUUNA AND BYAKUEI BEING WAGED OVER SPIRIT COMMUNICATION.
IN AN ATTEMPT TO RELEASE THE OTHER'S SPIRITUAL ARMOR!
GENRYU-SAI!
I SEALED AWAY YOUR MEMORIES AND VENGE-FUL SPIRIT.
WHY DO YOU OPPOSE ME STILL?!
ISN'T IT OBVIOUS?!
I MUST SAVE ALL THE SOULS STOLEN BY GARANDOU...
AND ANY-ONE WHO WOULD FALL PREY TO GARANDOU IF I LET IT BE!
AND MOST OF ALL...
TO SAVE THE FAMILY WHO GAVE ME LIFE...
THWAM
THAT MEANS MAHORO-SAN... AND EVEN YOU!
?!
THEY'RE PUSHING ME BACK?!
NO... THIS IS...

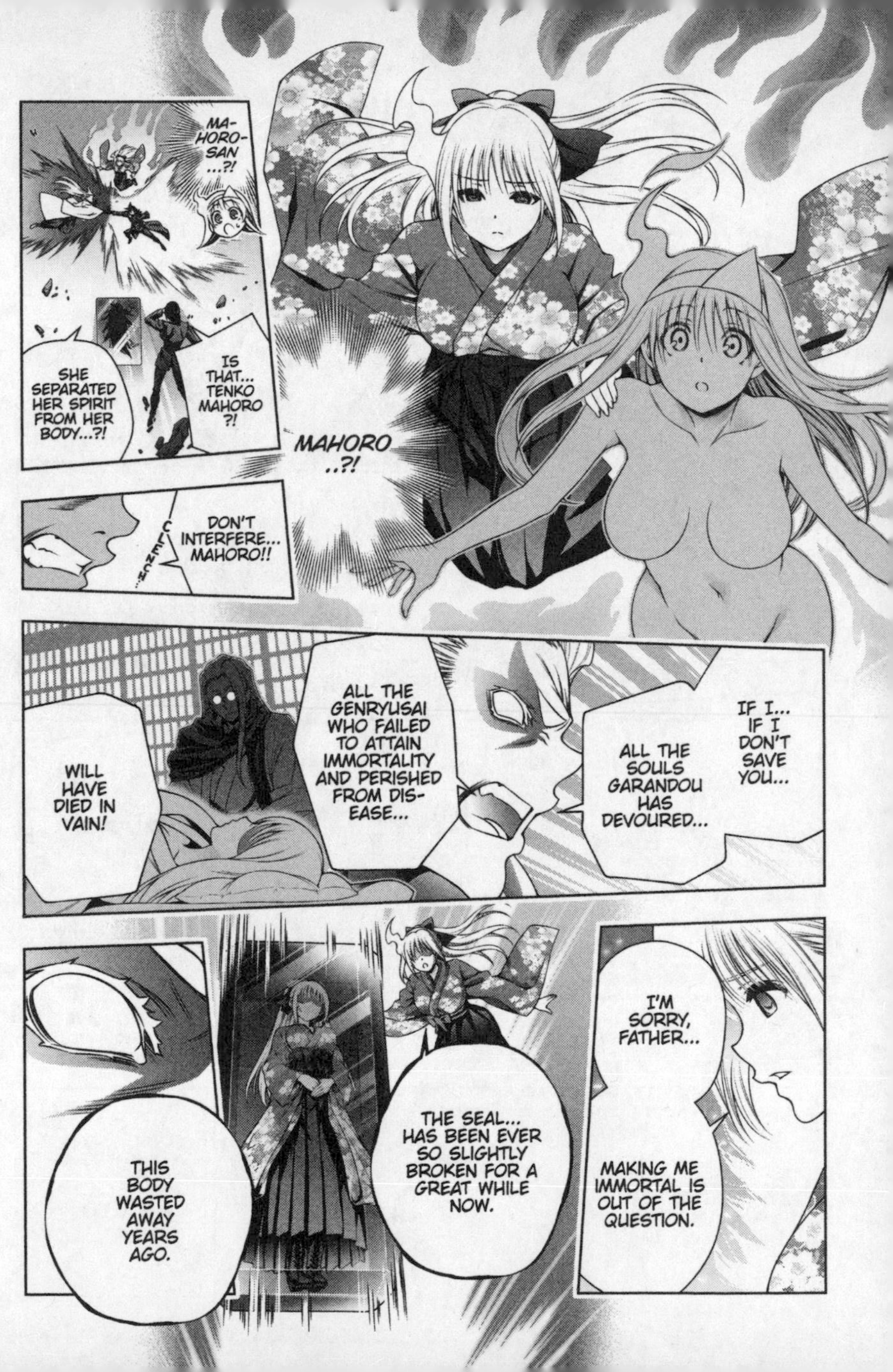
MAHORO ..?!
MA-HORO-SAN ...?!
IS THAT... TENKO MAHORO ?!
SHE SEPARATED HER SPIRIT FROM HER BODY...?!
CLENCH...
DON'T INTERFERE... MAHORO!!
IF I... IF I DON'T SAVE YOU...
ALL THE SOULS GARANDOU HAS DEVOURED...
ALL THE GENRYUSAI WHO FAILED TO ATTAIN IMMORTALITY AND PERISHED FROM DIS-EASE...
WILL HAVE DIED IN VAIN!
I'M SORRY, FATHER...
MAKING ME IMMORTAL IS OUT OF THE QUESTION.
THE SEAL... HAS BEEN EVER SO SLIGHTLY BROKEN FOR A GREAT WHILE NOW.
THIS BODY WASTED AWAY YEARS AGO.

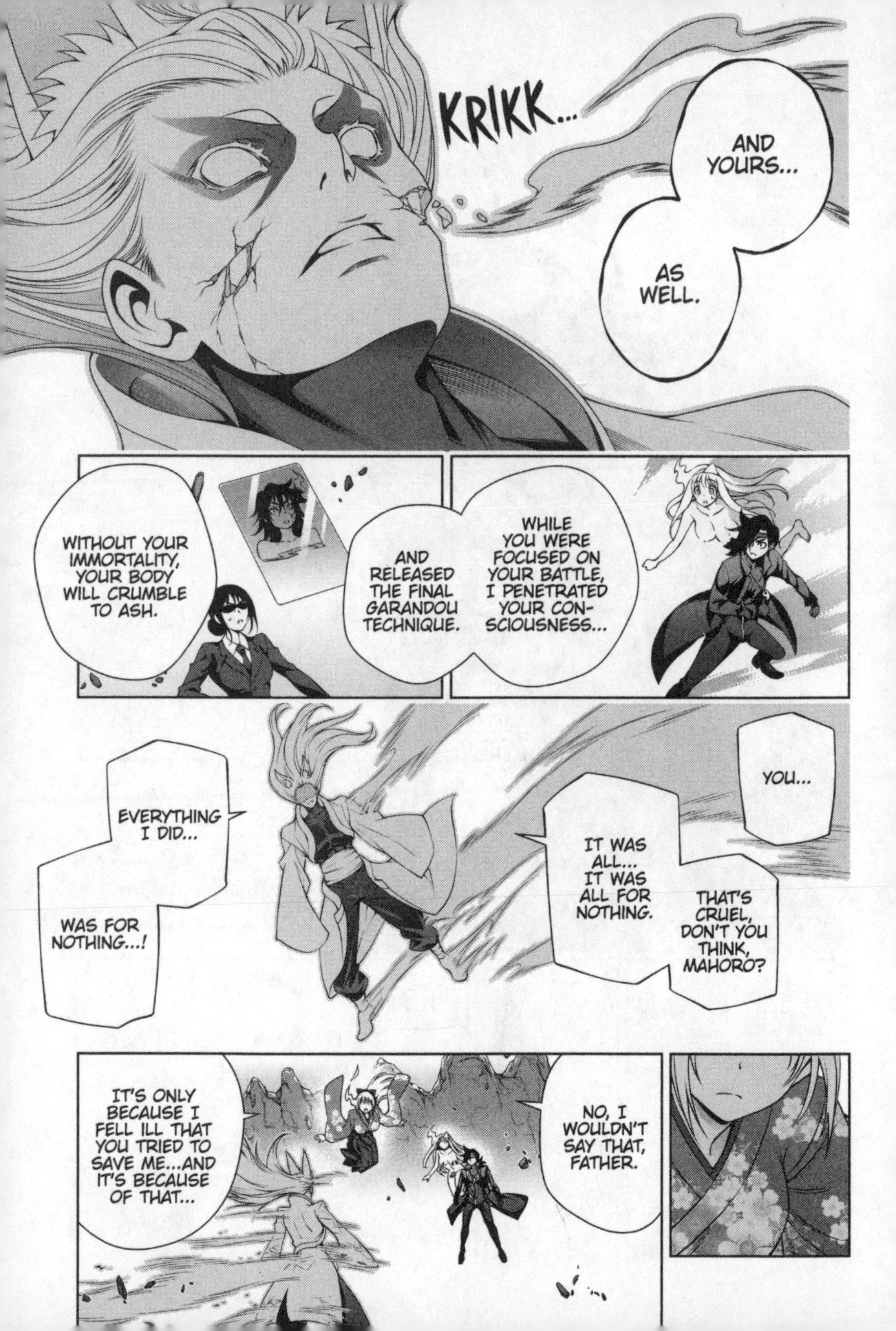
AND YOURS...
AS WELL.
KRIKK...
WHILE YOU WERE FOCUSED ON YOUR BATTLE, I PENETRATED YOUR CONSCIOUSNESS...
AND RELEASED THE FINAL GARANDOU TECHNIQUE.
WITHOUT YOUR IMMORTALITY, YOUR BODY WILL CRUMBLE TO ASH.
YOU...
THAT'S CRUEL, DON'T YOU THINK, MAHORO?
IT WAS ALL... IT WAS ALL FOR NOTHING.
EVERYTHING I DID...
WAS FOR NOTHING...!
NO, I WOULDN'T SAY THAT, FATHER.
IT'S ONLY BECAUSE I FELL ILL THAT YOU TRIED TO SAVE ME...AND IT'S BECAUSE OF THAT...

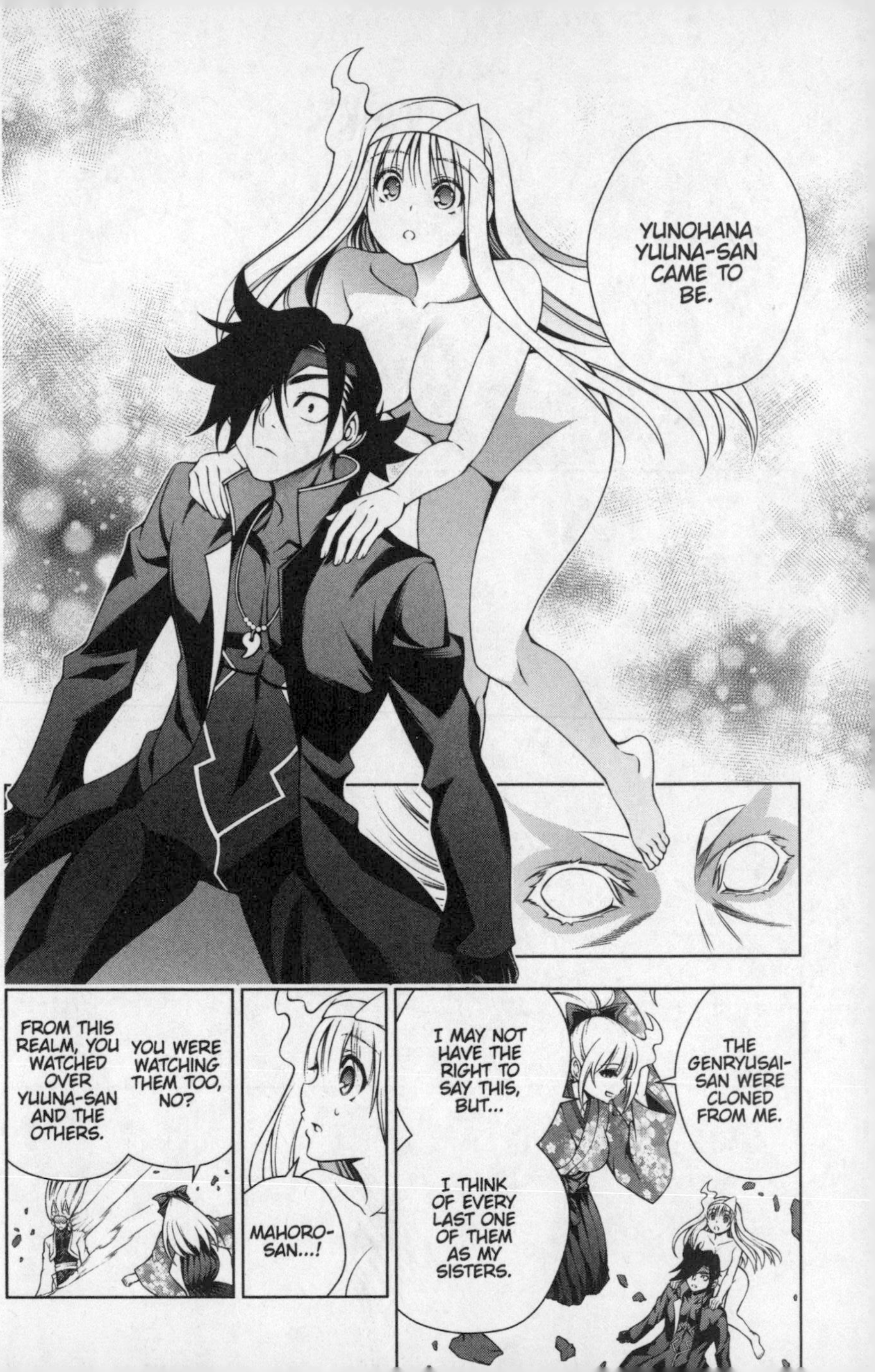
YUNOHANA YUUNA-SAN CAME TO BE.
THE GENRYUSAI-SAN WERE CLONED FROM ME.
I MAY NOT HAVE THE RIGHT TO SAY THIS, BUT...
I THINK OF EVERY LAST ONE OF THEM AS MY SISTERS.
MAHORO-SAN...!
YOU WERE WATCHING THEM TOO, NO?
FROM THIS REALM, YOU WATCHED OVER YUUNA-SAN AND THE OTHERS.

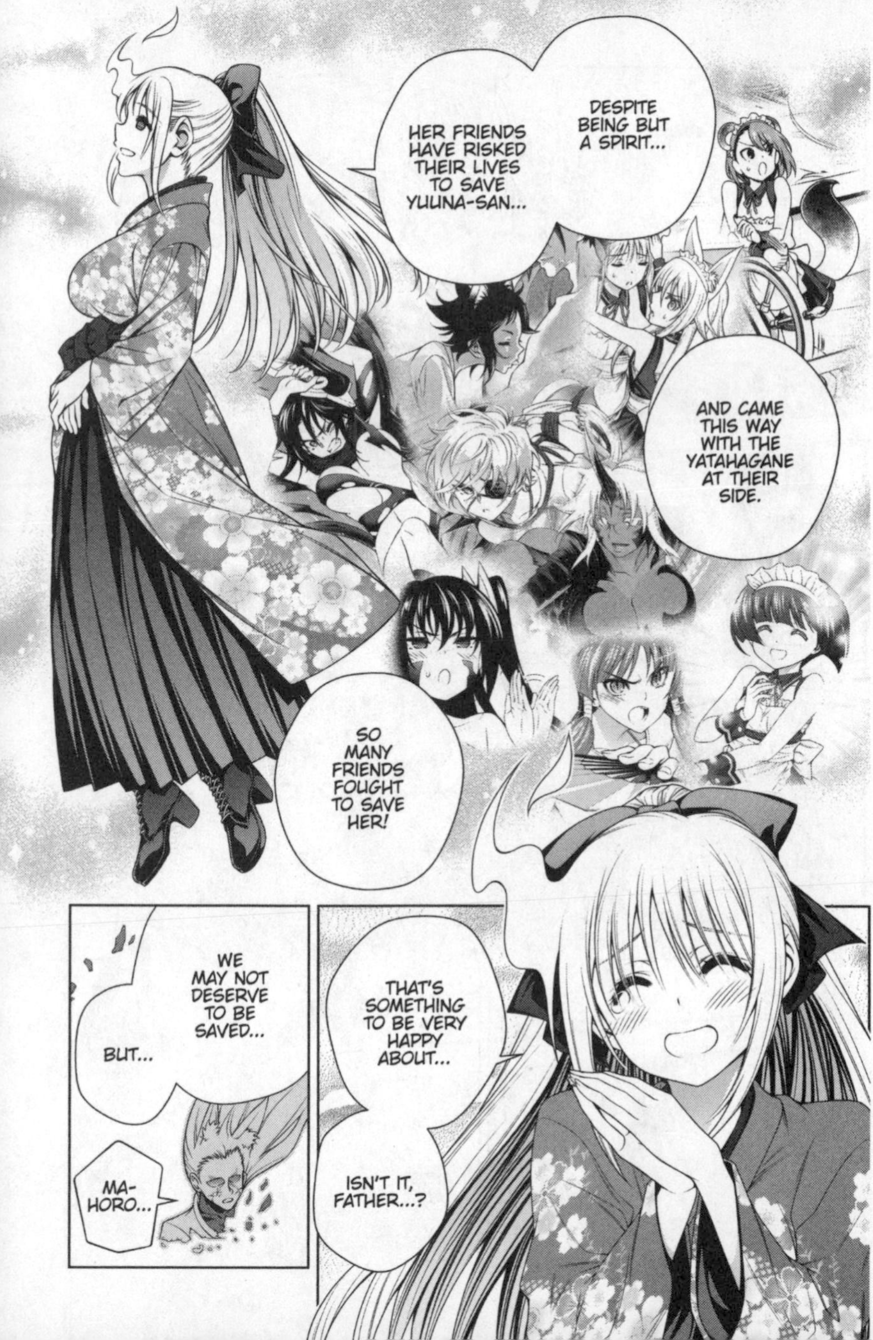
DESPITE BEING BUT A SPIRIT...
HER FRIENDS HAVE RISKED THEIR LIVES TO SAVE YUUNA-SAN...
AND CAME THIS WAY WITH THE YATAHAGANE AT THEIR SIDE.
SO MANY FRIENDS FOUGHT TO SAVE HER!
THAT'S SOMETHING TO BE VERY HAPPY ABOUT...
ISN'T IT, FATHER...?
WE MAY NOT DESERVE TO BE SAVED...
BUT...
MA-HORO...

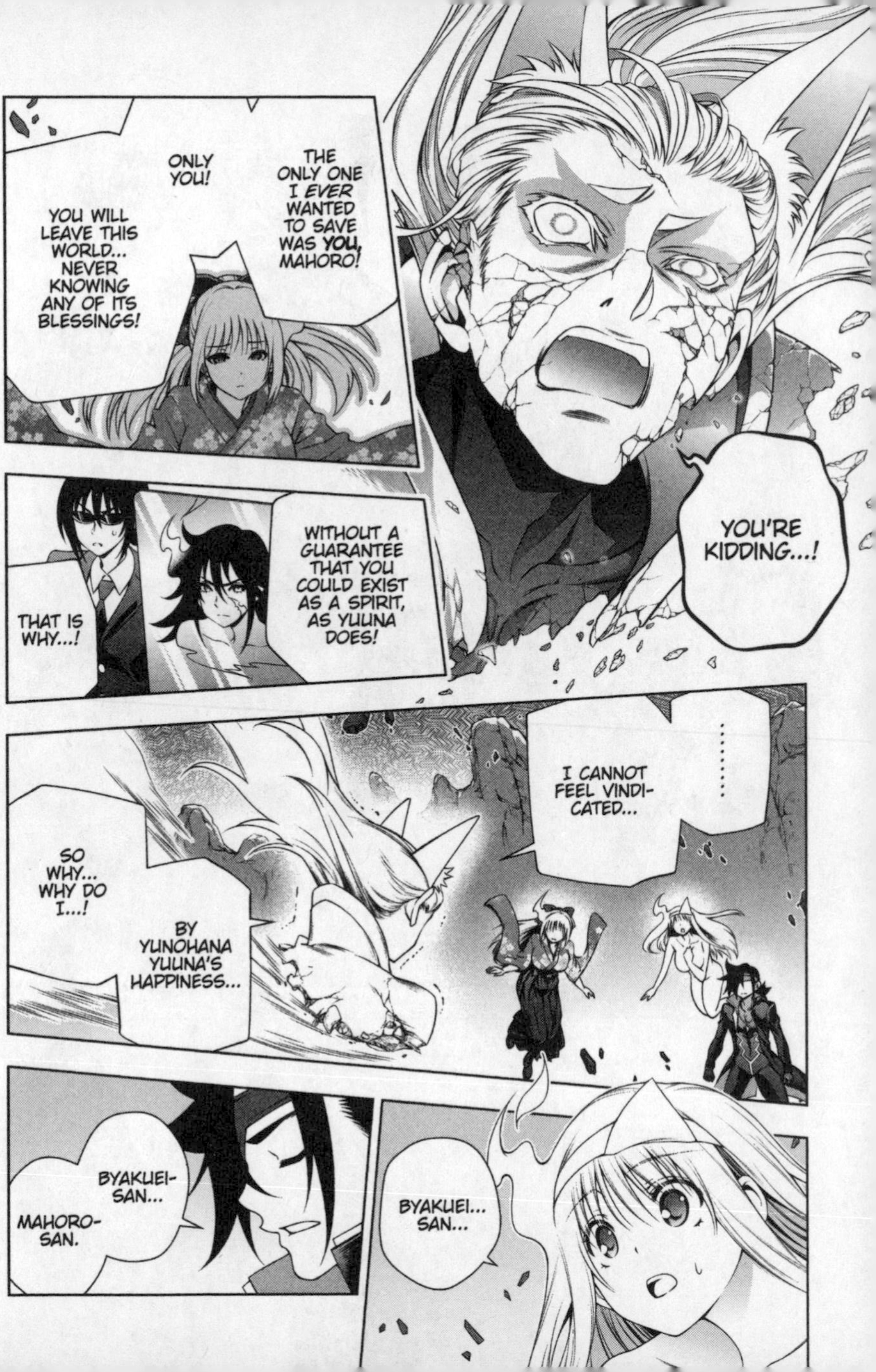
YOU'RE KIDDING...!
THE ONLY ONE I *EVER* WANTED TO SAVE WAS **YOU**, MAHORO!
ONLY YOU!
YOU WILL LEAVE THIS WORLD... NEVER KNOWING ANY OF ITS BLESSINGS!
WITHOUT A GUARANTEE THAT YOU COULD EXIST AS A SPIRIT, AS YUUNA DOES!
THAT IS WHY...!
......
I CANNOT FEEL VINDICATED...
BY YUNOHANA YUUNA'S HAPPINESS...
SO WHY... WHY DO I...!
BYAKUEI... SAN...
BYAKUEI-SAN...
MAHORO-SAN.

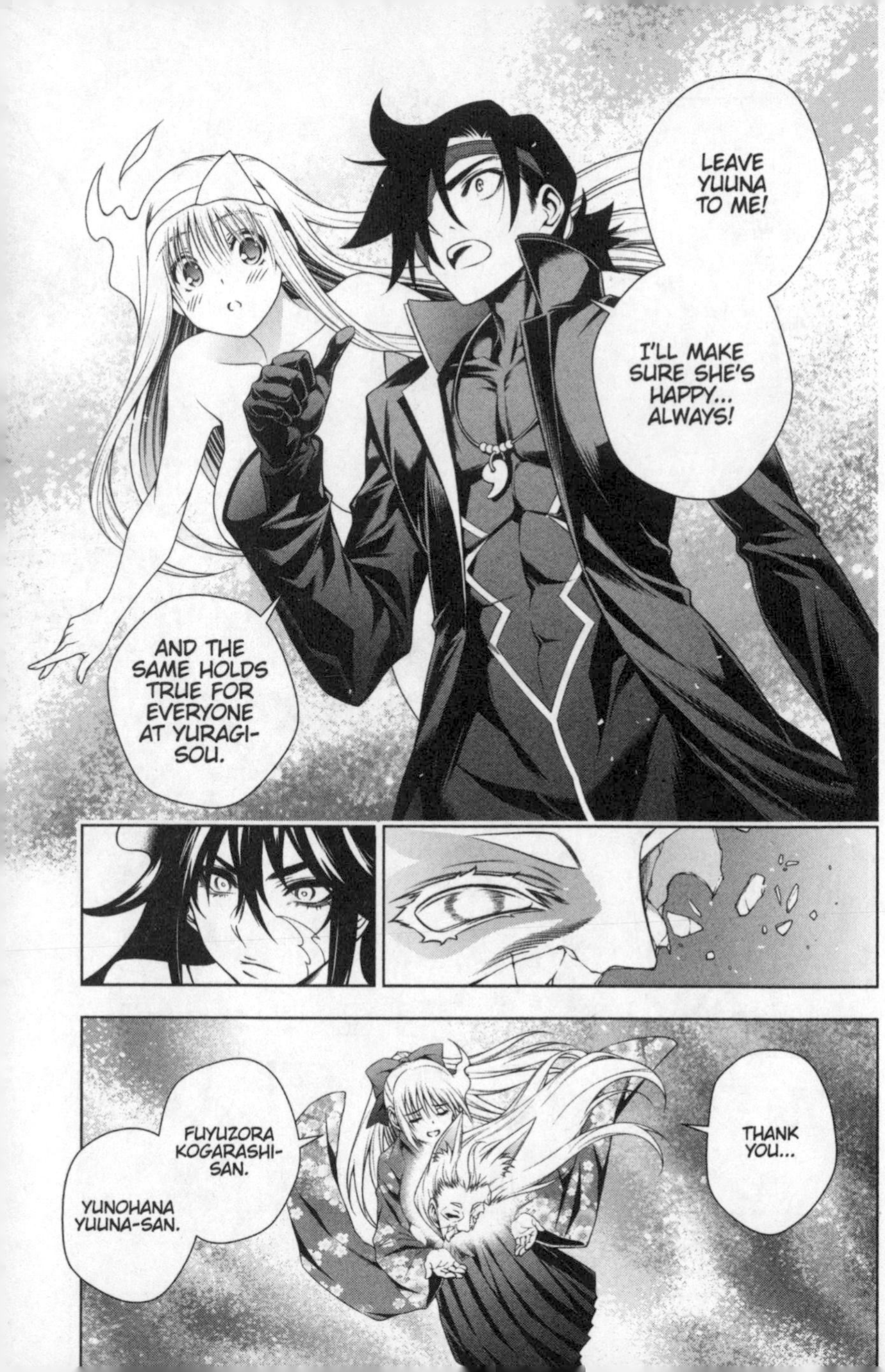
LEAVE YUUNA TO ME!
I'LL MAKE SURE SHE'S HAPPY... ALWAYS!
AND THE SAME HOLDS TRUE FOR EVERYONE AT YURAGI-SOU.
THANK YOU...
FUYUZORA KOGARASHI-SAN.
YUNOHANA YUUNA-SAN.

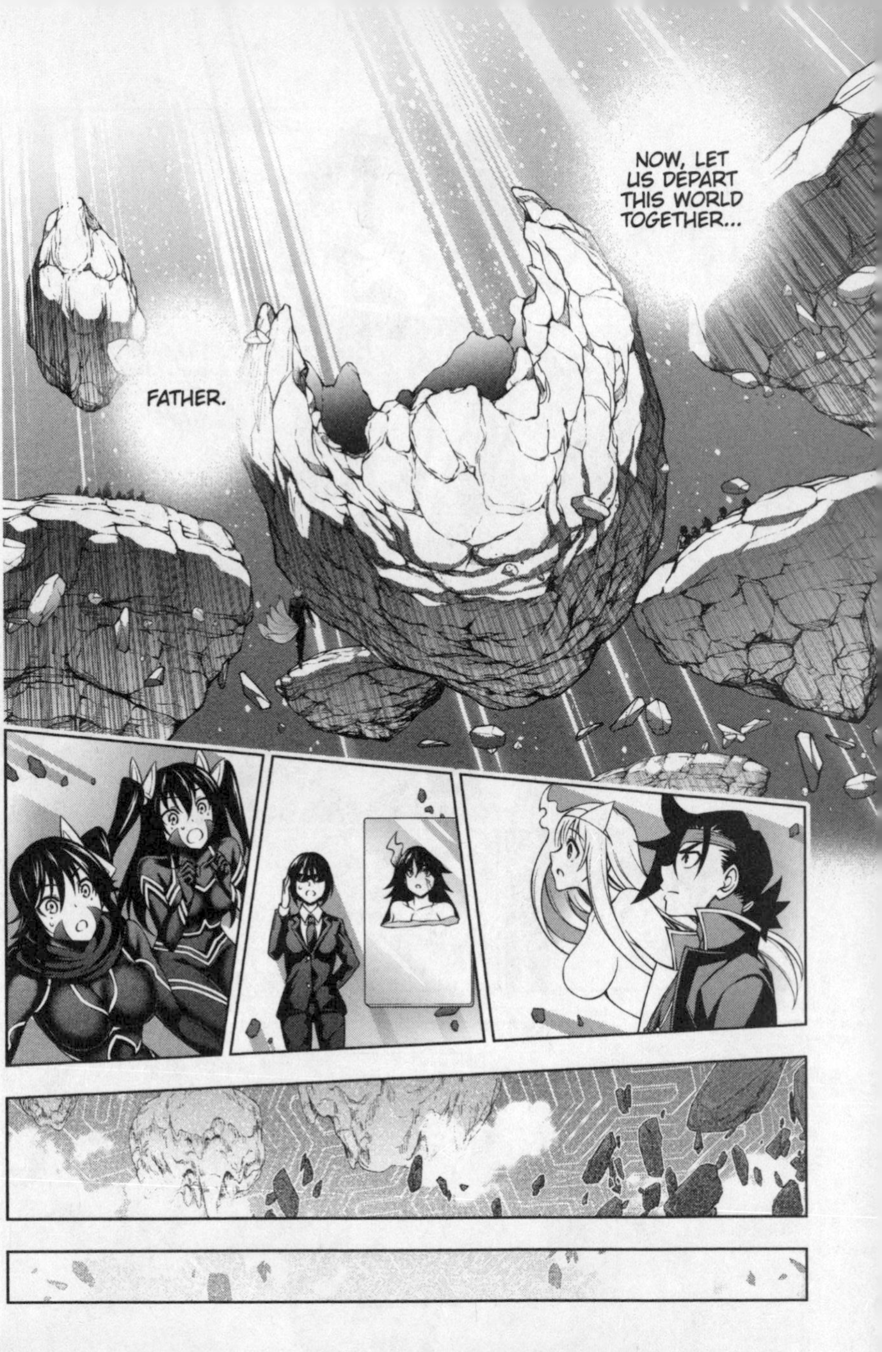
NOW, LET US DEPART THIS WORLD TOGETHER...
FATHER.

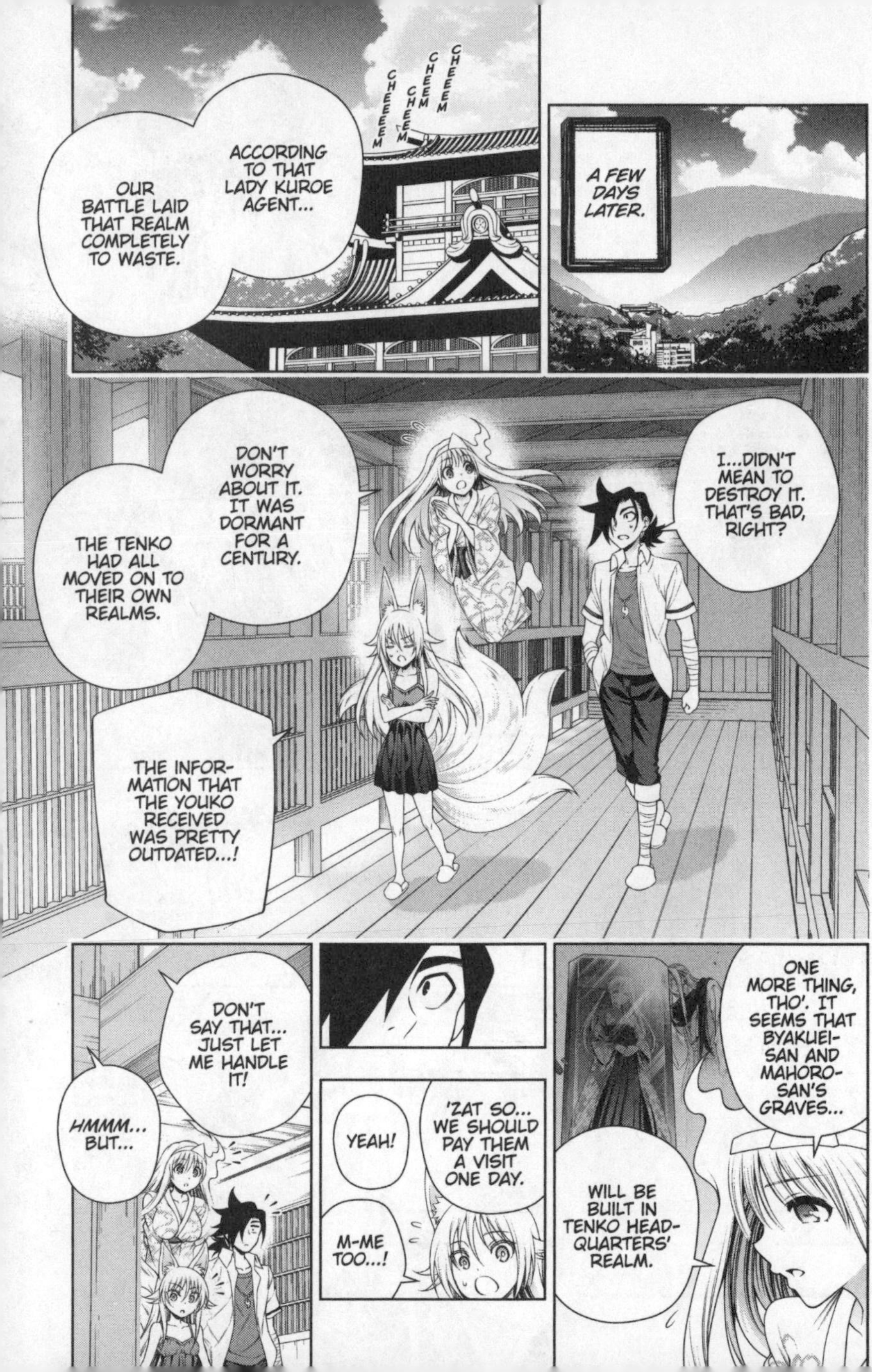
A FEW DAYS LATER.
CHEEEEM
CHEEM
CHEEEEM
ACCORDING TO THAT LADY KUROE AGENT...
OUR BATTLE LAID THAT REALM COMPLETELY TO WASTE.
I...DIDN'T MEAN TO DESTROY IT. THAT'S BAD, RIGHT?
DON'T WORRY ABOUT IT. IT WAS DORMANT FOR A CENTURY.
THE TENKO HAD ALL MOVED ON TO THEIR OWN REALMS.
THE INFOR-MATION THAT THE YOUKO RECEIVED WAS PRETTY OUTDATED...!
ONE MORE THING, THO'. IT SEEMS THAT BYAKUEI-SAN AND MAHORO-SAN'S GRAVES...
WILL BE BUILT IN TENKO HEAD-QUARTERS' REALM.
'ZAT SO... WE SHOULD PAY THEM A VISIT ONE DAY.
YEAH!
M-ME TOO...!
DON'T SAY THAT... JUST LET ME HANDLE IT!
HMMM... BUT...

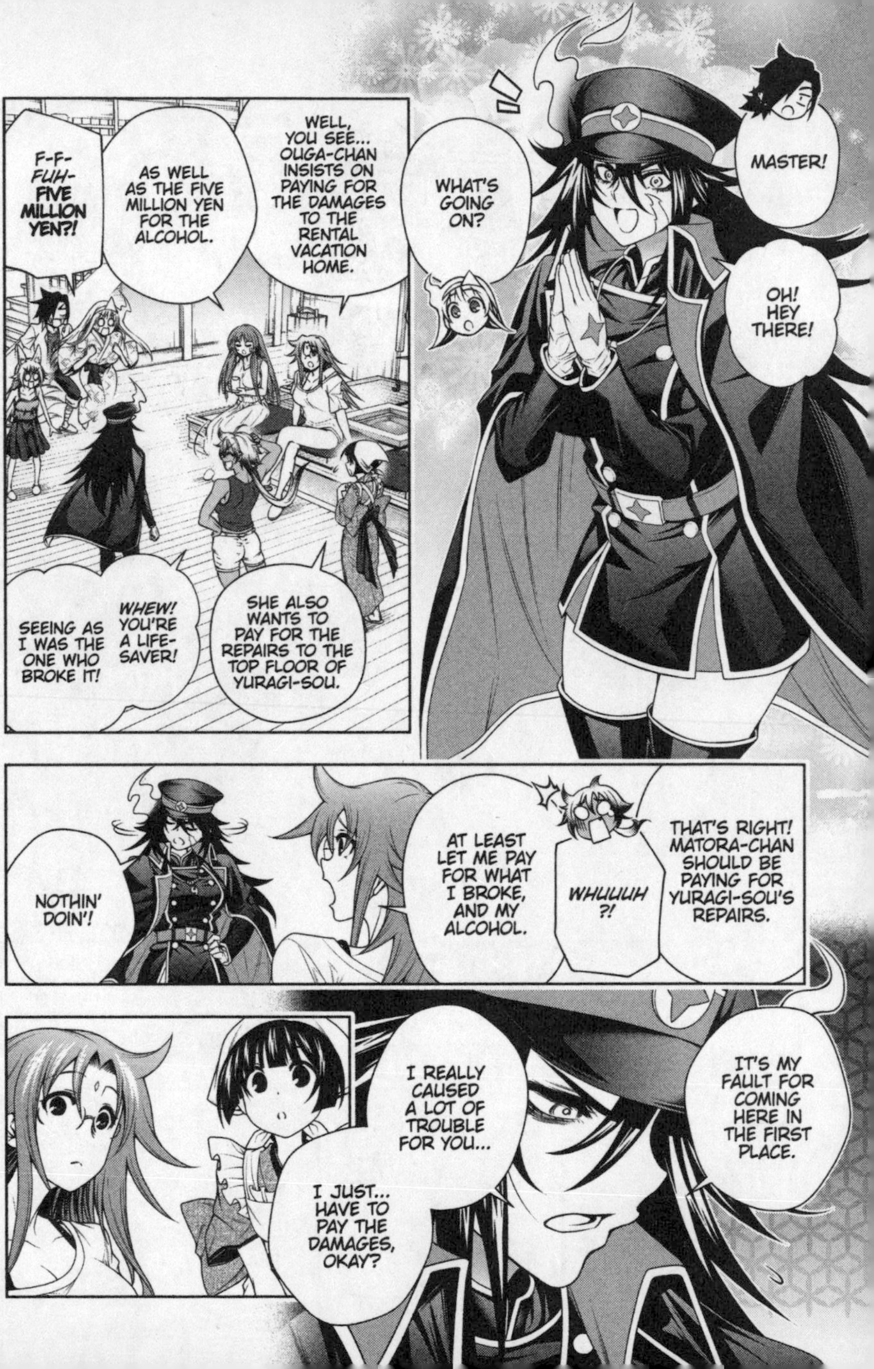
MASTER!
OH! HEY THERE!
WHAT'S GOING ON?
WELL, YOU SEE... OUGA-CHAN INSISTS ON PAYING FOR THE DAMAGES TO THE RENTAL VACATION HOME.
AS WELL AS THE FIVE MILLION YEN FOR THE ALCOHOL.
F-F-FUH-FIVE MILLION YEN?!
SHE ALSO WANTS TO PAY FOR THE REPAIRS TO THE TOP FLOOR OF YURAGI-SOU.
WHEW! YOU'RE A LIFE-SAVER!
SEEING AS I WAS THE ONE WHO BROKE IT!
THAT'S RIGHT! MATORA-CHAN SHOULD BE PAYING FOR YURAGI-SOU'S REPAIRS.
WHUUUH?!
AT LEAST LET ME PAY FOR WHAT I BROKE, AND MY ALCOHOL.
NOTHIN' DOIN'!
IT'S MY FAULT FOR COMING HERE IN THE FIRST PLACE.
I REALLY CAUSED A LOT OF TROUBLE FOR YOU...
I JUST... HAVE TO PAY THE DAMAGES, OKAY?

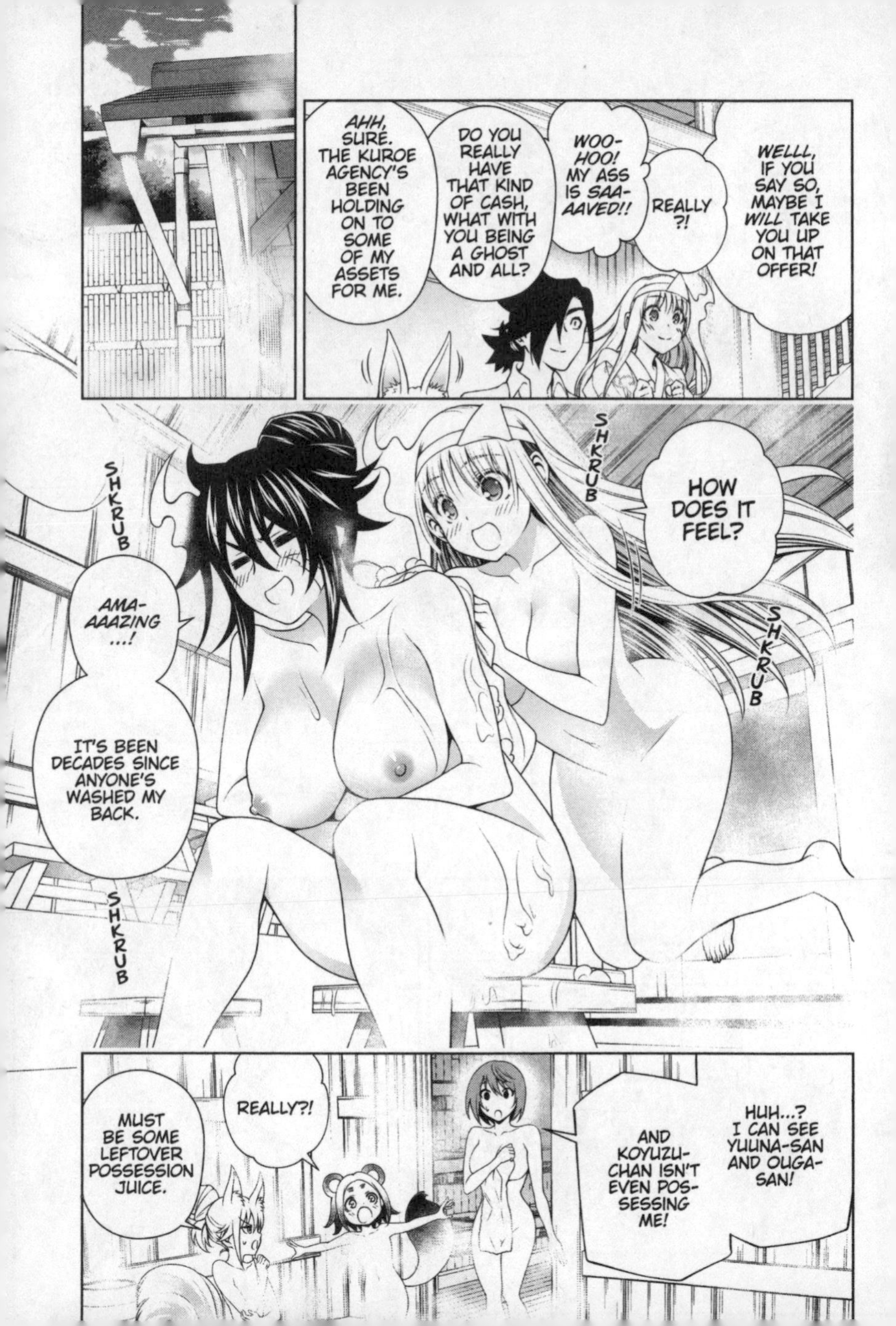
WELLL, IF YOU SAY SO, MAYBE I WILL TAKE YOU UP ON THAT OFFER!
REALLY?!
WOO-HOO! MY ASS IS SAA-AAVED!!
DO YOU REALLY HAVE THAT KIND OF CASH, WHAT WITH YOU BEING A GHOST AND ALL?
AHH, SURE. THE KUROE AGENCY'S BEEN HOLDING ON TO SOME OF MY ASSETS FOR ME.
SHKRUB
HOW DOES IT FEEL?
SHKRUB
SHKRUB
AMA-AAAZING ...!
IT'S BEEN DECADES SINCE ANYONE'S WASHED MY BACK.
SHKRUB
HUH...? I CAN SEE YUUNA-SAN AND OUGA-SAN!
AND KOYUZU-CHAN ISN'T EVEN POS-SESSING ME!
REALLY?!
MUST BE SOME LEFTOVER POSSESSION JUICE.

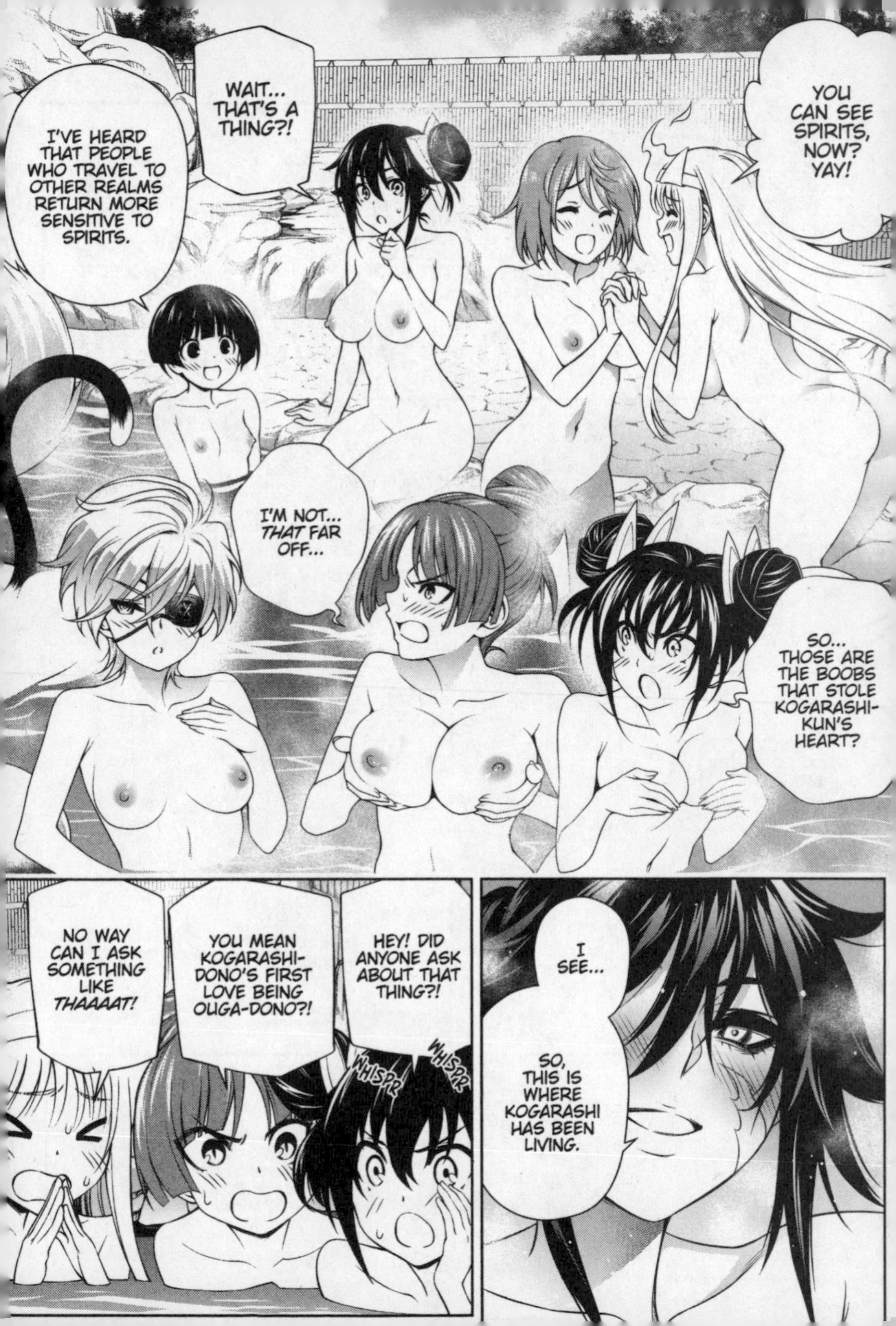
YOU CAN SEE SPIRITS, NOW? YAY!
WAIT... THAT'S A THING?!
I'VE HEARD THAT PEOPLE WHO TRAVEL TO OTHER REALMS RETURN MORE SENSITIVE TO SPIRITS.
SO... THOSE ARE THE BOOBS THAT STOLE KOGARASHI-KUN'S HEART?
I'M NOT... *THAT* FAR OFF...
I SEE...
SO, THIS IS WHERE KOGARASHI HAS BEEN LIVING.
HEY! DID ANYONE ASK ABOUT THAT THING?!
WHISPR
WHISPR
YOU MEAN KOGARASHI-DONO'S FIRST LOVE BEING OUGA-DONO?!
NO WAY CAN I ASK SOMETHING LIKE *THAAAAT!*

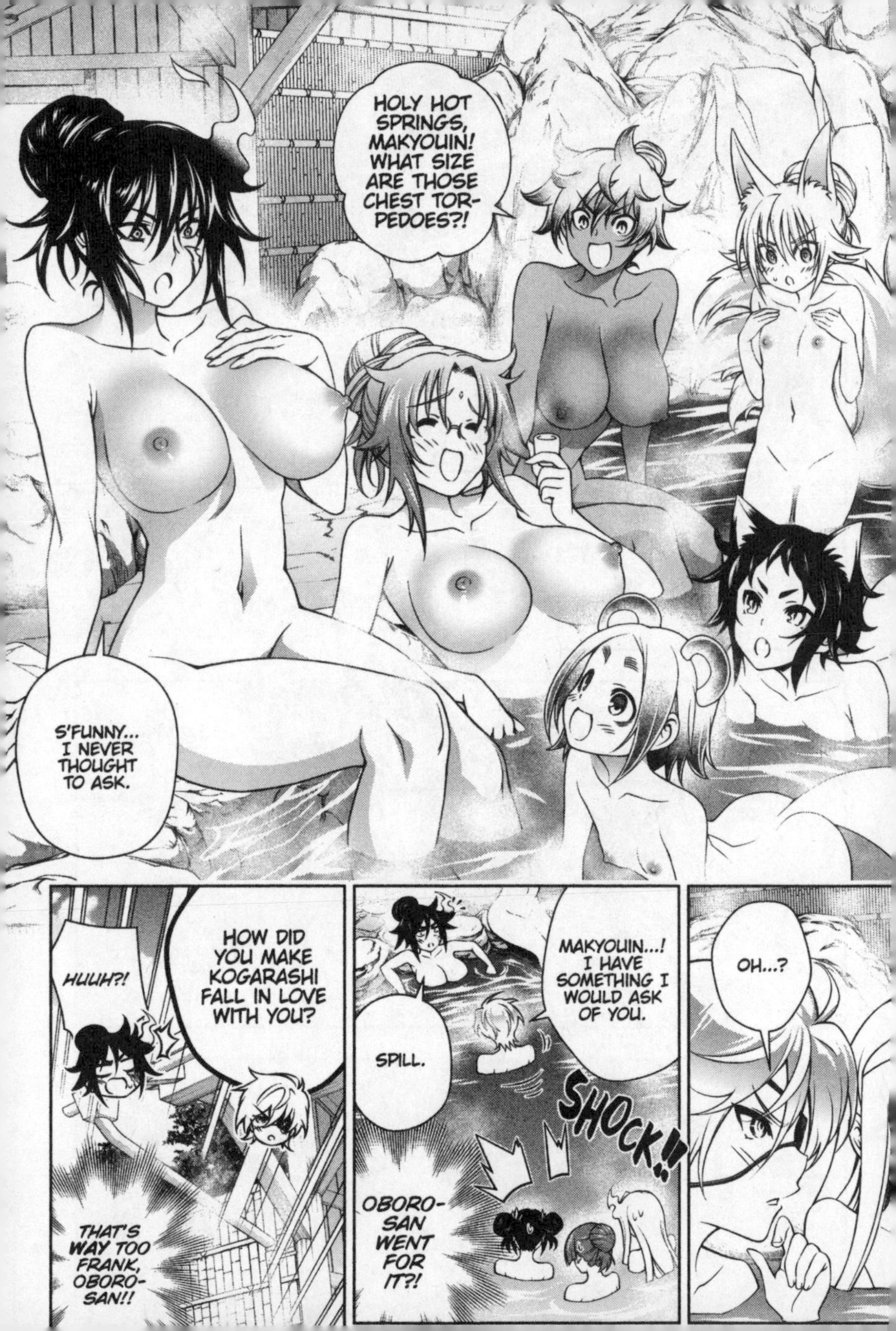
HOLY HOT SPRINGS, MAKYOUIN! WHAT SIZE ARE THOSE CHEST TOR-PEDOES?!
S'FUNNY... I NEVER THOUGHT TO ASK.
OH...?
MAKYOUIN...! I HAVE SOMETHING I WOULD ASK OF YOU.
SPILL.
SHOCK!!
OBORO-SAN WENT FOR IT?!
HOW DID YOU MAKE KOGARASHI FALL IN LOVE WITH YOU?
HUUH?!
THAT'S WAY TOO FRANK, OBORO-SAN!!

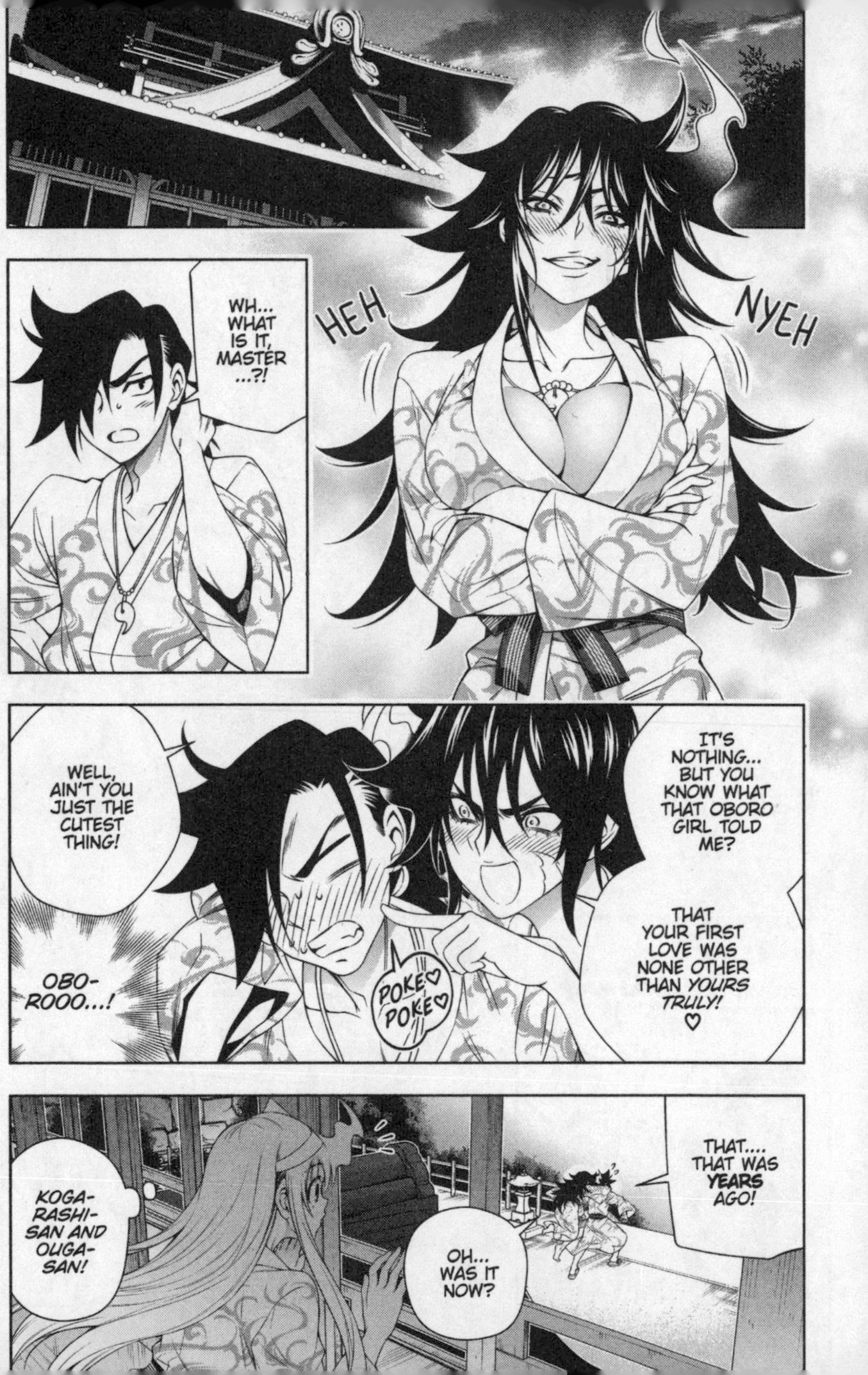
NYEH
HEH
WH... WHAT IS IT, MASTER ...?!
IT'S NOTHING... BUT YOU KNOW WHAT THAT OBORO GIRL TOLD ME?
THAT YOUR FIRST LOVE WAS NONE OTHER THAN *YOURS TRULY!* ♡
WELL, AIN'T YOU JUST THE CUTEST THING!
POKE♡ POKE♡
OBO-ROOO...!
THAT.... THAT WAS **YEARS** AGO!
OH... WAS IT NOW?
KOGA-RASHI-SAN AND OUGA-SAN!

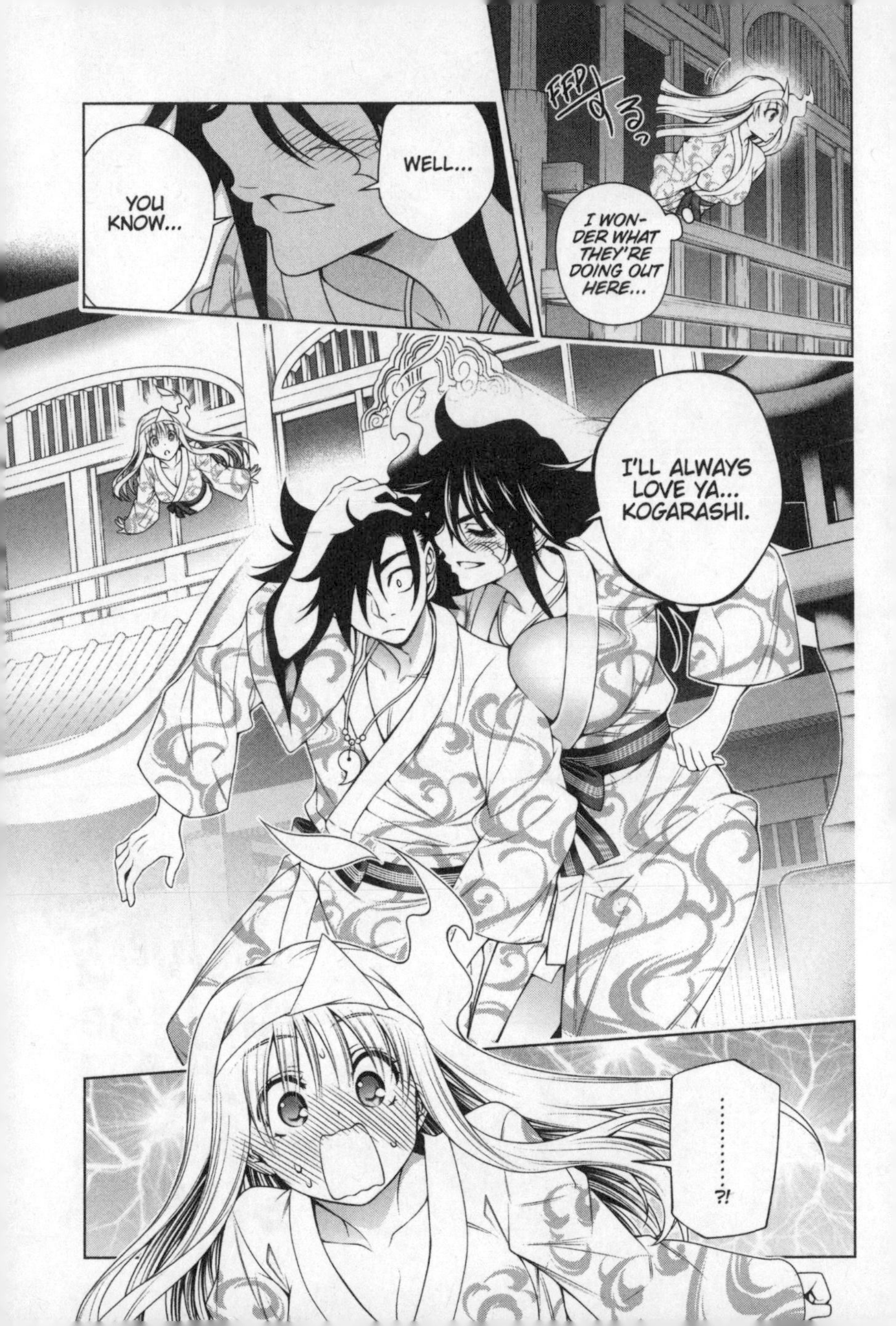
FFP
するっ
I WONDER WHAT THEY'RE DOING OUT HERE...
WELL...
YOU KNOW...
I'LL ALWAYS LOVE YA... KOGARASHI.
.........?!

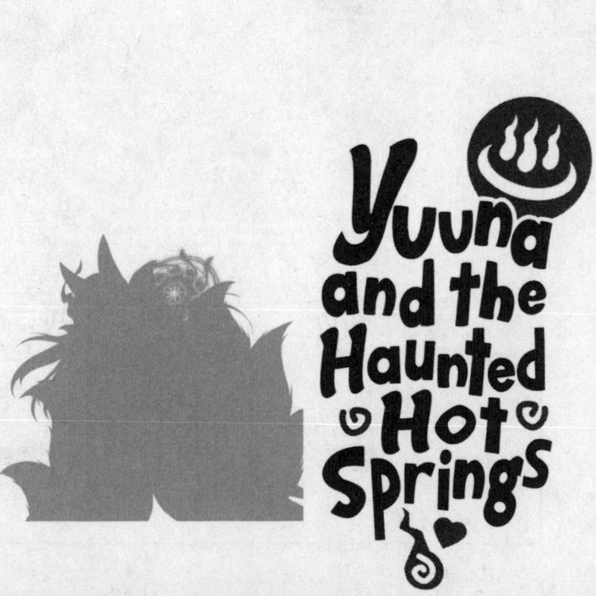

Yuuna and the Haunted Hot Springs

129 Ouga's Wish

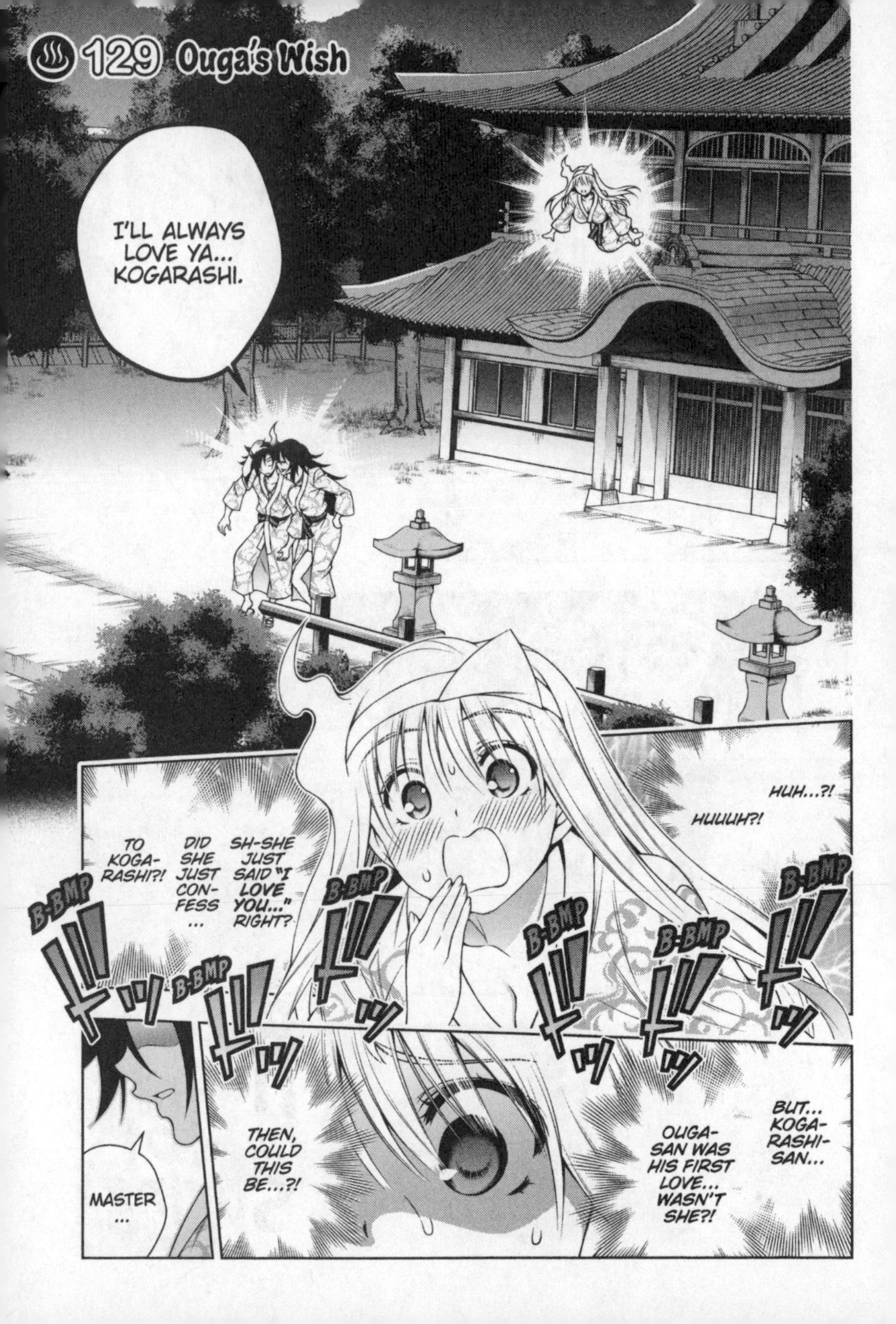
I'LL ALWAYS LOVE YA... KOGARASHI.
HUH...?!
HUUUH?!
SH-SHE JUST SAID "I LOVE YOU..." RIGHT?
DID SHE JUST CONFESS...
TO KOGA-RASHI?!
B-BMP
B-BMP
B-BMP
B-BMP
B-BMP
B-BMP
BUT... KOGA-RASHI-SAN...
OUGA-SAN WAS HIS FIRST LOVE... WASN'T SHE?!
THEN, COULD THIS BE...?!
MASTER...

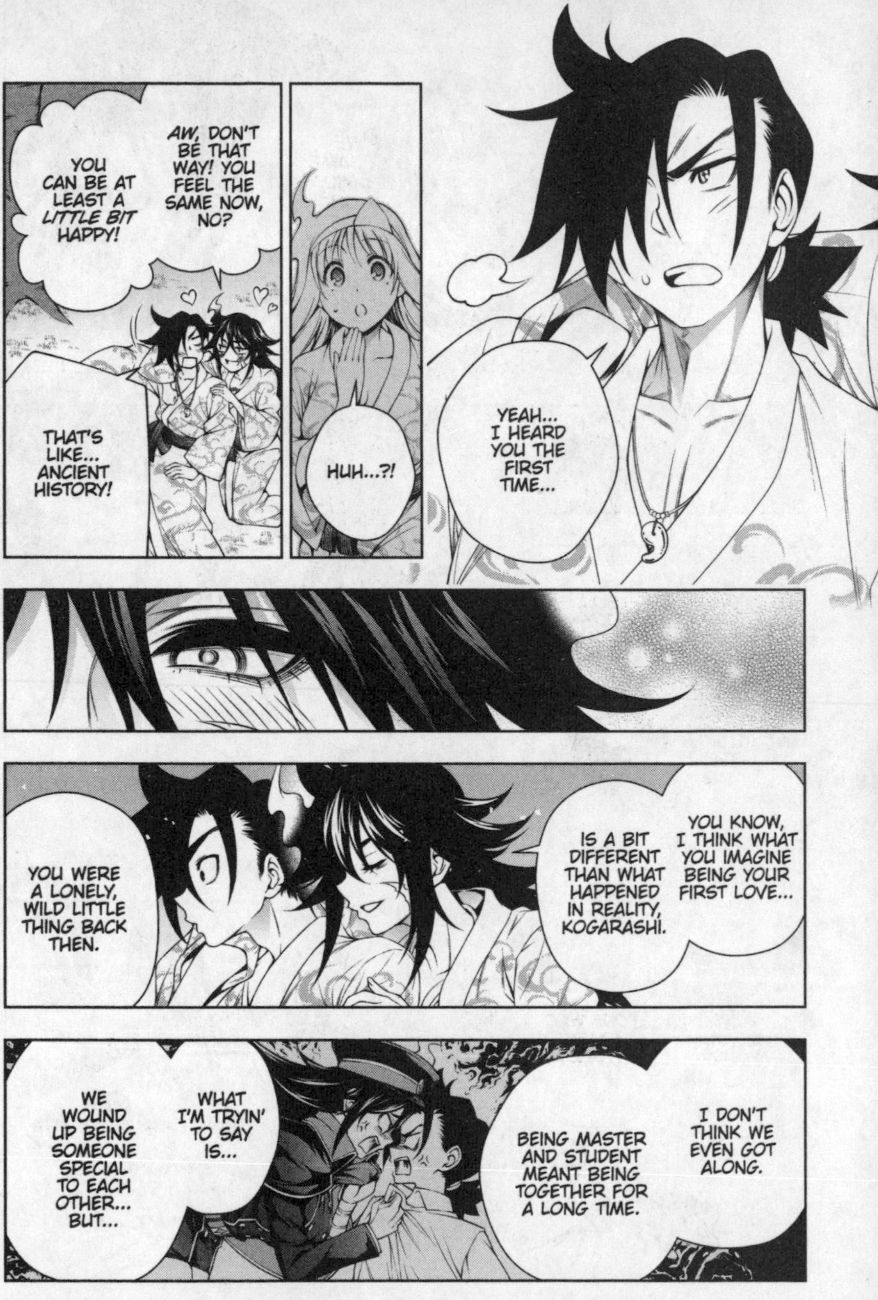
YEAH... I HEARD YOU THE FIRST TIME...
HUH...?!
AW, DON'T BE THAT WAY! YOU FEEL THE SAME NOW, NO?
YOU CAN BE AT LEAST A *LITTLE BIT* HAPPY!
THAT'S LIKE... ANCIENT HISTORY!
YOU KNOW, I THINK WHAT YOU IMAGINE BEING YOUR FIRST LOVE...
IS A BIT DIFFERENT THAN WHAT HAPPENED IN REALITY, KOGARASHI.
YOU WERE A LONELY, WILD LITTLE THING BACK THEN.
I DON'T THINK WE EVEN GOT ALONG.
BEING MASTER AND STUDENT MEANT BEING TOGETHER FOR A LONG TIME.
WHAT I'M TRYIN' TO SAY IS...
WE WOUND UP BEING SOMEONE SPECIAL TO EACH OTHER... BUT...

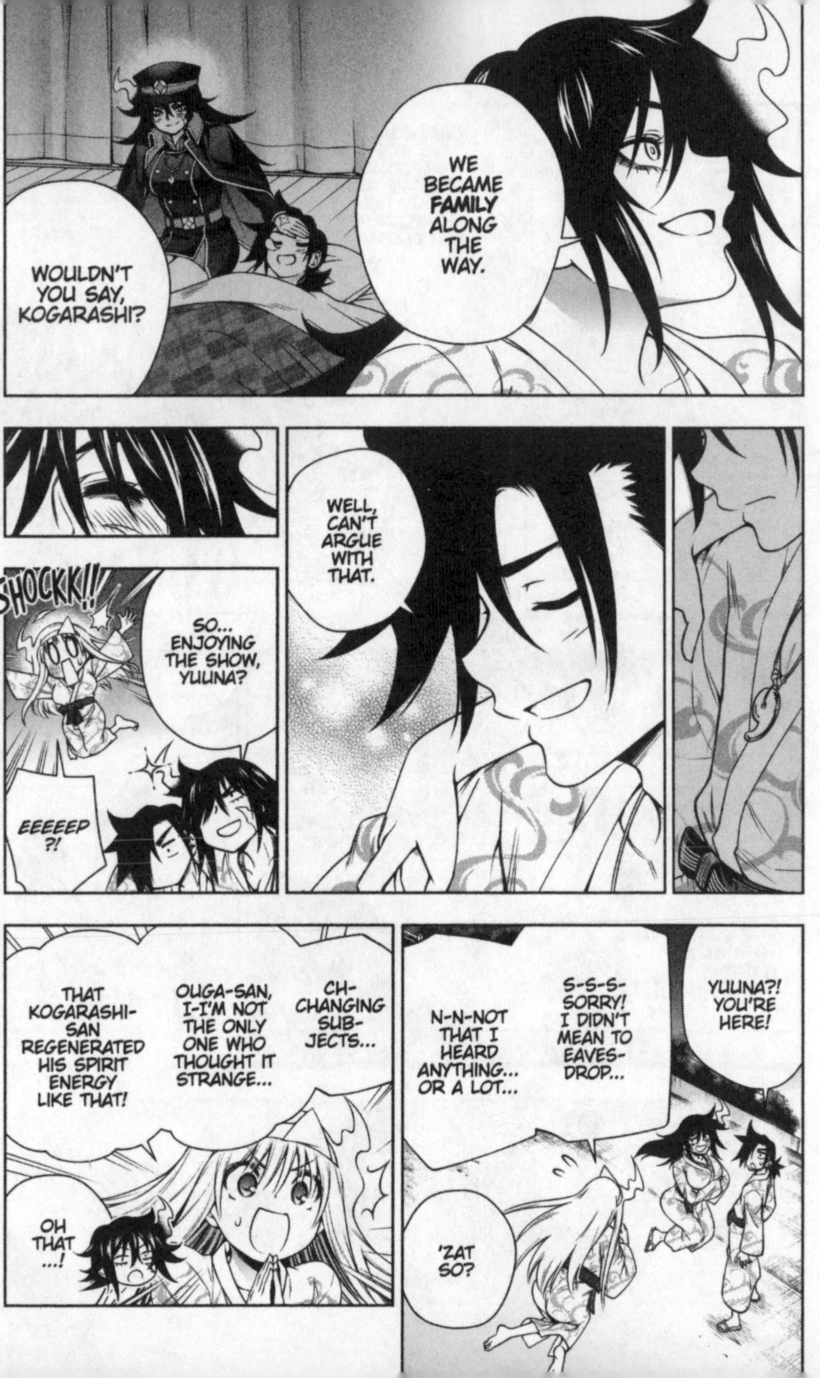
WE BECAME FAMILY ALONG THE WAY.
WOULDN'T YOU SAY, KOGARASHI?
WELL, CAN'T ARGUE WITH THAT.
SO... ENJOYING THE SHOW, YUUNA?
SHOCKK!!
EEEEEP?!
YUUNA?! YOU'RE HERE!
S-S-S-SORRY! I DIDN'T MEAN TO EAVES-DROP...
N-N-NOT THAT I HEARD ANYTHING... OR A LOT...
'ZAT SO?
CH-CHANGING SUB-JECTS...
OUGA-SAN, I-I'M NOT THE ONLY ONE WHO THOUGHT IT STRANGE...
THAT KOGARASHI-SAN REGENERATED HIS SPIRIT ENERGY LIKE THAT!
OH THAT ...!

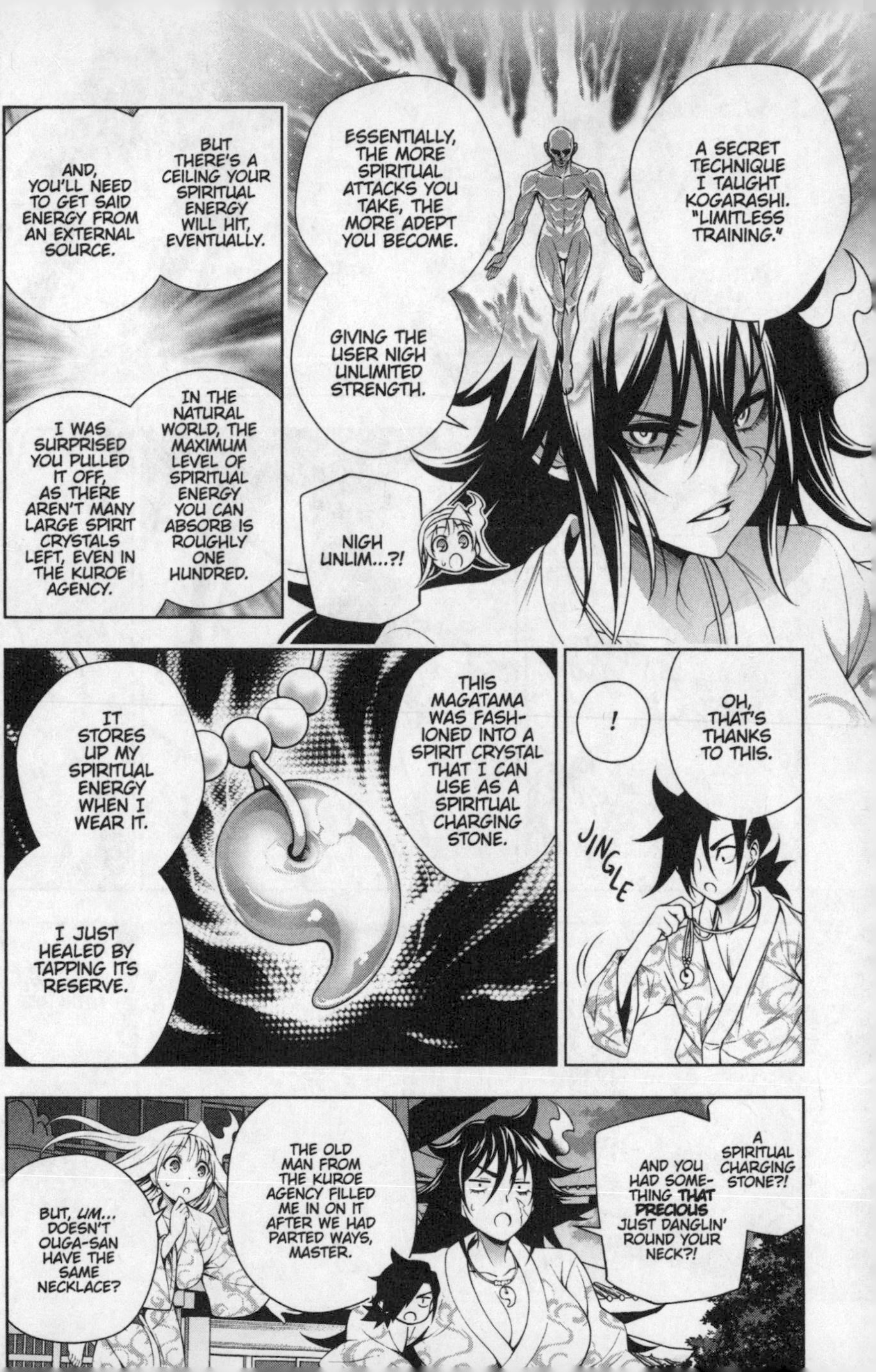
A SECRET TECHNIQUE I TAUGHT KOGARASHI. "LIMITLESS TRAINING."
ESSENTIALLY, THE MORE SPIRITUAL ATTACKS YOU TAKE, THE MORE ADEPT YOU BECOME.
GIVING THE USER NIGH UNLIMITED STRENGTH.
NIGH UNLIM...?!
BUT THERE'S A CEILING YOUR SPIRITUAL ENERGY WILL HIT, EVENTUALLY.
AND, YOU'LL NEED TO GET SAID ENERGY FROM AN EXTERNAL SOURCE.
IN THE NATURAL WORLD, THE MAXIMUM LEVEL OF SPIRITUAL ENERGY YOU CAN ABSORB IS ROUGHLY ONE HUNDRED.
I WAS SURPRISED YOU PULLED IT OFF, AS THERE AREN'T MANY LARGE SPIRIT CRYSTALS LEFT, EVEN IN THE KUROE AGENCY.
OH, THAT'S THANKS TO THIS.
!
JINGLE
THIS MAGATAMA WAS FASH-IONED INTO A SPIRIT CRYSTAL THAT I CAN USE AS A SPIRITUAL CHARGING STONE.
IT STORES UP MY SPIRITUAL ENERGY WHEN I WEAR IT.
I JUST HEALED BY TAPPING ITS RESERVE.
A SPIRITUAL CHARGING STONE?!
AND YOU HAD SOME-THING **THAT PRECIOUS** JUST DANGLIN' ROUND YOUR NECK?!
THE OLD MAN FROM THE KUROE AGENCY FILLED ME IN ON IT AFTER WE HAD PARTED WAYS, MASTER.
BUT, *UM*... DOESN'T OUGA-SAN HAVE THE SAME NECKLACE?

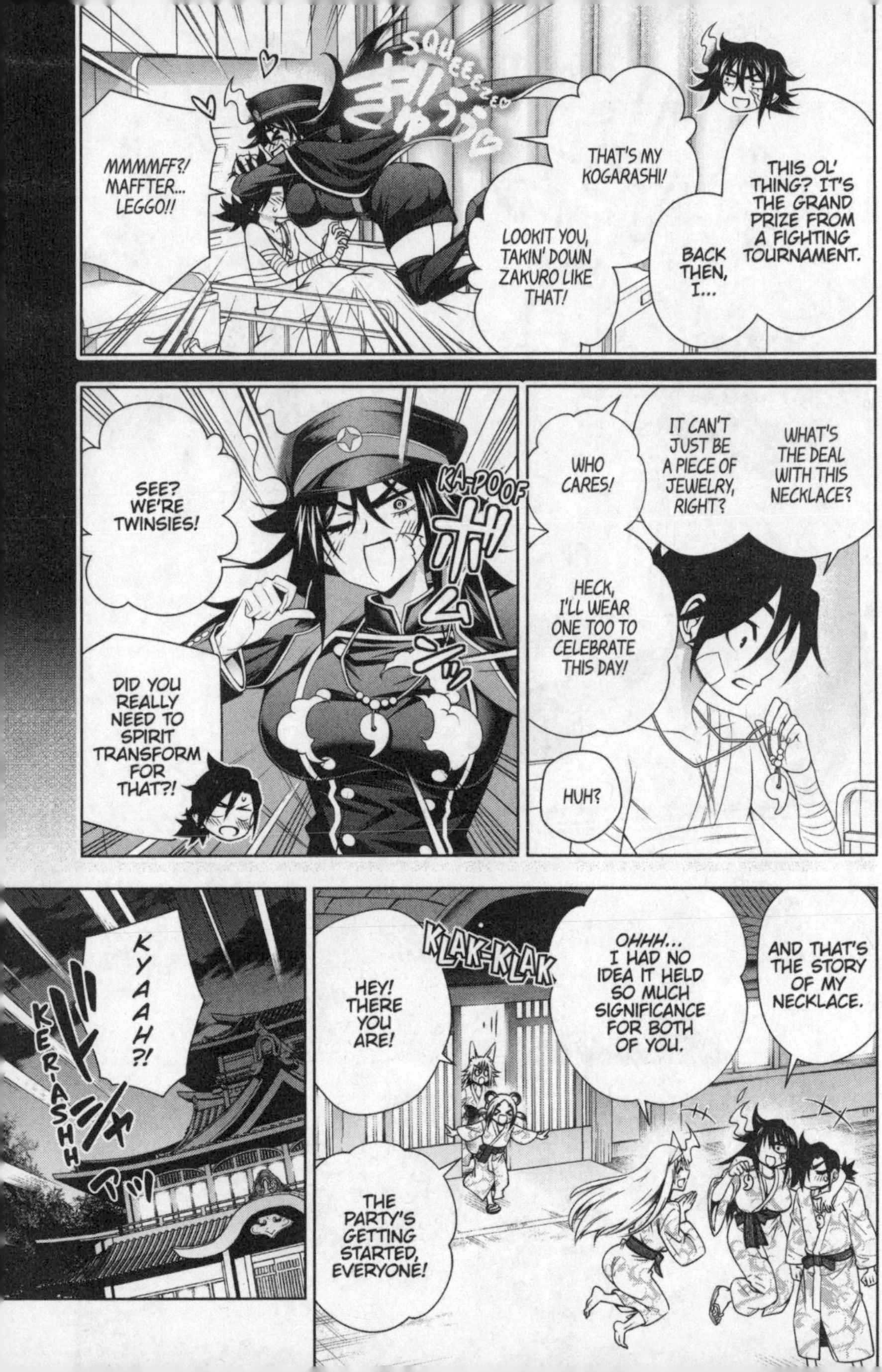
THIS OL' THING? IT'S THE GRAND PRIZE FROM A FIGHTING TOURNAMENT.
BACK THEN, I...
THAT'S MY KOGARASHI!
LOOKIT YOU, TAKIN' DOWN ZAKURO LIKE THAT!
SQUEEEEZE
MMMMFF?! MAFFTER... LEGGO!!
WHAT'S THE DEAL WITH THIS NECKLACE?
IT CAN'T JUST BE A PIECE OF JEWELRY, RIGHT?
WHO CARES!
HECK, I'LL WEAR ONE TOO TO CELEBRATE THIS DAY!
HUH?
KA-POOF
SEE? WE'RE TWINSIES!
DID YOU REALLY NEED TO SPIRIT TRANSFORM FOR THAT?!
AND THAT'S THE STORY OF MY NECKLACE.
OHHH... I HAD NO IDEA IT HELD SO MUCH SIGNIFICANCE FOR BOTH OF YOU.
KLAK-KLAK
HEY! THERE YOU ARE!
THE PARTY'S GETTING STARTED, EVERYONE!
KYAAAH?!
KERASHH

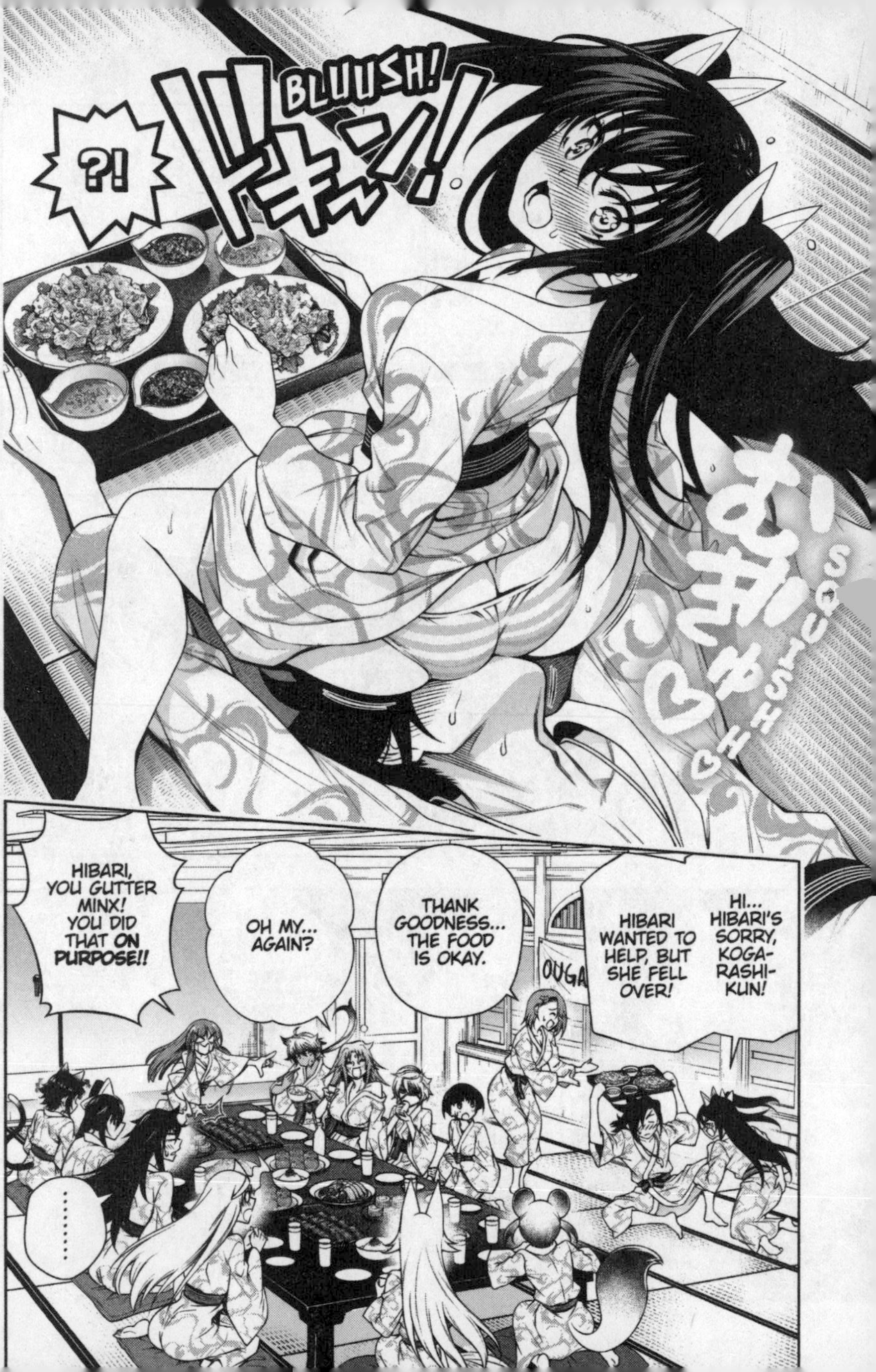
?!
BLUUSH!
ドキュン!
むぎゅ♡
SQUISH♡
HI... HIBARI'S SORRY, KOGA-RASHI-KUN!
HIBARI WANTED TO HELP, BUT SHE FELL OVER!
THANK GOODNESS... THE FOOD IS OKAY.
OH MY... AGAIN?
HIBARI, YOU GUTTER MINX! YOU DID THAT ON PURPOSE!!
......

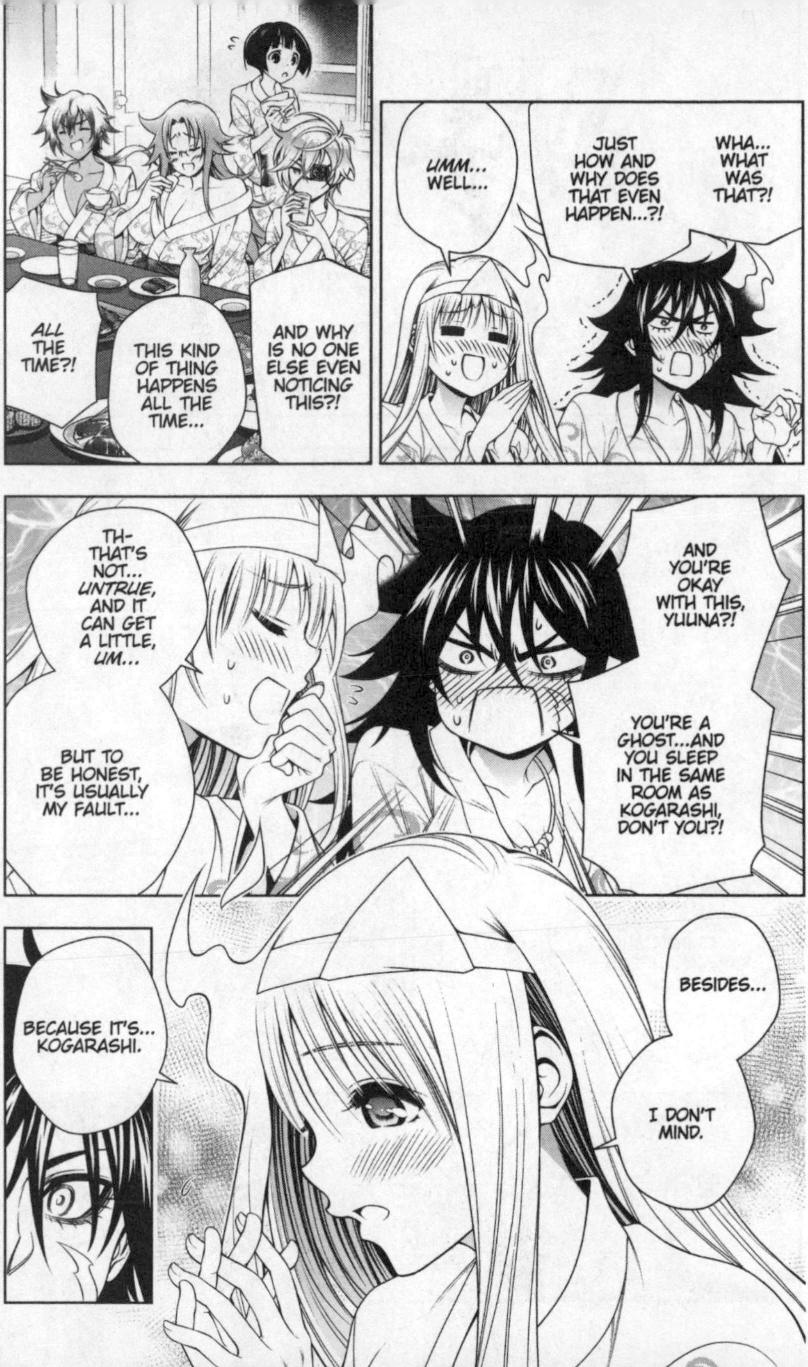
WHA... WHAT WAS THAT?!
JUST HOW AND WHY DOES THAT EVEN HAPPEN...?!
UMM... WELL...
AND WHY IS NO ONE ELSE EVEN NOTICING THIS?!
THIS KIND OF THING HAPPENS ALL THE TIME...
ALL THE TIME?!
AND YOU'RE OKAY WITH THIS, YUUNA?!
YOU'RE A GHOST...AND YOU SLEEP IN THE SAME ROOM AS KOGARASHI, DON'T YOU?!
TH-THAT'S NOT... UNTRUE, AND IT CAN GET A LITTLE, UM...
BUT TO BE HONEST, IT'S USUALLY MY FAULT...
BESIDES...
I DON'T MIND.
BECAUSE IT'S... KOGARASHI.

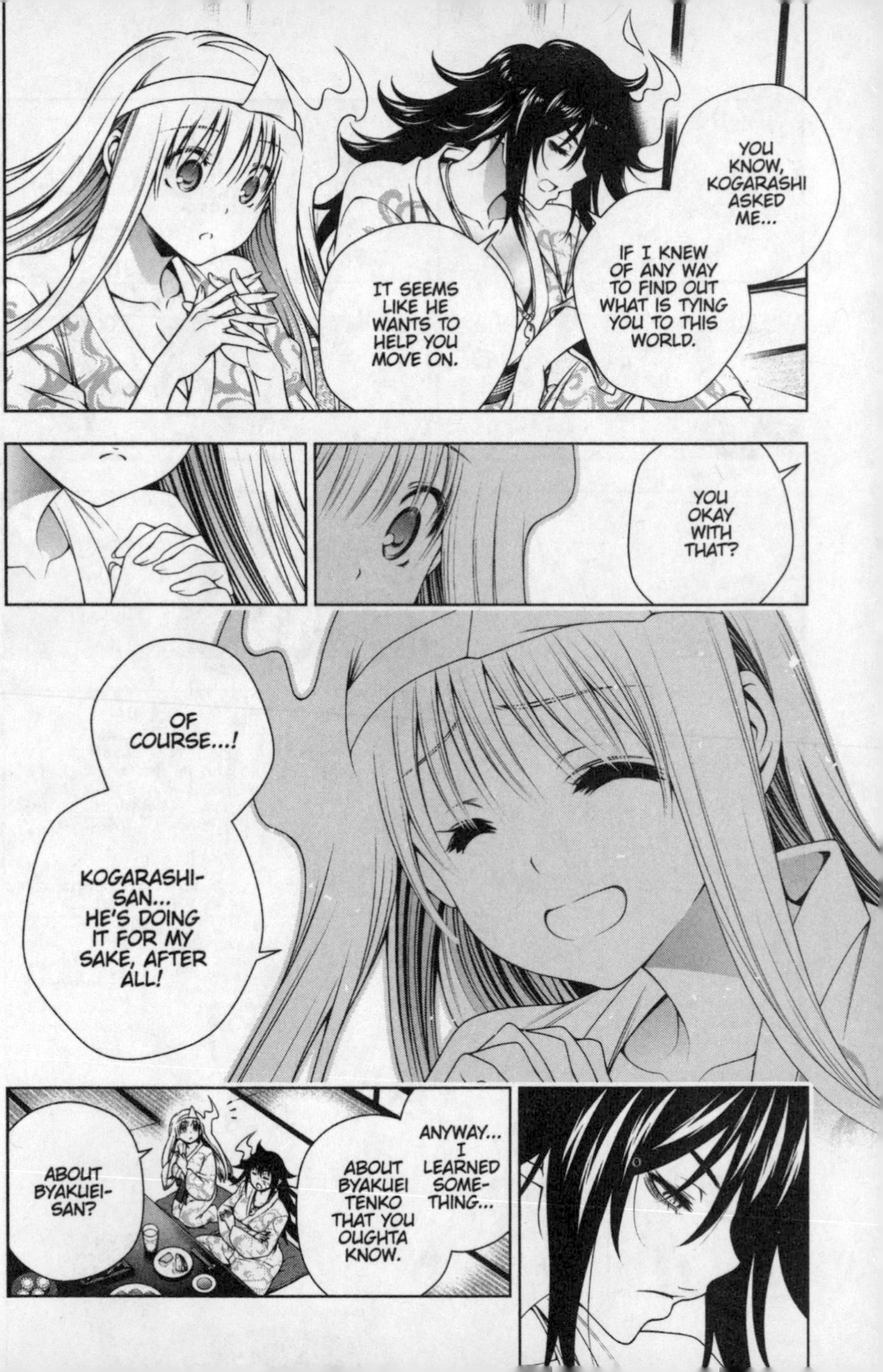
YOU KNOW, KOGARASHI ASKED ME...
IF I KNEW OF ANY WAY TO FIND OUT WHAT IS TYING YOU TO THIS WORLD.
IT SEEMS LIKE HE WANTS TO HELP YOU MOVE ON.
YOU OKAY WITH THAT?
OF COURSE...!
KOGARASHI-SAN... HE'S DOING IT FOR MY SAKE, AFTER ALL!
ANYWAY... I LEARNED SOME-THING...
ABOUT BYAKUEI TENKO THAT YOU OUGHTA KNOW.
ABOUT BYAKUEI-SAN?

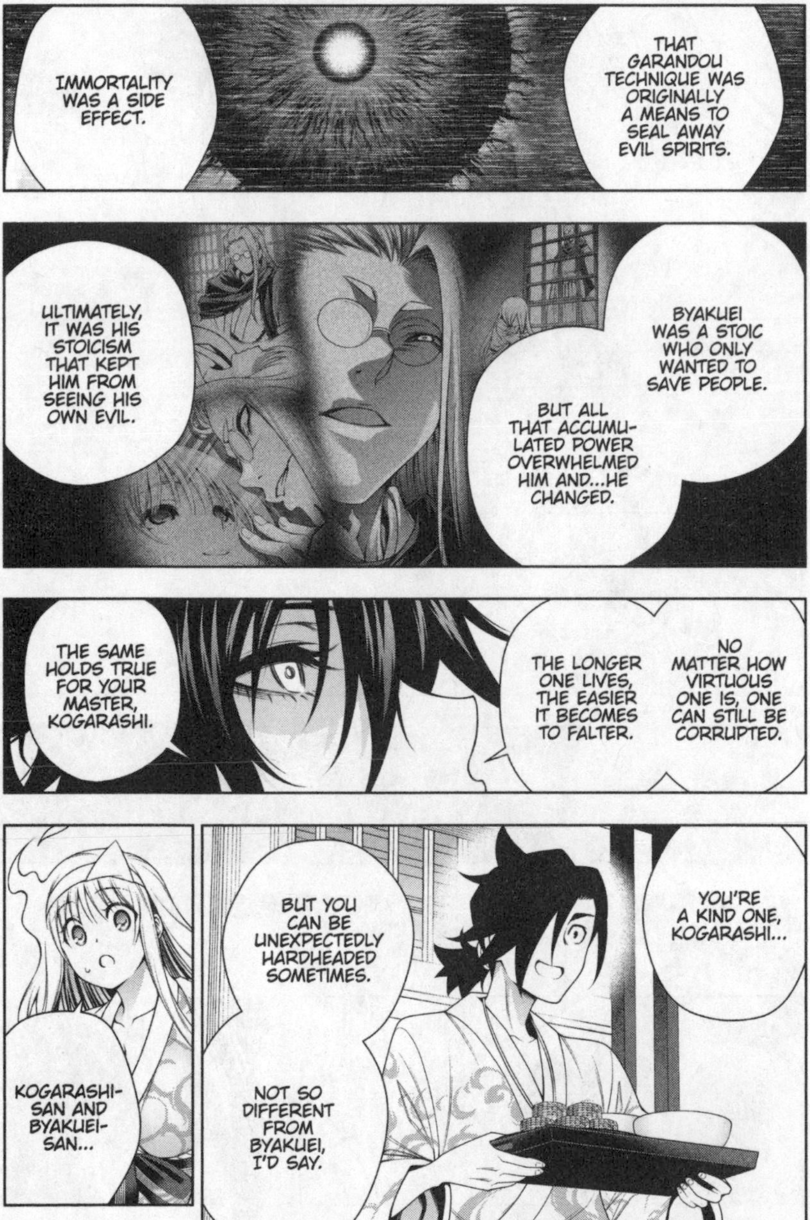
THAT GARANDOU TECHNIQUE WAS ORIGINALLY A MEANS TO SEAL AWAY EVIL SPIRITS.
IMMORTALITY WAS A SIDE EFFECT.
BYAKUEI WAS A STOIC WHO ONLY WANTED TO SAVE PEOPLE.
BUT ALL THAT ACCUMULATED POWER OVERWHELMED HIM AND...HE CHANGED.
ULTIMATELY, IT WAS HIS STOICISM THAT KEPT HIM FROM SEEING HIS OWN EVIL.
NO MATTER HOW VIRTUOUS ONE IS, ONE CAN STILL BE CORRUPTED.
THE LONGER ONE LIVES, THE EASIER IT BECOMES TO FALTER.
THE SAME HOLDS TRUE FOR YOUR MASTER, KOGARASHI.
YOU'RE A KIND ONE, KOGARASHI...
BUT YOU CAN BE UNEXPECTEDLY HARDHEADED SOMETIMES.
NOT SO DIFFERENT FROM BYAKUEI, I'D SAY.
KOGARASHI-SAN AND BYAKUEI-SAN...

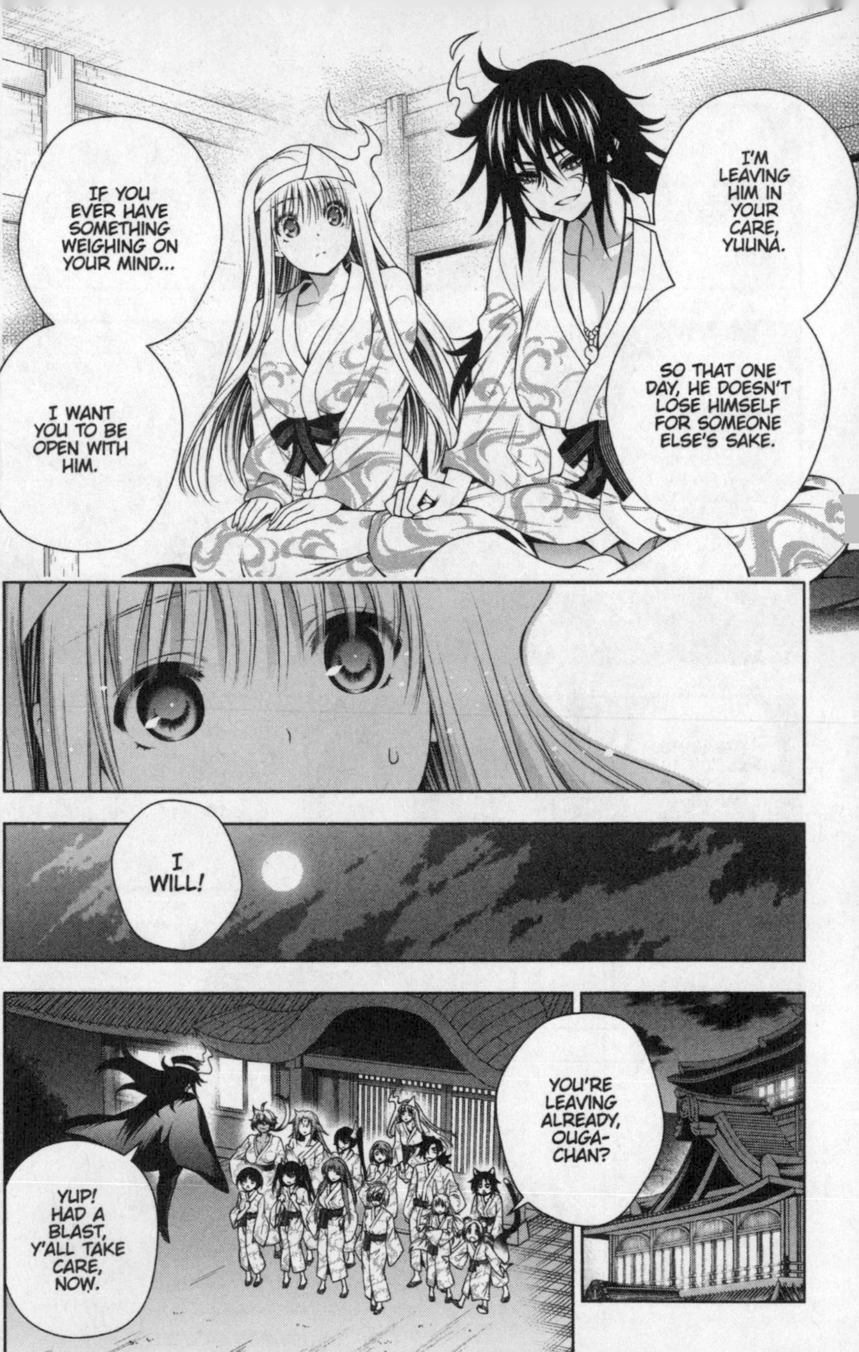
I'M LEAVING HIM IN YOUR CARE, YUUNA.
SO THAT ONE DAY, HE DOESN'T LOSE HIMSELF FOR SOMEONE ELSE'S SAKE.
IF YOU EVER HAVE SOMETHING WEIGHING ON YOUR MIND...
I WANT YOU TO BE OPEN WITH HIM.
I WILL!
YOU'RE LEAVING ALREADY, OUGA-CHAN?
YUP! HAD A BLAST, Y'ALL TAKE CARE, NOW.

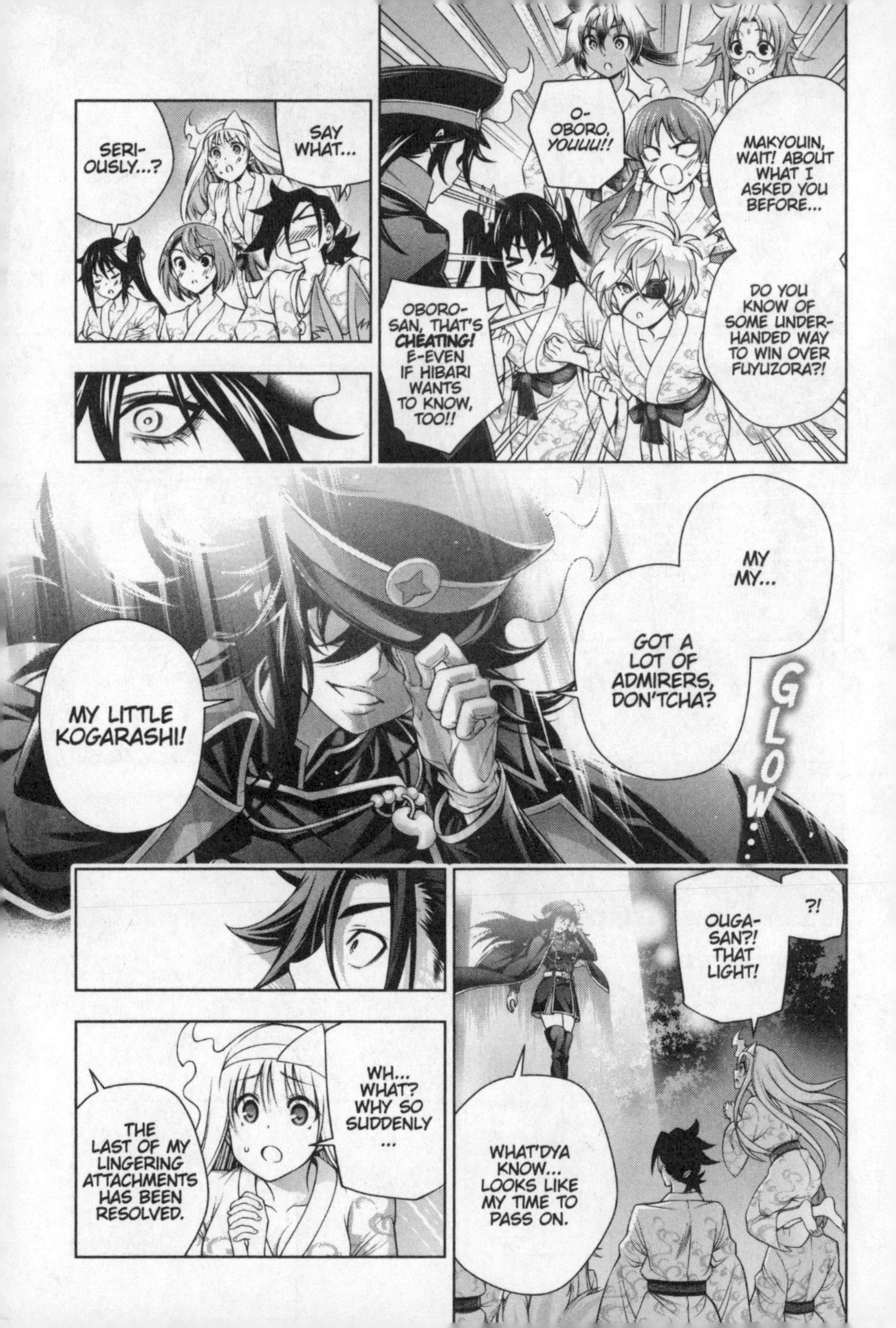
MAKYOUIN, WAIT! ABOUT WHAT I ASKED YOU BEFORE...
DO YOU KNOW OF SOME UNDER-HANDED WAY TO WIN OVER FUYUZORA?!
O-OBORO, YOUUU!!
OBORO-SAN, THAT'S CHEATING! E-EVEN IF HIBARI WANTS TO KNOW, TOO!!
SAY WHAT...
SERI-OUSLY...?
MY MY...
GOT A LOT OF ADMIRERS, DON'TCHA?
GLOW
MY LITTLE KOGARASHI!
?!
OUGA-SAN?! THAT LIGHT!
WHAT'DYA KNOW... LOOKS LIKE MY TIME TO PASS ON.
WH... WHAT? WHY SO SUDDENLY ...
THE LAST OF MY LINGERING ATTACHMENTS HAS BEEN RESOLVED.

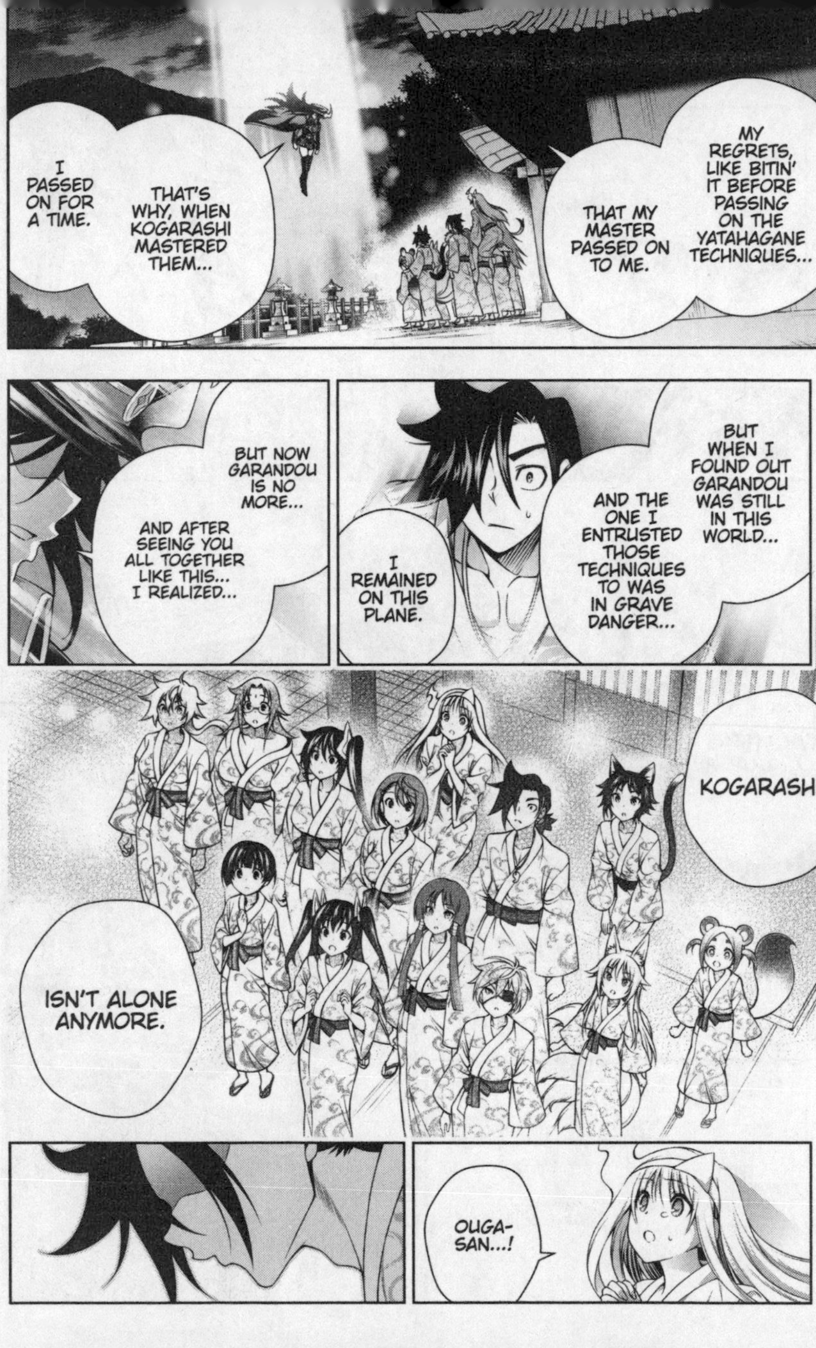
MY REGRETS, LIKE BITIN' IT BEFORE PASSING ON THE YATAHAGANE TECHNIQUES...
THAT MY MASTER PASSED ON TO ME.
THAT'S WHY, WHEN KOGARASHI MASTERED THEM...
I PASSED ON FOR A TIME.
BUT WHEN I FOUND OUT GARANDOU WAS STILL IN THIS WORLD...
AND THE ONE I ENTRUSTED THOSE TECHNIQUES TO WAS IN GRAVE DANGER...
I REMAINED ON THIS PLANE.
BUT NOW GARANDOU IS NO MORE...
AND AFTER SEEING YOU ALL TOGETHER LIKE THIS... I REALIZED...
KOGARASHI...
ISN'T ALONE ANYMORE.
OUGA-SAN...!

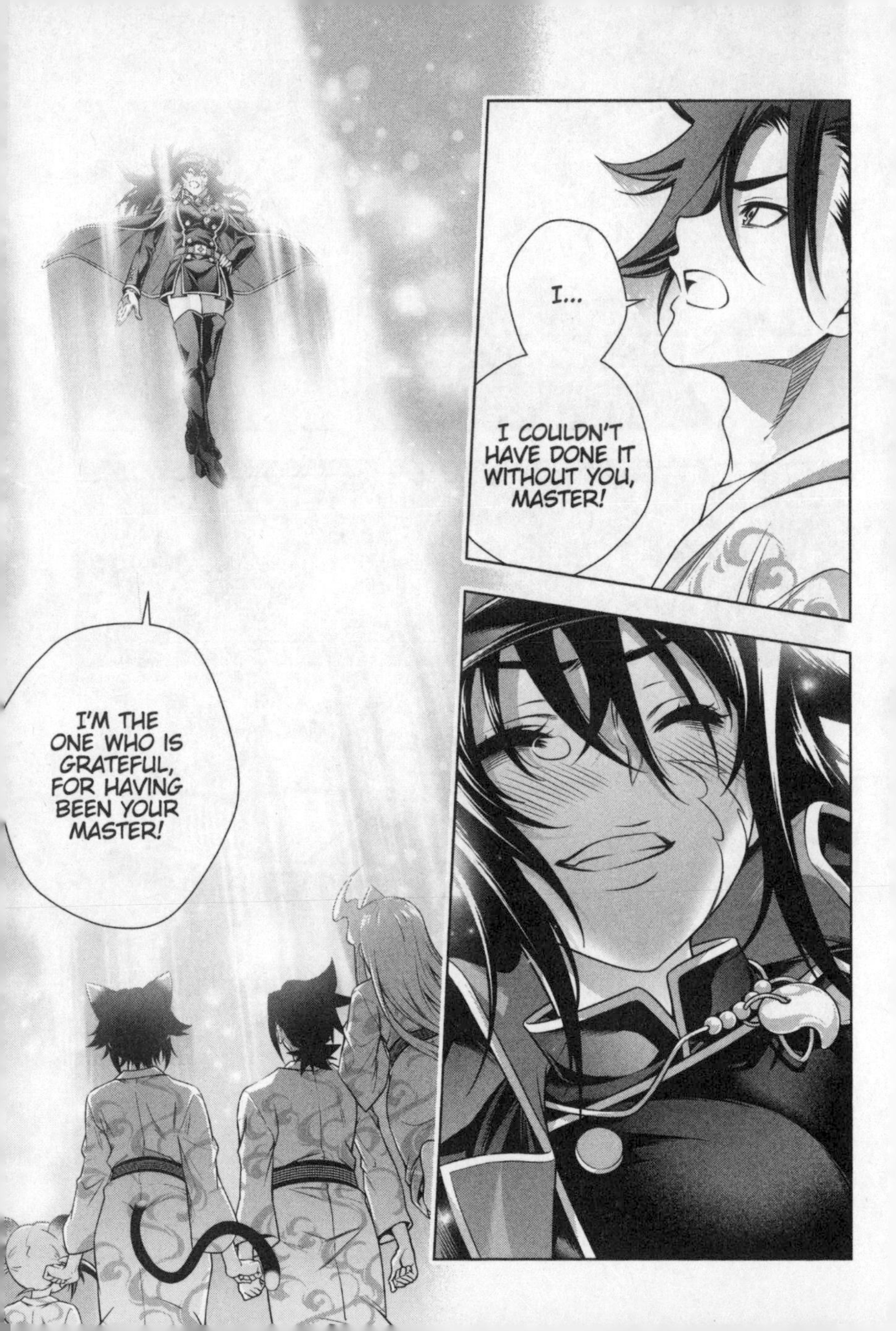
I...
I COULDN'T HAVE DONE IT WITHOUT YOU, MASTER!
I'M THE ONE WHO IS GRATEFUL, FOR HAVING BEEN YOUR MASTER!

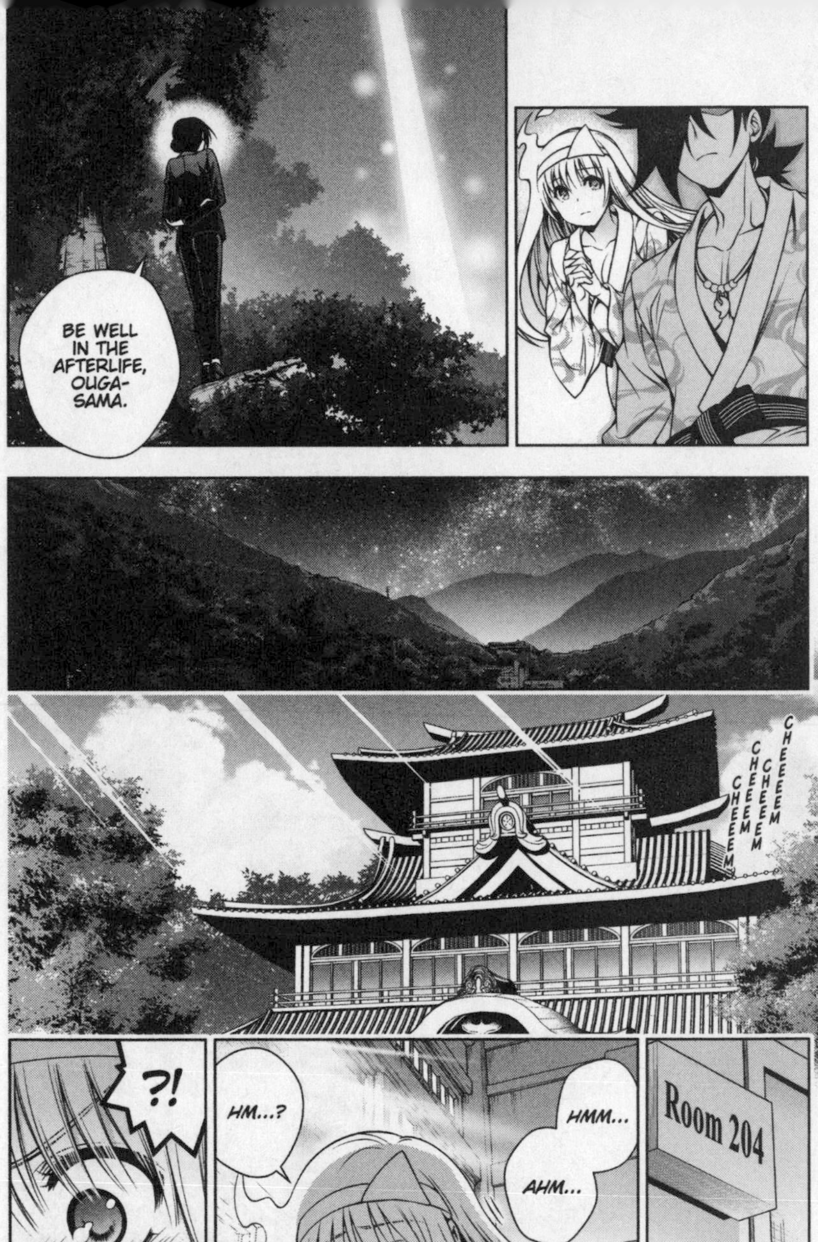
BE WELL IN THE AFTERLIFE, OUGA-SAMA.
CHEEEM CHEEEM CHEEEM CHEEEM
Room 204
HMM...
AHM...
HM...?
?!

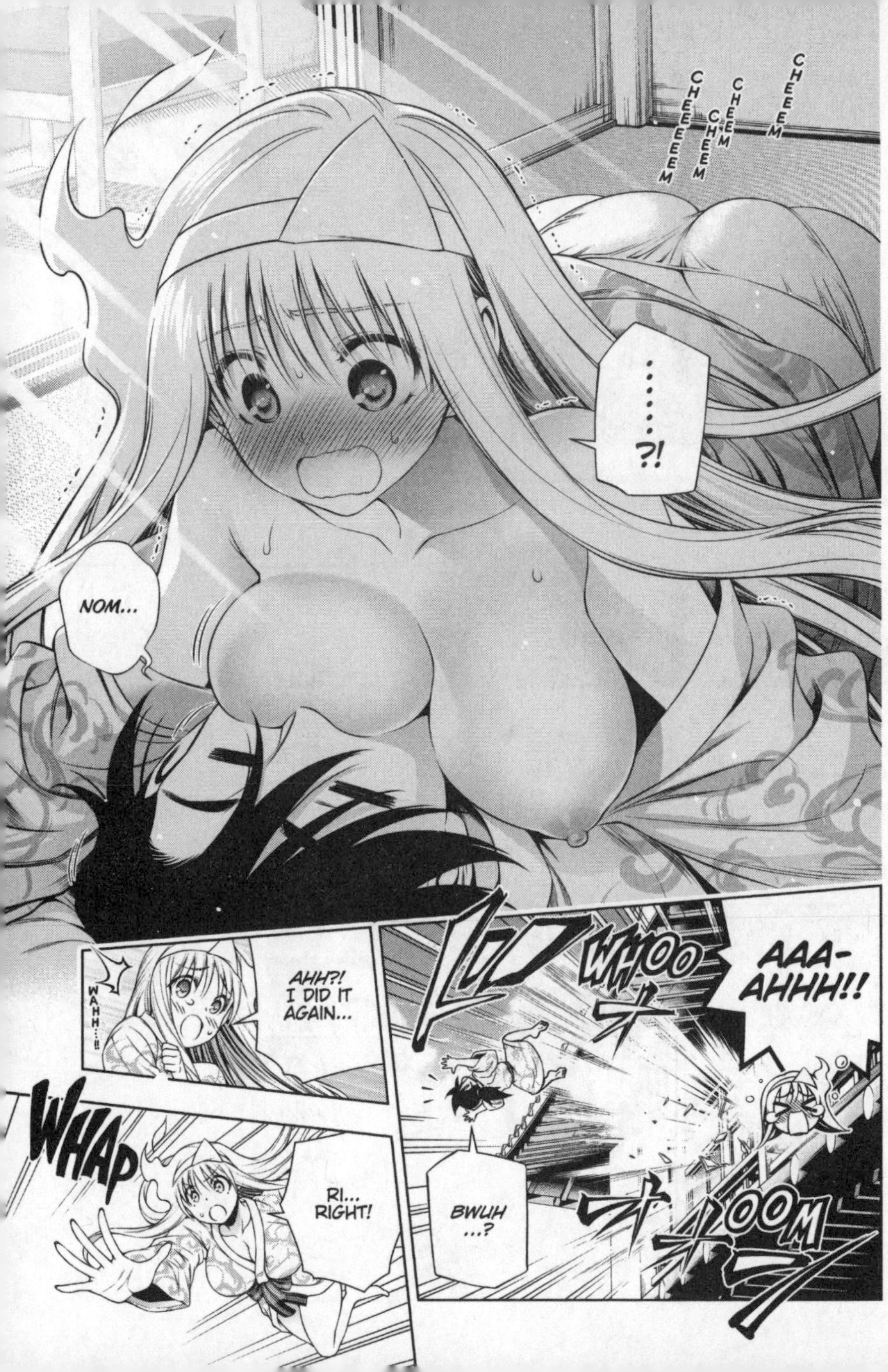
CHEEEM
CHEEM
CHEEM
CHEEEEEM
......?!
NOM...
AAA-AHHH!!
WHOO
BWUH ...?
ZOOM
AHH?! I DID IT AGAIN...
WAHH...!!
WHAP
RI... RIGHT!

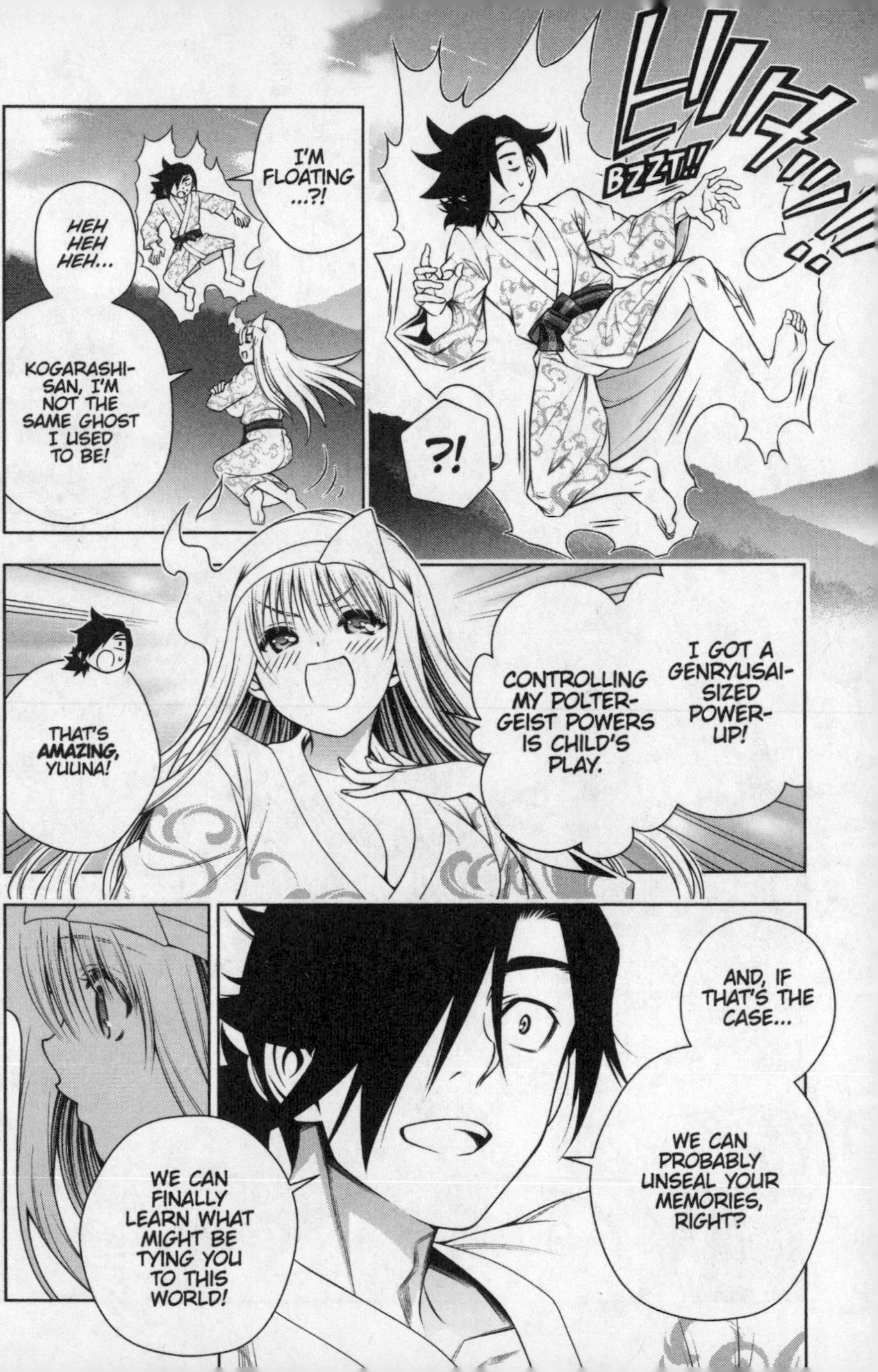
BZZT!!
?!
I'M FLOATING ...?!
HEH HEH HEH...
KOGARASHI-SAN, I'M NOT THE SAME GHOST I USED TO BE!
I GOT A GENRYUSAI-SIZED POWER-UP!
CONTROLLING MY POLTER-GEIST POWERS IS CHILD'S PLAY.
THAT'S AMAZING, YUUNA!
AND, IF THAT'S THE CASE...
WE CAN PROBABLY UNSEAL YOUR MEMORIES, RIGHT?
WE CAN FINALLY LEARN WHAT MIGHT BE TYING YOU TO THIS WORLD!

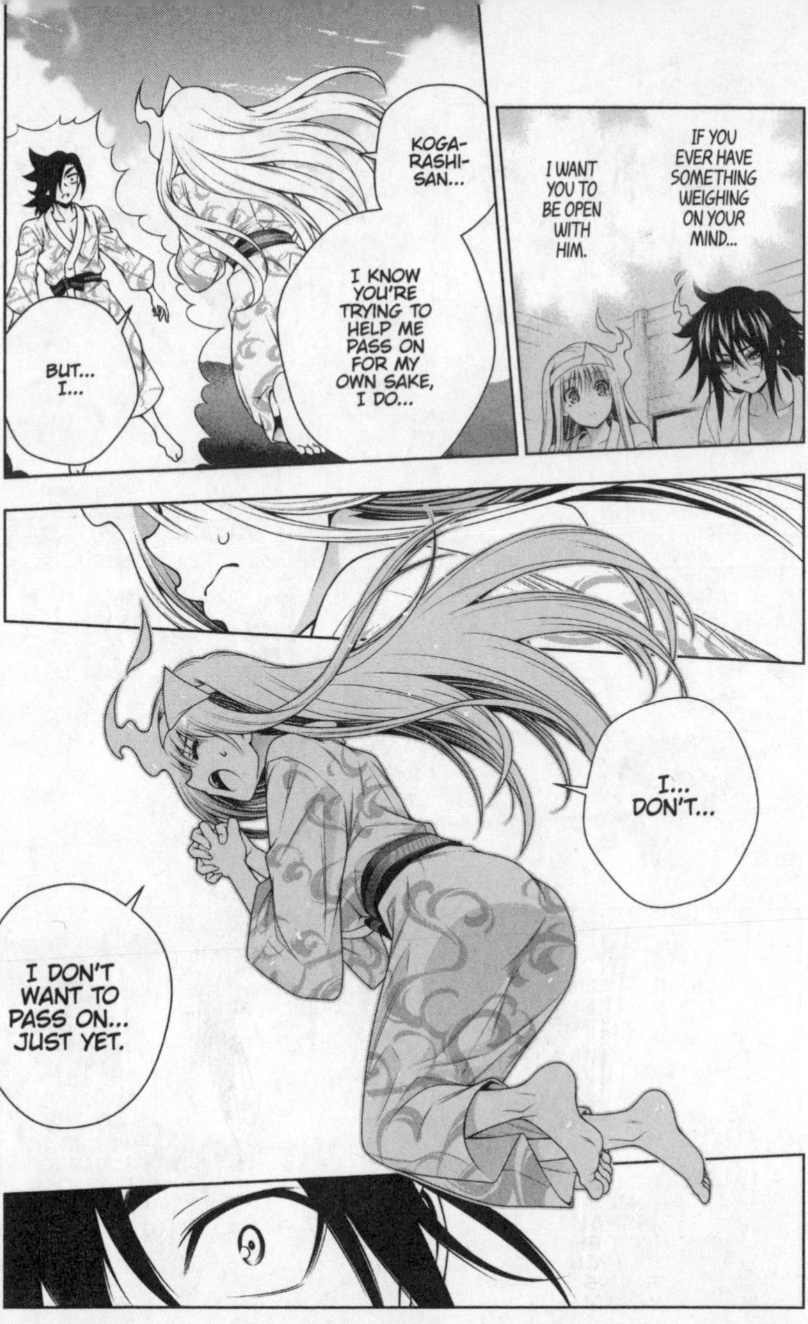
IF YOU EVER HAVE SOMETHING WEIGHING ON YOUR MIND...
I WANT YOU TO BE OPEN WITH HIM.
KOGA-RASHI-SAN...
I KNOW YOU'RE TRYING TO HELP ME PASS ON FOR MY OWN SAKE, I DO...
BUT... I...
I... DON'T...
I DON'T WANT TO PASS ON... JUST YET.

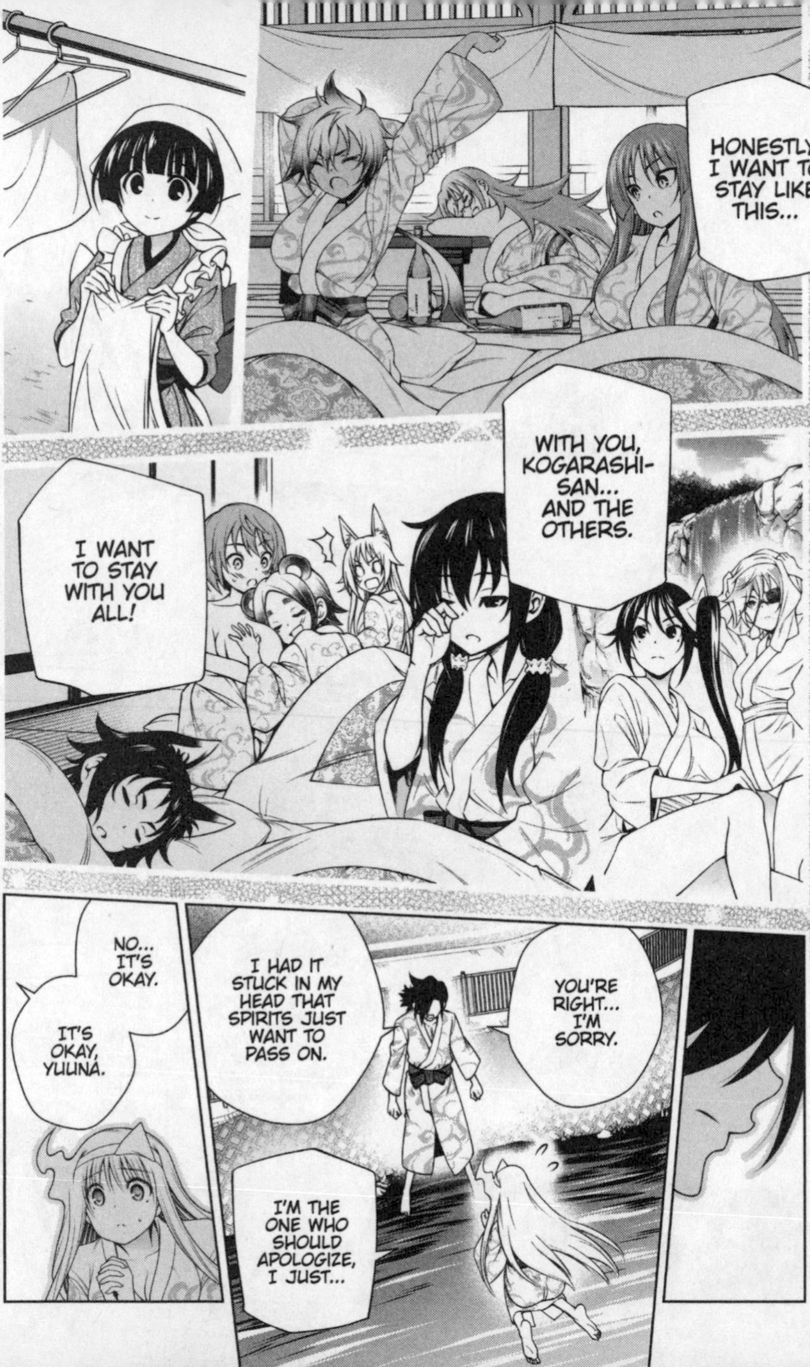
HONESTLY, I WANT TO STAY LIKE THIS...
WITH YOU, KOGARASHI-SAN... AND THE OTHERS.
I WANT TO STAY WITH YOU ALL!
YOU'RE RIGHT... I'M SORRY.
I HAD IT STUCK IN MY HEAD THAT SPIRITS JUST WANT TO PASS ON.
I'M THE ONE WHO SHOULD APOLOGIZE, I JUST...
NO... IT'S OKAY.
IT'S OKAY, YUUNA.

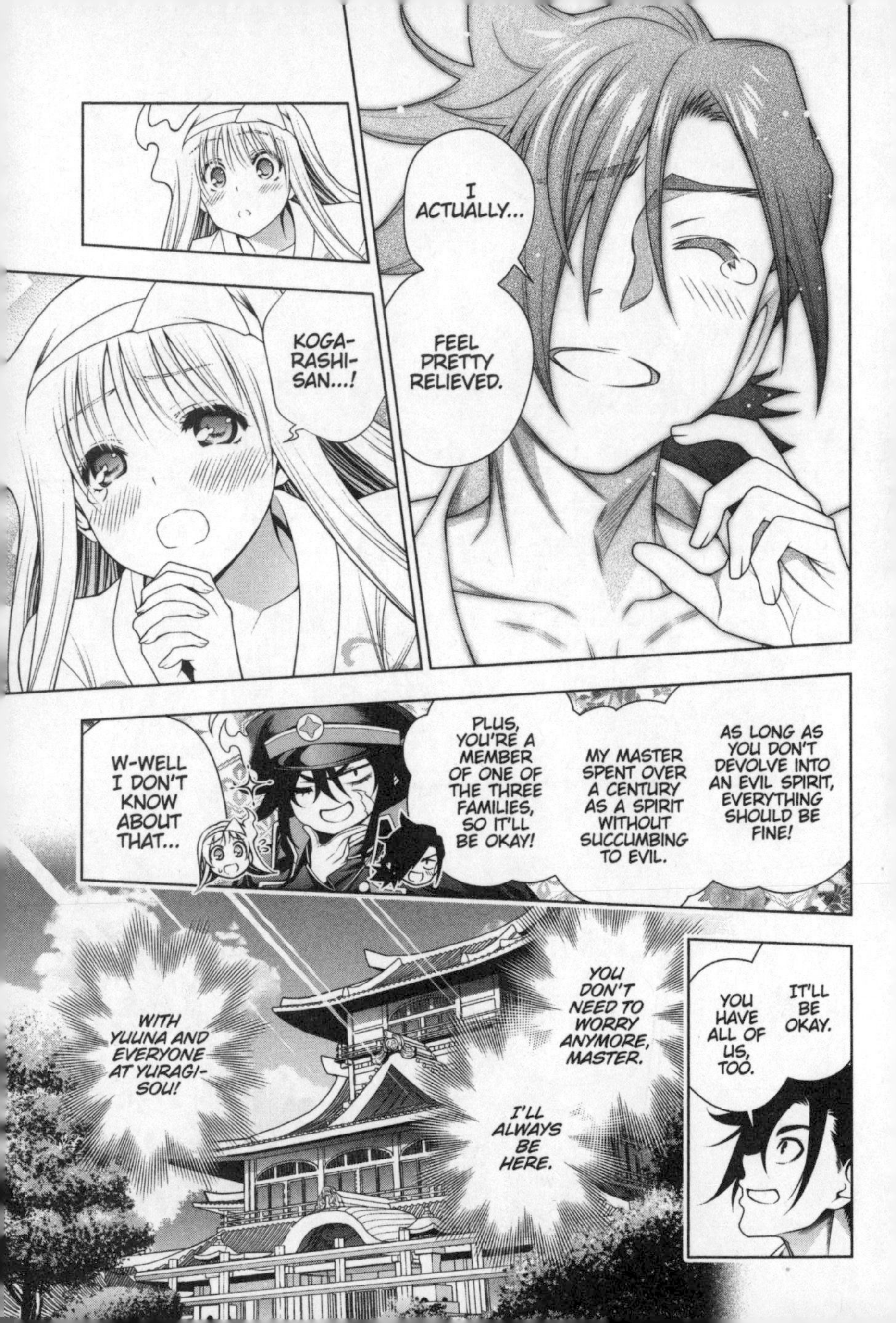
I ACTUALLY...
FEEL PRETTY RELIEVED.
KOGA-RASHI-SAN...!
AS LONG AS YOU DON'T DEVOLVE INTO AN EVIL SPIRIT, EVERYTHING SHOULD BE FINE!
MY MASTER SPENT OVER A CENTURY AS A SPIRIT WITHOUT SUCCUMBING TO EVIL.
PLUS, YOU'RE A MEMBER OF ONE OF THE THREE FAMILIES, SO IT'LL BE OKAY!
W-WELL I DON'T KNOW ABOUT THAT...
IT'LL BE OKAY.
YOU HAVE ALL OF US, TOO.
YOU DON'T NEED TO WORRY ANYMORE, MASTER.
I'LL ALWAYS BE HERE.
WITH YUUNA AND EVERYONE AT YURAGI-SOU!

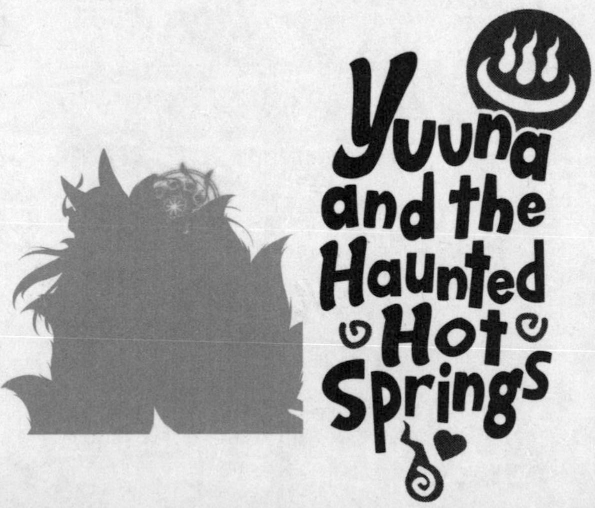

Yuuna and the Haunted Hot Springs

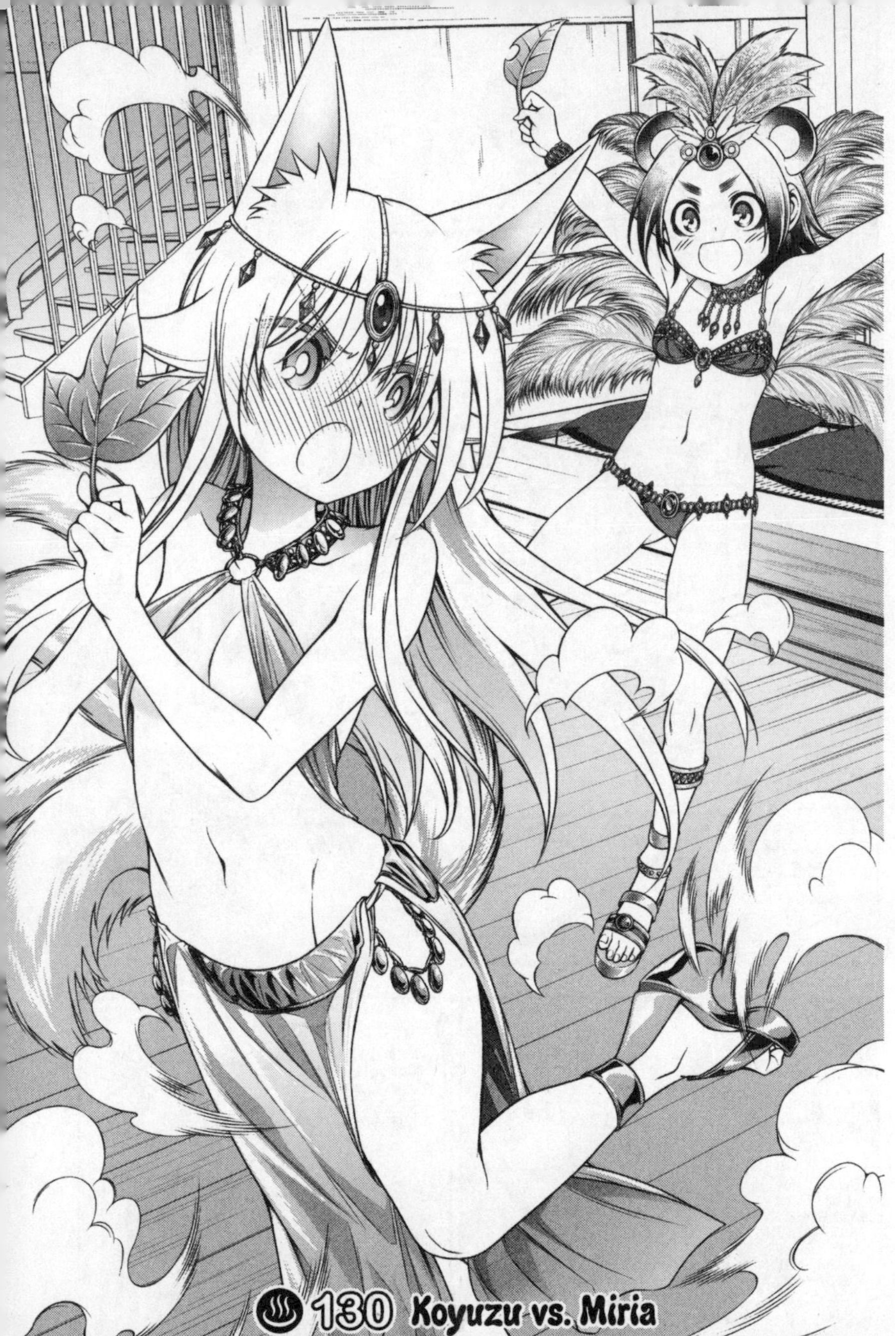

130 Koyuzu vs. Miria

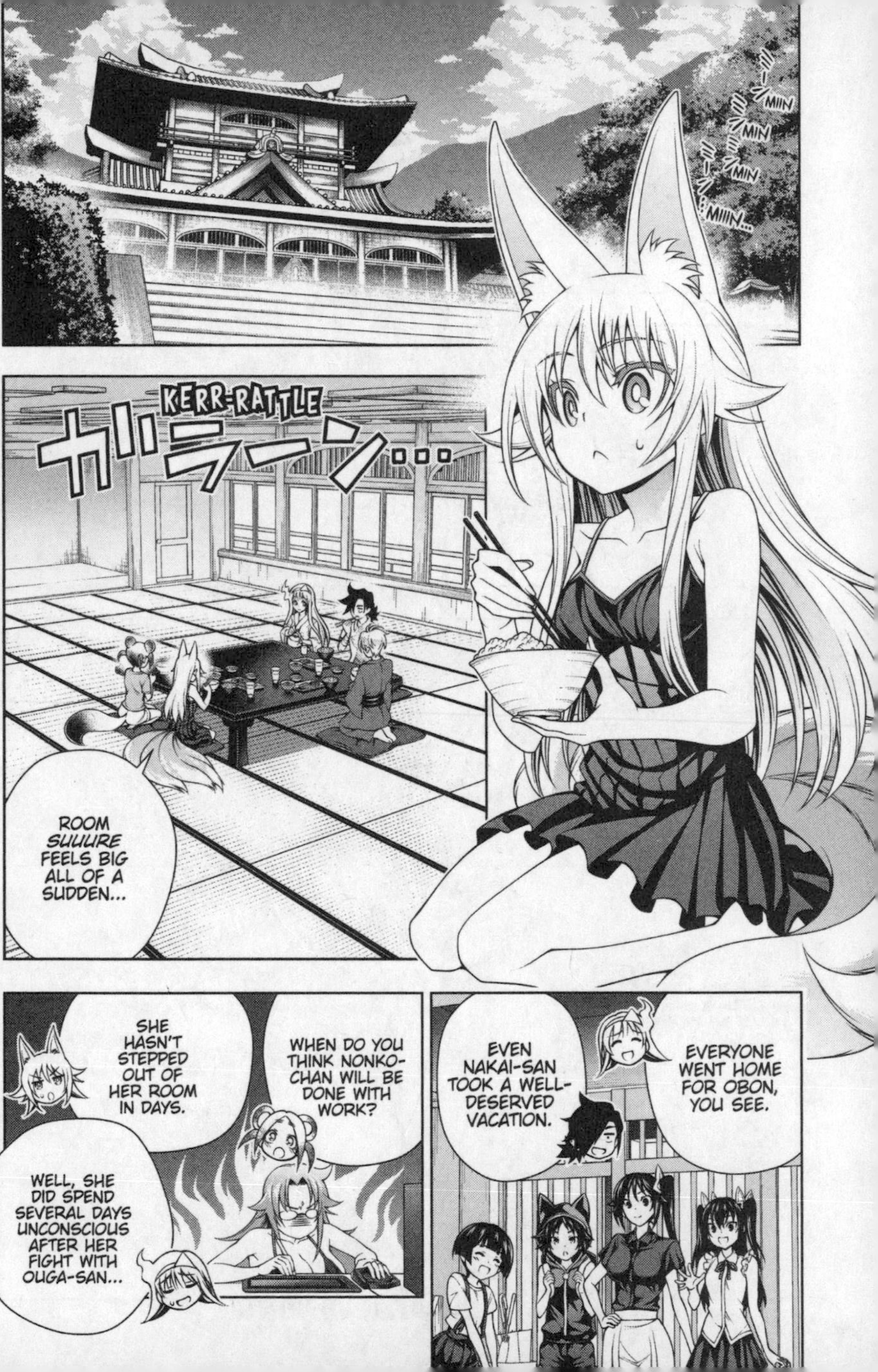

MIIN
MIN
MIN
MIIIN...
カラーン…
KERR-RATTLE
ROOM SUUURE FEELS BIG ALL OF A SUDDEN...
EVERYONE WENT HOME FOR OBON, YOU SEE.
EVEN NAKAI-SAN TOOK A WELL-DESERVED VACATION.
WHEN DO YOU THINK NONKO-CHAN WILL BE DONE WITH WORK?
SHE HASN'T STEPPED OUT OF HER ROOM IN DAYS.
WELL, SHE DID SPEND SEVERAL DAYS UNCONSCIOUS AFTER HER FIGHT WITH OUGA-SAN...

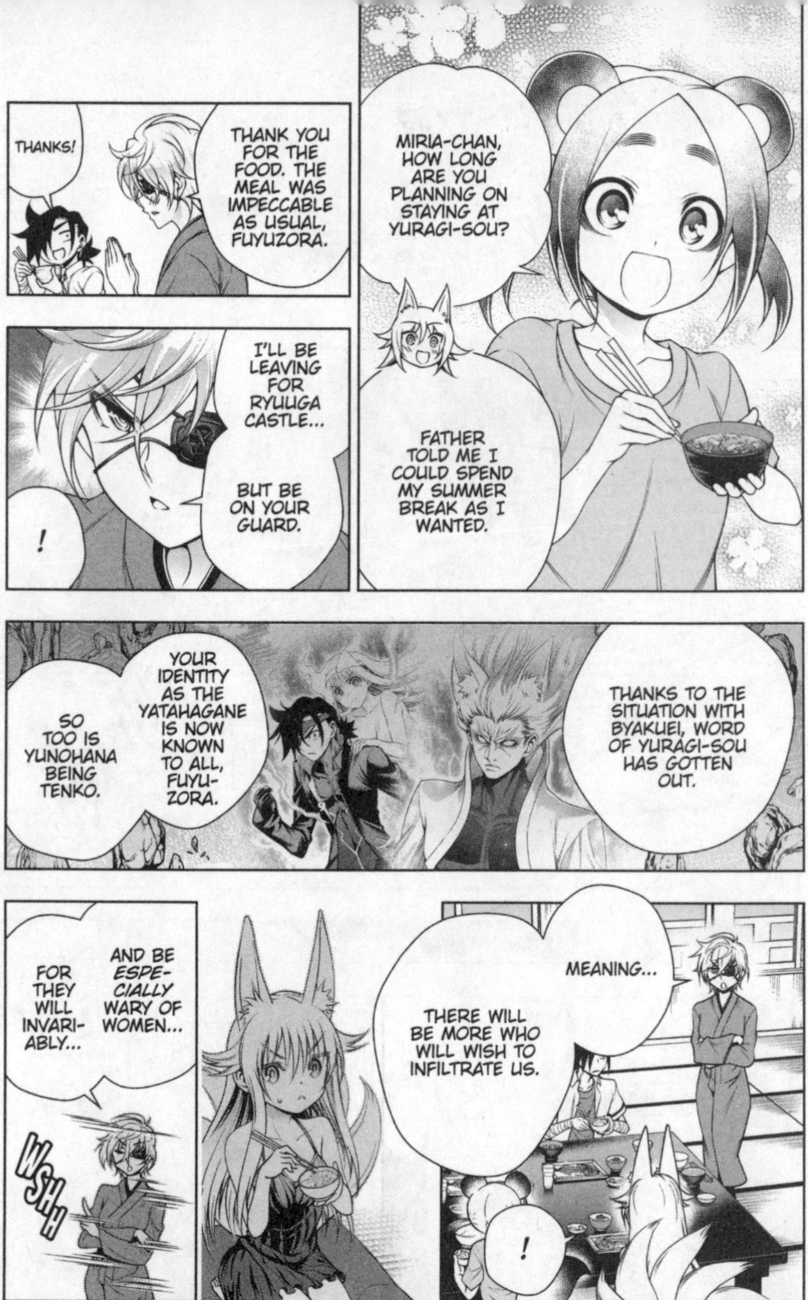
MIRIA-CHAN, HOW LONG ARE YOU PLANNING ON STAYING AT YURAGI-SOU?
FATHER TOLD ME I COULD SPEND MY SUMMER BREAK AS I WANTED.
THANK YOU FOR THE FOOD. THE MEAL WAS IMPECCABLE AS USUAL, FUYUZORA.
THANKS!
I'LL BE LEAVING FOR RYUUGA CASTLE...
BUT BE ON YOUR GUARD.
!
THANKS TO THE SITUATION WITH BYAKUEI, WORD OF YURAGI-SOU HAS GOTTEN OUT.
YOUR IDENTITY AS THE YATAHAGANE IS NOW KNOWN TO ALL, FUYU-ZORA.
SO TOO IS YUNOHANA BEING TENKO.
MEANING...
THERE WILL BE MORE WHO WILL WISH TO INFILTRATE US.
!
AND BE ESPE-CIALLY WARY OF WOMEN...
FOR THEY WILL INVARI-ABLY...
WSHH

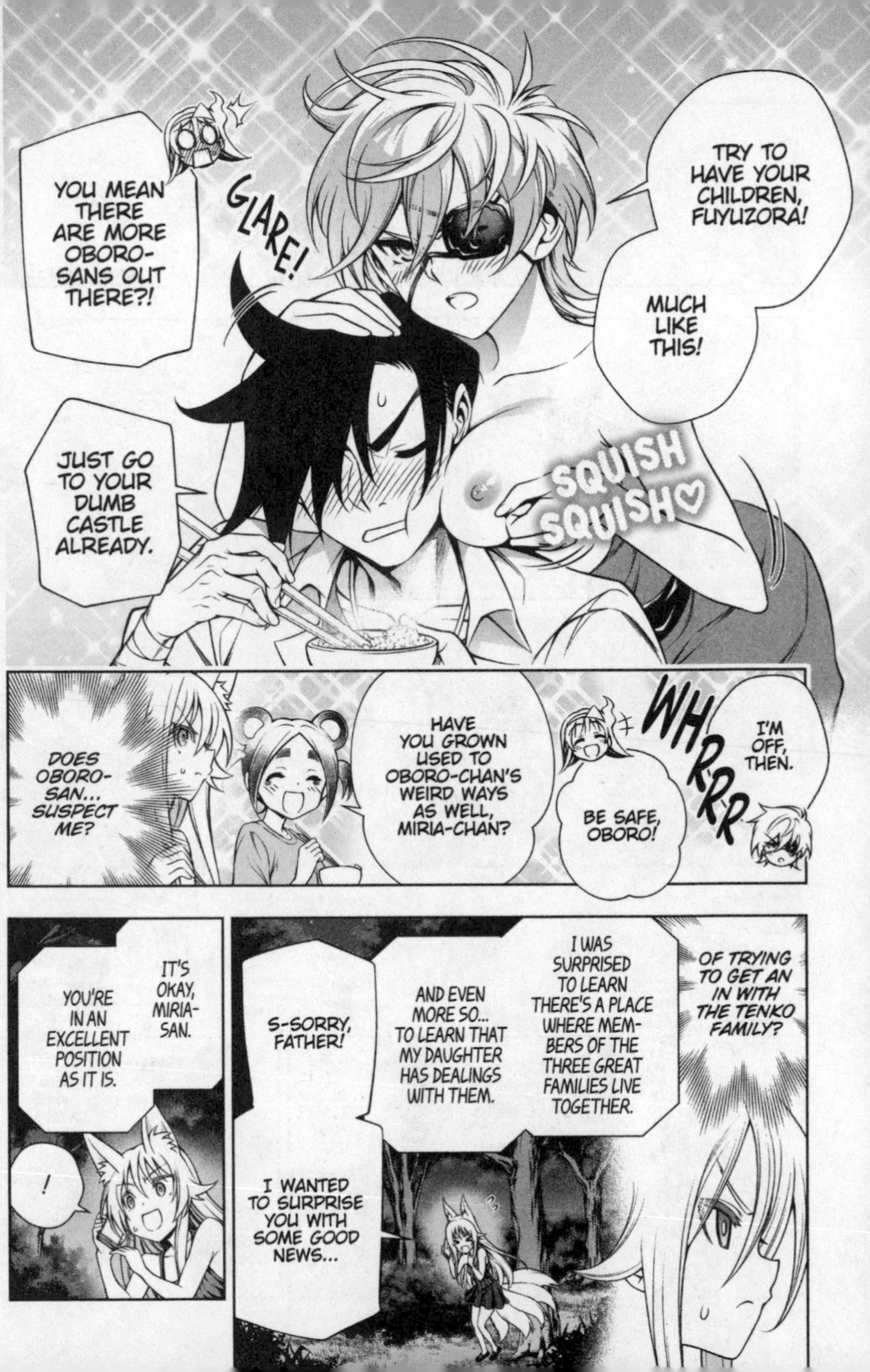
TRY TO HAVE YOUR CHILDREN, FUYUZORA!
MUCH LIKE THIS!
YOU MEAN THERE ARE MORE OBORO-SANS OUT THERE?!
GLARE!
SQUISH SQUISH♡
JUST GO TO YOUR DUMB CASTLE ALREADY.
I'M OFF, THEN.
WHRRR
BE SAFE, OBORO!
HAVE YOU GROWN USED TO OBORO-CHAN'S WEIRD WAYS AS WELL, MIRIA-CHAN?
DOES OBORO-SAN... SUSPECT ME?
OF TRYING TO GET AN IN WITH THE TENKO FAMILY?
I WAS SURPRISED TO LEARN THERE'S A PLACE WHERE MEMBERS OF THE THREE GREAT FAMILIES LIVE TOGETHER.
AND EVEN MORE SO... TO LEARN THAT MY DAUGHTER HAS DEALINGS WITH THEM.
S-SORRY, FATHER!
I WANTED TO SURPRISE YOU WITH SOME GOOD NEWS...
IT'S OKAY, MIRIA-SAN.
YOU'RE IN AN EXCELLENT POSITION AS IT IS.
!

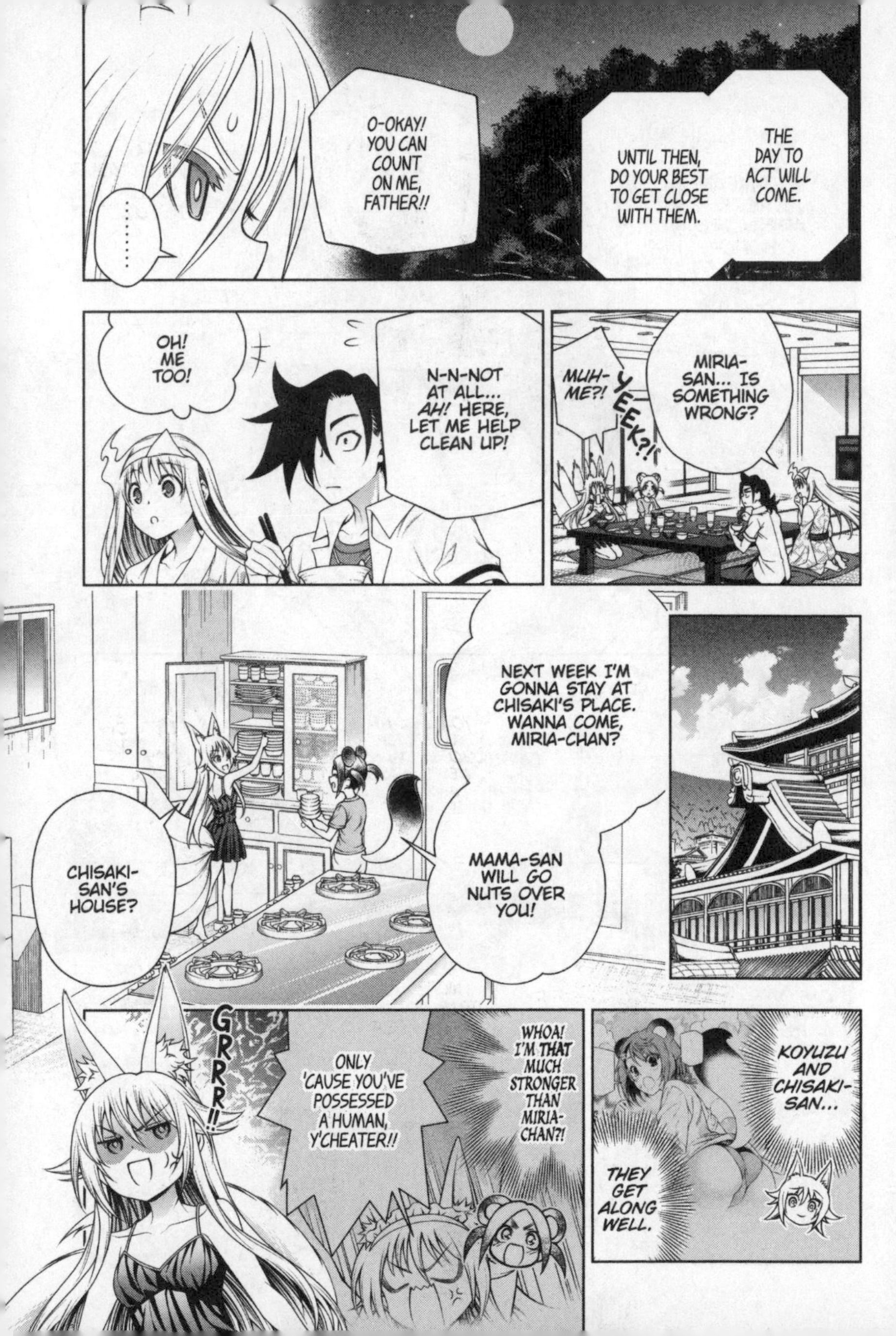
THE DAY TO ACT WILL COME.
UNTIL THEN, DO YOUR BEST TO GET CLOSE WITH THEM.
O-OKAY! YOU CAN COUNT ON ME, FATHER!!
......
MIRIA-SAN... IS SOMETHING WRONG?
MUH-ME?!
YEEK?!
N-N-NOT AT ALL... AH! HERE, LET ME HELP CLEAN UP!
OH! ME TOO!
NEXT WEEK I'M GONNA STAY AT CHISAKI'S PLACE. WANNA COME, MIRIA-CHAN?
MAMA-SAN WILL GO NUTS OVER YOU!
CHISAKI-SAN'S HOUSE?
KOYUZU AND CHISAKI-SAN...
THEY GET ALONG WELL.
WHOA! I'M THAT MUCH STRONGER THAN MIRIA-CHAN?!
ONLY 'CAUSE YOU'VE POSSESSED A HUMAN, Y'CHEATER!!
GRRRR!!

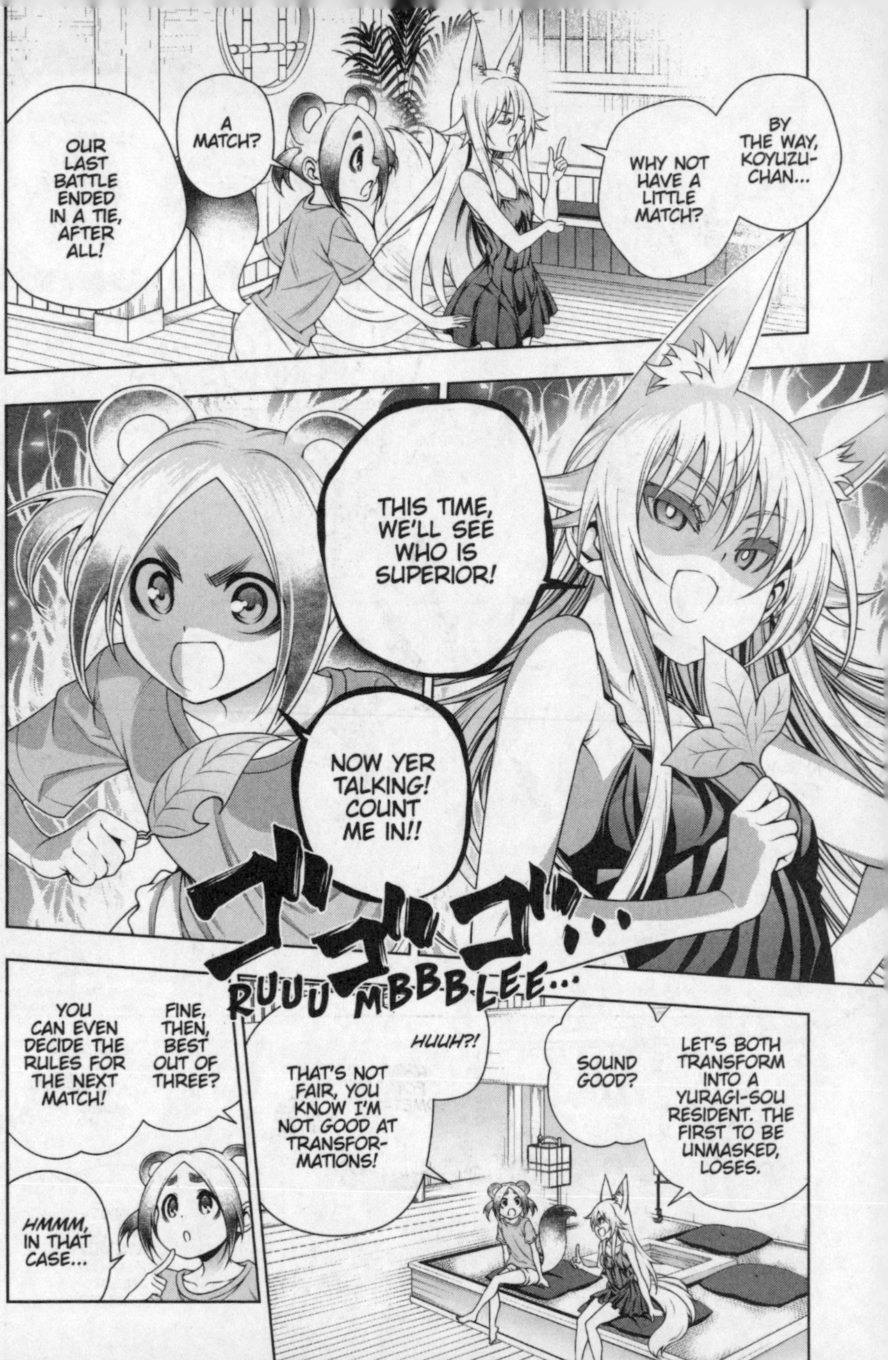
BY THE WAY, KOYUZU-CHAN...
WHY NOT HAVE A LITTLE MATCH?
A MATCH?
OUR LAST BATTLE ENDED IN A TIE, AFTER ALL!
THIS TIME, WE'LL SEE WHO IS SUPERIOR!
NOW YER TALKING! COUNT ME IN!!
RUUU MBBBLEE...
LET'S BOTH TRANSFORM INTO A YURAGI-SOU RESIDENT. THE FIRST TO BE UNMASKED, LOSES.
SOUND GOOD?
HUUH?!
THAT'S NOT FAIR, YOU KNOW I'M NOT GOOD AT TRANSFORMATIONS!
FINE, THEN, BEST OUT OF THREE?
YOU CAN EVEN DECIDE THE RULES FOR THE NEXT MATCH!
HMMM, IN THAT CASE...

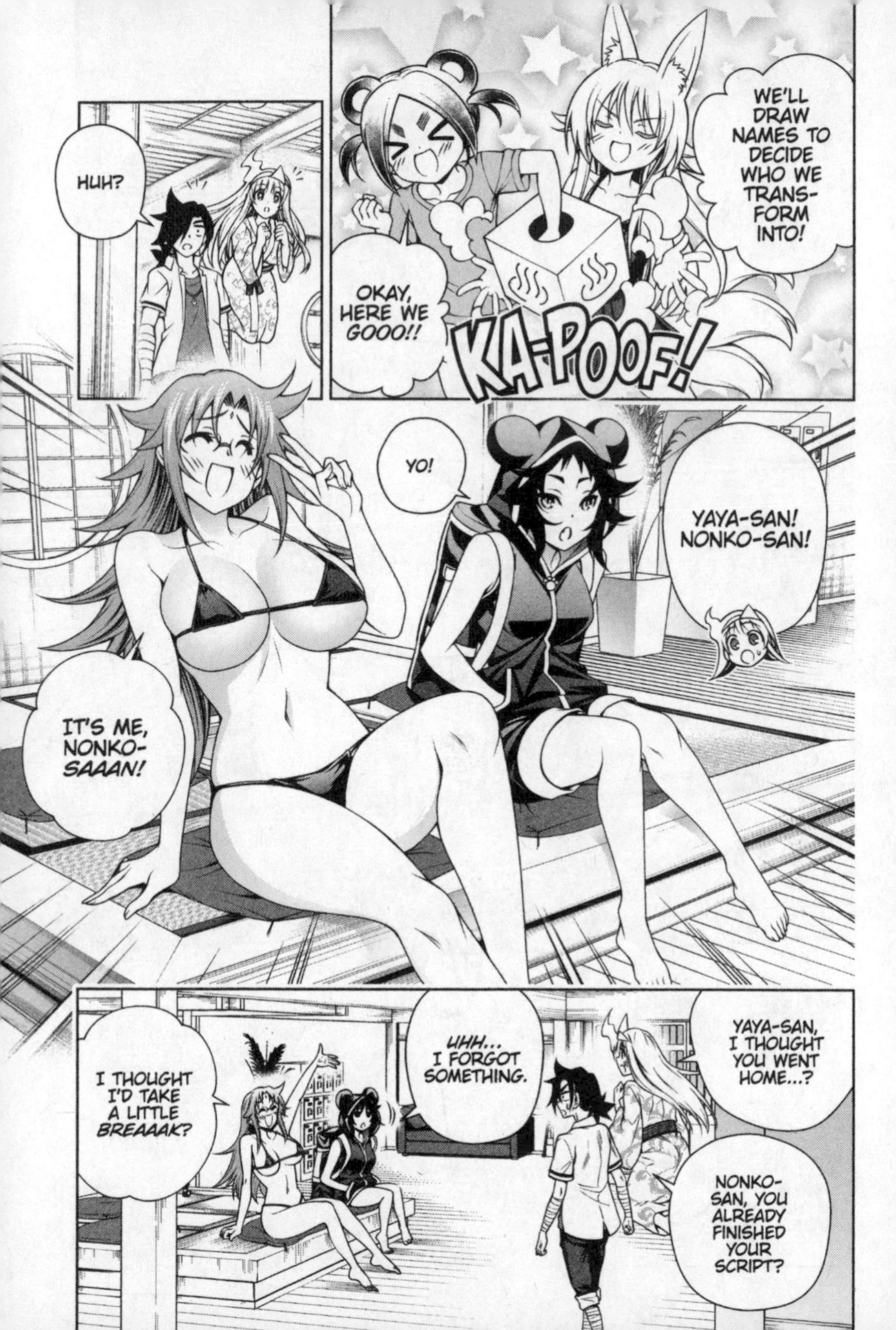
WE'LL DRAW NAMES TO DECIDE WHO WE TRANS-FORM INTO!
OKAY, HERE WE GOOO!!
KA-POOF!
HUH?
YAYA-SAN! NONKO-SAN!
YO!
IT'S ME, NONKO-SAAAN!
YAYA-SAN, I THOUGHT YOU WENT HOME...?
NONKO-SAN, YOU ALREADY FINISHED YOUR SCRIPT?
UHH... I FORGOT SOMETHING.
I THOUGHT I'D TAKE A LITTLE BREAAAK?

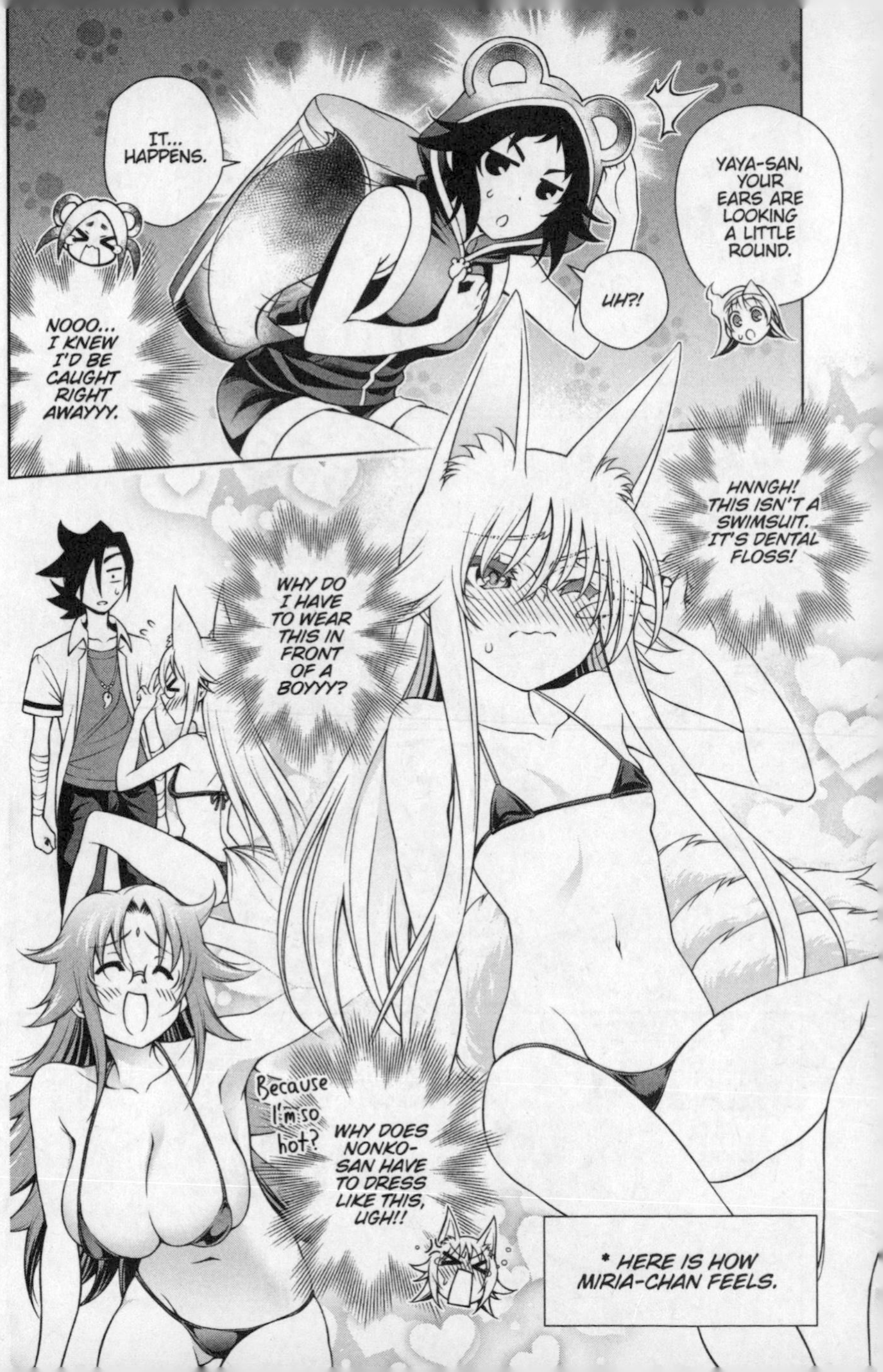
YAYA-SAN, YOUR EARS ARE LOOKING A LITTLE ROUND.
UH?!
IT... HAPPENS.
NOOO... I KNEW I'D BE CAUGHT RIGHT AWAYYY.
HNNGH! THIS ISN'T A SWIMSUIT. IT'S DENTAL FLOSS!
WHY DO I HAVE TO WEAR THIS IN FRONT OF A BOYYY?
WHY DOES NONKO-SAN HAVE TO DRESS LIKE THIS, UGH!!
Because I'm so hot?
* HERE IS HOW MIRIA-CHAN FEELS.

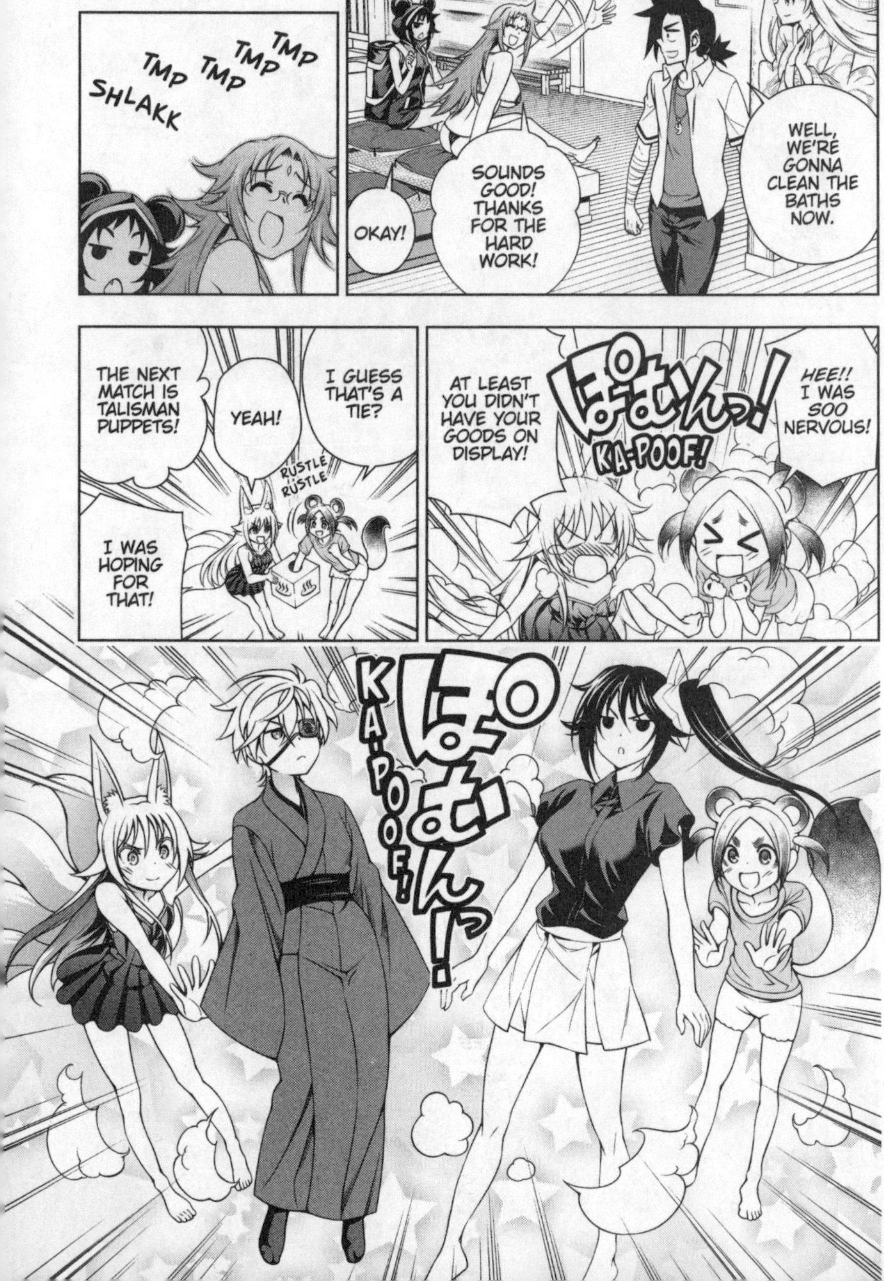
WELL, WE'RE GONNA CLEAN THE BATHS NOW.
SOUNDS GOOD! THANKS FOR THE HARD WORK!
OKAY!
TMP TMP TMP TMP
SHLAKK
HEE!! I WAS SOO NERVOUS!
ぽむんっ!
KA-POOF!
AT LEAST YOU DIDN'T HAVE YOUR GOODS ON DISPLAY!
I GUESS THAT'S A TIE?
YEAH!
THE NEXT MATCH IS TALISMAN PUPPETS!
RUSTLE RUSTLE
I WAS HOPING FOR THAT!
ぽむんっ!
KA-POOF!

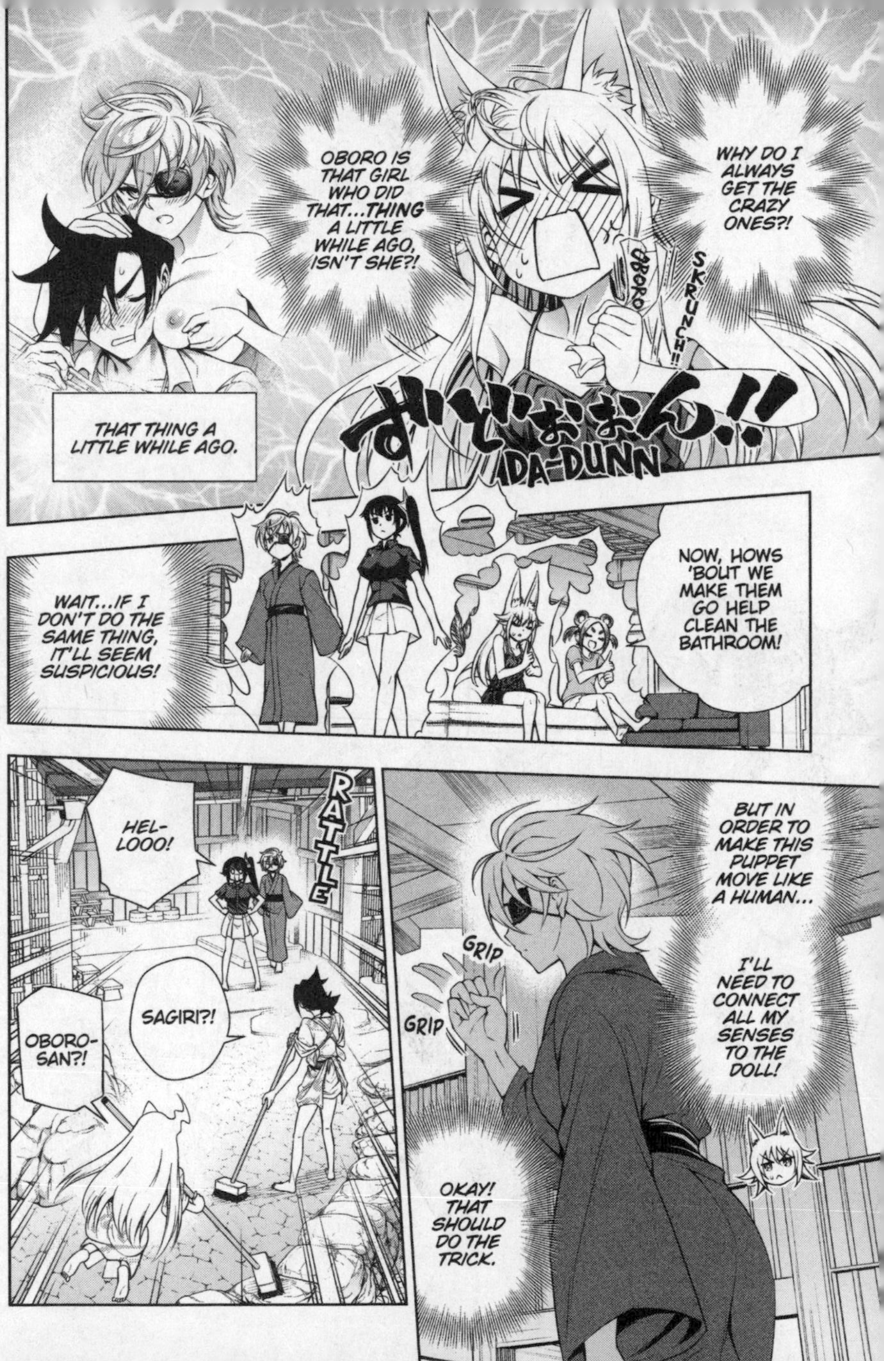
WHY DO I ALWAYS GET THE CRAZY ONES?!
OBORO
SKRUNCH!!
OBORO IS THAT GIRL WHO DID THAT...THING A LITTLE WHILE AGO, ISN'T SHE?!
THAT THING A LITTLE WHILE AGO.
DA-DUNN
NOW, HOWS 'BOUT WE MAKE THEM GO HELP CLEAN THE BATHROOM!
WAIT...IF I DON'T DO THE SAME THING, IT'LL SEEM SUSPICIOUS!
BUT IN ORDER TO MAKE THIS PUPPET MOVE LIKE A HUMAN...
I'LL NEED TO CONNECT ALL MY SENSES TO THE DOLL!
GRIP
GRIP
OKAY! THAT SHOULD DO THE TRICK.
RATTLE
HEL-LOOO!
SAGIRI?!
OBORO-SAN?!

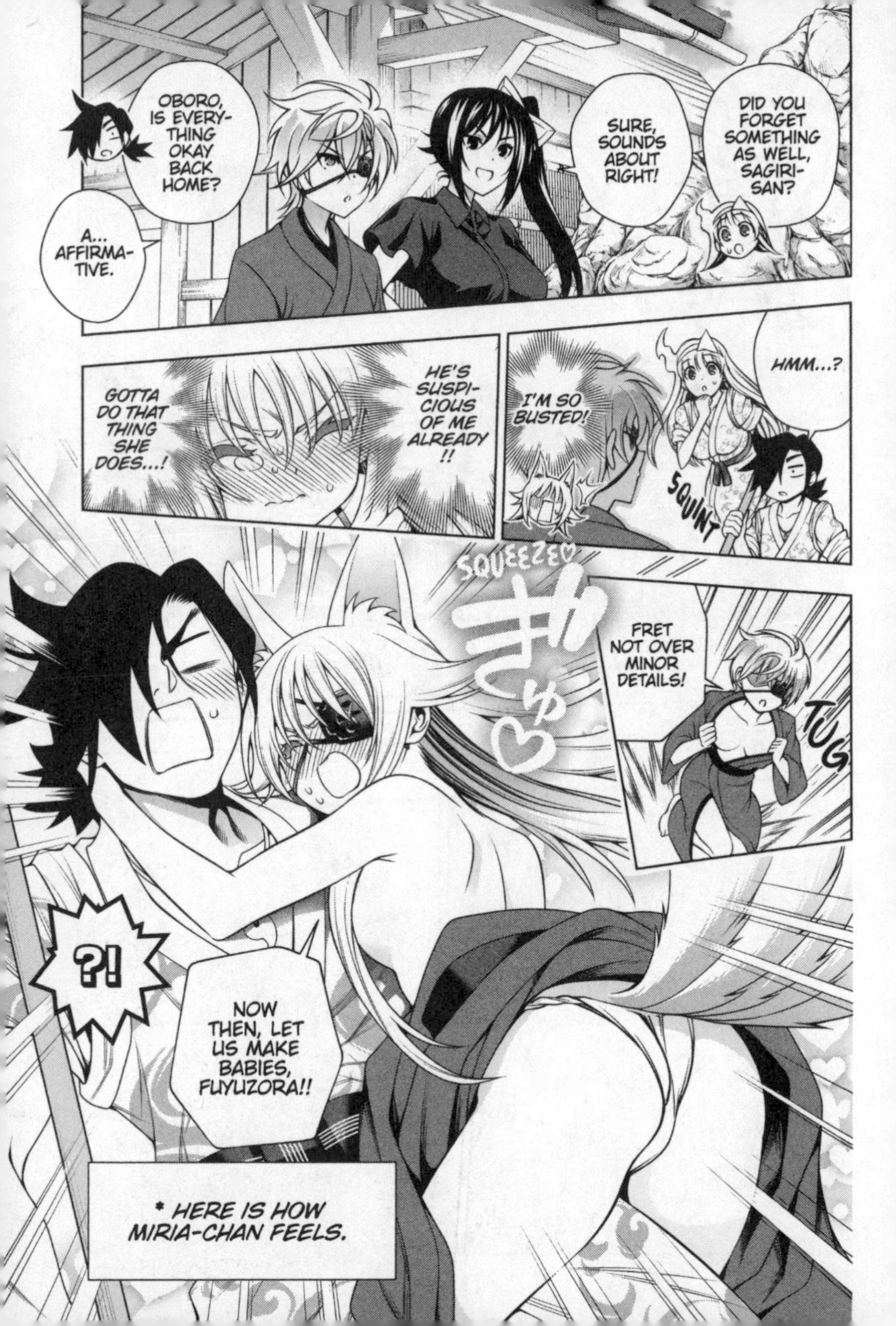
DID YOU FORGET SOMETHING AS WELL, SAGIRI-SAN?
SURE, SOUNDS ABOUT RIGHT!
OBORO, IS EVERY-THING OKAY BACK HOME?
A... AFFIRMA-TIVE.
HMM...?
I'M SO BUSTED!
SQUINT
HE'S SUSPI-CIOUS OF ME ALREADY !!
GOTTA DO THAT THING SHE DOES...!
FRET NOT OVER MINOR DETAILS!
TUG
SQUEEZE♡
きゅ♡
?!
NOW THEN, LET US MAKE BABIES, FUYUZORA!!
* HERE IS HOW MIRIA-CHAN FEELS.

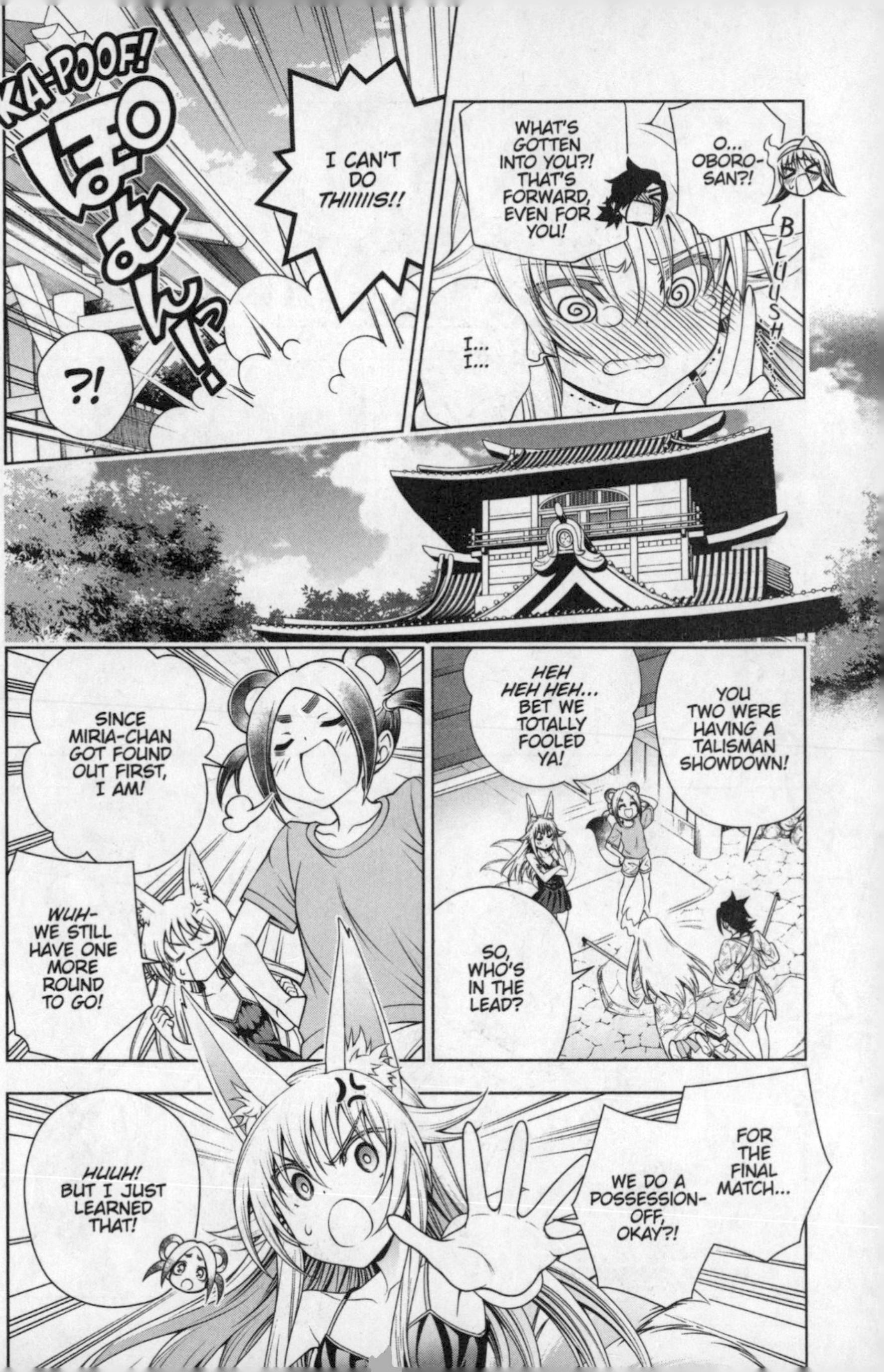
O... OBORO-SAN?!
BLUSH
WHAT'S GOTTEN INTO YOU?! THAT'S FORWARD, EVEN FOR YOU!
I... I...
I CAN'T DO THIIIIIS!!
KA-POOF!
?!
YOU TWO WERE HAVING A TALISMAN SHOWDOWN!
HEH HEH HEH... BET WE TOTALLY FOOLED YA!
SO, WHO'S IN THE LEAD?
SINCE MIRIA-CHAN GOT FOUND OUT FIRST, I AM!
WUH- WE STILL HAVE ONE MORE ROUND TO GO!
FOR THE FINAL MATCH...
WE DO A POSSESSION-OFF, OKAY?!
HUUH! BUT I JUST LEARNED THAT!

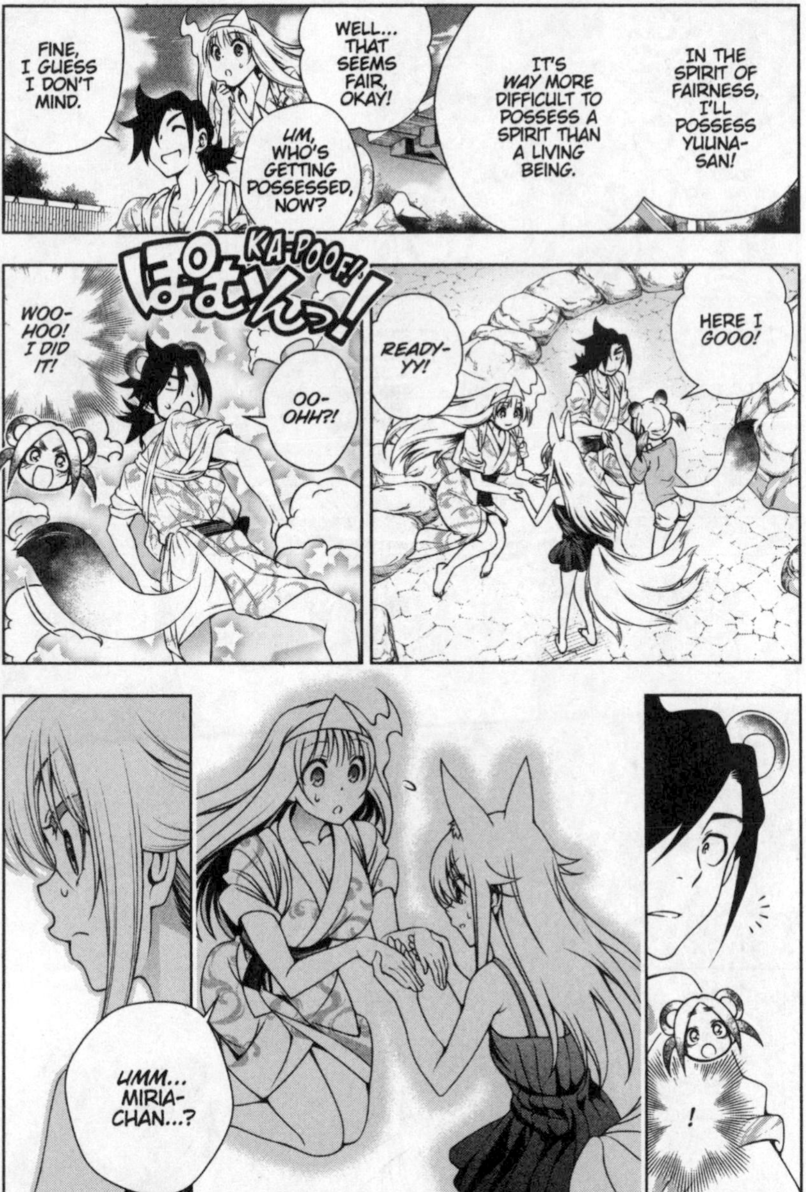
IN THE SPIRIT OF FAIRNESS, I'LL POSSESS YUUNA-SAN!
IT'S WAY MORE DIFFICULT TO POSSESS A SPIRIT THAN A LIVING BEING.
WELL... THAT SEEMS FAIR, OKAY!
UM, WHO'S GETTING POSSESSED, NOW?
FINE, I GUESS I DON'T MIND.
HERE I GOOO!
READY-YY!
ぽむんっ!
KA-POOF!
OO-OHH?!
WOO-HOO! I DID IT!
!
UMM... MIRIA-CHAN...?

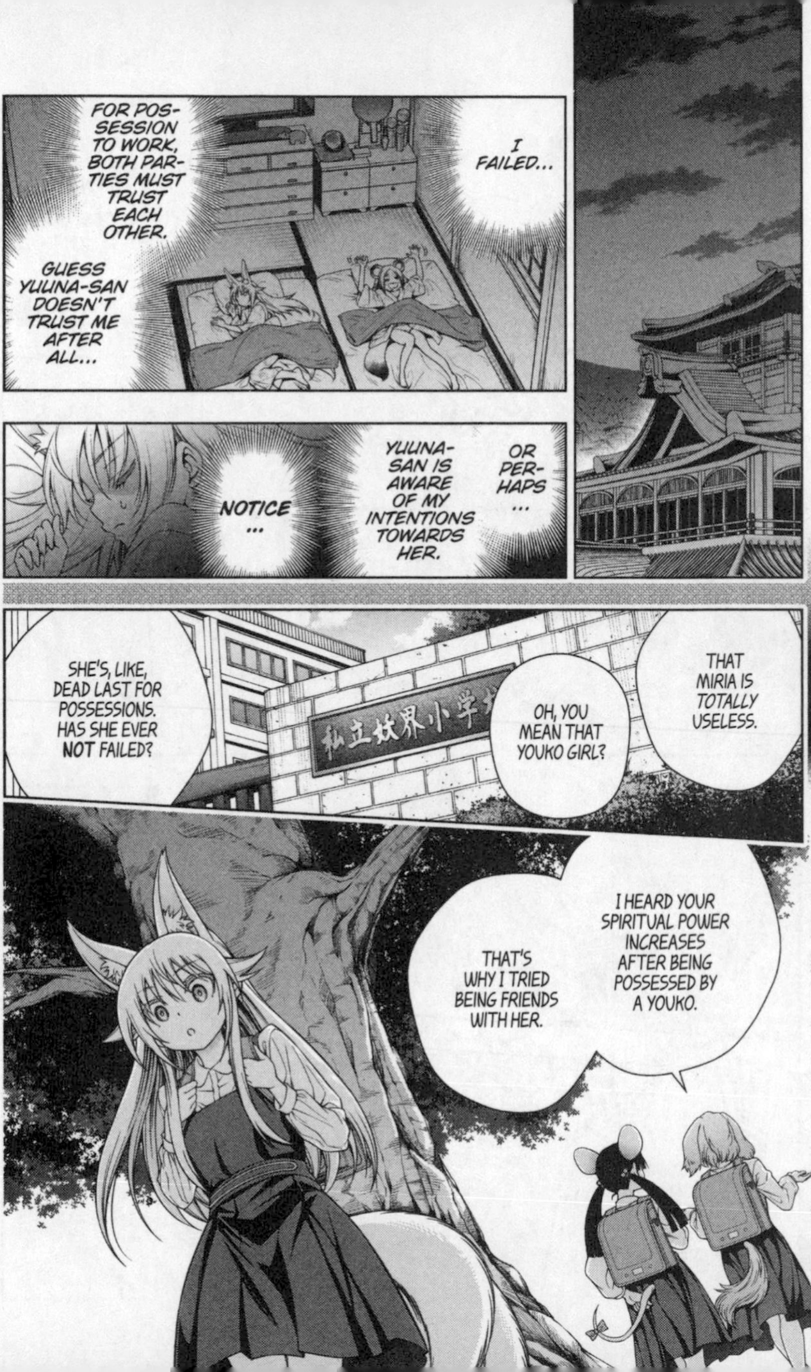
I FAILED...
FOR POSSESSION TO WORK, BOTH PARTIES MUST TRUST EACH OTHER.
GUESS YUUNA-SAN DOESN'T TRUST ME AFTER ALL...
OR PERHAPS...
YUUNA-SAN IS AWARE OF MY INTENTIONS TOWARDS HER.
NOTICE...
THAT MIRIA IS TOTALLY USELESS.
OH, YOU MEAN THAT YOUKO GIRL?
私立妖界小学
SHE'S, LIKE, DEAD LAST FOR POSSESSIONS. HAS SHE EVER **NOT** FAILED?
I HEARD YOUR SPIRITUAL POWER INCREASES AFTER BEING POSSESSED BY A YOUKO.
THAT'S WHY I TRIED BEING FRIENDS WITH HER.

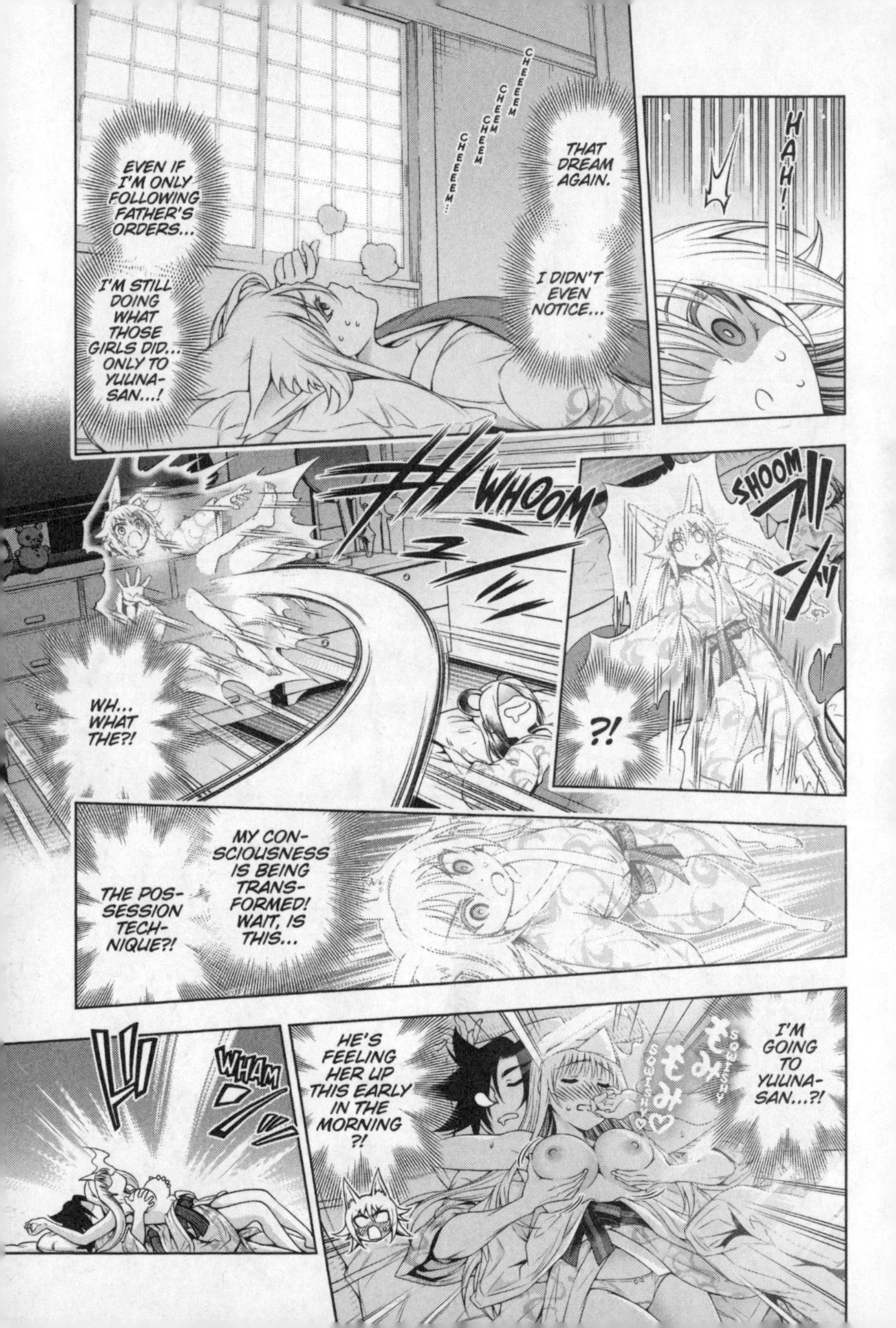
HAH!
THAT DREAM AGAIN.
I DIDN'T EVEN NOTICE...
CHEEEEM CHEEM CHEEM CHEEEEM...
EVEN IF I'M ONLY FOLLOWING FATHER'S ORDERS...
I'M STILL DOING WHAT THOSE GIRLS DID... ONLY TO YUUNA-SAN...!
SHOOM
?!
WHOOM
WH... WHAT THE?!
MY CONSCIOUSNESS IS BEING TRANSFORMED! WAIT, IS THIS...
THE POSSESSION TECHNIQUE?!
I'M GOING TO YUUNA-SAN...?!
もみ もみ
HE'S FEELING HER UP THIS EARLY IN THE MORNING?!
WHAM

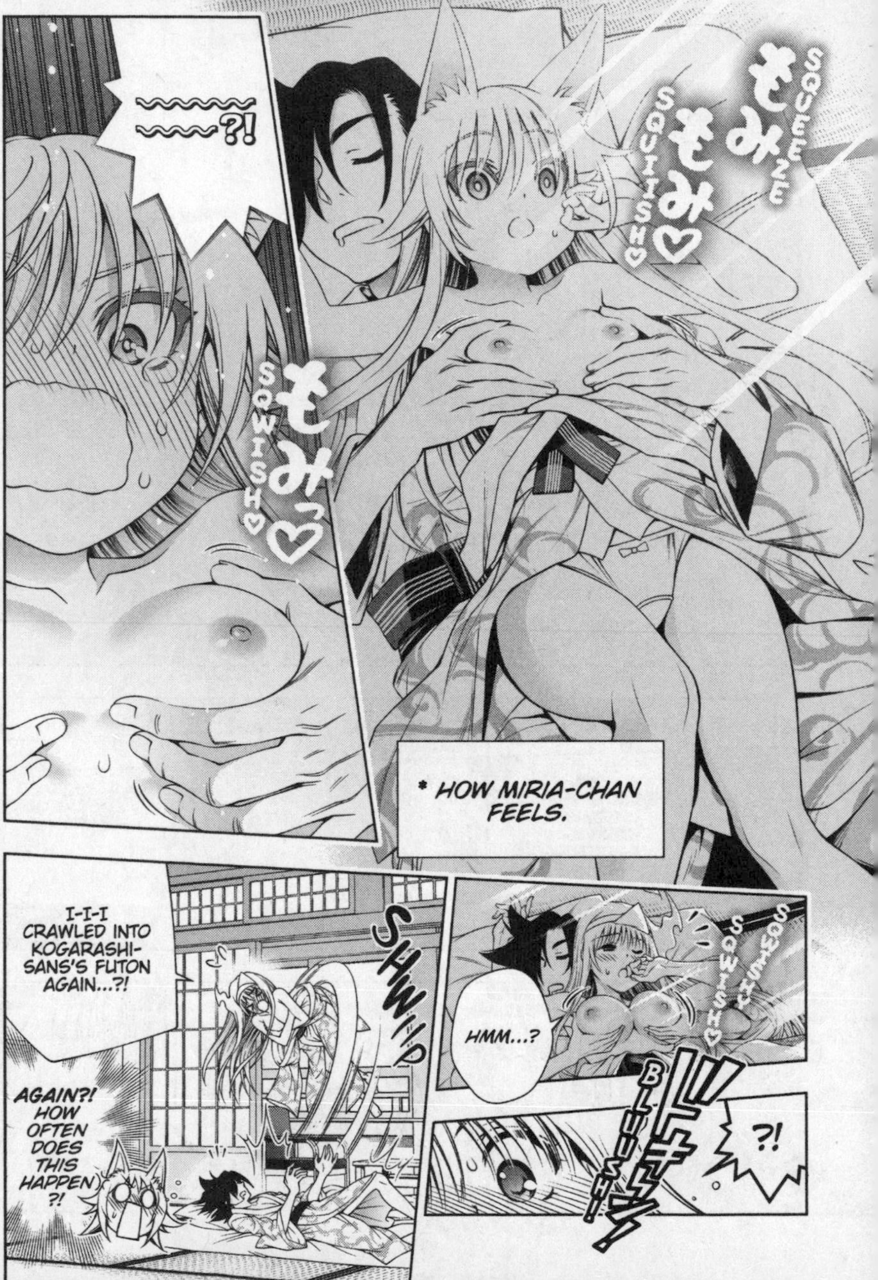
もみ
SQUEEZE
もみ♡
SQUISH♡
* HOW MIRIA-CHAN FEELS.
~~~~~~~ ~~~~?!
もみっ♡
SQWISH♡
SQWISH♡
HMM...?
?!
BLUUSH!
SHW!!
I-I-I CRAWLED INTO KOGARASHI-SANS'S FUTON AGAIN...?!
AGAIN?! HOW OFTEN DOES THIS HAPPEN?!
~~~~~~~

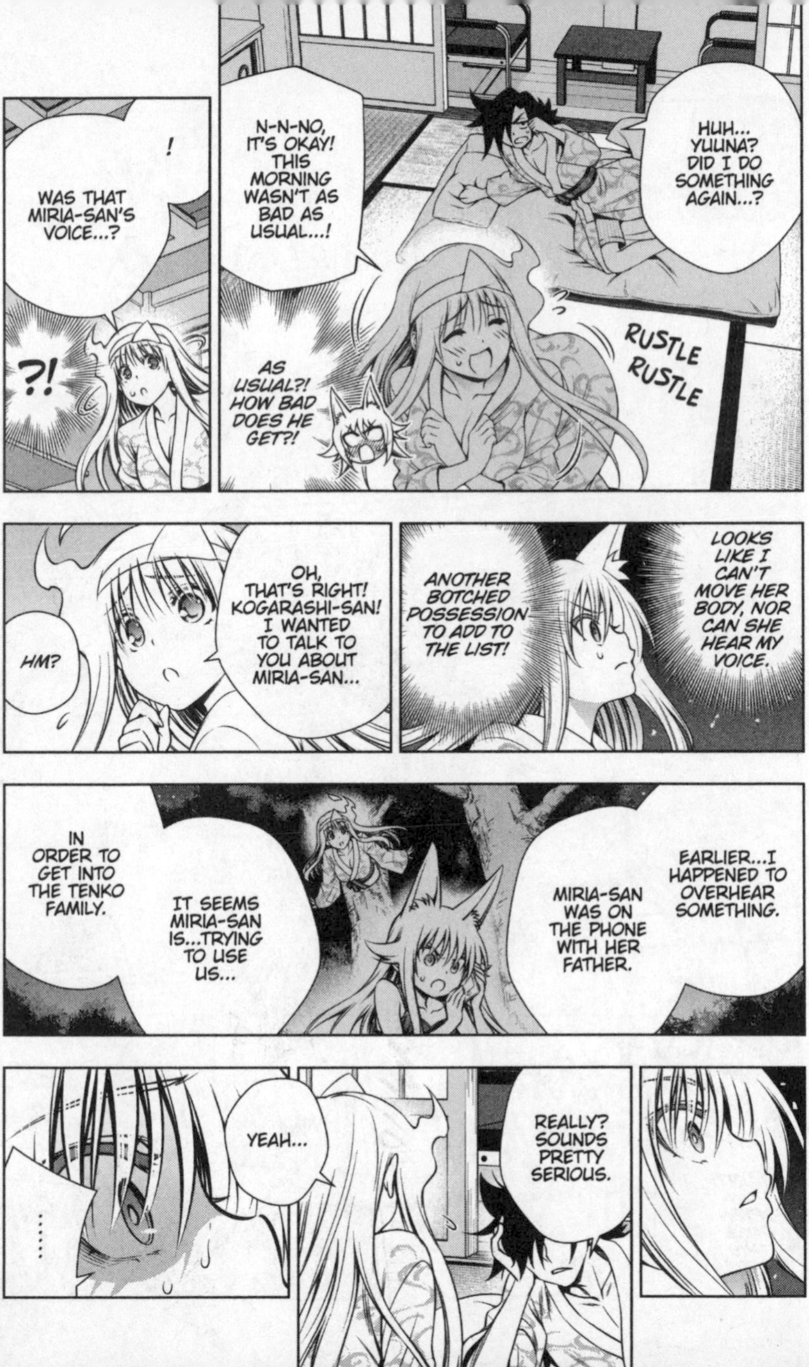
HUH... YUUNA? DID I DO SOMETHING AGAIN...?
RUSTLE RUSTLE
N-N-NO, IT'S OKAY! THIS MORNING WASN'T AS BAD AS USUAL...!
AS USUAL?! HOW BAD DOES HE GET?!
!
WAS THAT MIRIA-SAN'S VOICE...?
?!
LOOKS LIKE I CAN'T MOVE HER BODY, NOR CAN SHE HEAR MY VOICE.
ANOTHER BOTCHED POSSESSION TO ADD TO THE LIST!
OH, THAT'S RIGHT! KOGARASHI-SAN! I WANTED TO TALK TO YOU ABOUT MIRIA-SAN...
HM?
EARLIER...I HAPPENED TO OVERHEAR SOMETHING.
MIRIA-SAN WAS ON THE PHONE WITH HER FATHER.
IT SEEMS MIRIA-SAN IS...TRYING TO USE US...
IN ORDER TO GET INTO THE TENKO FAMILY.
REALLY? SOUNDS PRETTY SERIOUS.
YEAH...
......

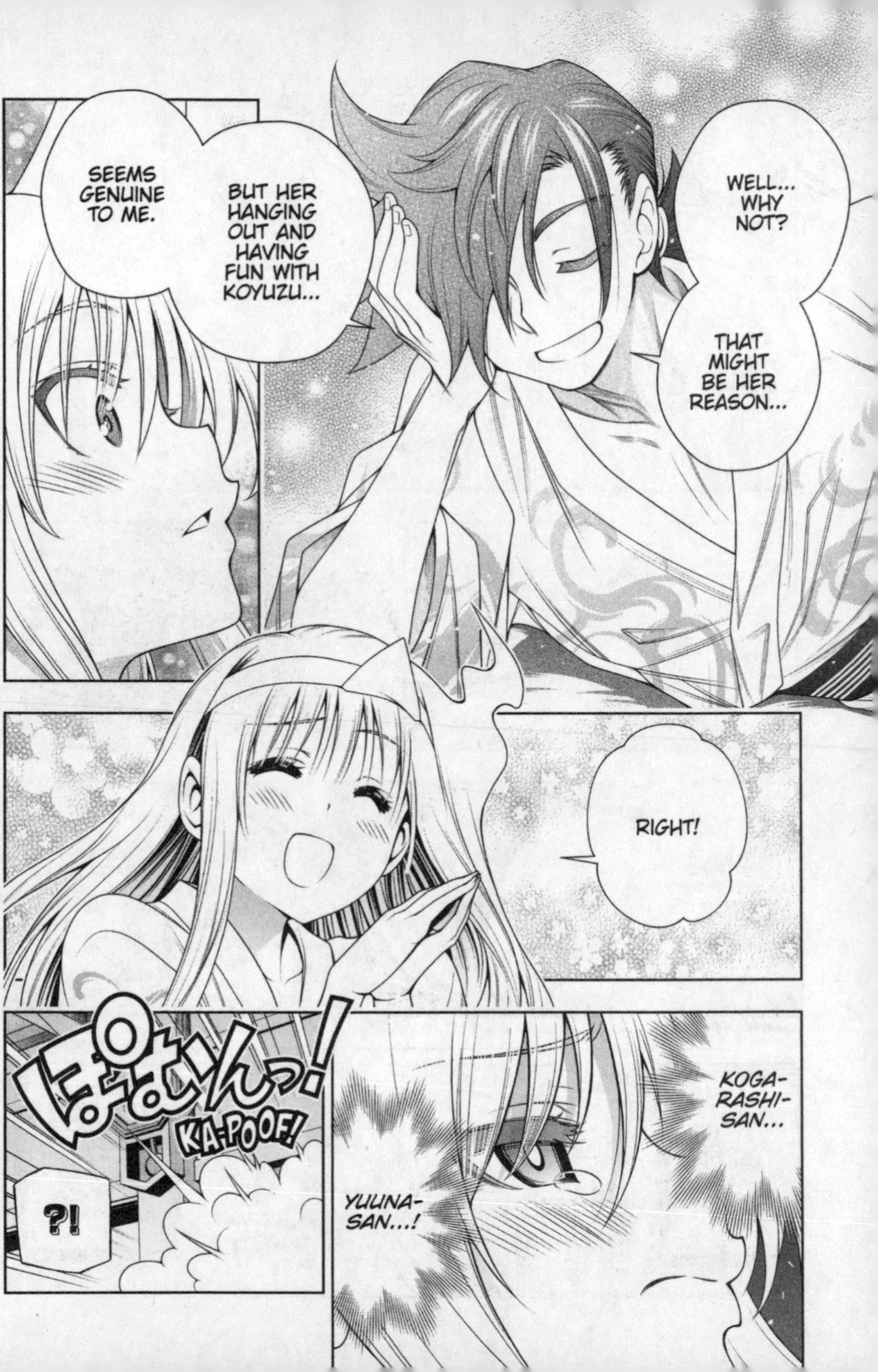
WELL... WHY NOT?
THAT MIGHT BE HER REASON...
SEEMS GENUINE TO ME.
BUT HER HANGING OUT AND HAVING FUN WITH KOYUZU...
RIGHT!
KOGA-RASHI-SAN...
YUUNA-SAN...!
KA-POOF!
?!

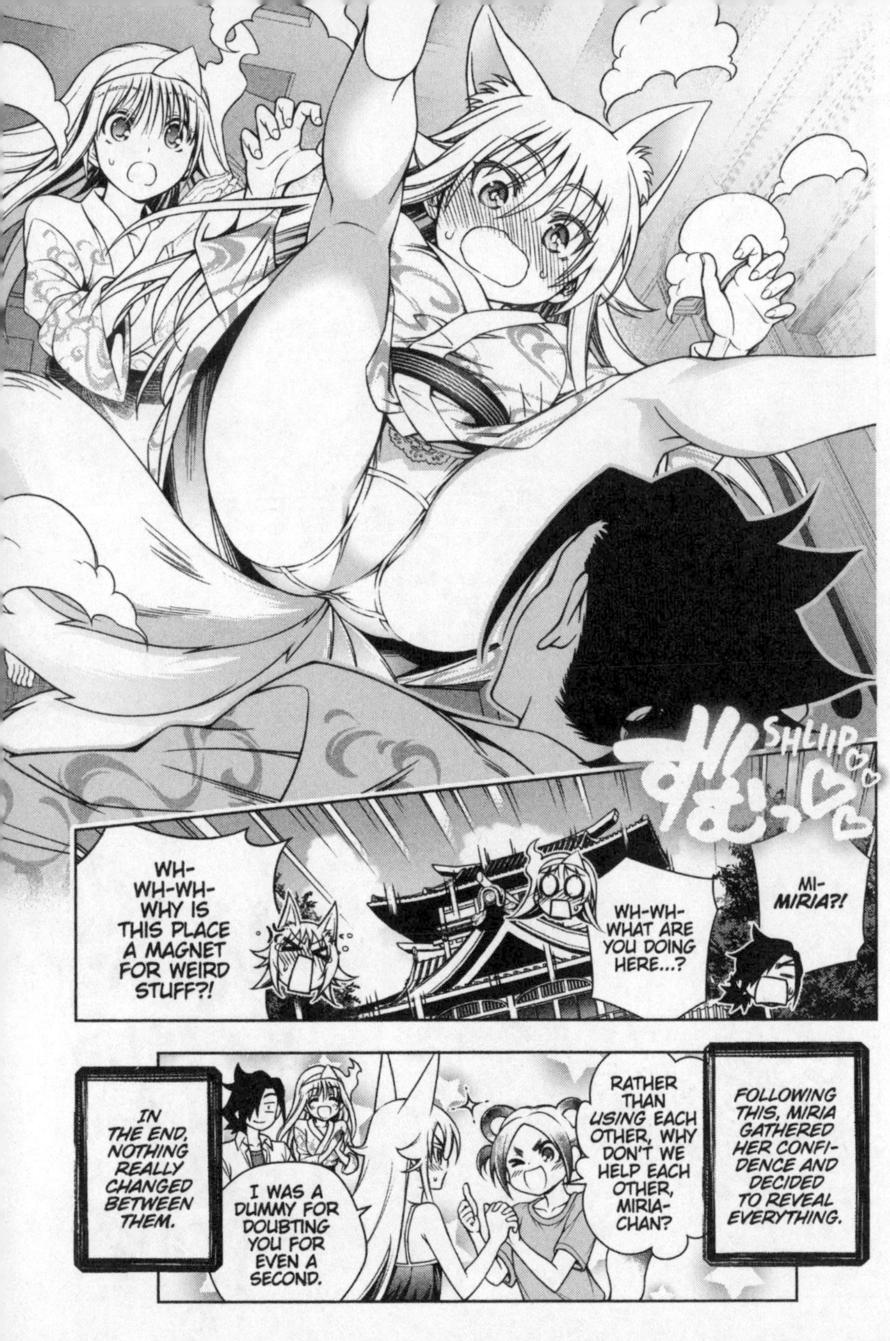
SHLIIP
すむっ
MI-MIRIA?!
WH-WH-WHAT ARE YOU DOING HERE...?
WH-WH-WH-WHY IS THIS PLACE A MAGNET FOR WEIRD STUFF?!
FOLLOWING THIS, MIRIA GATHERED HER CONFIDENCE AND DECIDED TO REVEAL EVERYTHING.
RATHER THAN USING EACH OTHER, WHY DON'T WE HELP EACH OTHER, MIRIA-CHAN?
I WAS A DUMMY FOR DOUBTING YOU FOR EVEN A SECOND.
IN THE END, NOTHING REALLY CHANGED BETWEEN THEM.

Yuuna and the Haunted Hot Springs

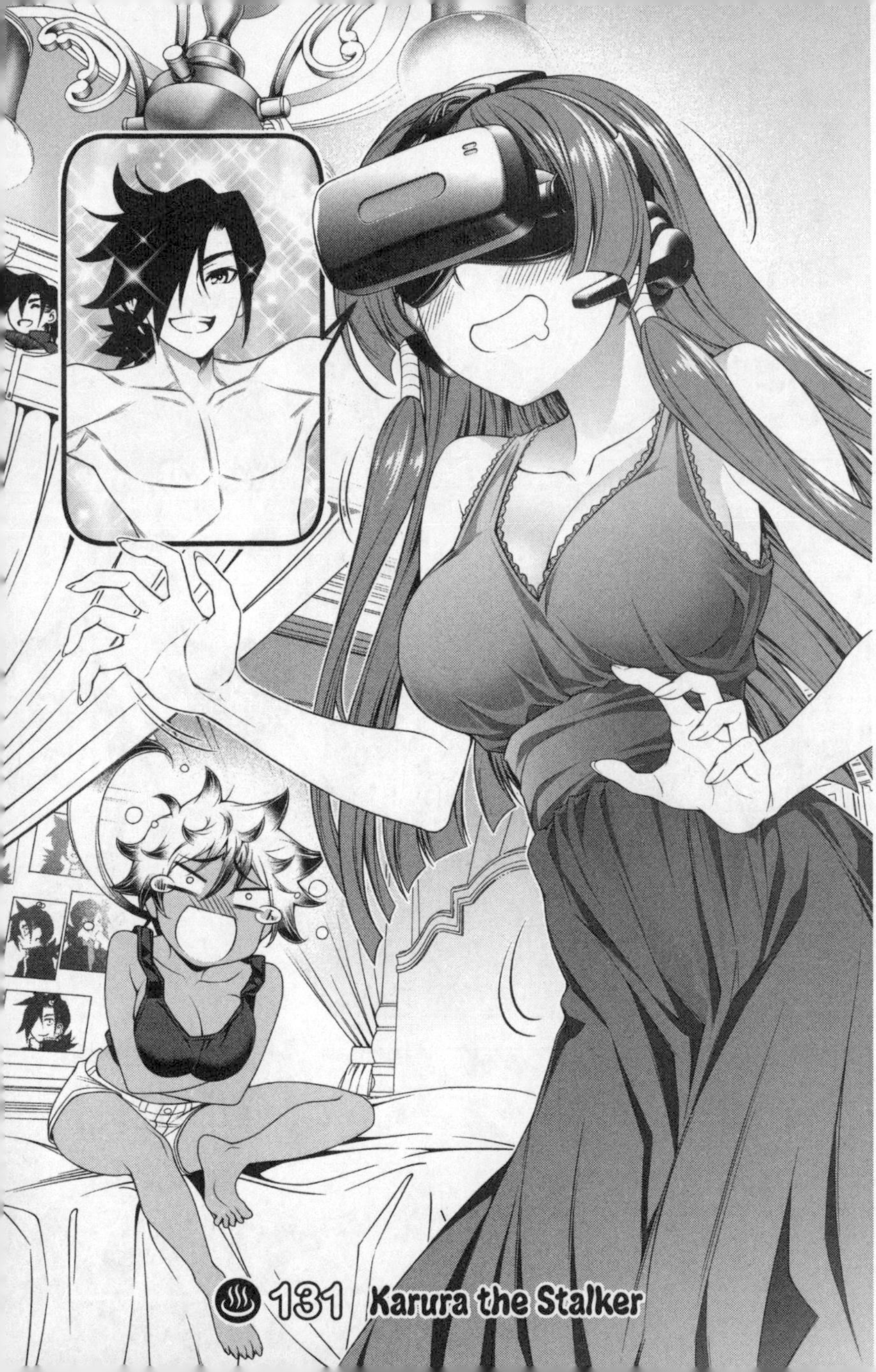
131 Karura the Stalker

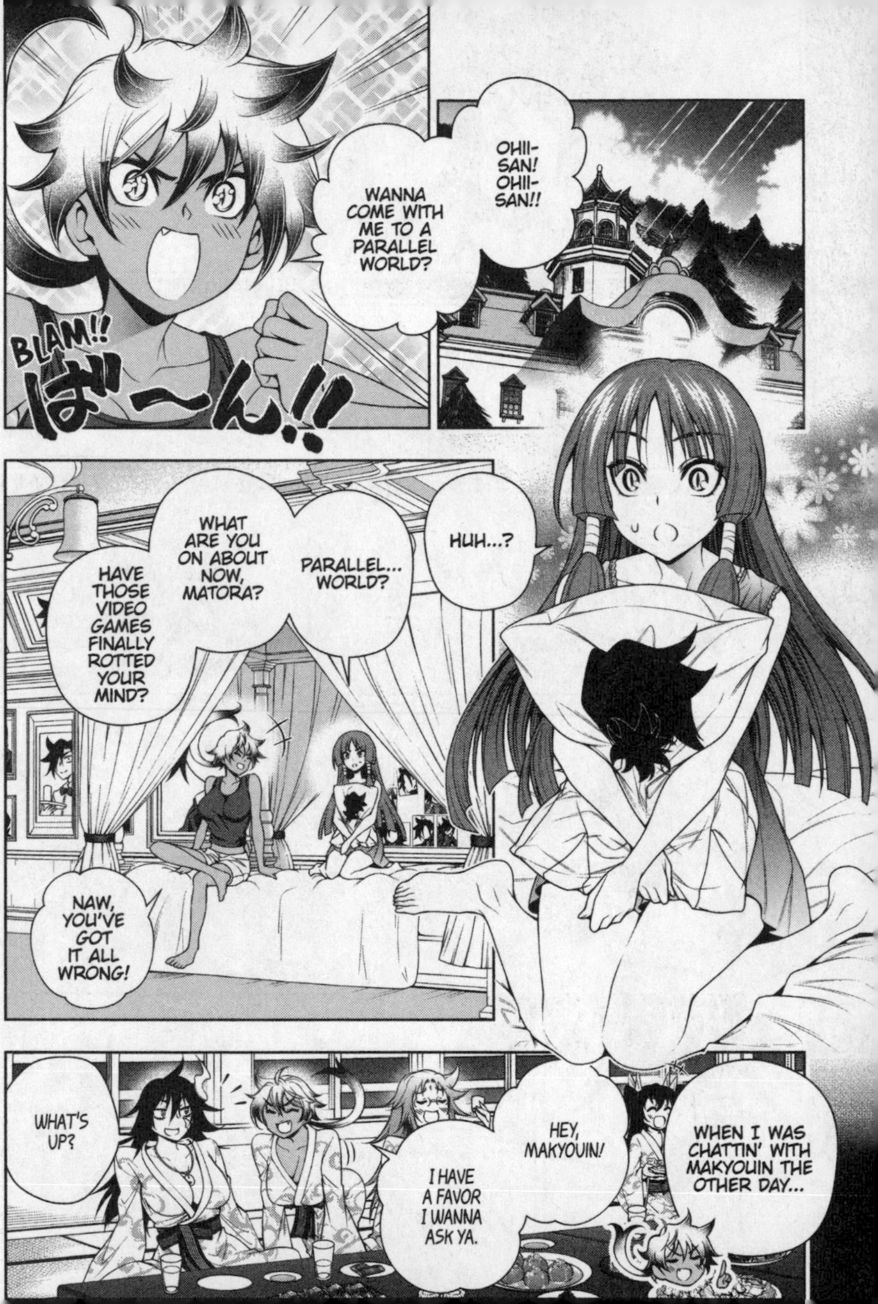
OHII-SAN! OHII-SAN!!
WANNA COME WITH ME TO A PARALLEL WORLD?
BLAM!!
ば〜ん!!
HUH...?
PARALLEL... WORLD?
WHAT ARE YOU ON ABOUT NOW, MATORA?
HAVE THOSE VIDEO GAMES FINALLY ROTTED YOUR MIND?
NAW, YOU'VE GOT IT ALL WRONG!
WHEN I WAS CHATTIN' WITH MAKYOUIN THE OTHER DAY...
HEY, MAKYOUIN!
I HAVE A FAVOR I WANNA ASK YA.
WHAT'S UP?

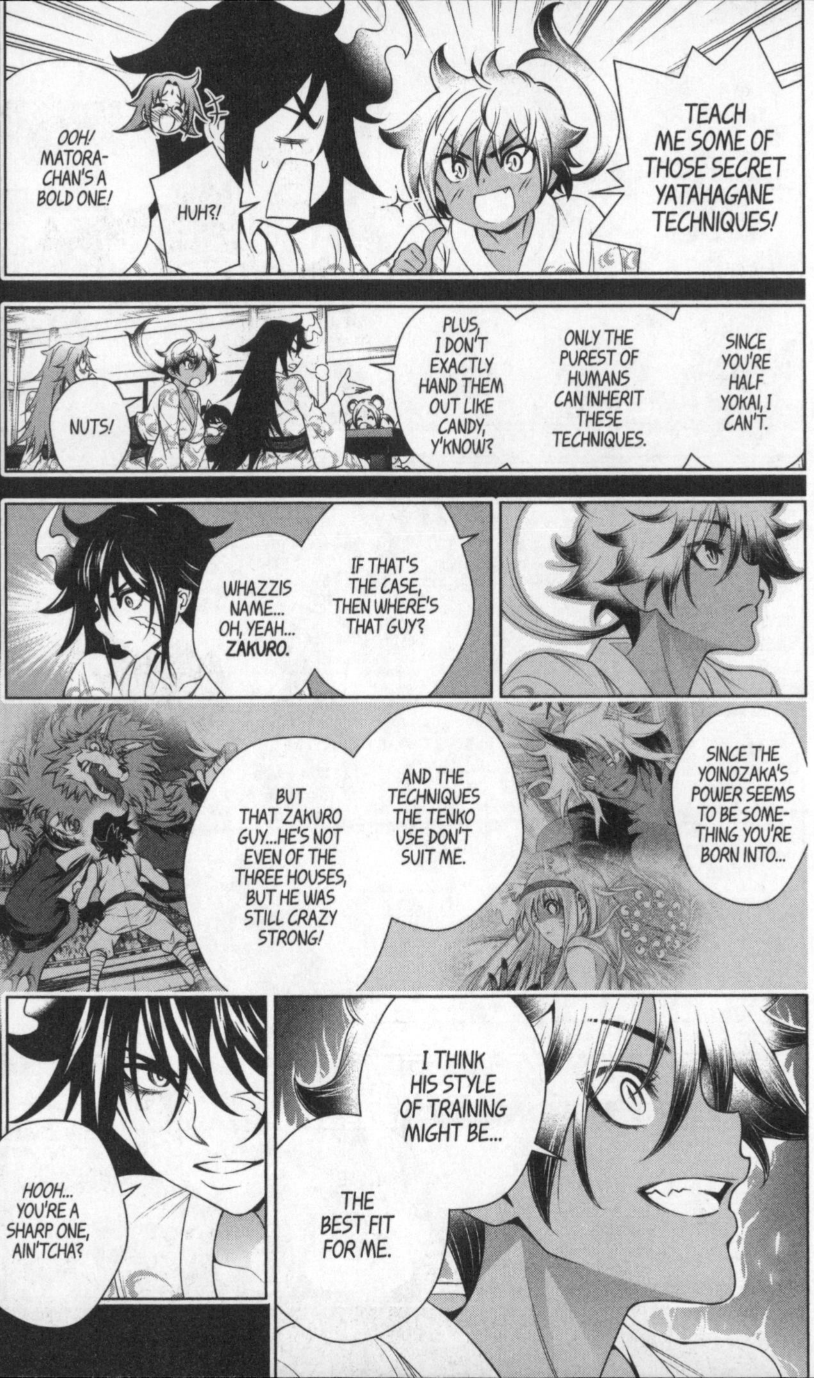
TEACH ME SOME OF THOSE SECRET YATAHAGANE TECHNIQUES!
HUH?!
OOH! MATORA-CHAN'S A BOLD ONE!
SINCE YOU'RE HALF YOKAI, I CAN'T.
ONLY THE PUREST OF HUMANS CAN INHERIT THESE TECHNIQUES.
PLUS, I DON'T EXACTLY HAND THEM OUT LIKE CANDY, Y'KNOW?
NUTS!
IF THAT'S THE CASE, THEN WHERE'S THAT GUY?
WHAZZIS NAME... OH, YEAH... **ZAKURO.**
SINCE THE YOINOZAKA'S POWER SEEMS TO BE SOME-THING YOU'RE BORN INTO...
AND THE TECHNIQUES THE TENKO USE DON'T SUIT ME.
BUT THAT ZAKURO GUY...HE'S NOT EVEN OF THE THREE HOUSES, BUT HE WAS STILL CRAZY STRONG!
I THINK HIS STYLE OF TRAINING MIGHT BE...
THE BEST FIT FOR ME.
HOOH... YOU'RE A SHARP ONE, AIN'TCHA?

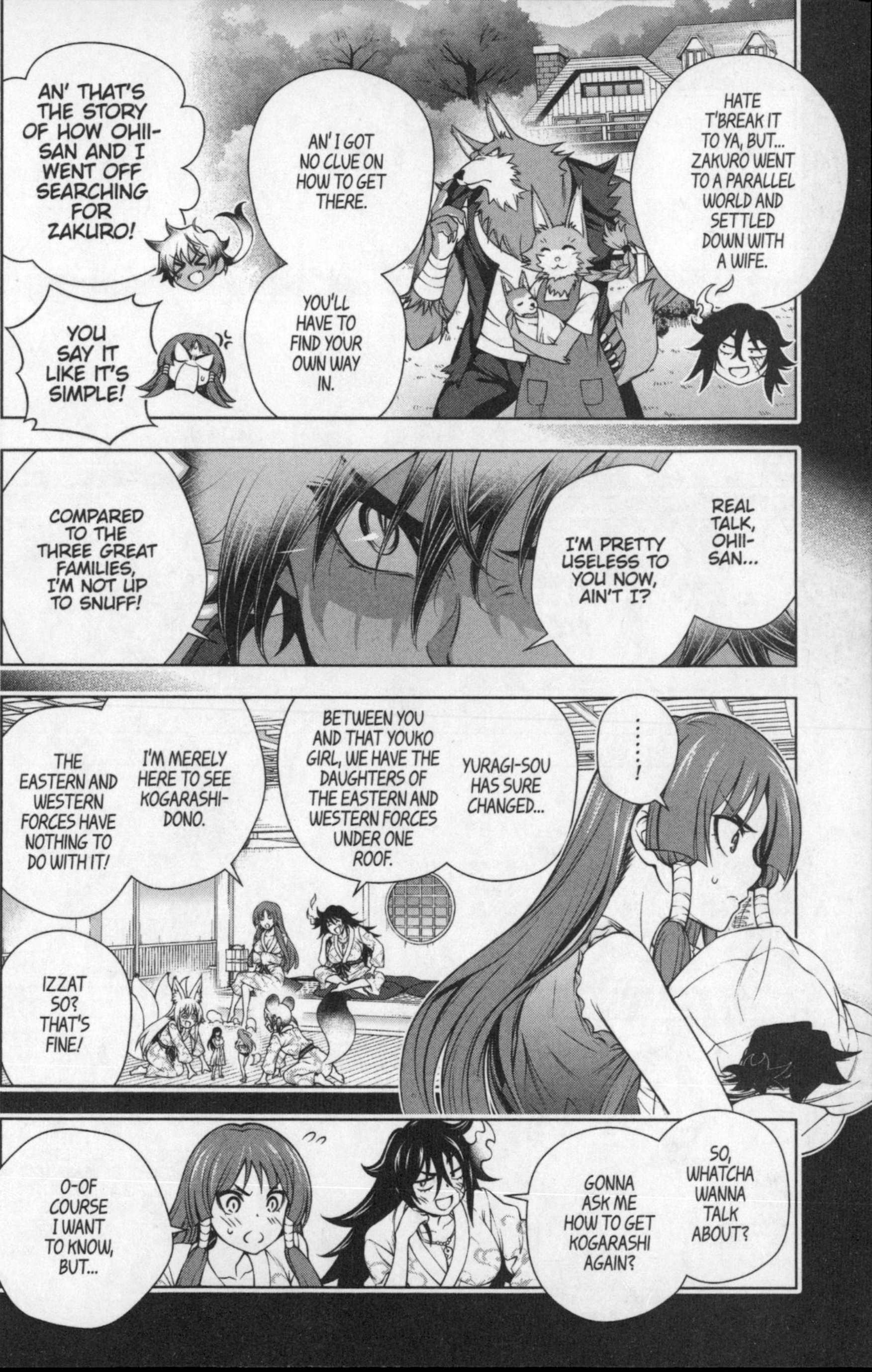
HATE T'BREAK IT TO YA, BUT... ZAKURO WENT TO A PARALLEL WORLD AND SETTLED DOWN WITH A WIFE.
AN' I GOT NO CLUE ON HOW TO GET THERE.
YOU'LL HAVE TO FIND YOUR OWN WAY IN.
AN' THAT'S THE STORY OF HOW OHII-SAN AND I WENT OFF SEARCHING FOR ZAKURO!
YOU SAY IT LIKE IT'S SIMPLE!
REAL TALK, OHII-SAN...
I'M PRETTY USELESS TO YOU NOW, AIN'T I?
COMPARED TO THE THREE GREAT FAMILIES, I'M NOT UP TO SNUFF!
......!
YURAGI-SOU HAS SURE CHANGED...
BETWEEN YOU AND THAT YOUKO GIRL, WE HAVE THE DAUGHTERS OF THE EASTERN AND WESTERN FORCES UNDER ONE ROOF.
I'M MERELY HERE TO SEE KOGARASHI-DONO.
THE EASTERN AND WESTERN FORCES HAVE NOTHING TO DO WITH IT!
IZZAT SO? THAT'S FINE!
SO, WHATCHA WANNA TALK ABOUT?
GONNA ASK ME HOW TO GET KOGARASHI AGAIN?
O-OF COURSE I WANT TO KNOW, BUT...

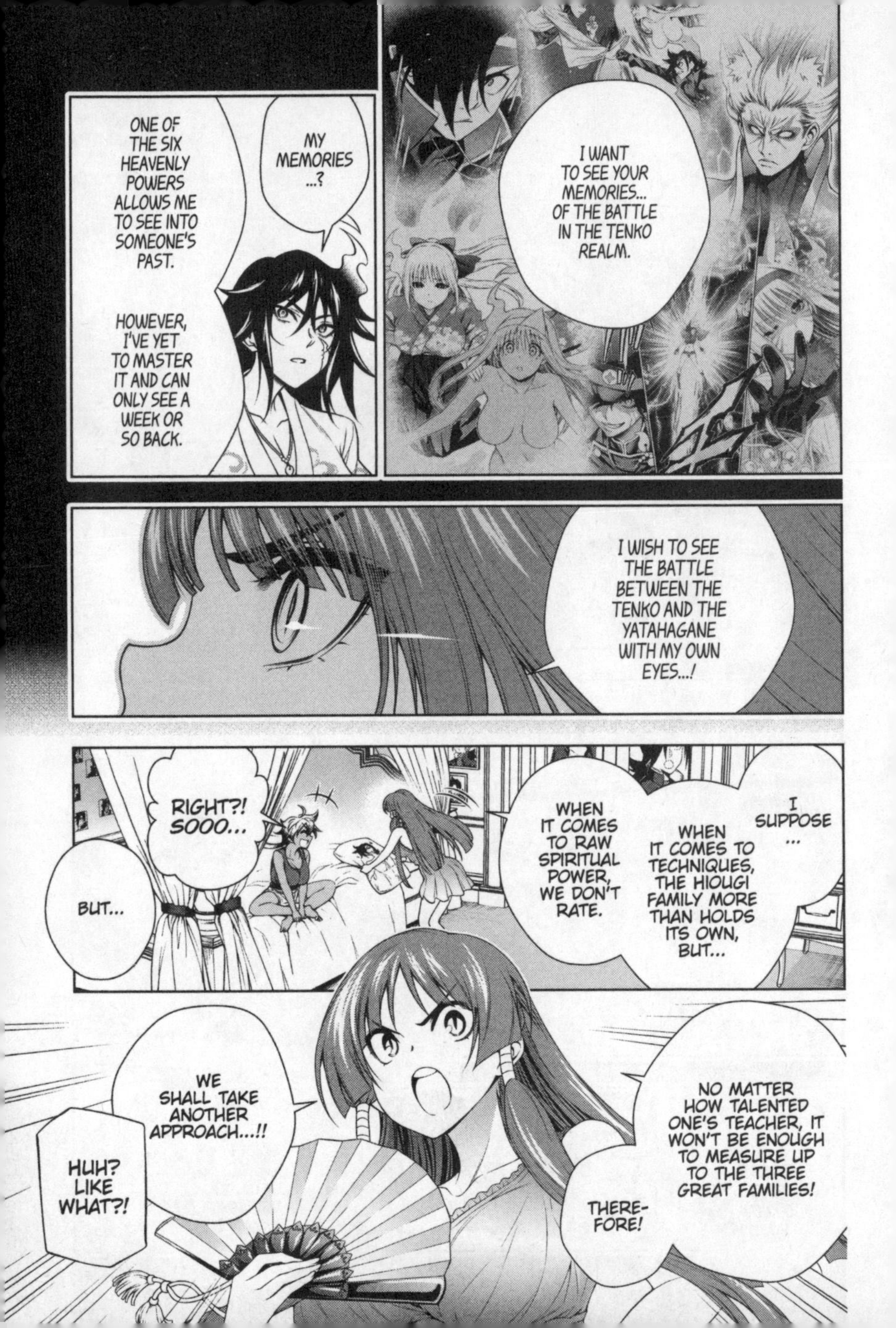
I WANT TO SEE YOUR MEMORIES... OF THE BATTLE IN THE TENKO REALM.
MY MEMORIES ...?
ONE OF THE SIX HEAVENLY POWERS ALLOWS ME TO SEE INTO SOMEONE'S PAST.
HOWEVER, I'VE YET TO MASTER IT AND CAN ONLY SEE A WEEK OR SO BACK.
I WISH TO SEE THE BATTLE BETWEEN THE TENKO AND THE YATAHAGANE WITH MY OWN EYES...!
I SUPPOSE ...
WHEN IT COMES TO TECHNIQUES, THE HIOUGI FAMILY MORE THAN HOLDS ITS OWN, BUT...
WHEN IT COMES TO RAW SPIRITUAL POWER, WE DON'T RATE.
RIGHT?! SOOO...
BUT...
NO MATTER HOW TALENTED ONE'S TEACHER, IT WON'T BE ENOUGH TO MEASURE UP TO THE THREE GREAT FAMILIES!
THERE-FORE!
WE SHALL TAKE ANOTHER APPROACH...!!
HUH? LIKE WHAT?!

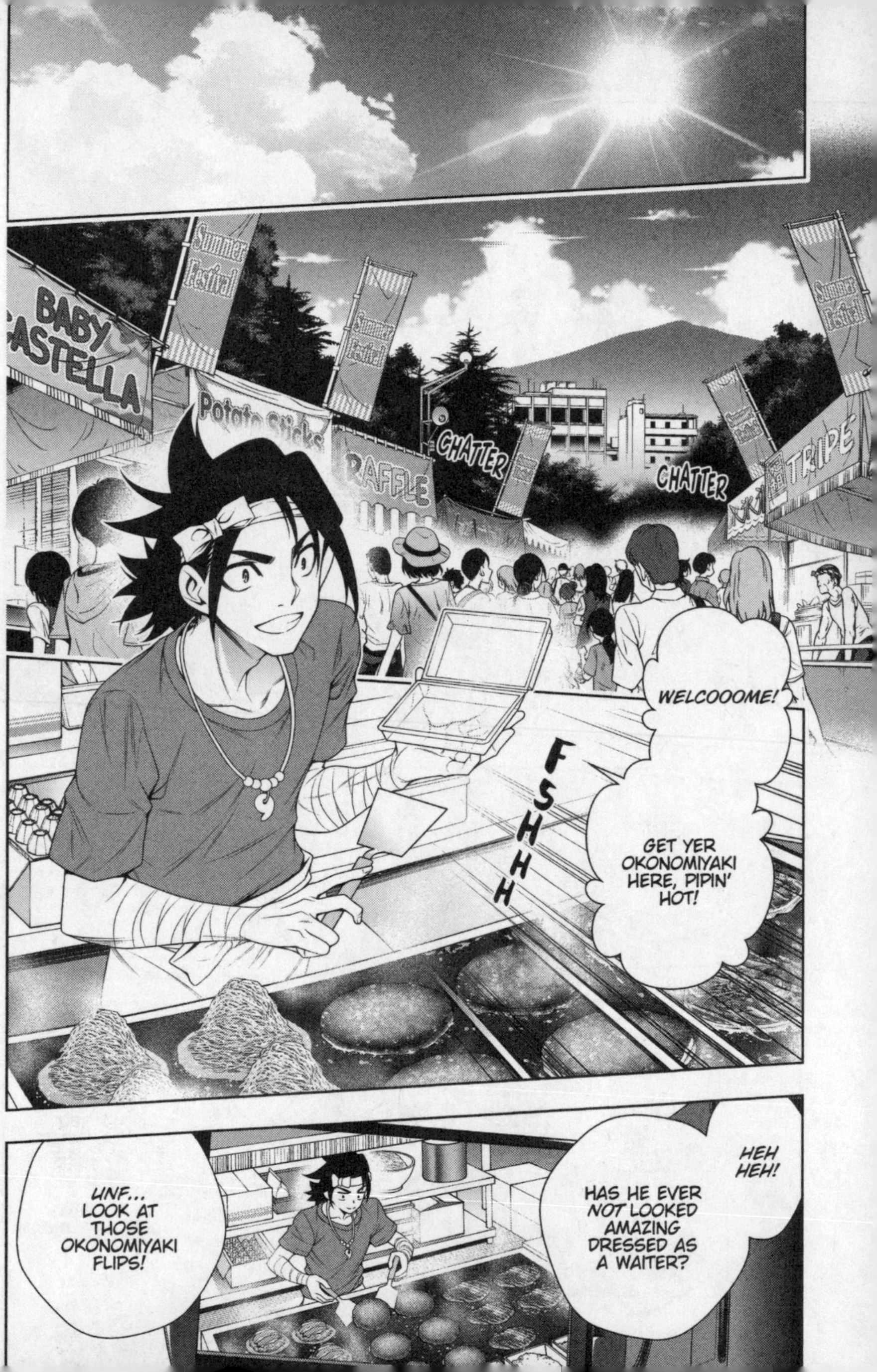
TRIPE
Summer Festival
CHATTER
CHATTER
RAFFLE
Potato Sticks
BABY CASTELLA
WELCOOOME!
GET YER OKONOMIYAKI HERE, PIPIN' HOT!
FSHHHH
HEH HEH!
HAS HE EVER *NOT* LOOKED AMAZING DRESSED AS A WAITER?
UNF... LOOK AT THOSE OKONOMIYAKI FLIPS!

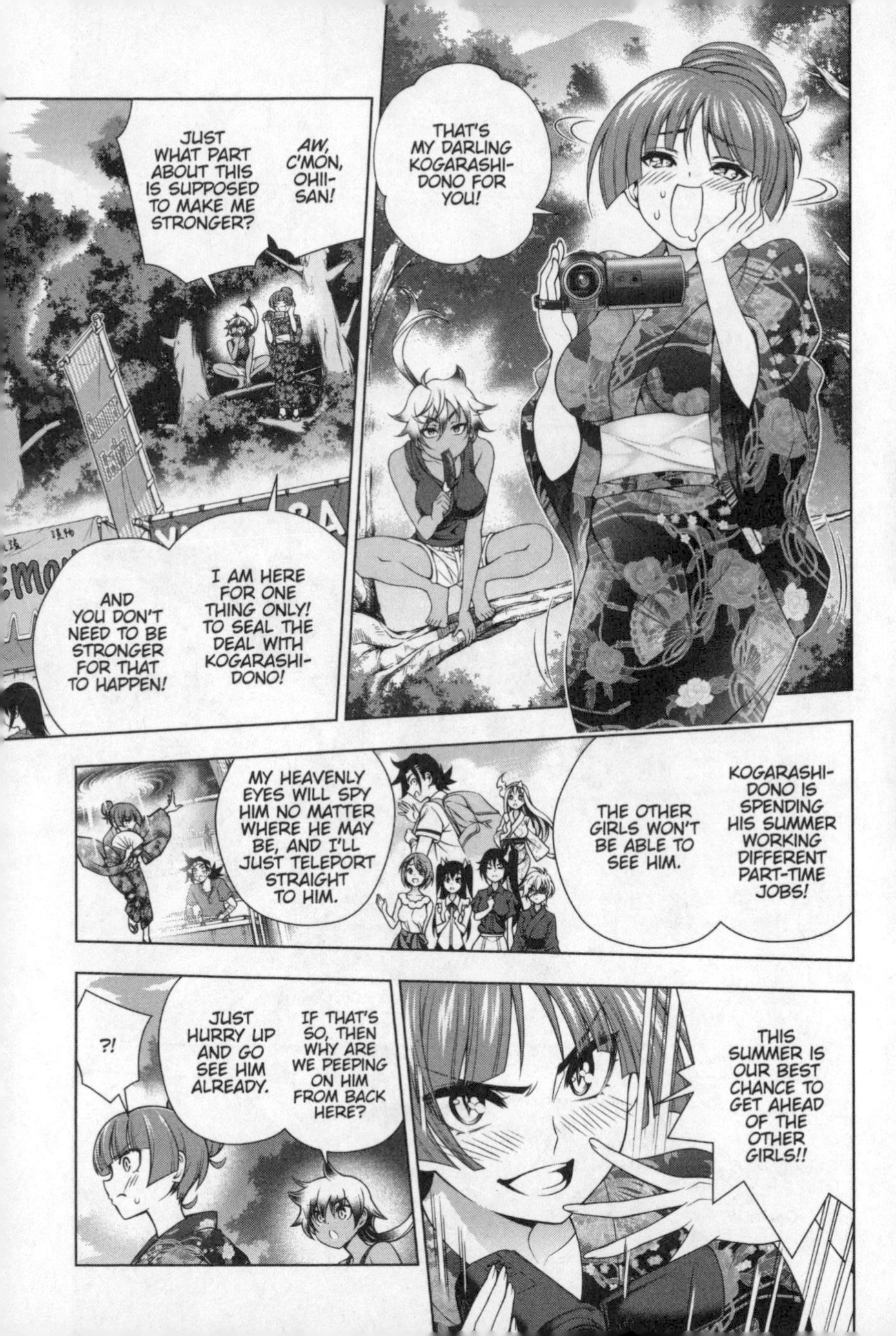
THAT'S MY DARLING KOGARASHI-DONO FOR YOU!
AW, C'MON, OHII-SAN!
JUST WHAT PART ABOUT THIS IS SUPPOSED TO MAKE ME STRONGER?
I AM HERE FOR ONE THING ONLY! TO SEAL THE DEAL WITH KOGARASHI-DONO!
AND YOU DON'T NEED TO BE STRONGER FOR THAT TO HAPPEN!
KOGARASHI-DONO IS SPENDING HIS SUMMER WORKING DIFFERENT PART-TIME JOBS!
THE OTHER GIRLS WON'T BE ABLE TO SEE HIM.
MY HEAVENLY EYES WILL SPY HIM NO MATTER WHERE HE MAY BE, AND I'LL JUST TELEPORT STRAIGHT TO HIM.
THIS SUMMER IS OUR BEST CHANCE TO GET AHEAD OF THE OTHER GIRLS!!
IF THAT'S SO, THEN WHY ARE WE PEEPING ON HIM FROM BACK HERE?
JUST HURRY UP AND GO SEE HIM ALREADY.
?!

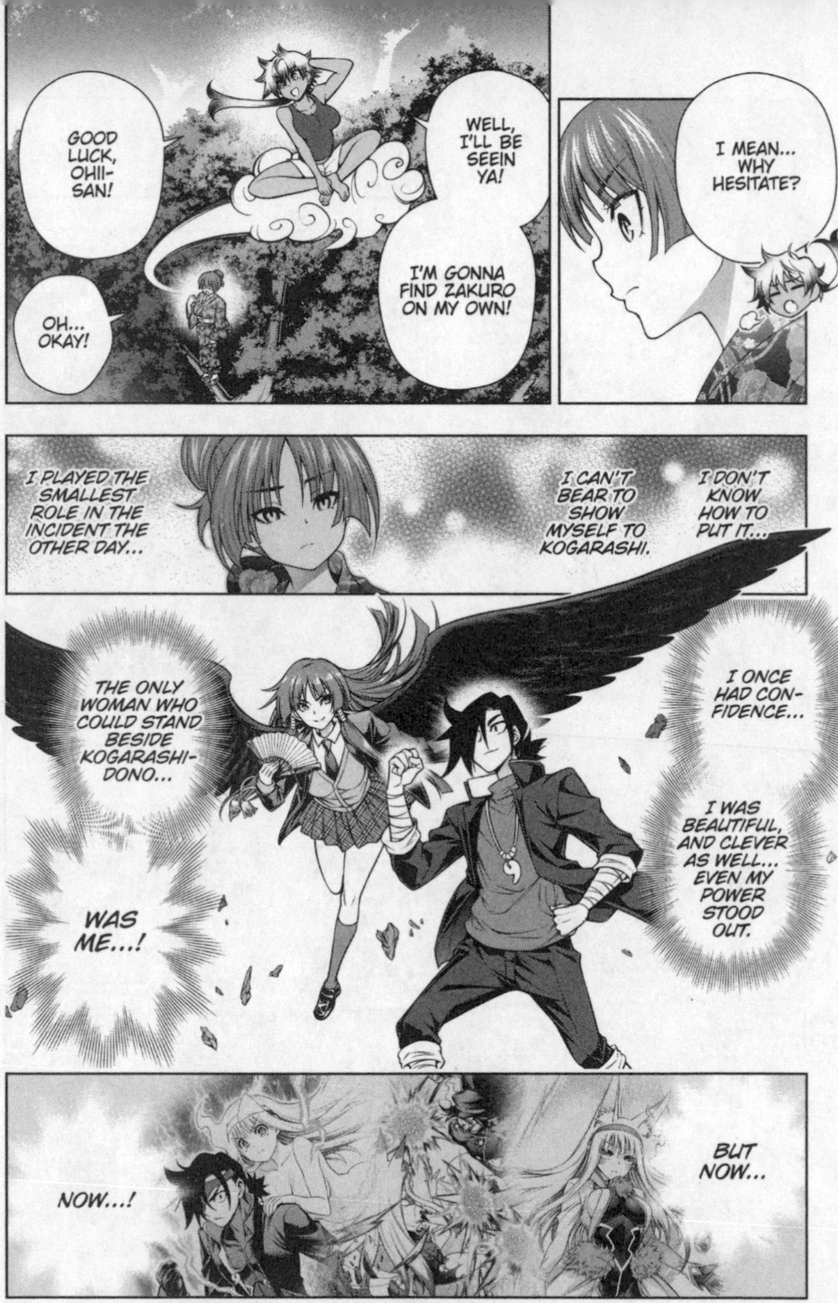
I MEAN... WHY HESITATE?
WELL, I'LL BE SEEIN YA!
I'M GONNA FIND ZAKURO ON MY OWN!
GOOD LUCK, OHII-SAN!
OH... OKAY!
I DON'T KNOW HOW TO PUT IT...
I CAN'T BEAR TO SHOW MYSELF TO KOGARASHI.
I PLAYED THE SMALLEST ROLE IN THE INCIDENT THE OTHER DAY...
I ONCE HAD CON-FIDENCE...
I WAS BEAUTIFUL, AND CLEVER AS WELL... EVEN MY POWER STOOD OUT.
THE ONLY WOMAN WHO COULD STAND BESIDE KOGARASHI-DONO...
WAS ME...!
BUT NOW...
NOW...!

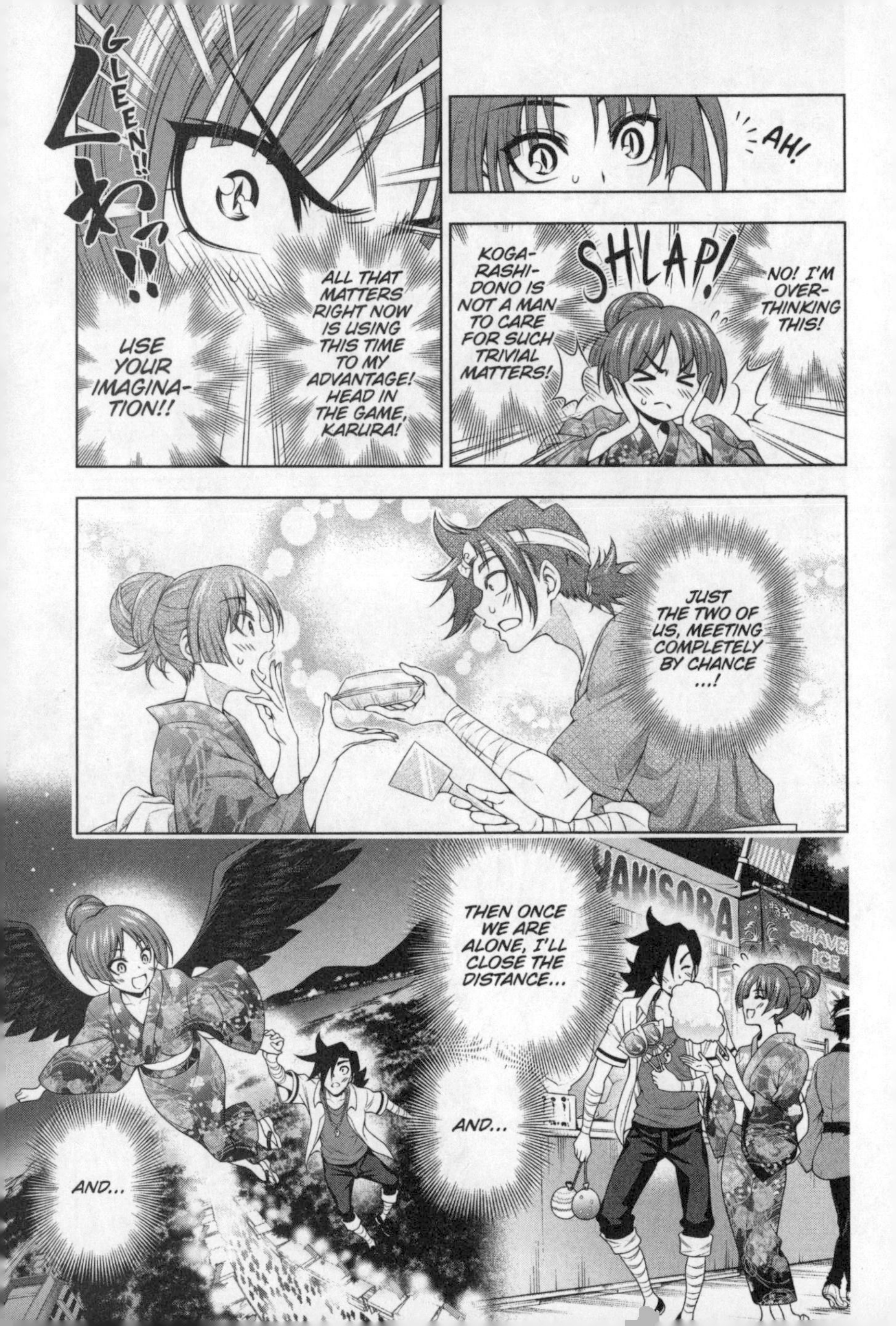
AH!
NO! I'M OVER-THINKING THIS!
SHLAP!
KOGA-RASHI-DONO IS NOT A MAN TO CARE FOR SUCH TRIVIAL MATTERS!
GLEEN!!
ALL THAT MATTERS RIGHT NOW IS USING THIS TIME TO MY ADVANTAGE! HEAD IN THE GAME, KARURA!
USE YOUR IMAGINA-TION!!
JUST THE TWO OF US, MEETING COMPLETELY BY CHANCE ...!
YAKISOBA
SHAVE ICE
THEN ONCE WE ARE ALONE, I'LL CLOSE THE DISTANCE...
AND...
AND...

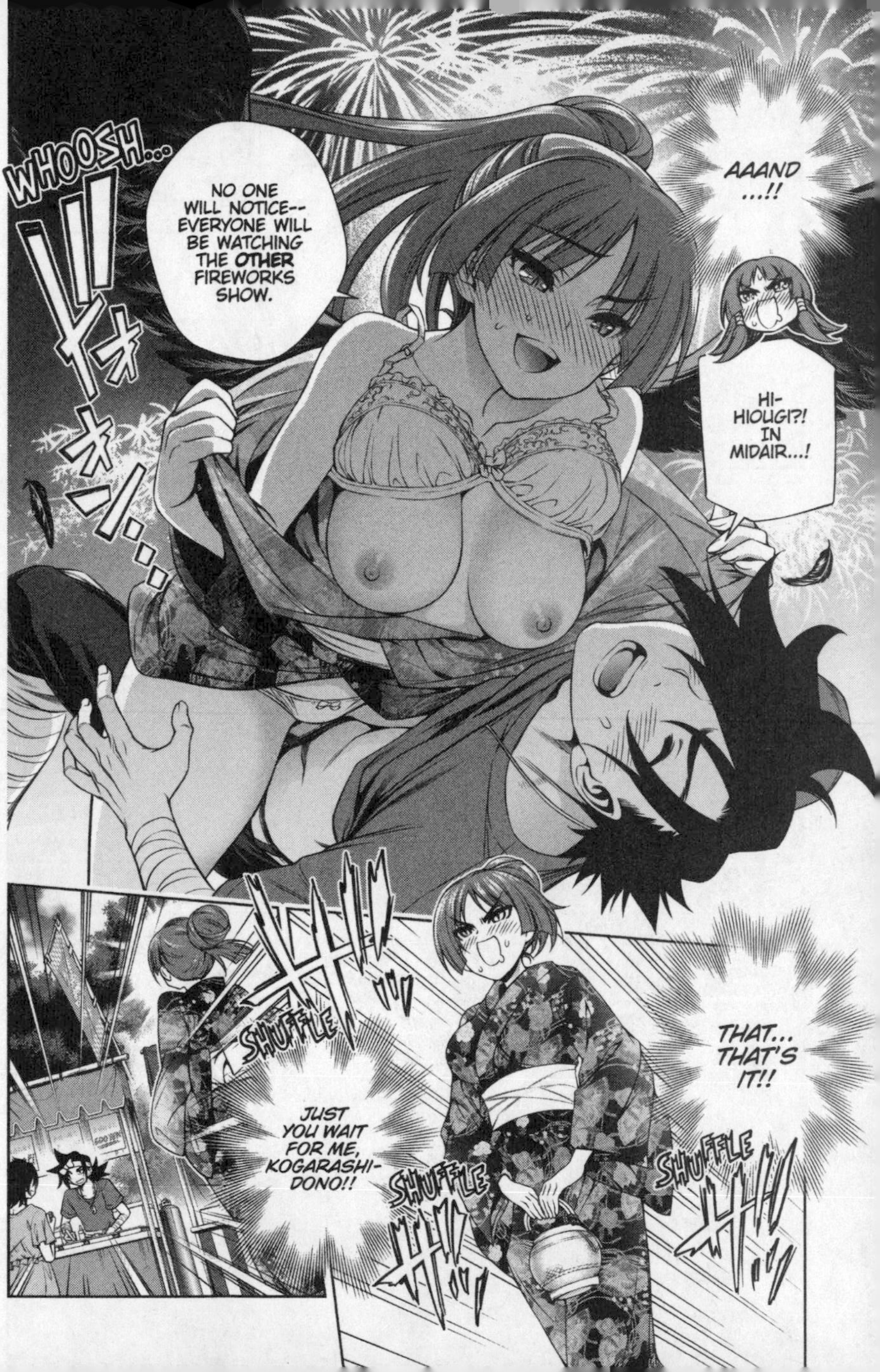
AAAND ...!!
HI-HIOUGI?! IN MIDAIR...!
NO ONE WILL NOTICE-- EVERYONE WILL BE WATCHING THE **OTHER** FIREWORKS SHOW.
WHOOSH...
THAT... THAT'S IT!!
SHUFFLE
JUST YOU WAIT FOR ME, KOGARASHI-DONO!!
SHUFFLE
SHUFFLE

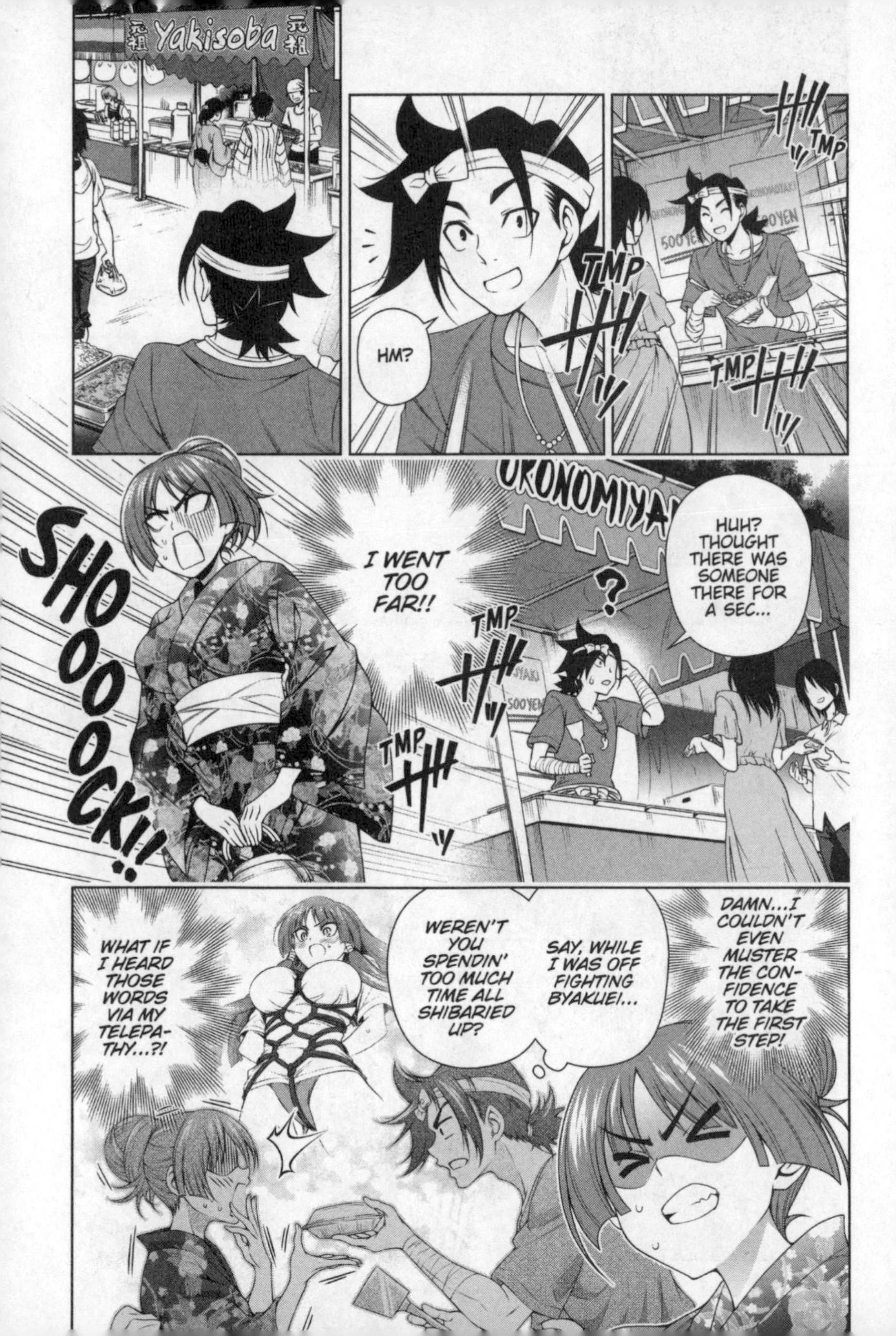
TMP
TMP
TMP
HM?
元祖 Yakisoba 元祖
OKONOMIYA
HUH? THOUGHT THERE WAS SOMEONE THERE FOR A SEC...
?
TMP
TMP
I WENT TOO FAR!!
SHOOOOCK!!
DAMN...I COULDN'T EVEN MUSTER THE CON-FIDENCE TO TAKE THE FIRST STEP!
SAY, WHILE I WAS OFF FIGHTING BYAKUEI...
WEREN'T YOU SPENDIN' TOO MUCH TIME ALL SHIBARIED UP?
WHAT IF I HEARD THOSE WORDS VIA MY TELEPA-THY...?!

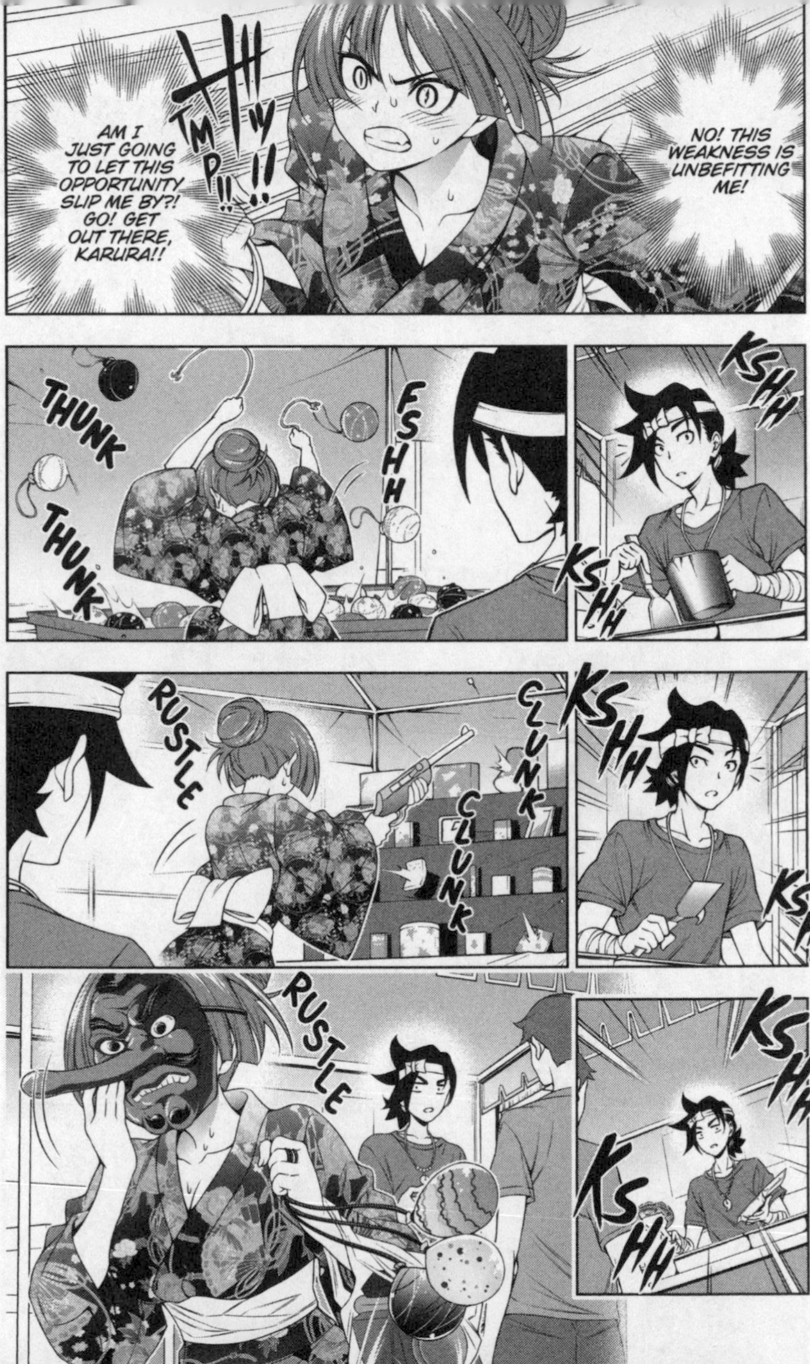
NO! THIS WEAKNESS IS UNBEFITTING ME!
TMP!!
AM I JUST GOING TO LET THIS OPPORTUNITY SLIP ME BY?! GO! GET OUT THERE, KARURA!!
KSHH
KSHH
FSHH
THUNK
THUNK
KSHH
KSHH
CLUNK
CLUNK
RUSTLE
KSHH
KSHH
RUSTLE

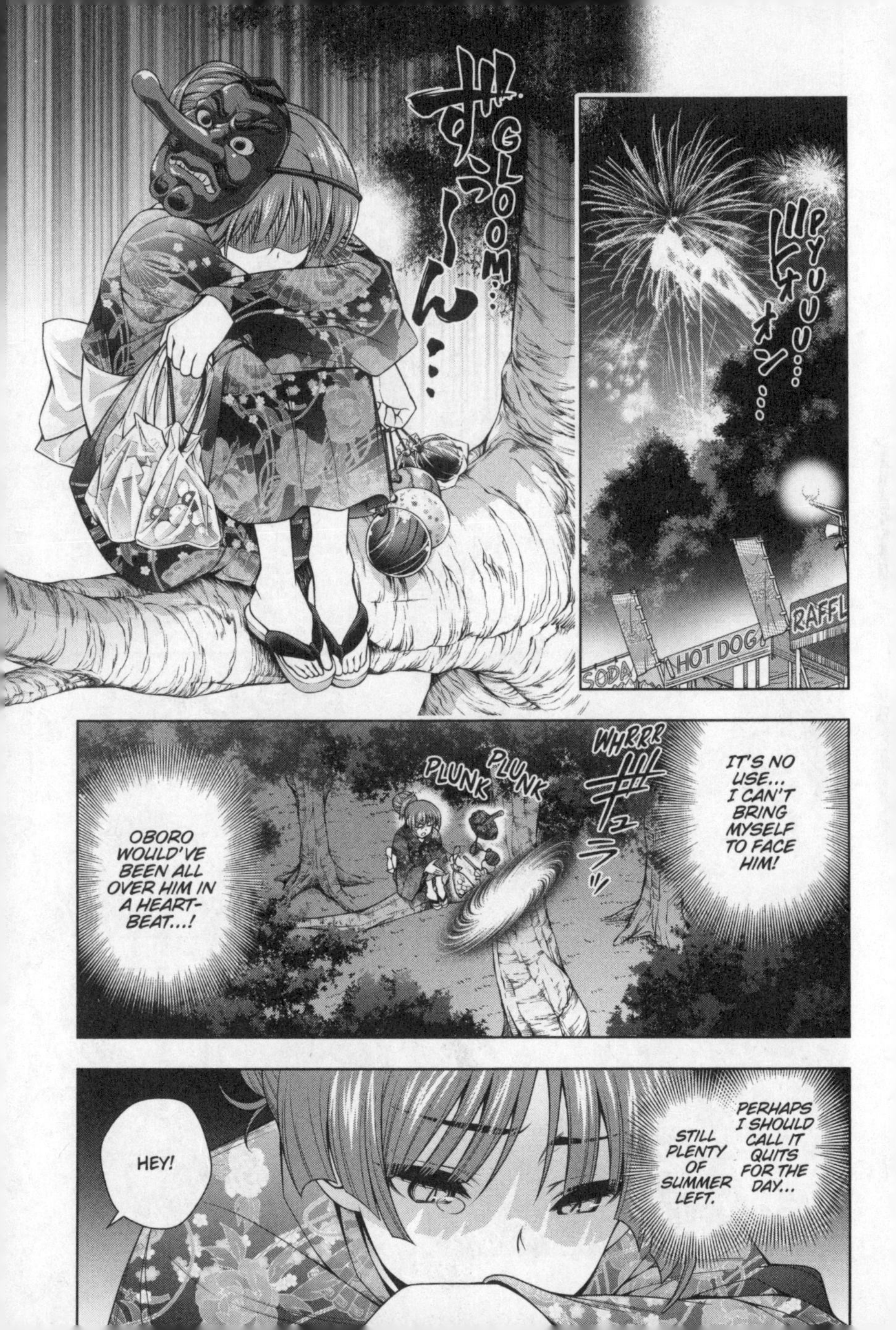
PYUUU...
ヒュォオン...
RAFFL
HOT DOG
SODA
GLOOM...
ずう～ん...
IT'S NO USE... I CAN'T BRING MYSELF TO FACE HIM!
WHRRR
PLUNK
PLUNK
OBORO WOULD'VE BEEN ALL OVER HIM IN A HEART-BEAT...!
PERHAPS I SHOULD CALL IT QUITS FOR THE DAY...
STILL PLENTY OF SUMMER LEFT.
HEY!

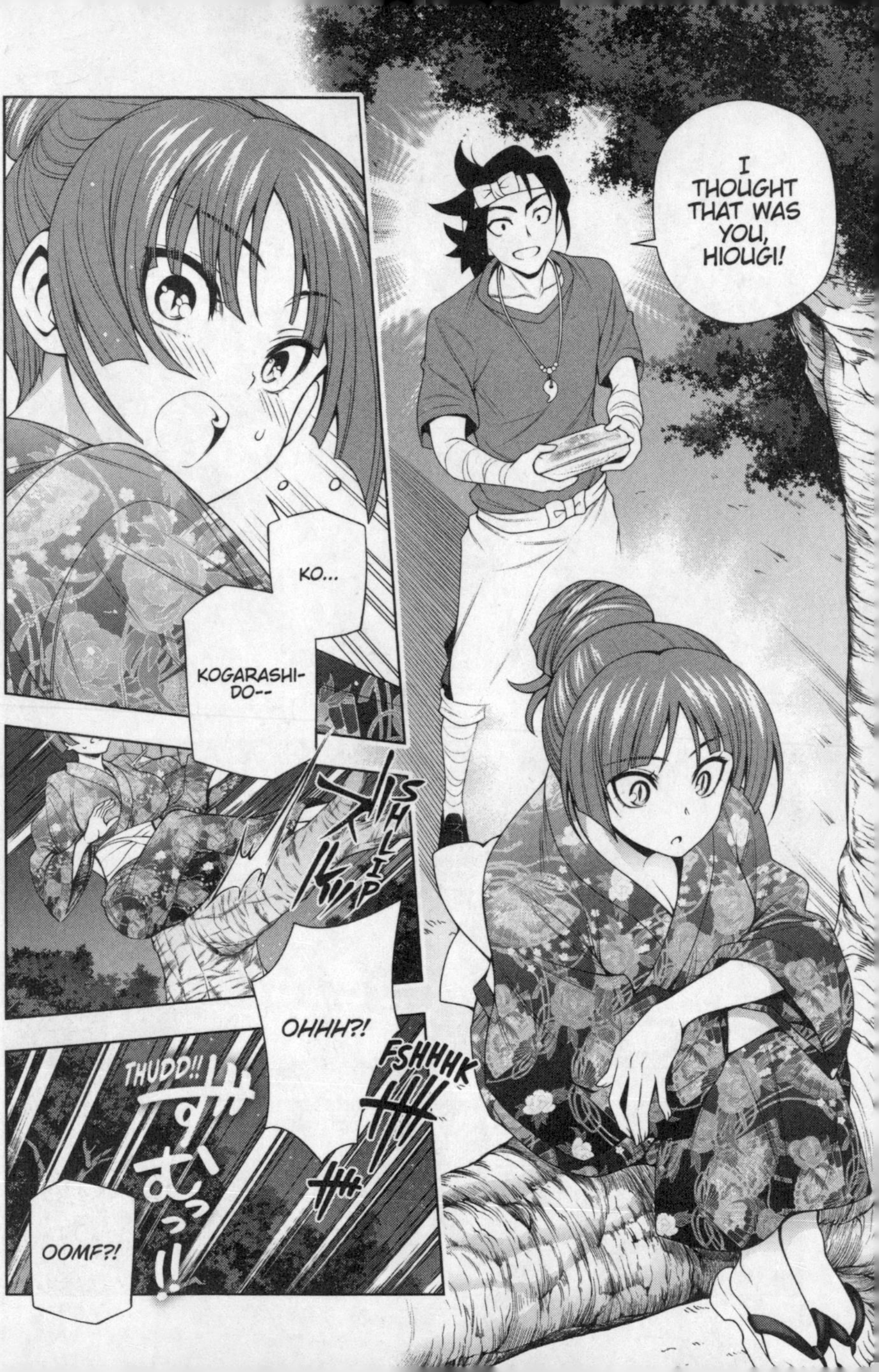
I THOUGHT THAT WAS YOU, HIOUGI!
KO...
KOGARASHI-DO--
SHLIP
OHHH?!
FSHHHK
THUDD!!
OOMF?!

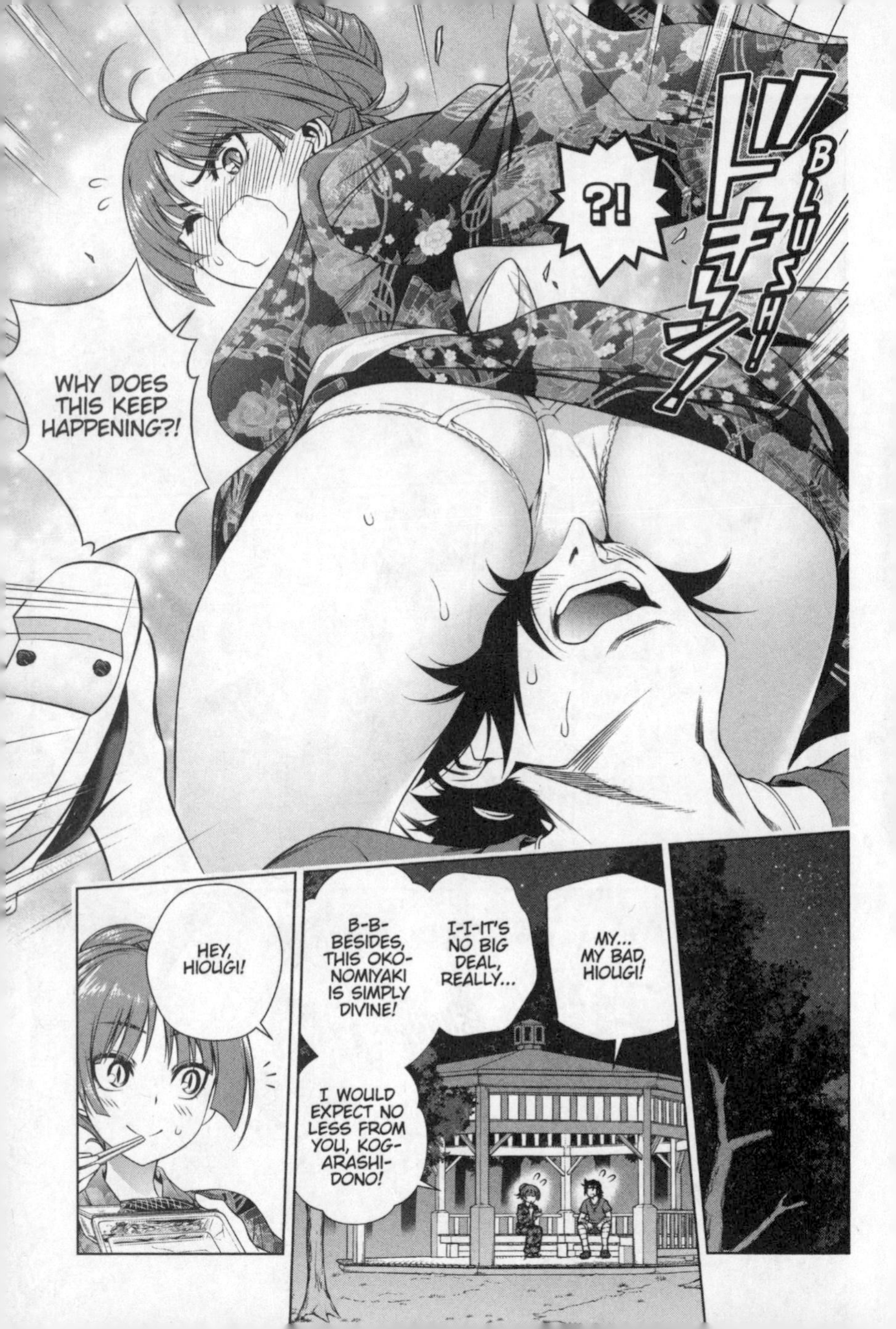
BLUSH!
?!
WHY DOES THIS KEEP HAPPENING?!
MY... MY BAD, HIOUGI!
I-I-IT'S NO BIG DEAL, REALLY...
B-B-BESIDES, THIS OKO-NOMIYAKI IS SIMPLY DIVINE!
I WOULD EXPECT NO LESS FROM YOU, KOG-ARASHI-DONO!
HEY, HIOUGI!

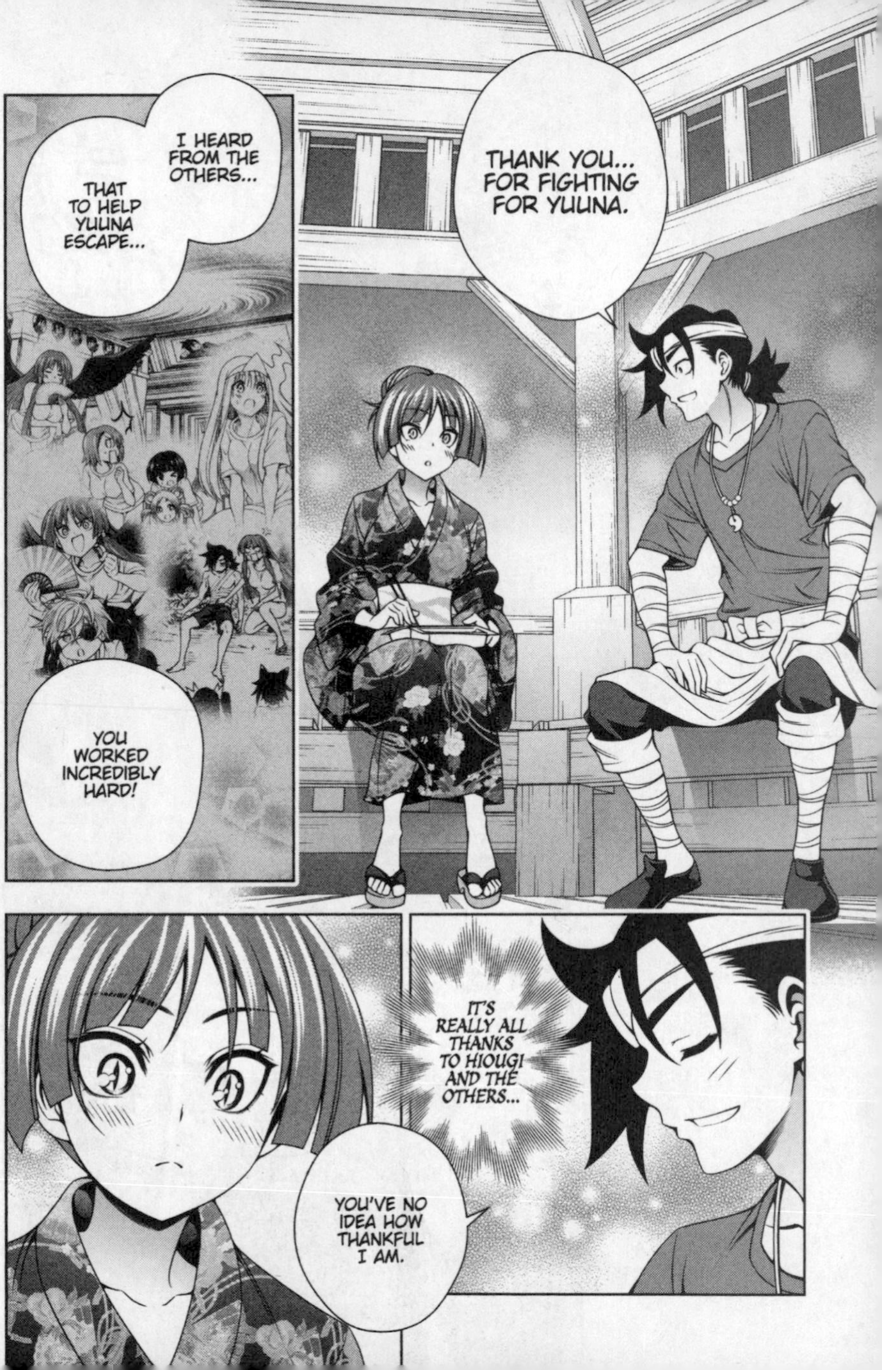
THANK YOU... FOR FIGHTING FOR YUUNA.
I HEARD FROM THE OTHERS...
THAT TO HELP YUUNA ESCAPE...
YOU WORKED INCREDIBLY HARD!
IT'S REALLY ALL THANKS TO HIOUGI AND THE OTHERS...
YOU'VE NO IDEA HOW THANKFUL I AM.

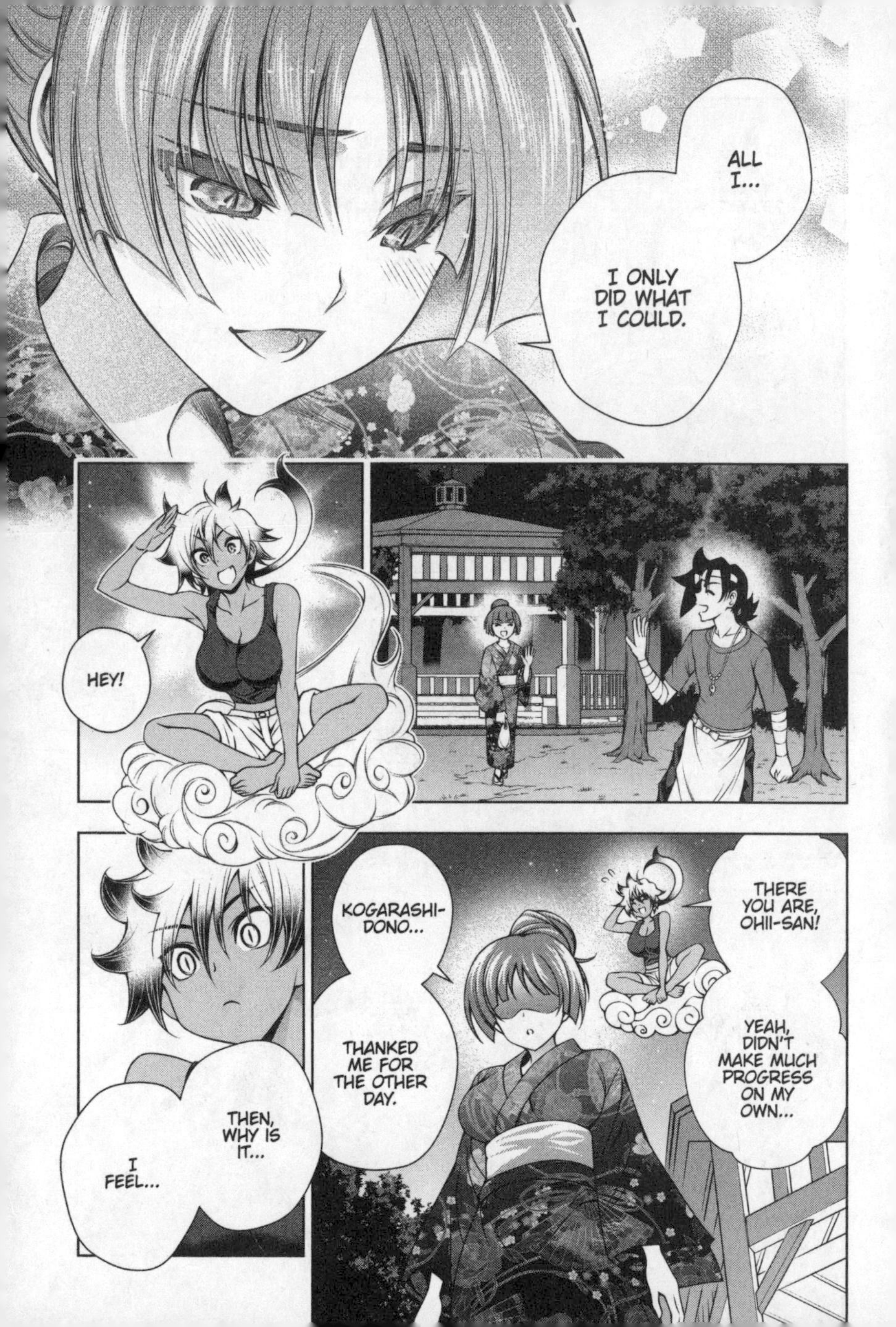
ALL I...
I ONLY DID WHAT I COULD.
HEY!
THERE YOU ARE, OHII-SAN!
YEAH, DIDN'T MAKE MUCH PROGRESS ON MY OWN...
KOGARASHI-DONO...
THANKED ME FOR THE OTHER DAY.
THEN, WHY IS IT...
I FEEL...

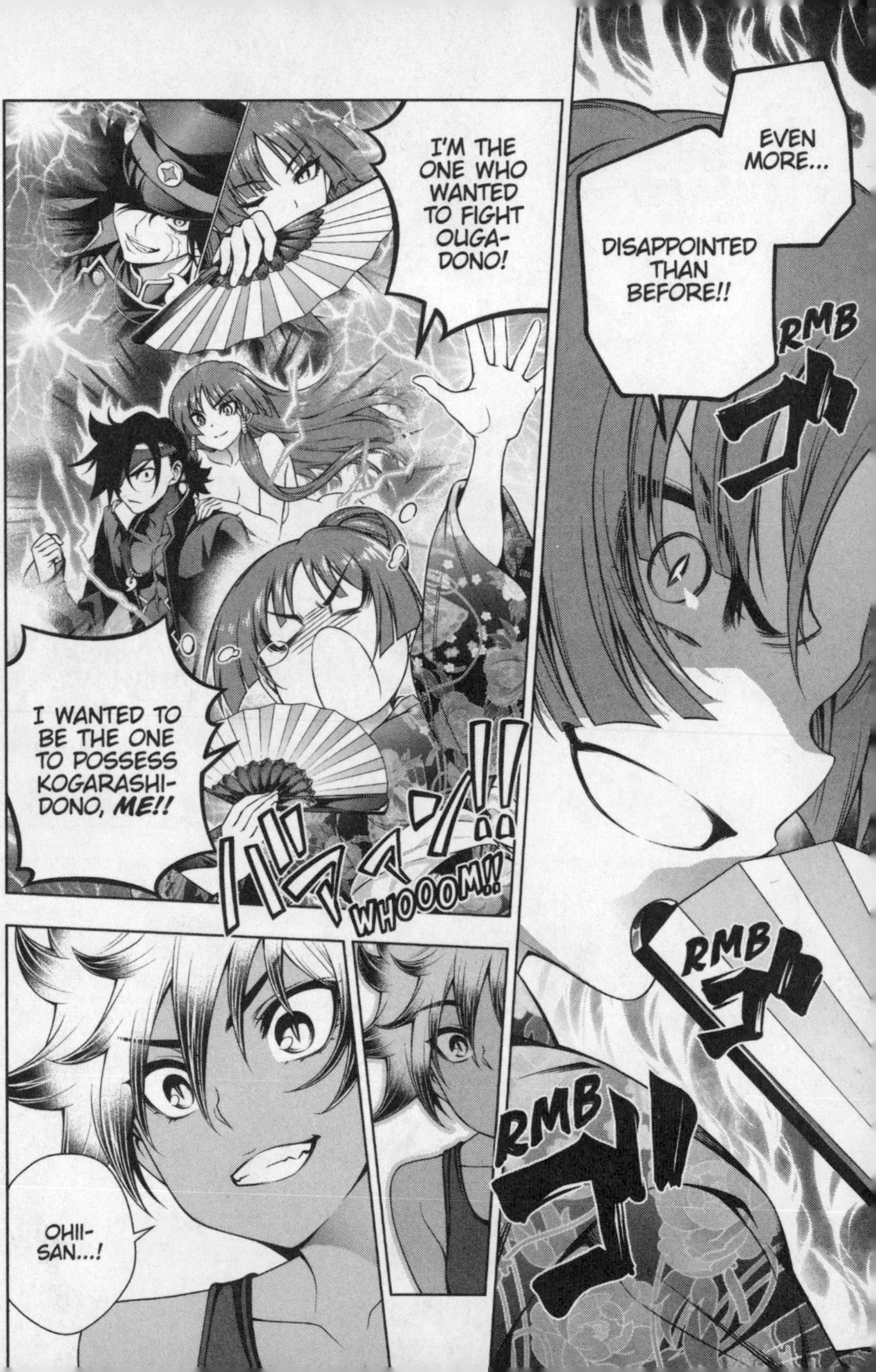
EVEN MORE...
DISAPPOINTED THAN BEFORE!!
RMB
RMB
RMB
I'M THE ONE WHO WANTED TO FIGHT OUGA-DONO!
I WANTED TO BE THE ONE TO POSSESS KOGARASHI-DONO, ME!!
WHOOOM!!
OHII-SAN...!

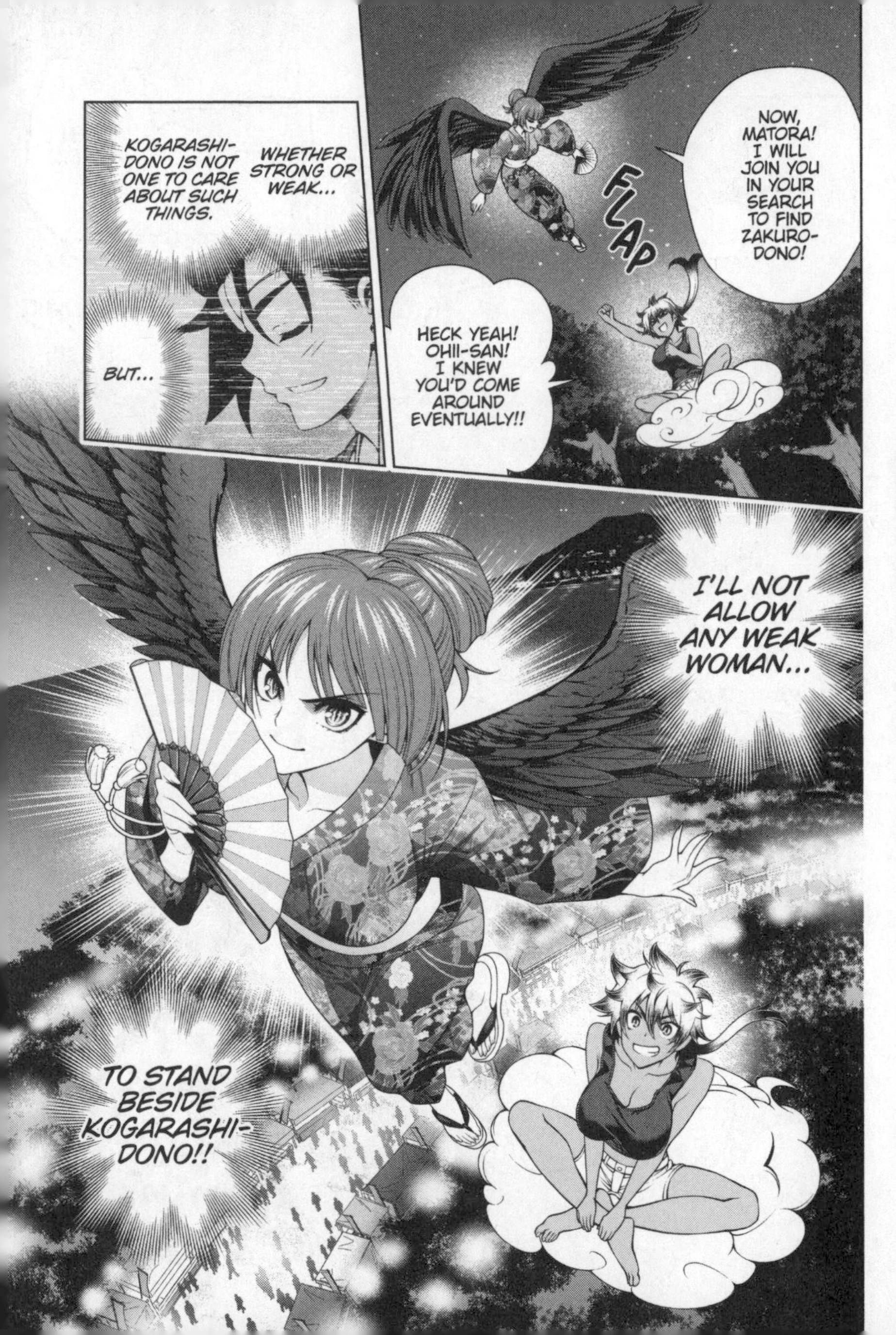
NOW, MATORA! I WILL JOIN YOU IN YOUR SEARCH TO FIND ZAKURO-DONO!
FLAP
HECK YEAH! OHII-SAN! I KNEW YOU'D COME AROUND EVENTUALLY!!
WHETHER STRONG OR WEAK...
KOGARASHI-DONO IS NOT ONE TO CARE ABOUT SUCH THINGS.
BUT...
I'LL NOT ALLOW ANY WEAK WOMAN...
TO STAND BESIDE KOGARASHI-DONO!!

Yuuna and the Haunted Hot Springs

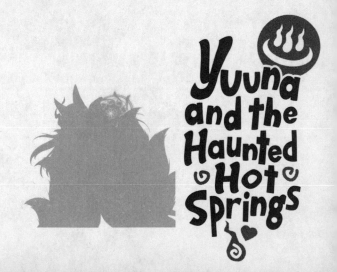

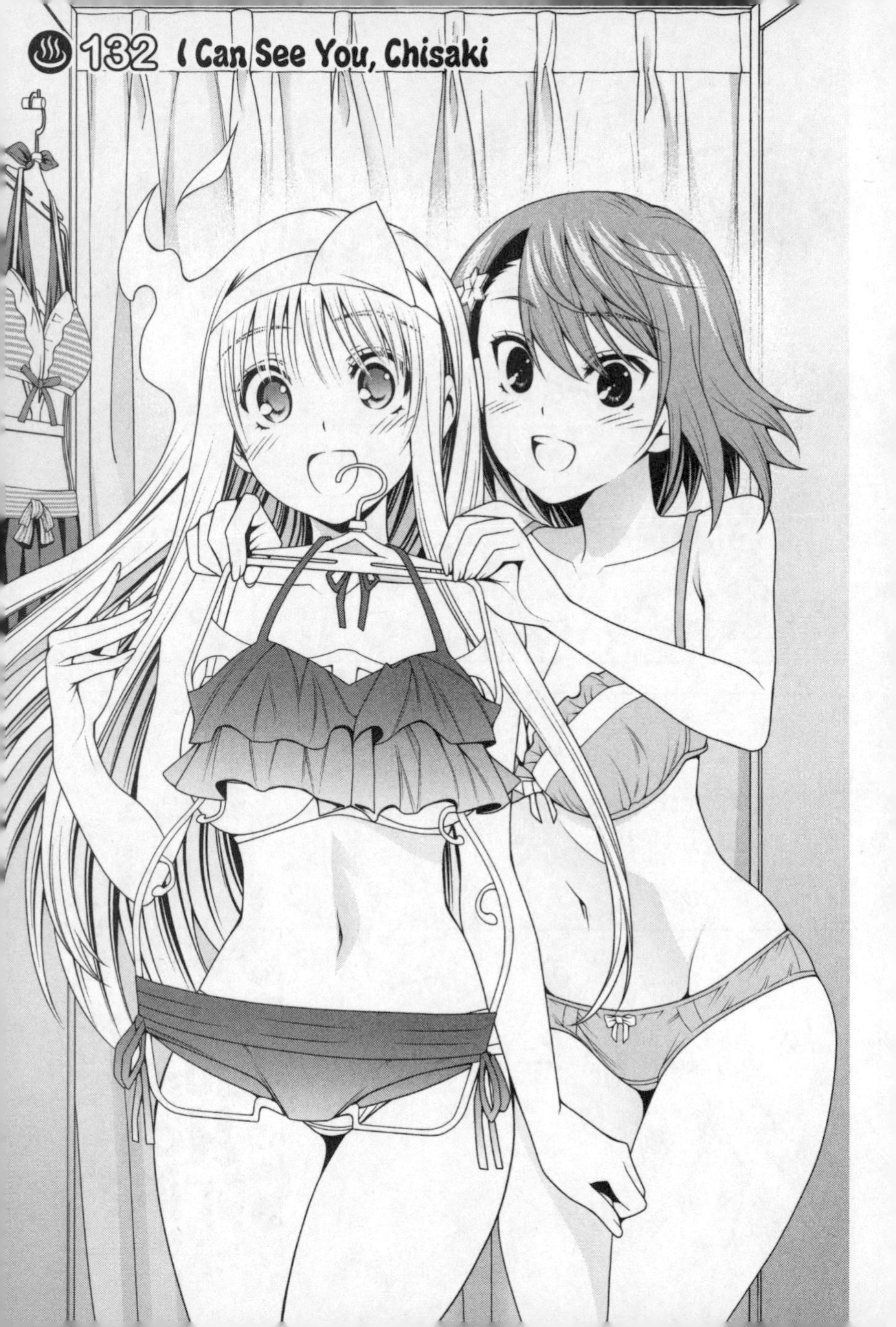
132 I Can See You, Chisaki

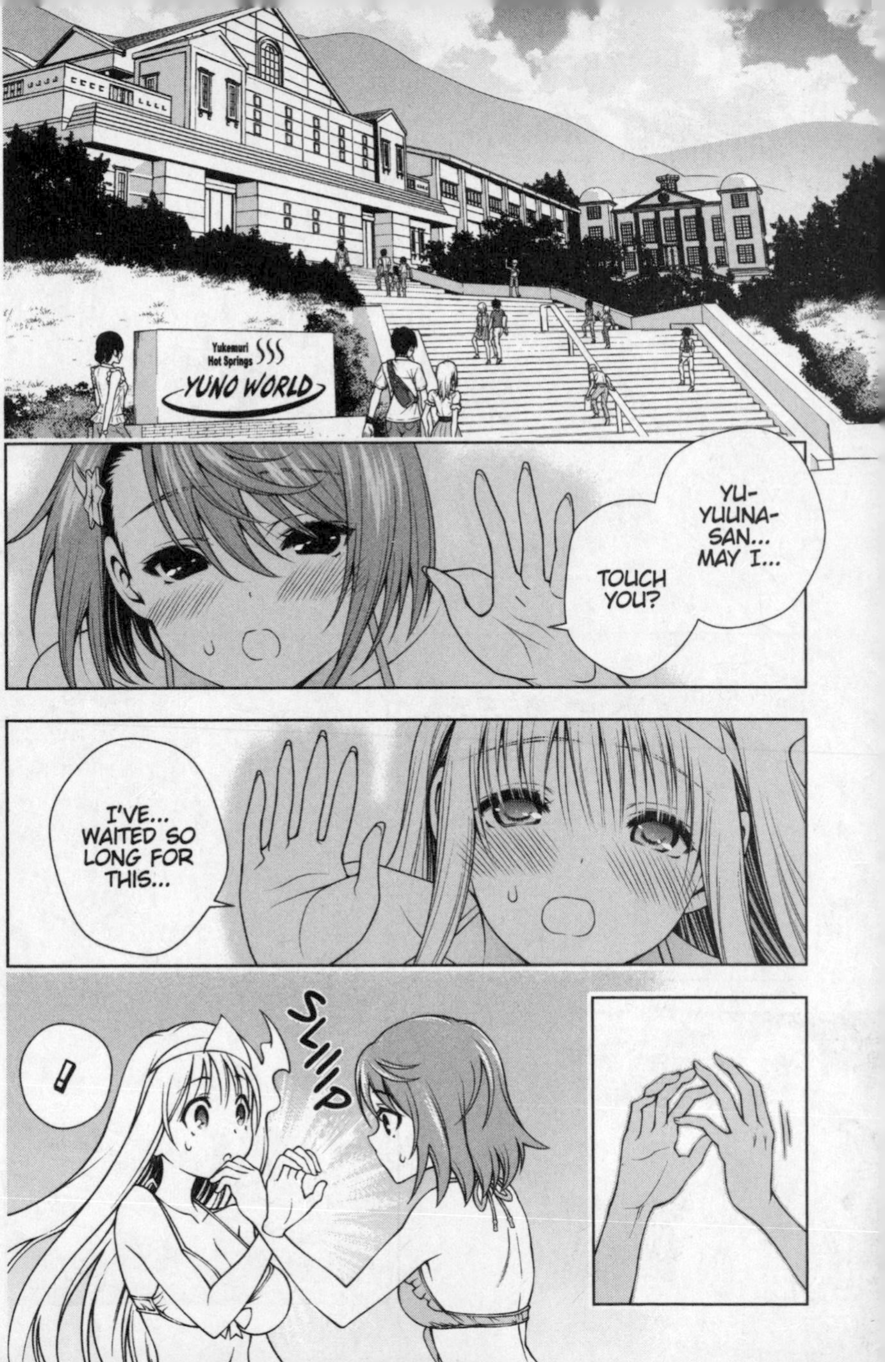
Yukemuri Hot Springs
YUNO WORLD
YU-YUUNA-SAN... MAY I...
TOUCH YOU?
I'VE... WAITED SO LONG FOR THIS...
SLIIIP
!

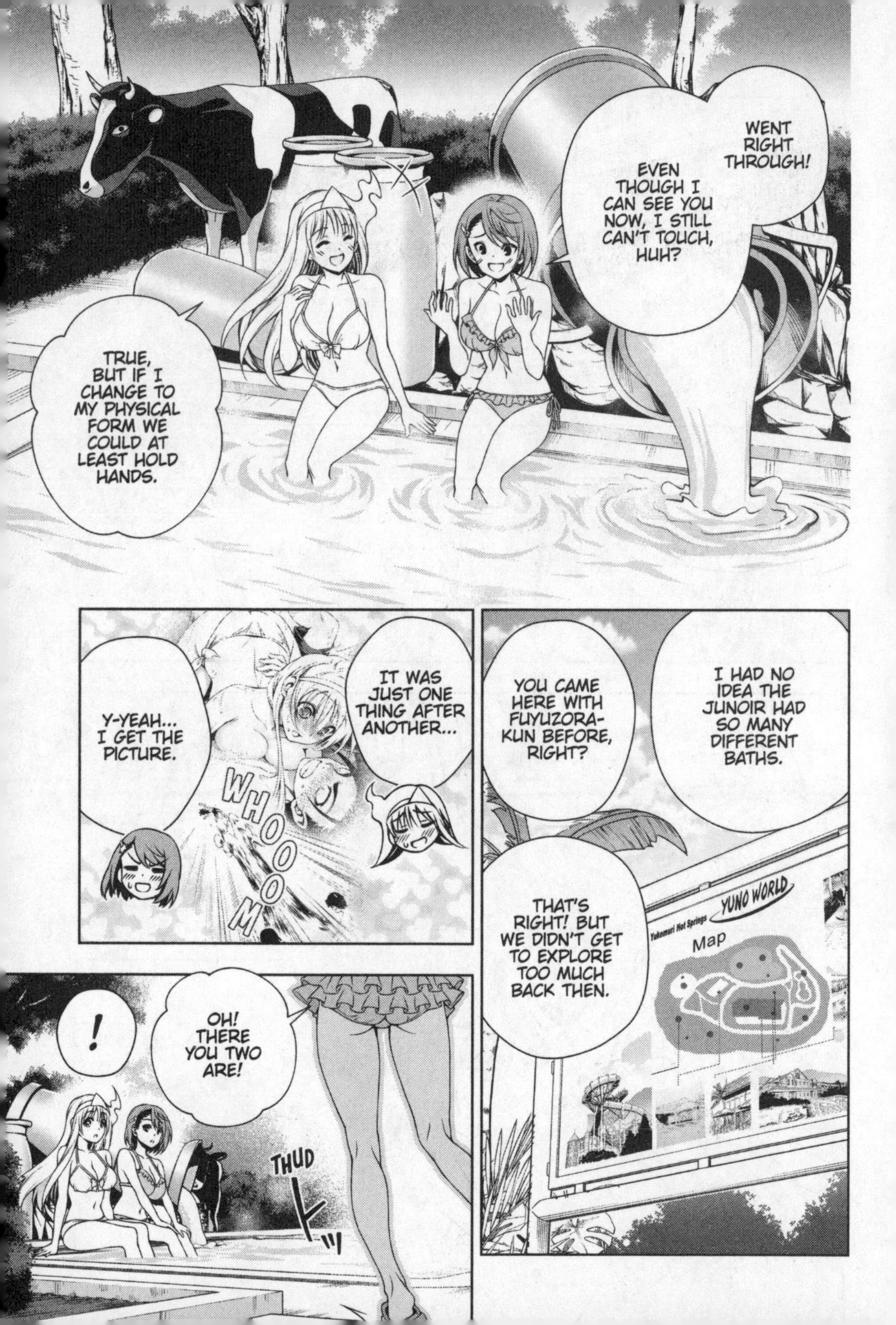
WENT RIGHT THROUGH!
EVEN THOUGH I CAN SEE YOU NOW, I STILL CAN'T TOUCH, HUH?
TRUE, BUT IF I CHANGE TO MY PHYSICAL FORM WE COULD AT LEAST HOLD HANDS.
I HAD NO IDEA THE JUNOIR HAD SO MANY DIFFERENT BATHS.
YOU CAME HERE WITH FUYUZORA-KUN BEFORE, RIGHT?
THAT'S RIGHT! BUT WE DIDN'T GET TO EXPLORE TOO MUCH BACK THEN.
Yukemuri Hot Springs
YUNO WORLD
Map
IT WAS JUST ONE THING AFTER ANOTHER...
Y-YEAH... I GET THE PICTURE.
WHOOOOM
OH! THERE YOU TWO ARE!
!
THUD

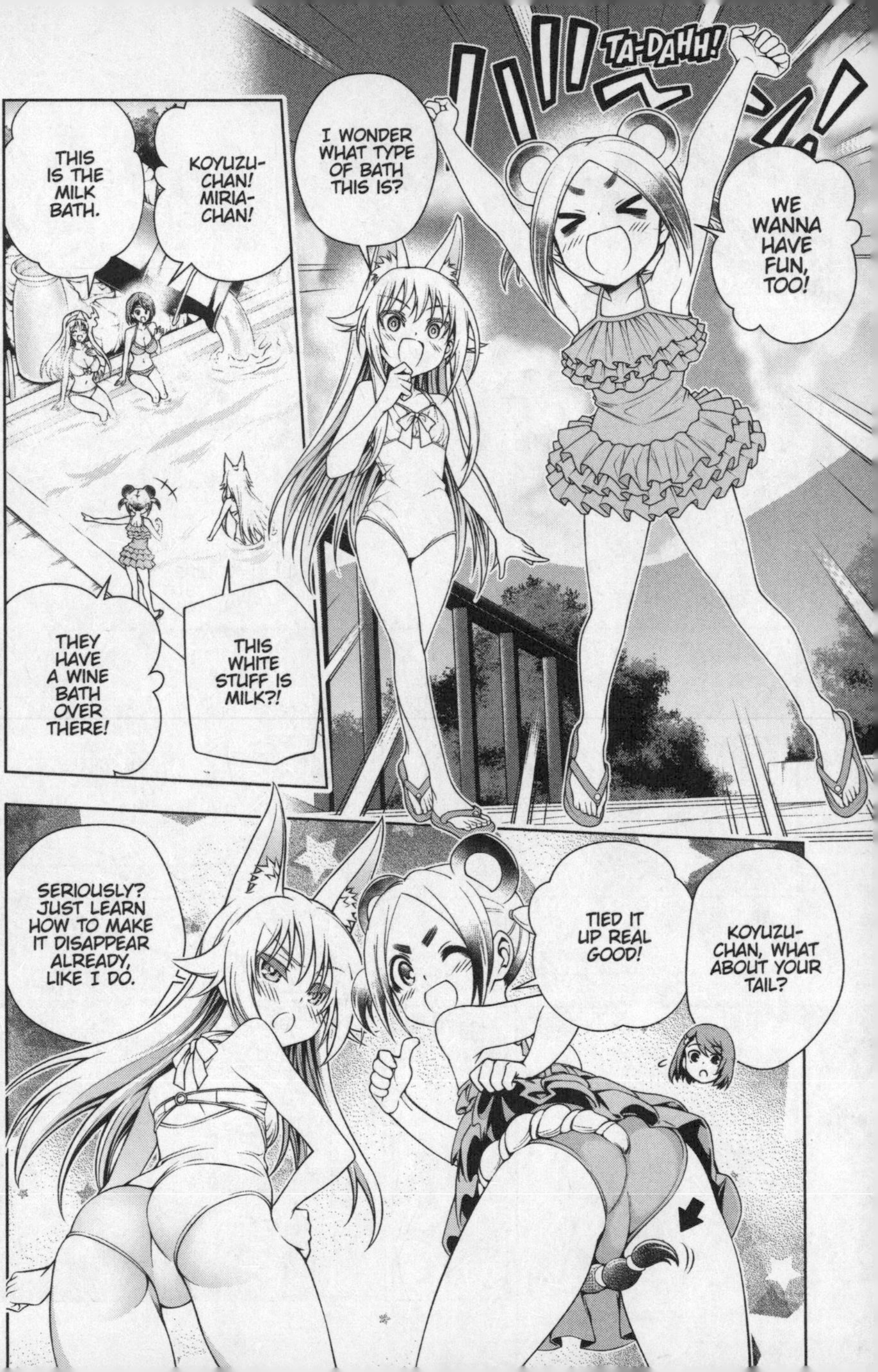
TA-DAHH!
WE WANNA HAVE FUN, TOO!
I WONDER WHAT TYPE OF BATH THIS IS?
KOYUZU-CHAN! MIRIA-CHAN!
THIS IS THE MILK BATH.
THIS WHITE STUFF IS MILK?!
THEY HAVE A WINE BATH OVER THERE!
KOYUZU-CHAN, WHAT ABOUT YOUR TAIL?
TIED IT UP REAL GOOD!
SERIOUSLY? JUST LEARN HOW TO MAKE IT DISAPPEAR ALREADY, LIKE I DO.

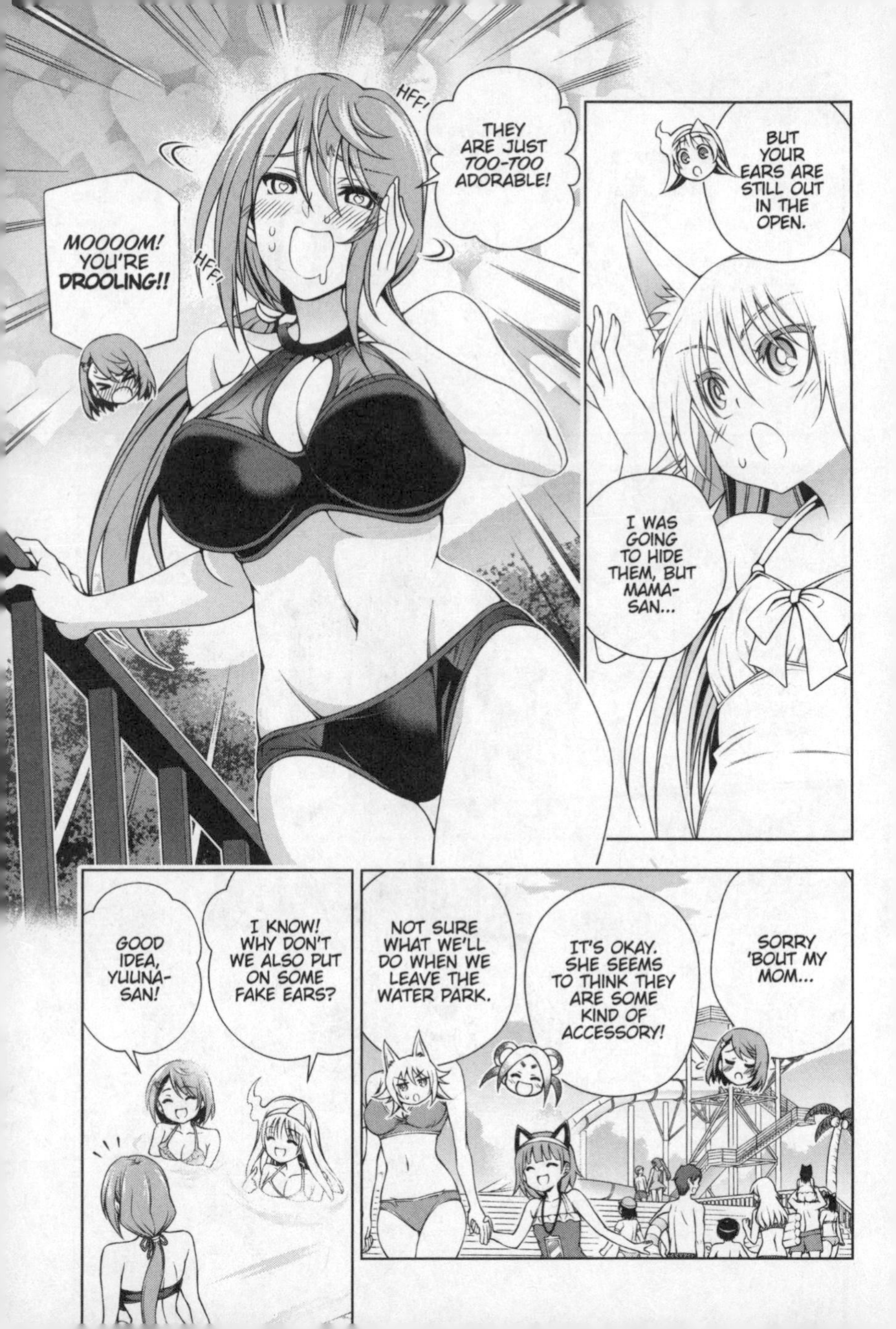
BUT YOUR EARS ARE STILL OUT IN THE OPEN.
I WAS GOING TO HIDE THEM, BUT MAMA-SAN...
HFF!
THEY ARE JUST *TOO-TOO* ADORABLE!
HFF!
MOOOOM! YOU'RE **DROOLING!!**
SORRY 'BOUT MY MOM...
IT'S OKAY. SHE SEEMS TO THINK THEY ARE SOME KIND OF ACCESSORY!
NOT SURE WHAT WE'LL DO WHEN WE LEAVE THE WATER PARK.
I KNOW! WHY DON'T WE ALSO PUT ON SOME FAKE EARS?
GOOD IDEA, YUUNA-SAN!

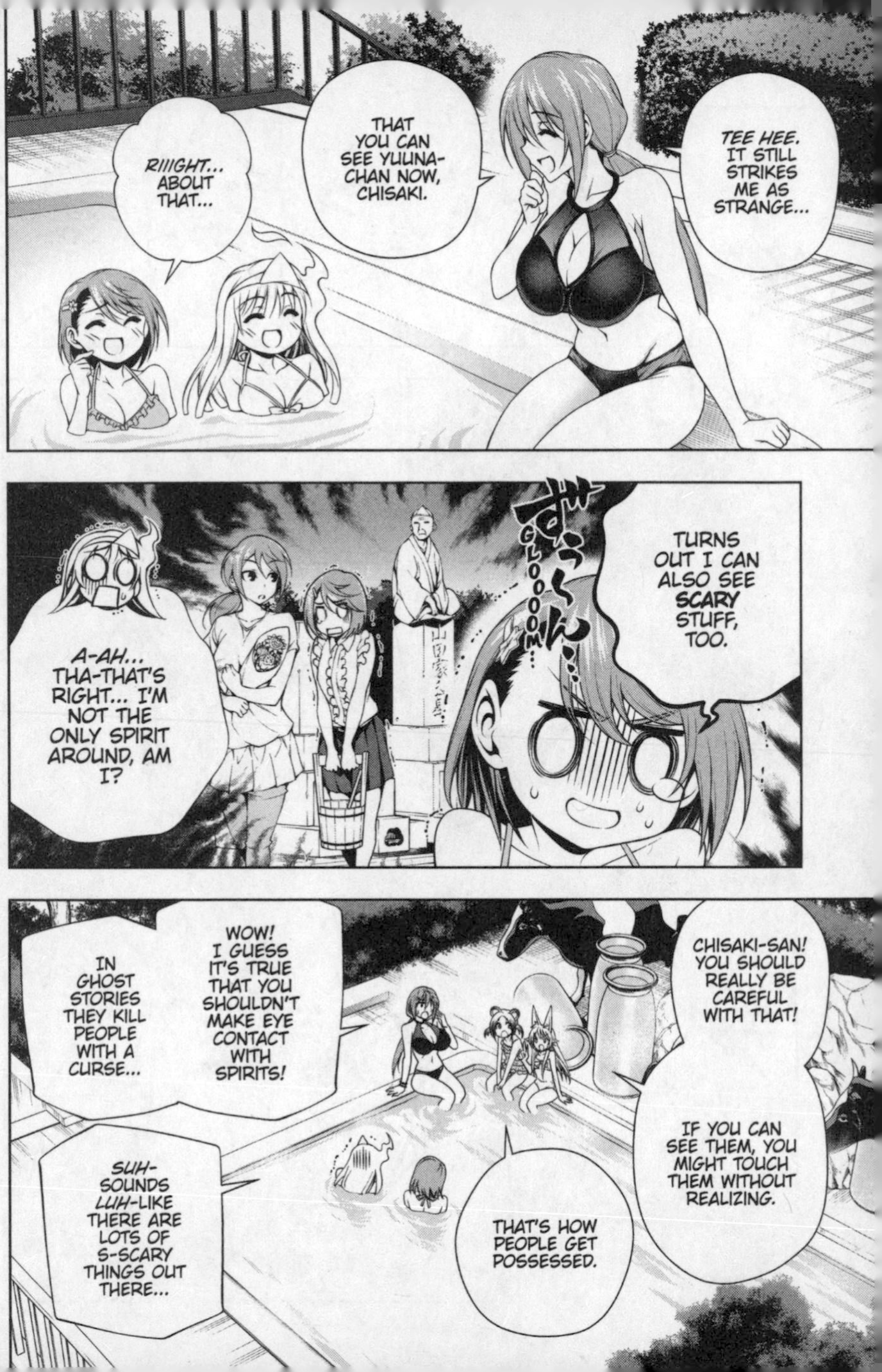
TEE HEE. IT STILL STRIKES ME AS STRANGE...
THAT YOU CAN SEE YUUNA-CHAN NOW, CHISAKI.
RIIIGHT... ABOUT THAT...
GLOOOOOM
TURNS OUT I CAN ALSO SEE **SCARY** STUFF, TOO.
A-AH... THA-THAT'S RIGHT... I'M NOT THE ONLY SPIRIT AROUND, AM I?
CHISAKI-SAN! YOU SHOULD REALLY BE CAREFUL WITH THAT!
IF YOU CAN SEE THEM, YOU MIGHT TOUCH THEM WITHOUT REALIZING.
THAT'S HOW PEOPLE GET POSSESSED.
WOW! I GUESS IT'S TRUE THAT YOU SHOULDN'T MAKE EYE CONTACT WITH SPIRITS!
IN GHOST STORIES THEY KILL PEOPLE WITH A CURSE...
SUH- SOUNDS *LUH-*LIKE THERE ARE LOTS OF S-SCARY THINGS OUT THERE...

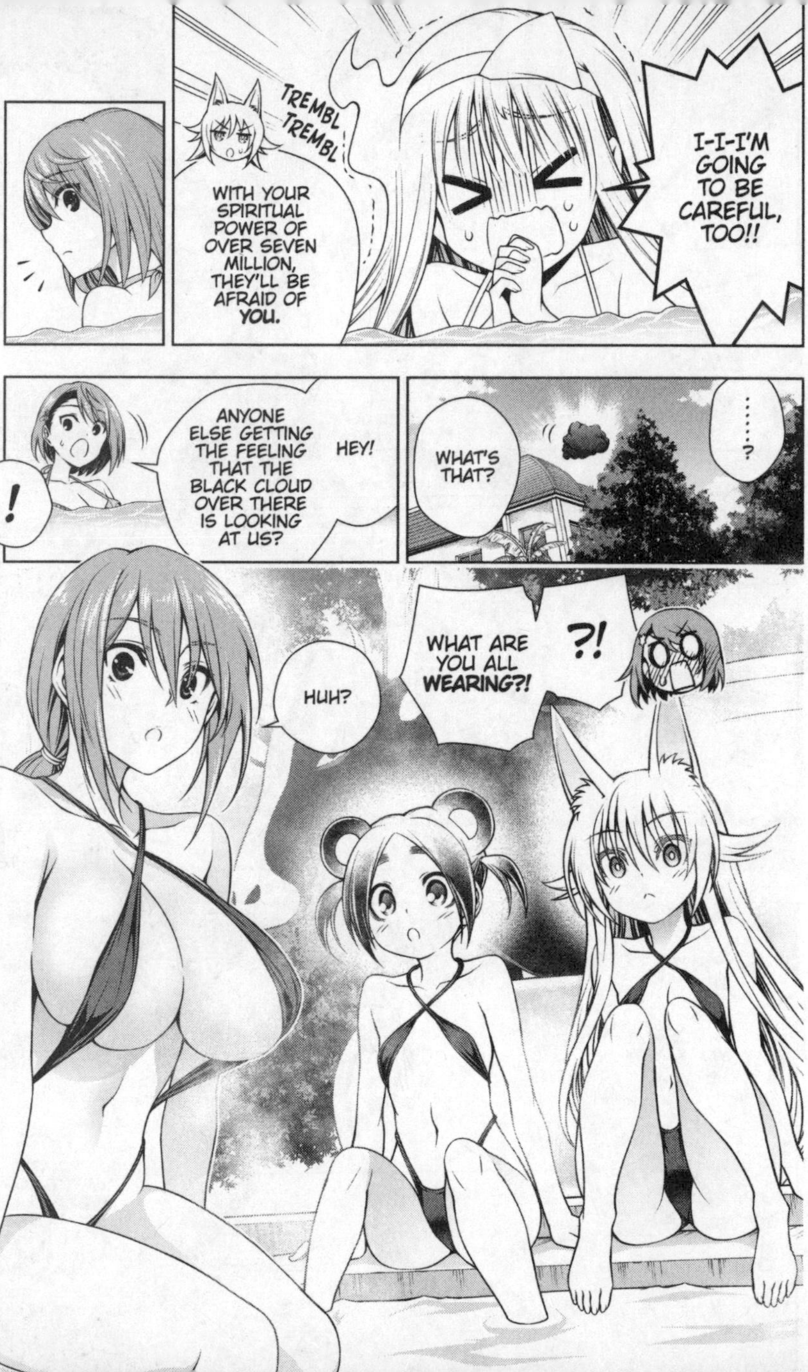
I-I-I'M GOING TO BE CAREFUL, TOO!!
TREMBL TREMBL
WITH YOUR SPIRITUAL POWER OF OVER SEVEN MILLION, THEY'LL BE AFRAID OF YOU.
......?
WHAT'S THAT?
HEY!
ANYONE ELSE GETTING THE FEELING THAT THE BLACK CLOUD OVER THERE IS LOOKING AT US?
!
?!
WHAT ARE YOU ALL WEARING?!
HUH?

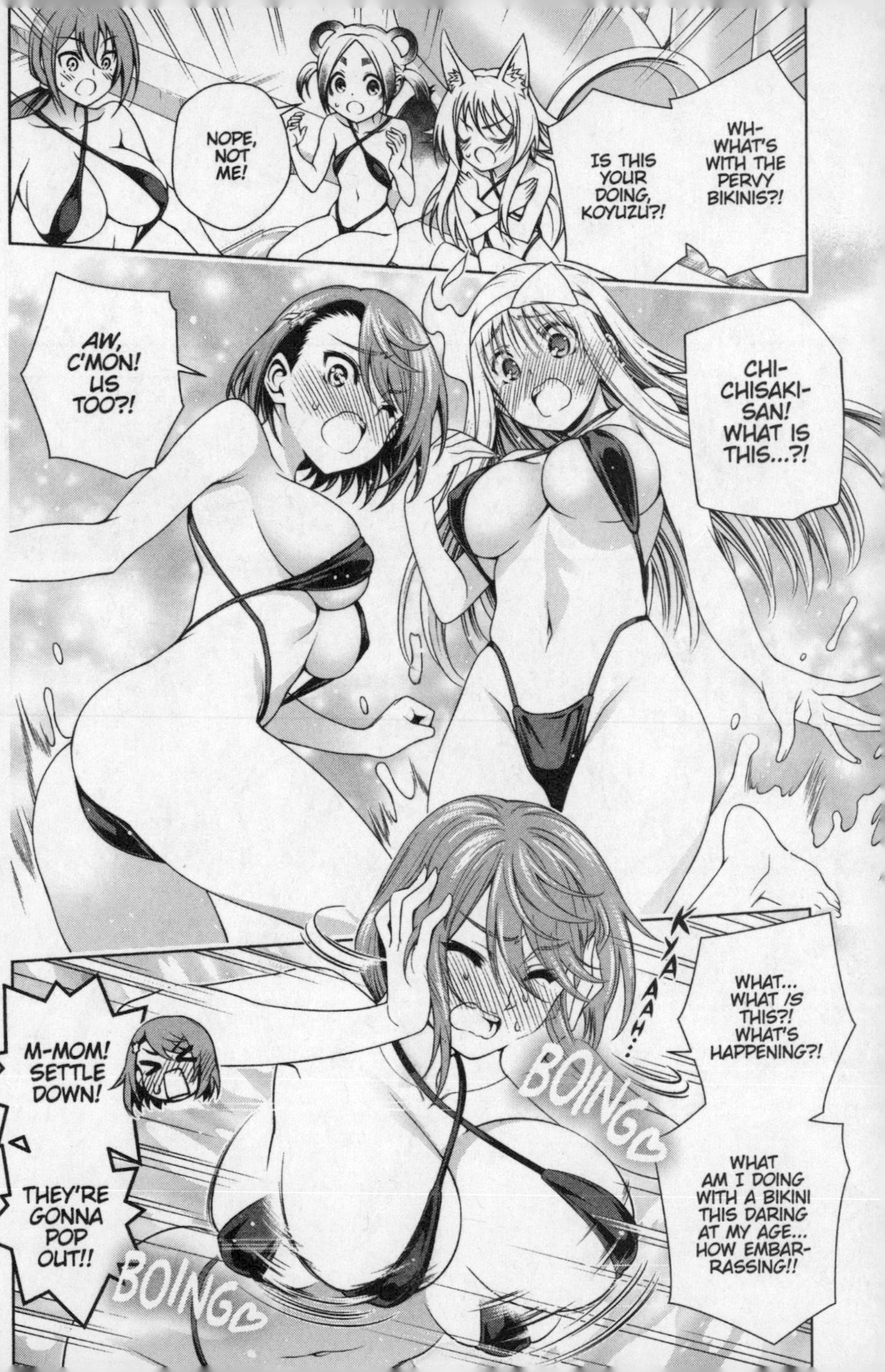
WH-WHAT'S WITH THE PERVY BIKINIS?!
IS THIS YOUR DOING, KOYUZU?!
NOPE, NOT ME!
CHI-CHISAKI-SAN! WHAT IS THIS...?!
AW, C'MON! US TOO?!
KYAAAH...
WHAT... WHAT IS THIS?! WHAT'S HAPPENING?!
BOING
WHAT AM I DOING WITH A BIKINI THIS DARING AT MY AGE... HOW EMBARRASSING!!
M-MOM! SETTLE DOWN!
THEY'RE GONNA POP OUT!!
BOING

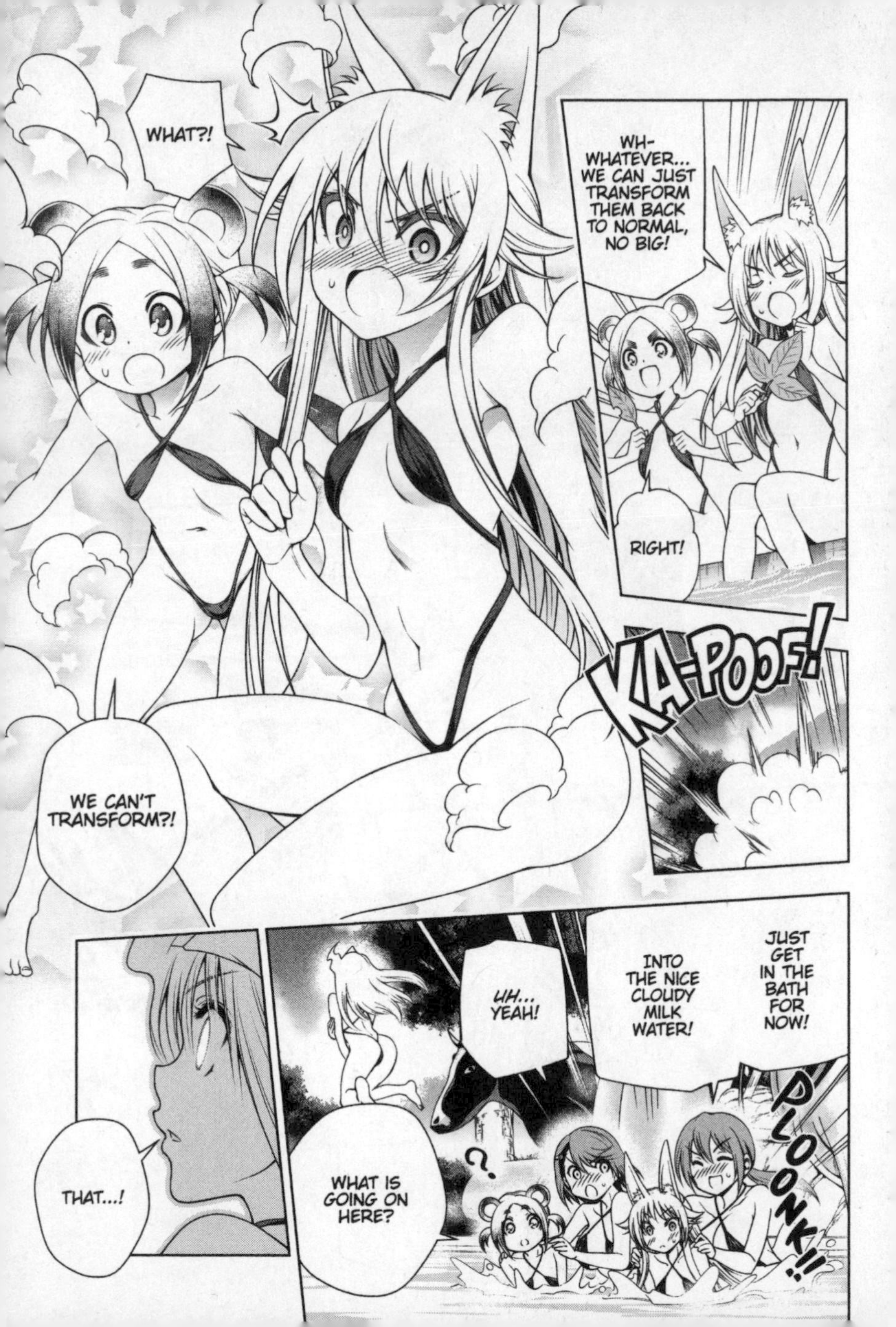
WH- WHATEVER... WE CAN JUST TRANSFORM THEM BACK TO NORMAL, NO BIG!
RIGHT!
KA-POOF!
WHAT?!
WE CAN'T TRANSFORM?!
JUST GET IN THE BATH FOR NOW!
INTO THE NICE CLOUDY MILK WATER!
UH... YEAH!
PLOONK!!
?
WHAT IS GOING ON HERE?
THAT...!

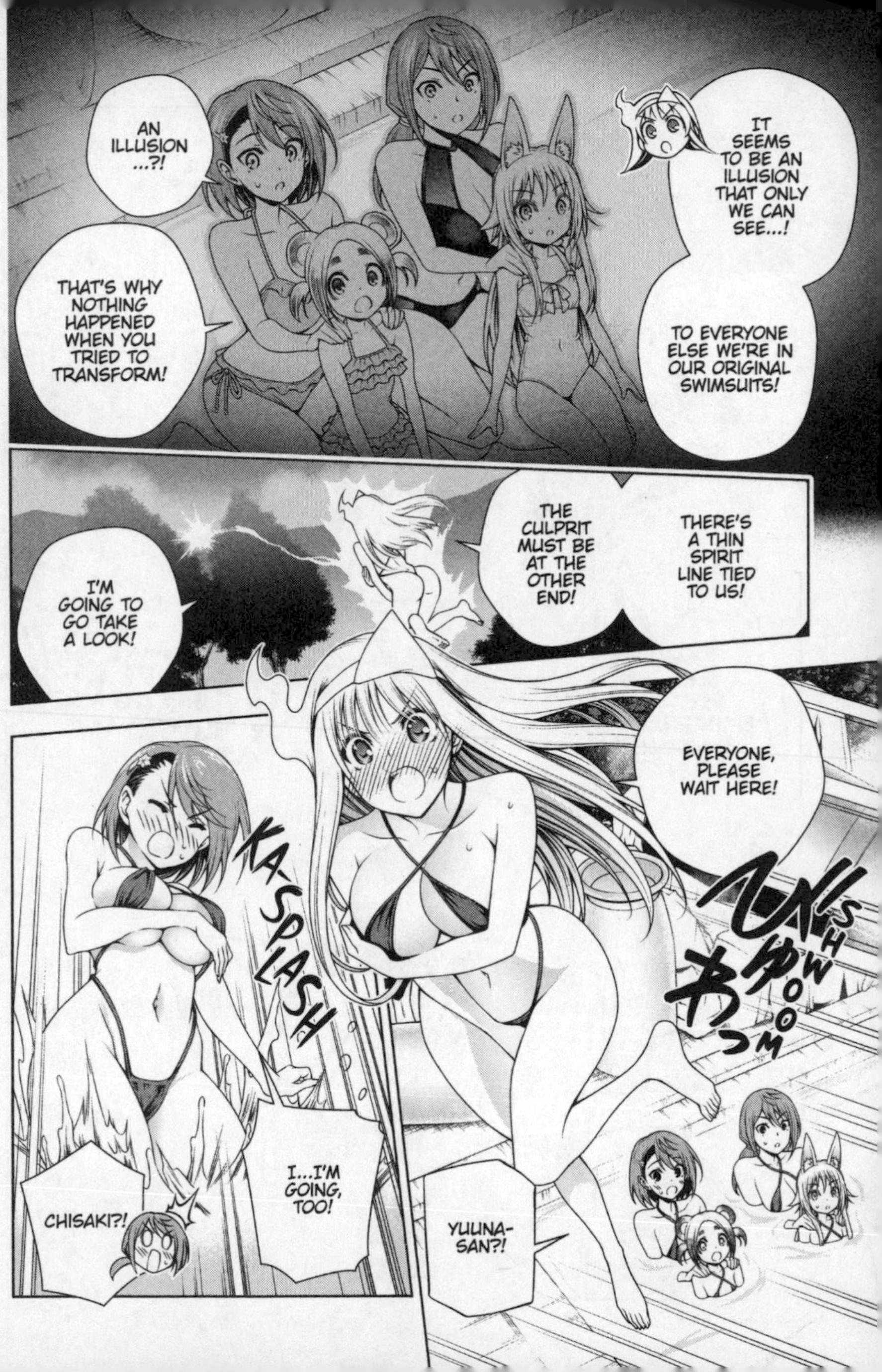
IT SEEMS TO BE AN ILLUSION THAT ONLY WE CAN SEE...!
TO EVERYONE ELSE WE'RE IN OUR ORIGINAL SWIMSUITS!
AN ILLUSION ...?!
THAT'S WHY NOTHING HAPPENED WHEN YOU TRIED TO TRANSFORM!
THERE'S A THIN SPIRIT LINE TIED TO US!
THE CULPRIT MUST BE AT THE OTHER END!
I'M GOING TO GO TAKE A LOOK!
EVERYONE, PLEASE WAIT HERE!
SHWOOOM
KA-SPLASH
YUUNA-SAN?!
I...I'M GOING, TOO!
CHISAKI?!

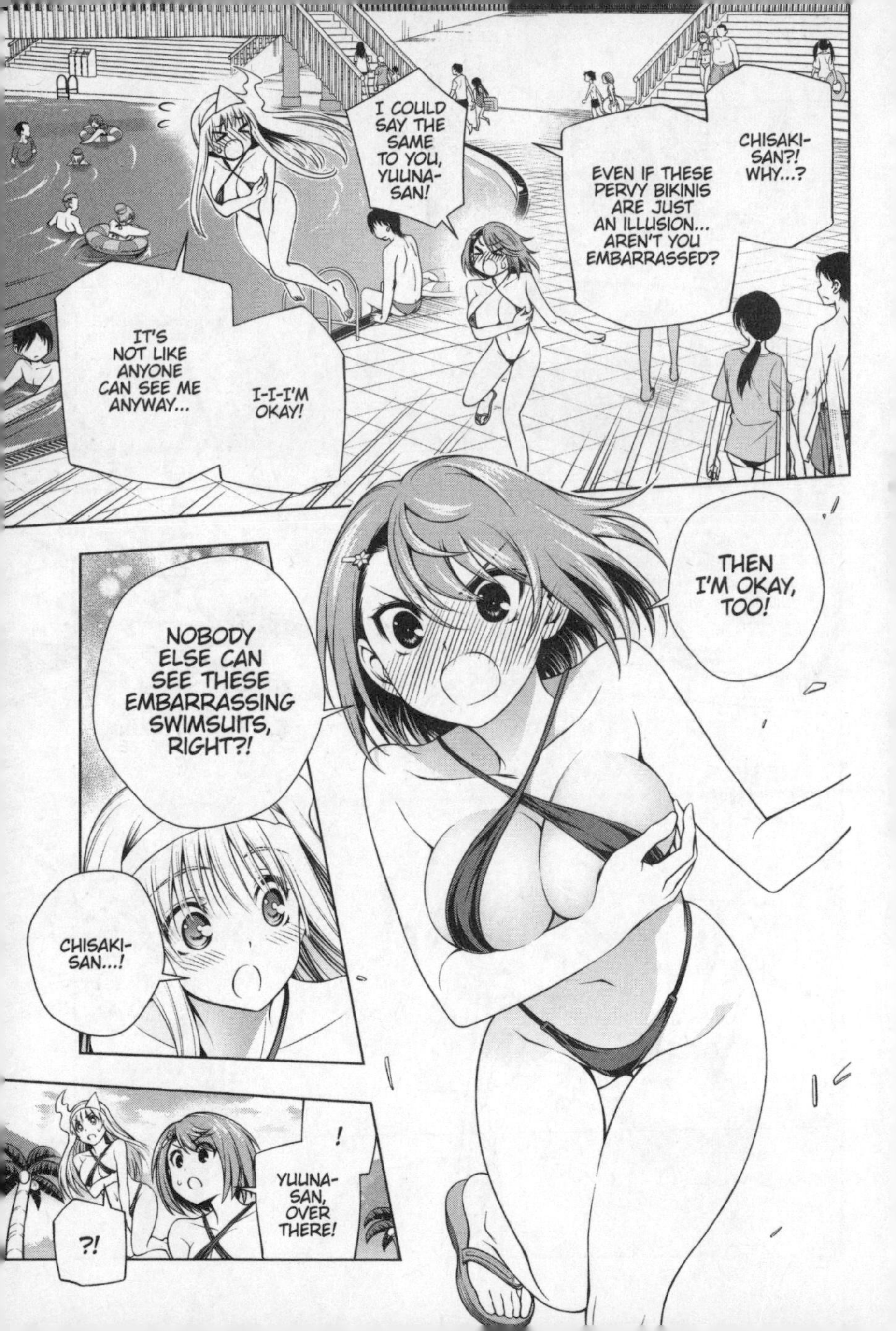
CHISAKI-SAN?! WHY...?
EVEN IF THESE PERVY BIKINIS ARE JUST AN ILLUSION... AREN'T YOU EMBARRASSED?
I COULD SAY THE SAME TO YOU, YUUNA-SAN!
I-I-I'M OKAY!
IT'S NOT LIKE ANYONE CAN SEE ME ANYWAY...
THEN I'M OKAY, TOO!
NOBODY ELSE CAN SEE THESE EMBARRASSING SWIMSUITS, RIGHT?!
CHISAKI-SAN...!
!
YUUNA-SAN, OVER THERE!
?!

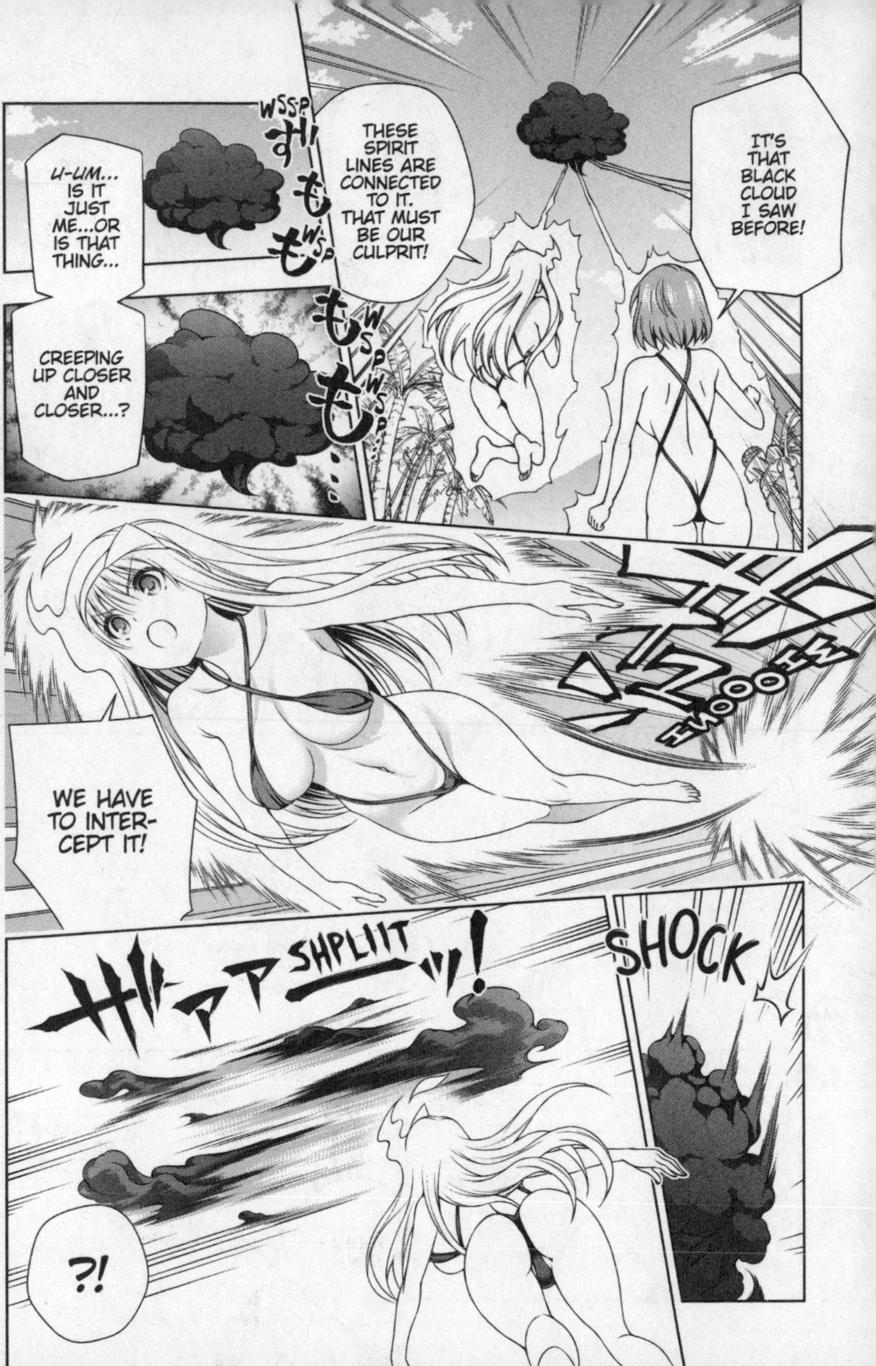
IT'S THAT BLACK CLOUD I SAW BEFORE!
THESE SPIRIT LINES ARE CONNECTED TO IT. THAT MUST BE OUR CULPRIT!
WSS-P
WSP
U-UM... IS IT JUST ME...OR IS THAT THING...
CREEPING UP CLOSER AND CLOSER...?
WSP
WSP...
WHOOSH
WE HAVE TO INTER-CEPT IT!
SHOCK
SHPLIIT
?!

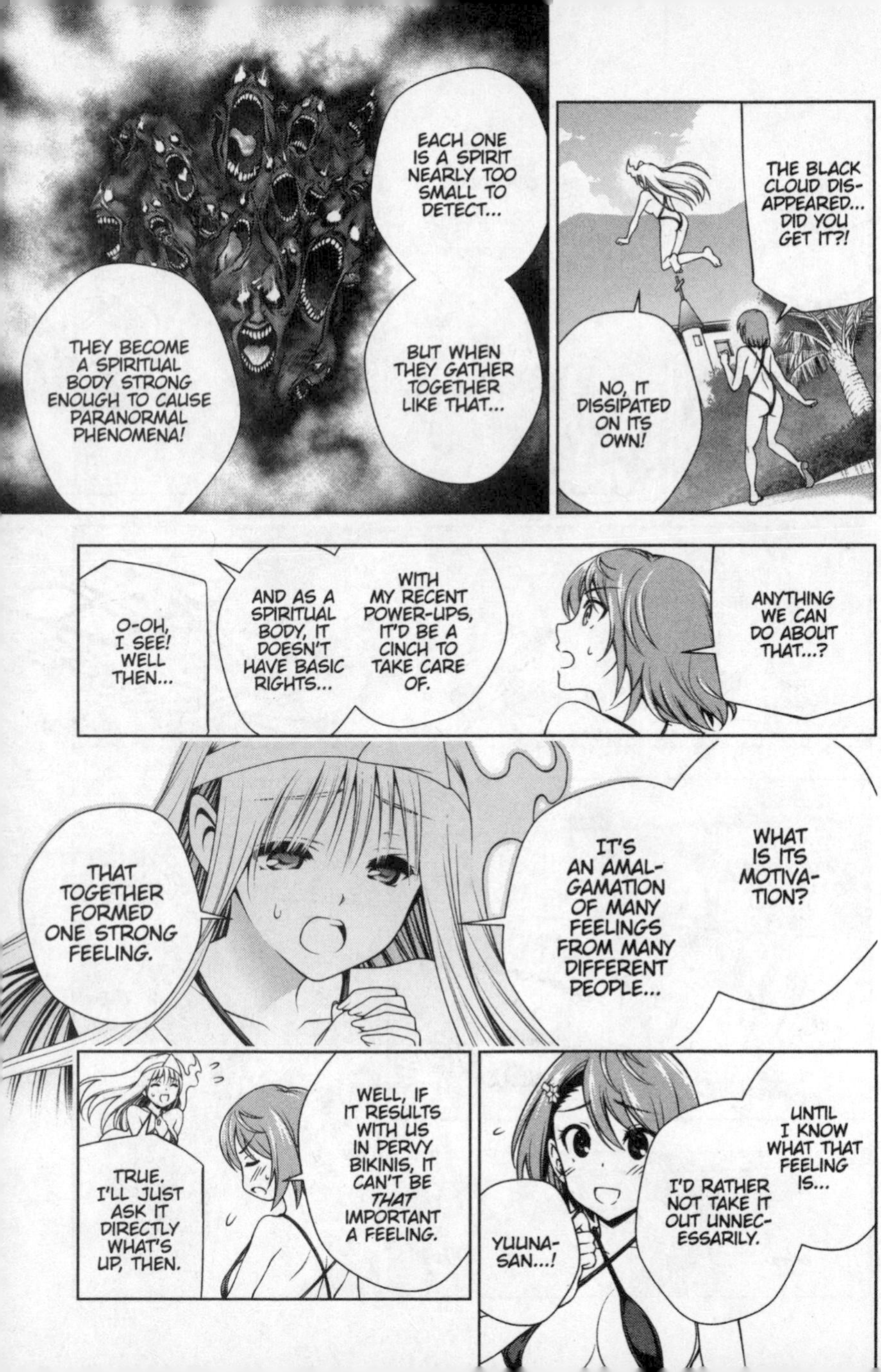
THE BLACK CLOUD DIS-APPEARED... DID YOU GET IT?!
NO, IT DISSIPATED ON ITS OWN!
EACH ONE IS A SPIRIT NEARLY TOO SMALL TO DETECT...
BUT WHEN THEY GATHER TOGETHER LIKE THAT...
THEY BECOME A SPIRITUAL BODY STRONG ENOUGH TO CAUSE PARANORMAL PHENOMENA!
ANYTHING WE CAN DO ABOUT THAT...?
WITH MY RECENT POWER-UPS, IT'D BE A CINCH TO TAKE CARE OF.
AND AS A SPIRITUAL BODY, IT DOESN'T HAVE BASIC RIGHTS...
O-OH, I SEE! WELL THEN...
WHAT IS ITS MOTIVA-TION?
IT'S AN AMAL-GAMATION OF MANY FEELINGS FROM MANY DIFFERENT PEOPLE...
THAT TOGETHER FORMED ONE STRONG FEELING.
UNTIL I KNOW WHAT THAT FEELING IS...
I'D RATHER NOT TAKE IT OUT UNNEC-ESSARILY.
YUUNA-SAN...!
WELL, IF IT RESULTS WITH US IN PERVY BIKINIS, IT CAN'T BE *THAT* IMPORTANT A FEELING.
TRUE. I'LL JUST ASK IT DIRECTLY WHAT'S UP, THEN.

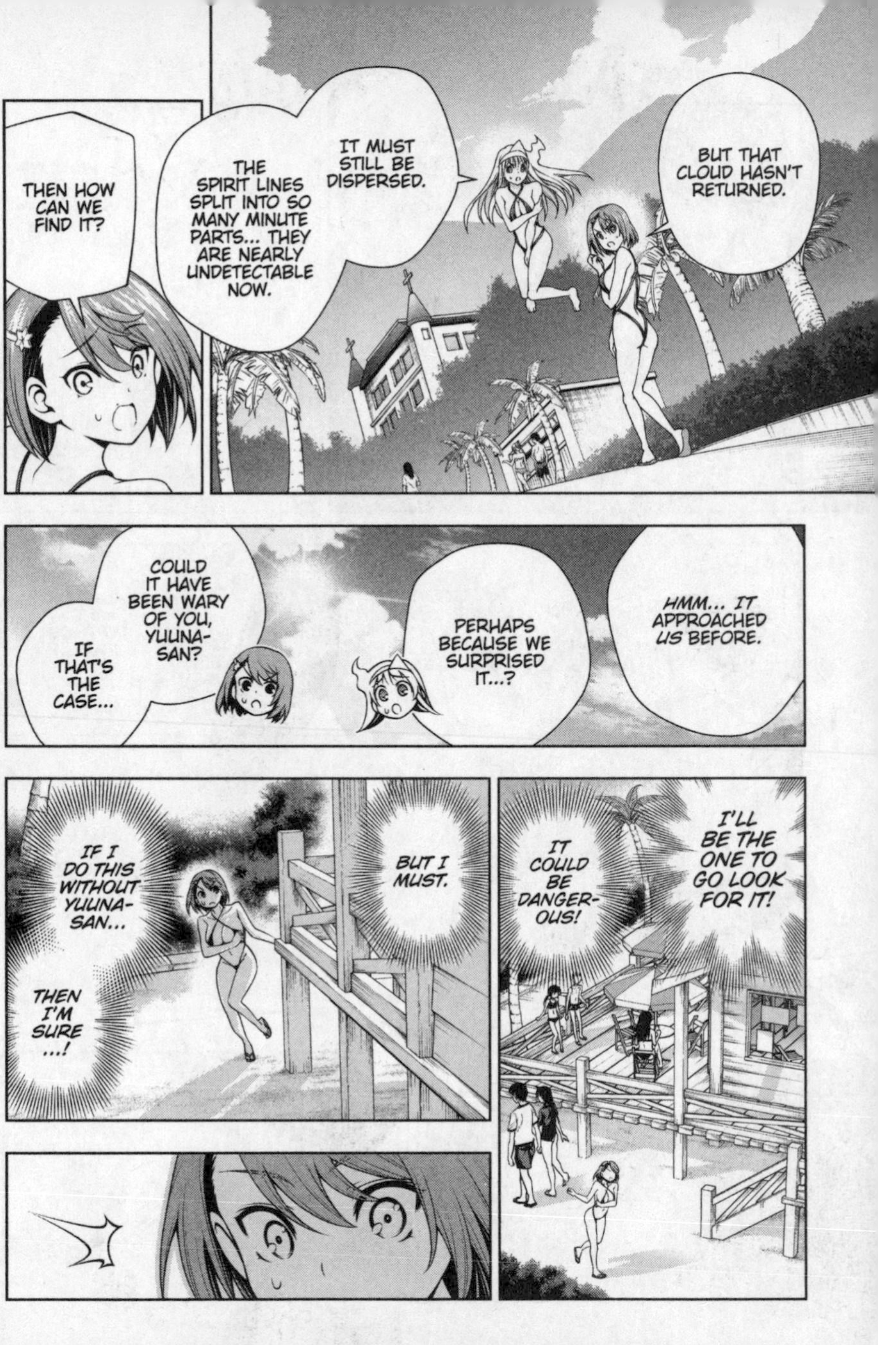
BUT THAT CLOUD HASN'T RETURNED.
IT MUST STILL BE DISPERSED.
THE SPIRIT LINES SPLIT INTO SO MANY MINUTE PARTS... THEY ARE NEARLY UNDETECTABLE NOW.
THEN HOW CAN WE FIND IT?
HMM... IT APPROACHED US BEFORE.
PERHAPS BECAUSE WE SURPRISED IT...?
COULD IT HAVE BEEN WARY OF YOU, YUUNA-SAN?
IF THAT'S THE CASE...
I'LL BE THE ONE TO GO LOOK FOR IT!
IT COULD BE DANGER-OUS!
BUT I MUST.
IF I DO THIS WITHOUT YUUNA-SAN...
THEN I'M SURE ...!

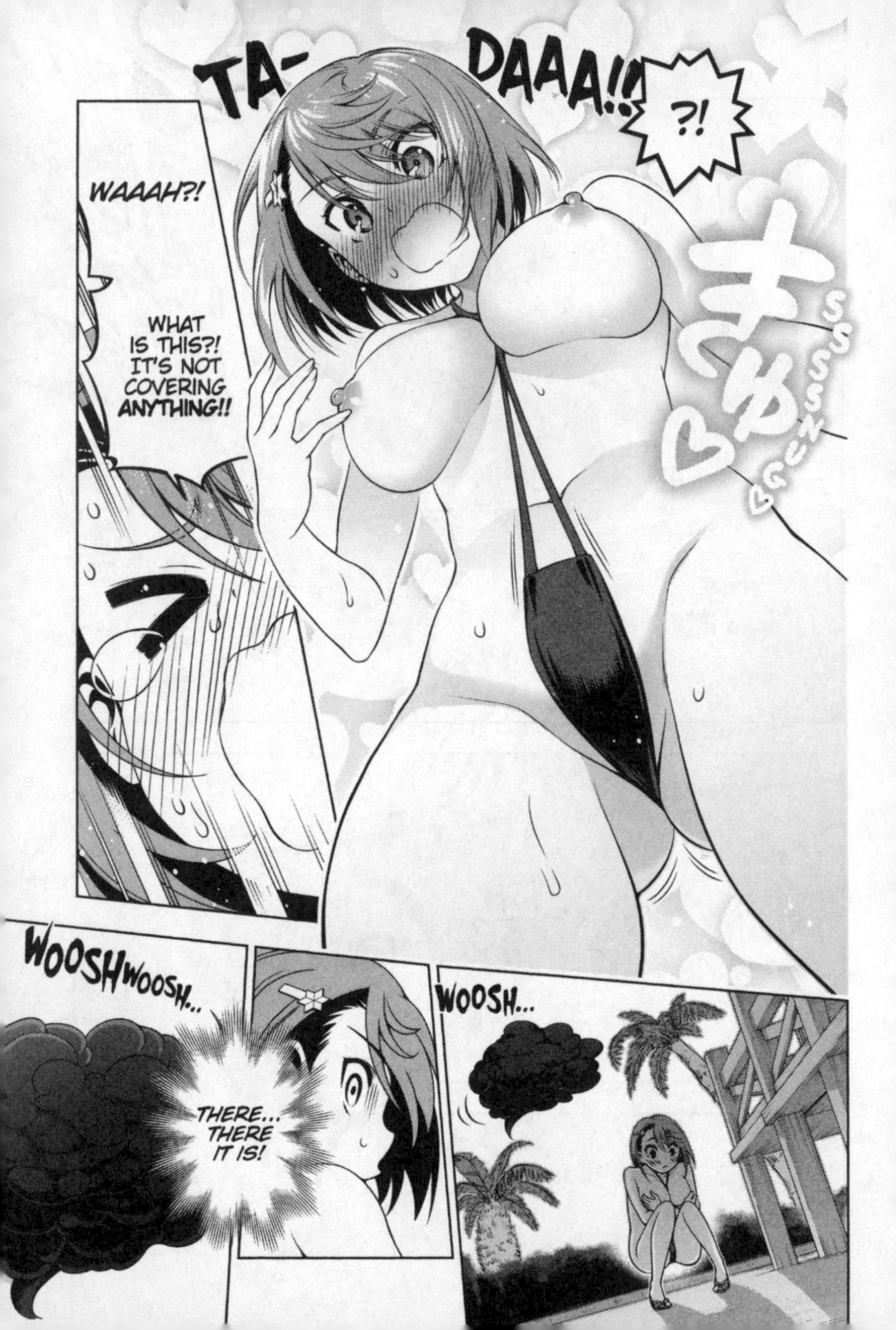
TA-DAAAA!!
?!
きゅ♡
WAAAH?!
WHAT IS THIS?! IT'S NOT COVERING ANYTHING!!
WOOSH...
THERE... THERE IT IS!
WOOSHWOOSH...

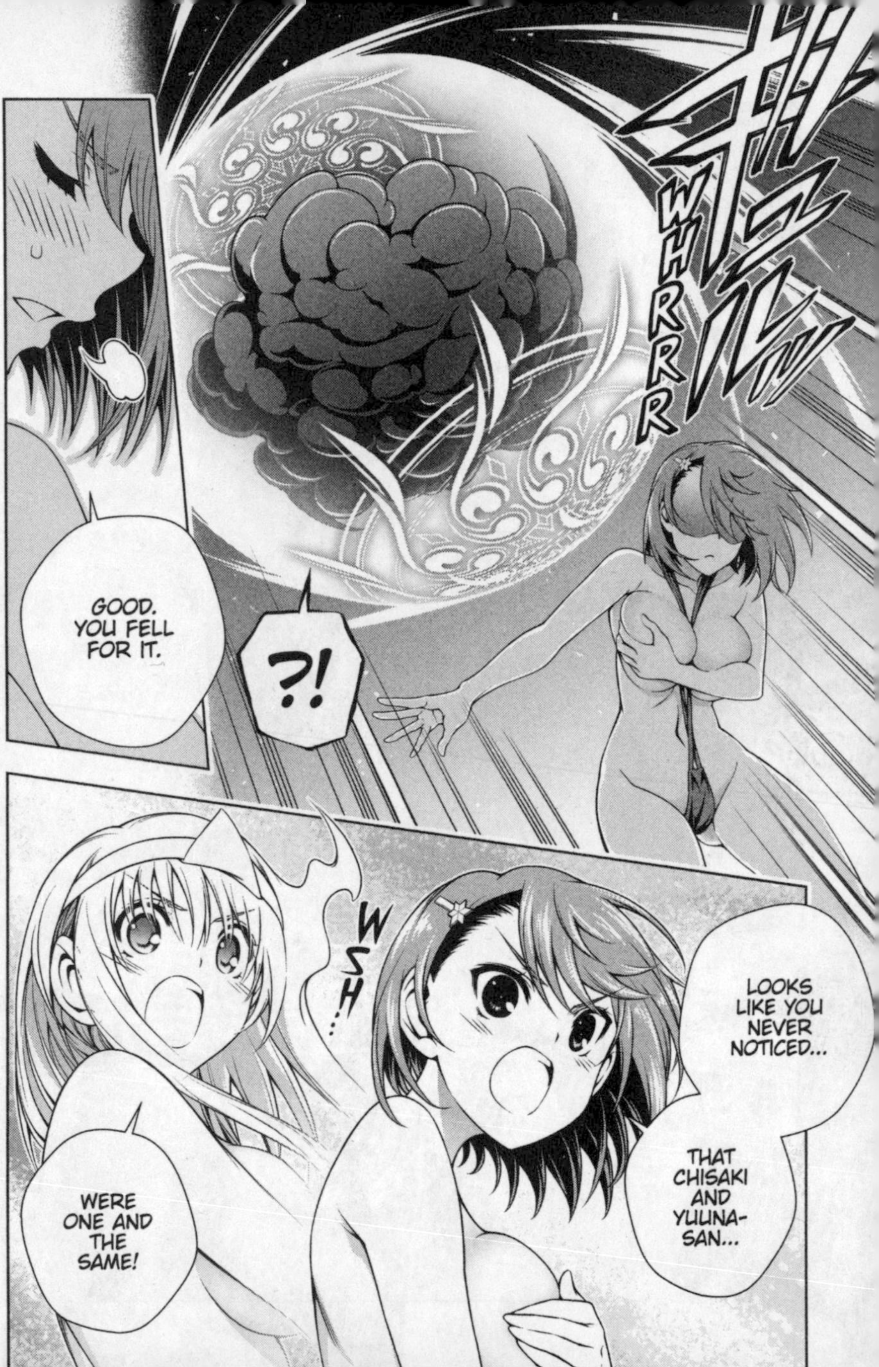
WHRRRR
?!
GOOD. YOU FELL FOR IT.
LOOKS LIKE YOU NEVER NOTICED...
THAT CHISAKI AND YUUNA-SAN...
WSH...
WERE ONE AND THE SAME!

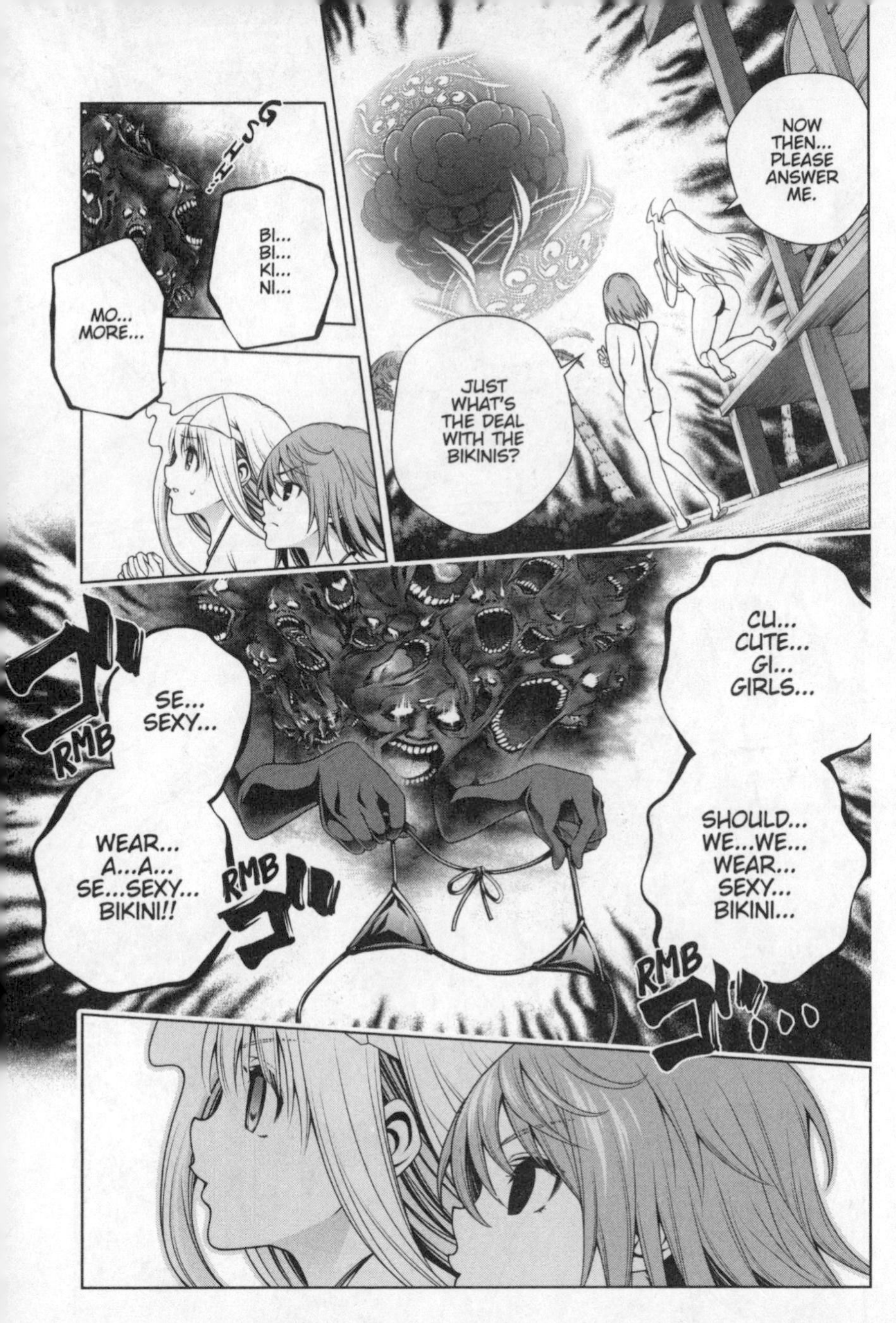

NOW THEN... PLEASE ANSWER ME.
JUST WHAT'S THE DEAL WITH THE BIKINIS?
BI... BI... KI... NI...
MO... MORE...
CU... CUTE... GI... GIRLS...
SHOULD... WE...WE... WEAR... SEXY... BIKINI...
RMB
SE... SEXY...
WEAR... A...A... SE...SEXY... BIKINI!!
RMB
RMB

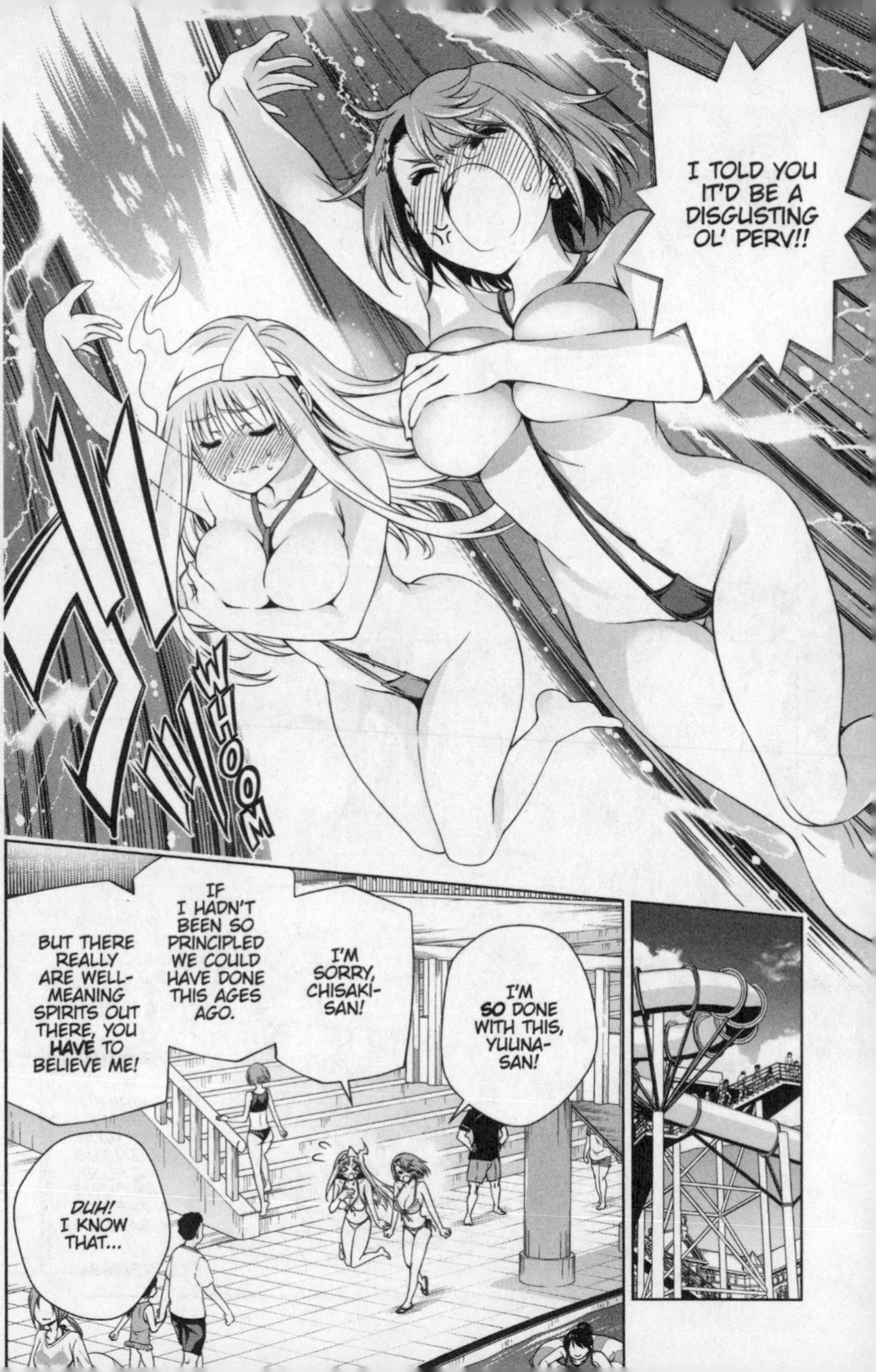
I TOLD YOU IT'D BE A DISGUSTING OL' PERV!!
WHOOMM
I'M SO DONE WITH THIS, YUUNA-SAN!
I'M SORRY, CHISAKI-SAN!
IF I HADN'T BEEN SO PRINCIPLED WE COULD HAVE DONE THIS AGES AGO.
BUT THERE REALLY ARE WELL-MEANING SPIRITS OUT THERE, YOU HAVE TO BELIEVE ME!
DUH! I KNOW THAT...

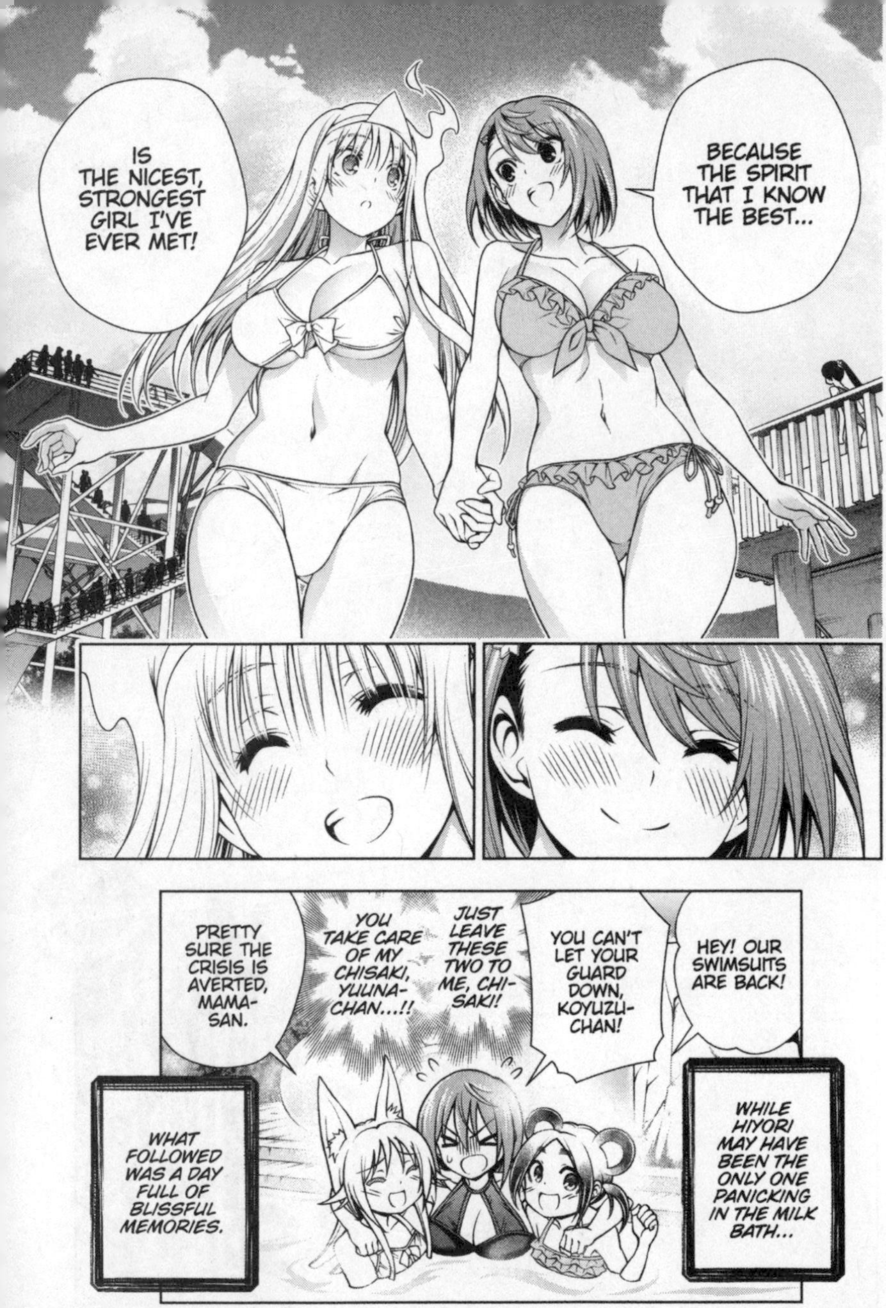
BECAUSE THE SPIRIT THAT I KNOW THE BEST...
IS THE NICEST, STRONGEST GIRL I'VE EVER MET!
HEY! OUR SWIMSUITS ARE BACK!
YOU CAN'T LET YOUR GUARD DOWN, KOYUZU-CHAN!
JUST LEAVE THESE TWO TO ME, CHISAKI!
YOU TAKE CARE OF MY CHISAKI, YUUNA-CHAN...!!
PRETTY SURE THE CRISIS IS AVERTED, MAMA-SAN.
WHILE HIYORI MAY HAVE BEEN THE ONLY ONE PANICKING IN THE MILK BATH...
WHAT FOLLOWED WAS A DAY FULL OF BLISSFUL MEMORIES.

Yuuna and the Haunted Hot Springs

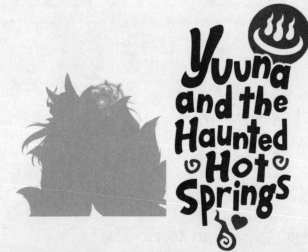

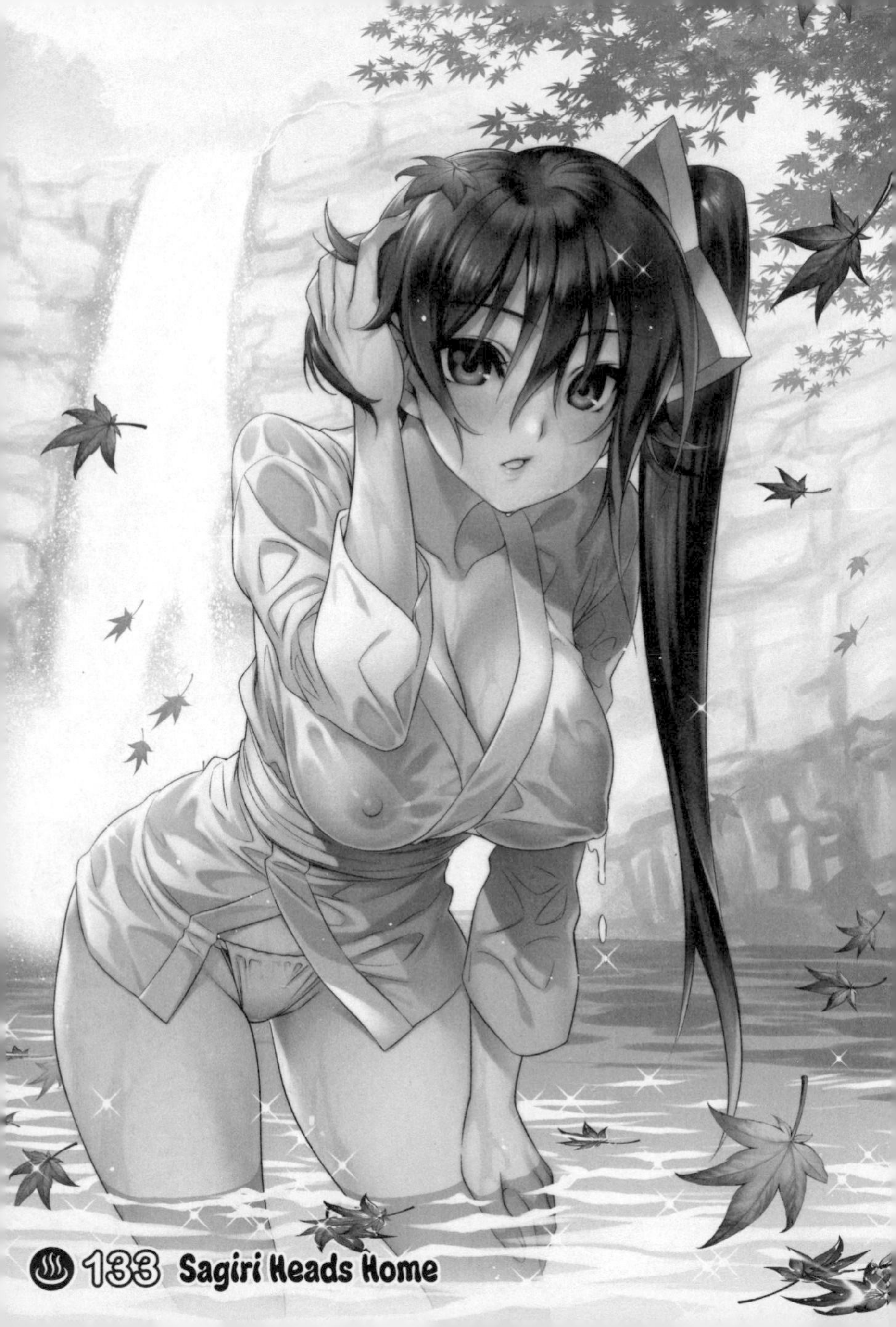

133 Sagiri Heads Home

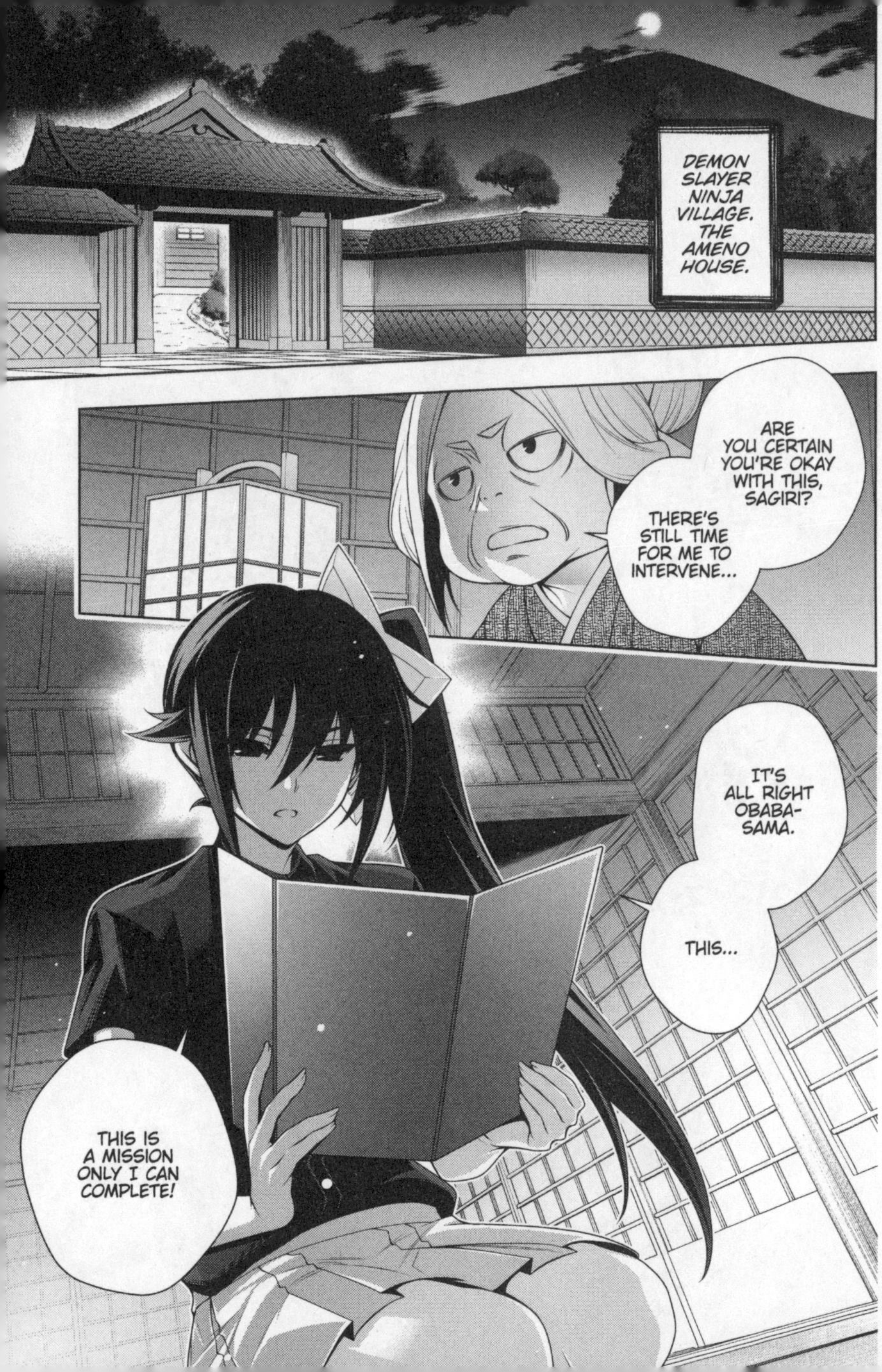
DEMON SLAYER NINJA VILLAGE. THE AMENO HOUSE.
ARE YOU CERTAIN YOU'RE OKAY WITH THIS, SAGIRI?
THERE'S STILL TIME FOR ME TO INTERVENE...
IT'S ALL RIGHT OBABA-SAMA.
THIS...
THIS IS A MISSION ONLY I CAN COMPLETE!

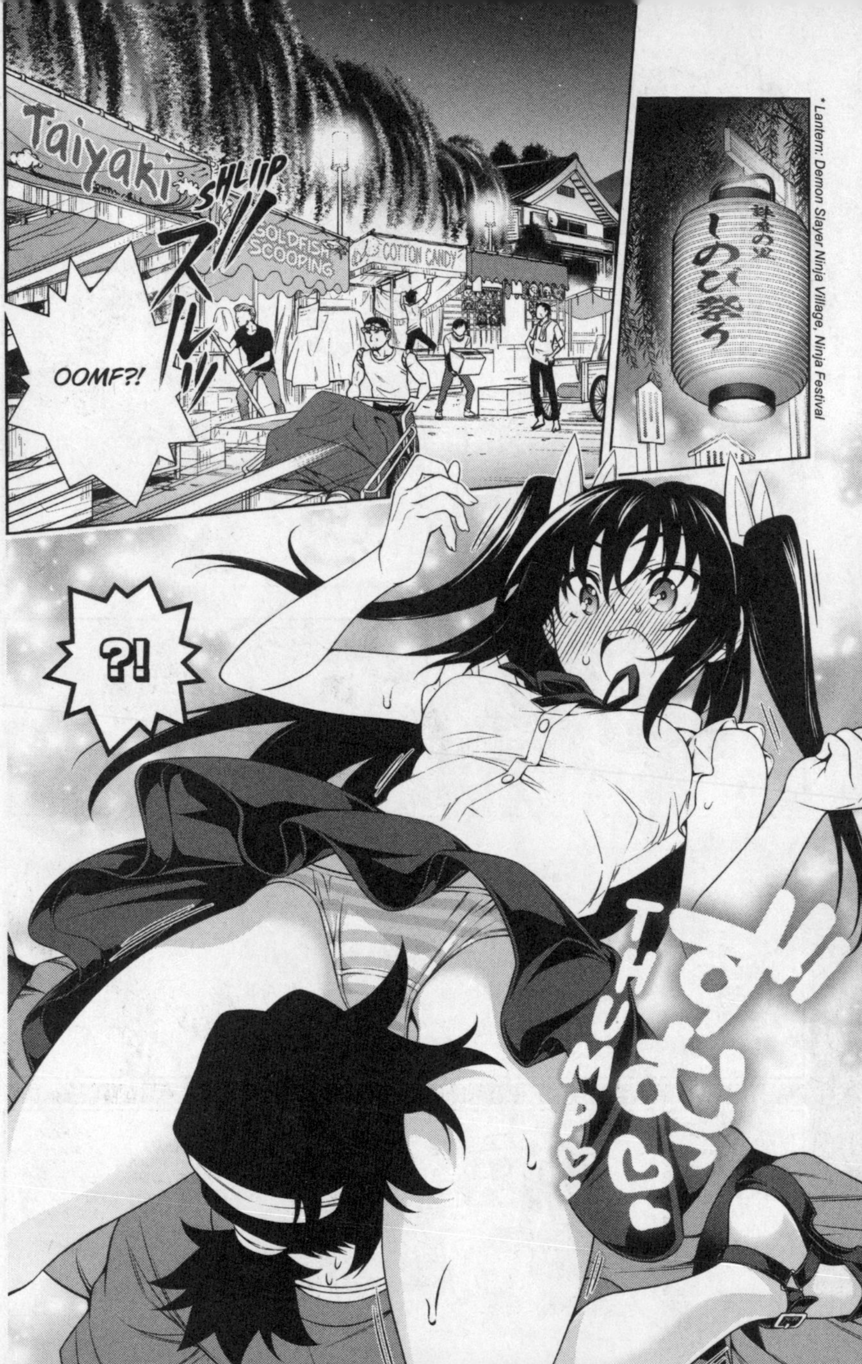
しのび祭り
Taiyaki
SHLIIP
スルッ
GOLDFISH SCOOPING
COTTON CANDY
OOMF?!
?!
ずむっ♡
THUMP♡
*Lantern: Demon Slayer Ninja Village, Ninja Festival

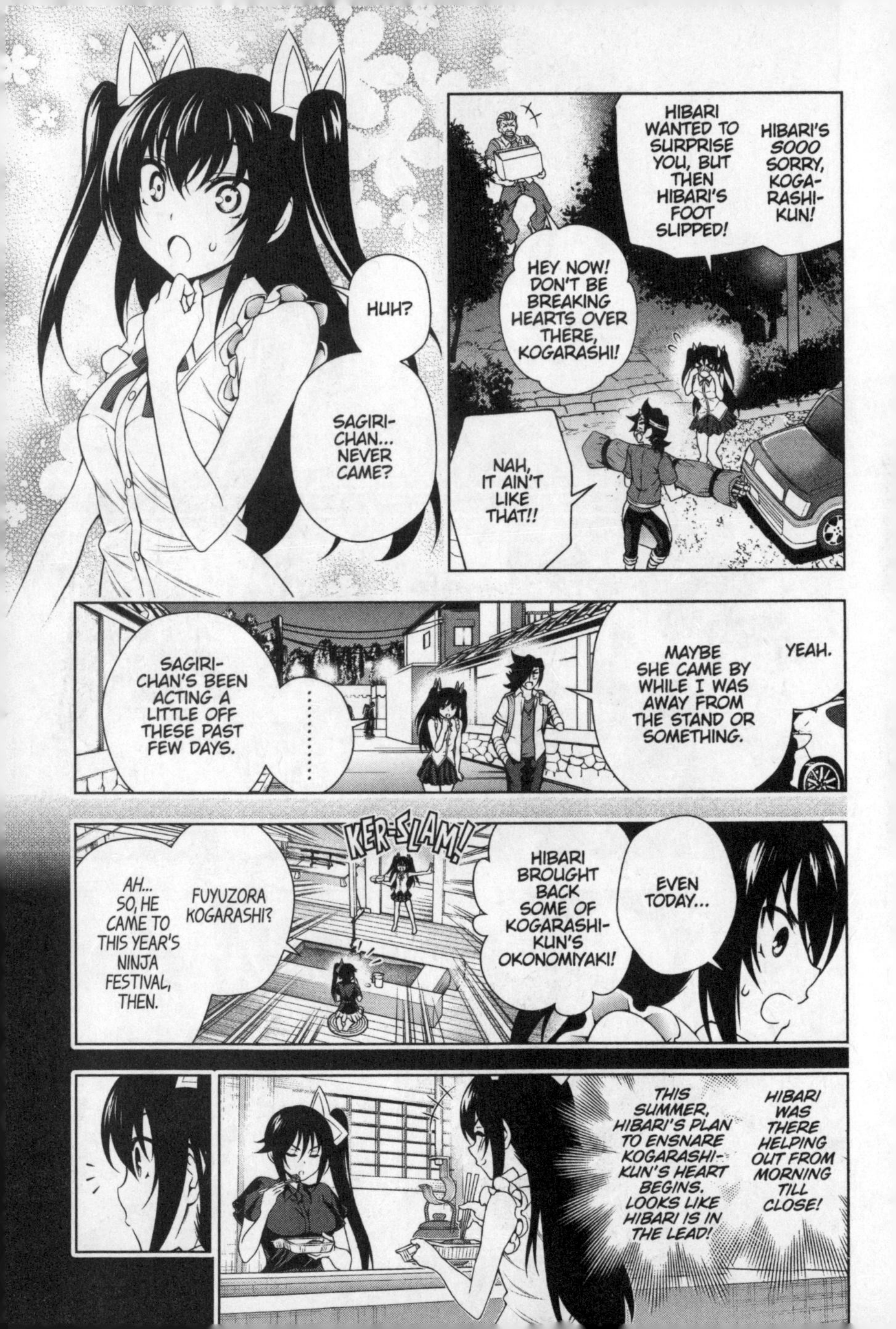
HIBARI'S SOOO SORRY, KOGA-RASHI-KUN!
HIBARI WANTED TO SURPRISE YOU, BUT THEN HIBARI'S FOOT SLIPPED!
HEY NOW! DON'T BE BREAKING HEARTS OVER THERE, KOGARASHI!
NAH, IT AIN'T LIKE THAT!!
HUH?
SAGIRI-CHAN... NEVER CAME?
YEAH.
MAYBE SHE CAME BY WHILE I WAS AWAY FROM THE STAND OR SOMETHING.
......
SAGIRI-CHAN'S BEEN ACTING A LITTLE OFF THESE PAST FEW DAYS.
EVEN TODAY...
HIBARI BROUGHT BACK SOME OF KOGARASHI-KUN'S OKONOMIYAKI!
KER-SLAM!
FUYUZORA KOGARASHI?
AH... SO, HE CAME TO THIS YEAR'S NINJA FESTIVAL, THEN.
HIBARI WAS THERE HELPING OUT FROM MORNING TILL CLOSE!
THIS SUMMER, HIBARI'S PLAN TO ENSNARE KOGARASHI-KUN'S HEART BEGINS. LOOKS LIKE HIBARI IS IN THE LEAD!

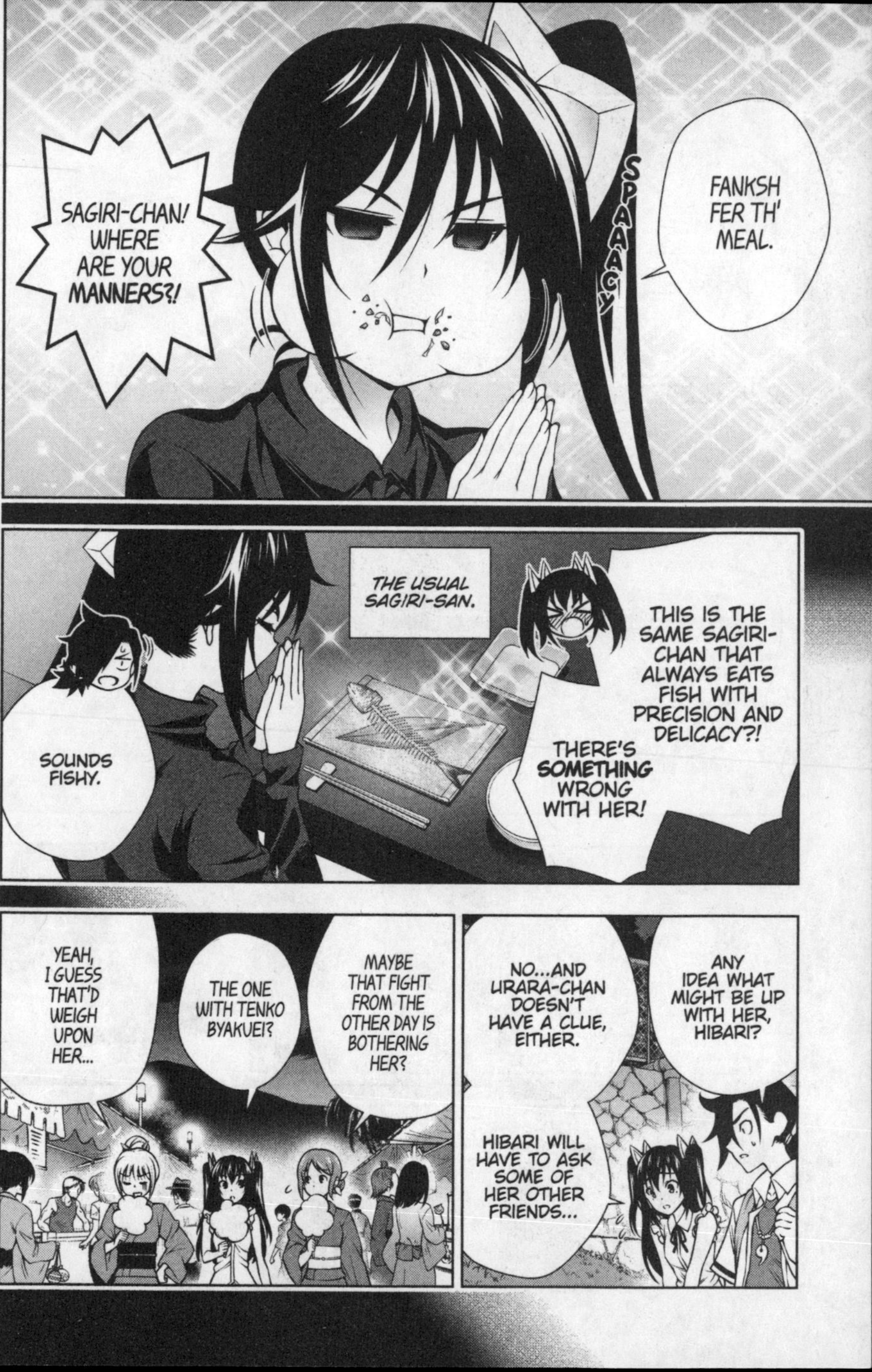
FANKSH FER TH' MEAL.
SPAAACY
SAGIRI-CHAN! WHERE ARE YOUR MANNERS?!
THIS IS THE SAME SAGIRI-CHAN THAT ALWAYS EATS FISH WITH PRECISION AND DELICACY?!
THERE'S **SOMETHING** WRONG WITH HER!
THE USUAL SAGIRI-SAN.
SOUNDS FISHY.
ANY IDEA WHAT MIGHT BE UP WITH HER, HIBARI?
NO...AND URARA-CHAN DOESN'T HAVE A CLUE, EITHER.
HIBARI WILL HAVE TO ASK SOME OF HER OTHER FRIENDS...
MAYBE THAT FIGHT FROM THE OTHER DAY IS BOTHERING HER?
THE ONE WITH TENKO BYAKUEI?
YEAH, I GUESS THAT'D WEIGH UPON HER...

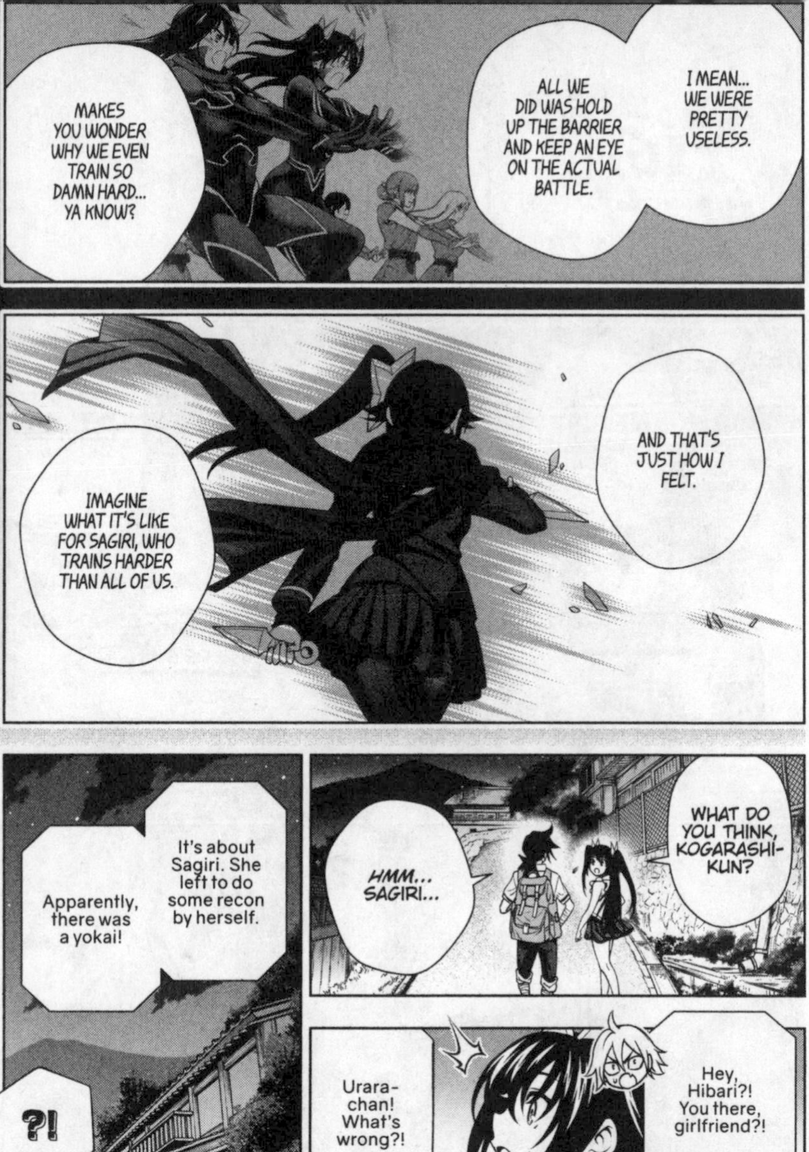
I MEAN... WE WERE PRETTY USELESS.
ALL WE DID WAS HOLD UP THE BARRIER AND KEEP AN EYE ON THE ACTUAL BATTLE.
MAKES YOU WONDER WHY WE EVEN TRAIN SO DAMN HARD... YA KNOW?
AND THAT'S JUST HOW I FELT.
IMAGINE WHAT IT'S LIKE FOR SAGIRI, WHO TRAINS HARDER THAN ALL OF US.
WHAT DO YOU THINK, KOGARASHI-KUN?
HMM... SAGIRI...
Hey, Hibari?! You there, girlfriend?!
Urara-chan! What's wrong?!
It's about Sagiri. She left to do some recon by herself.
Apparently, there was a yokai!
?!

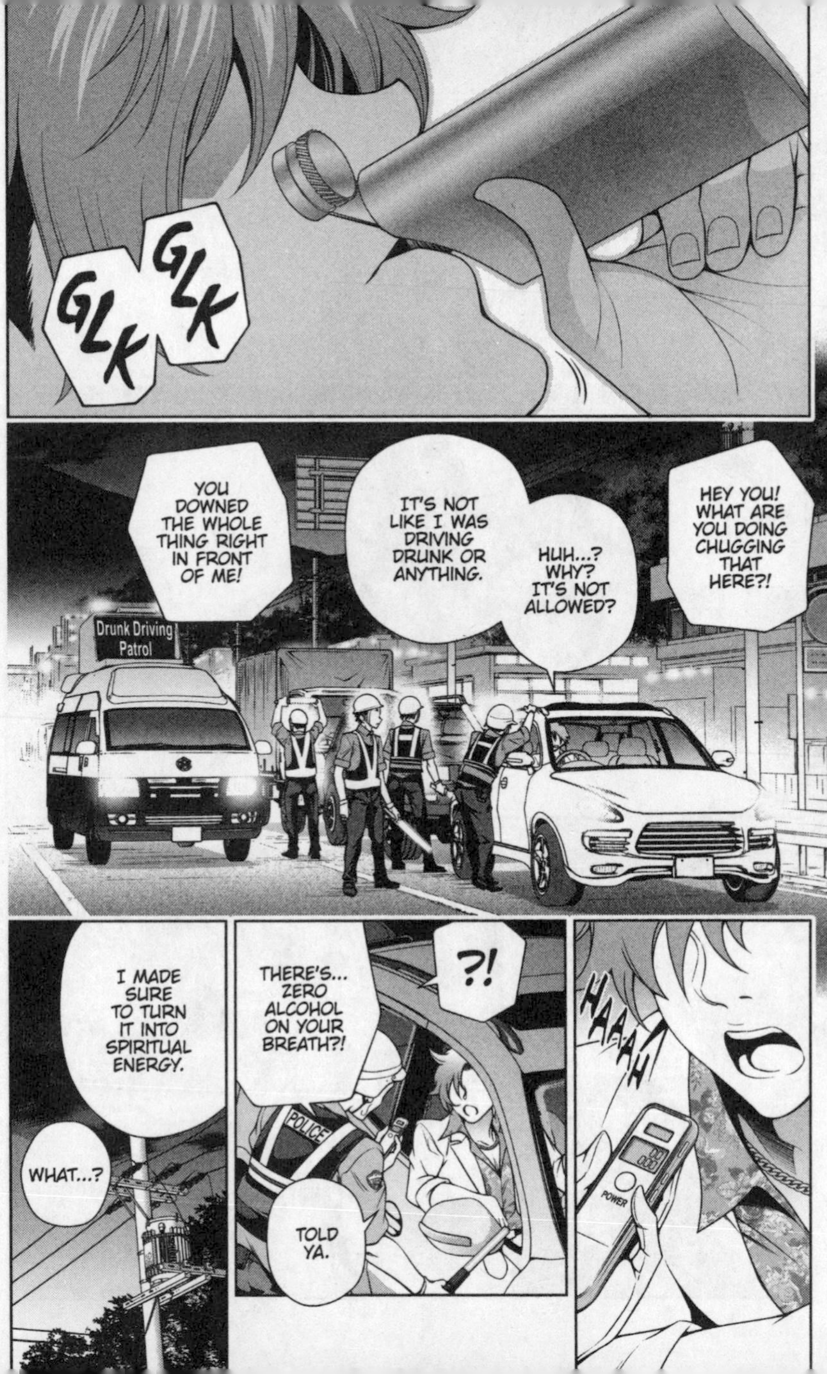
GLK
GLK
HEY YOU! WHAT ARE YOU DOING CHUGGING THAT HERE?!
HUH...? WHY? IT'S NOT ALLOWED?
IT'S NOT LIKE I WAS DRIVING DRUNK OR ANYTHING.
YOU DOWNED THE WHOLE THING RIGHT IN FRONT OF ME!
Drunk Driving Patrol
HAAAAH
POWER
?!
THERE'S... ZERO ALCOHOL ON YOUR BREATH?!
POLICE
TOLD YA.
I MADE SURE TO TURN IT INTO SPIRITUAL ENERGY.
WHAT...?

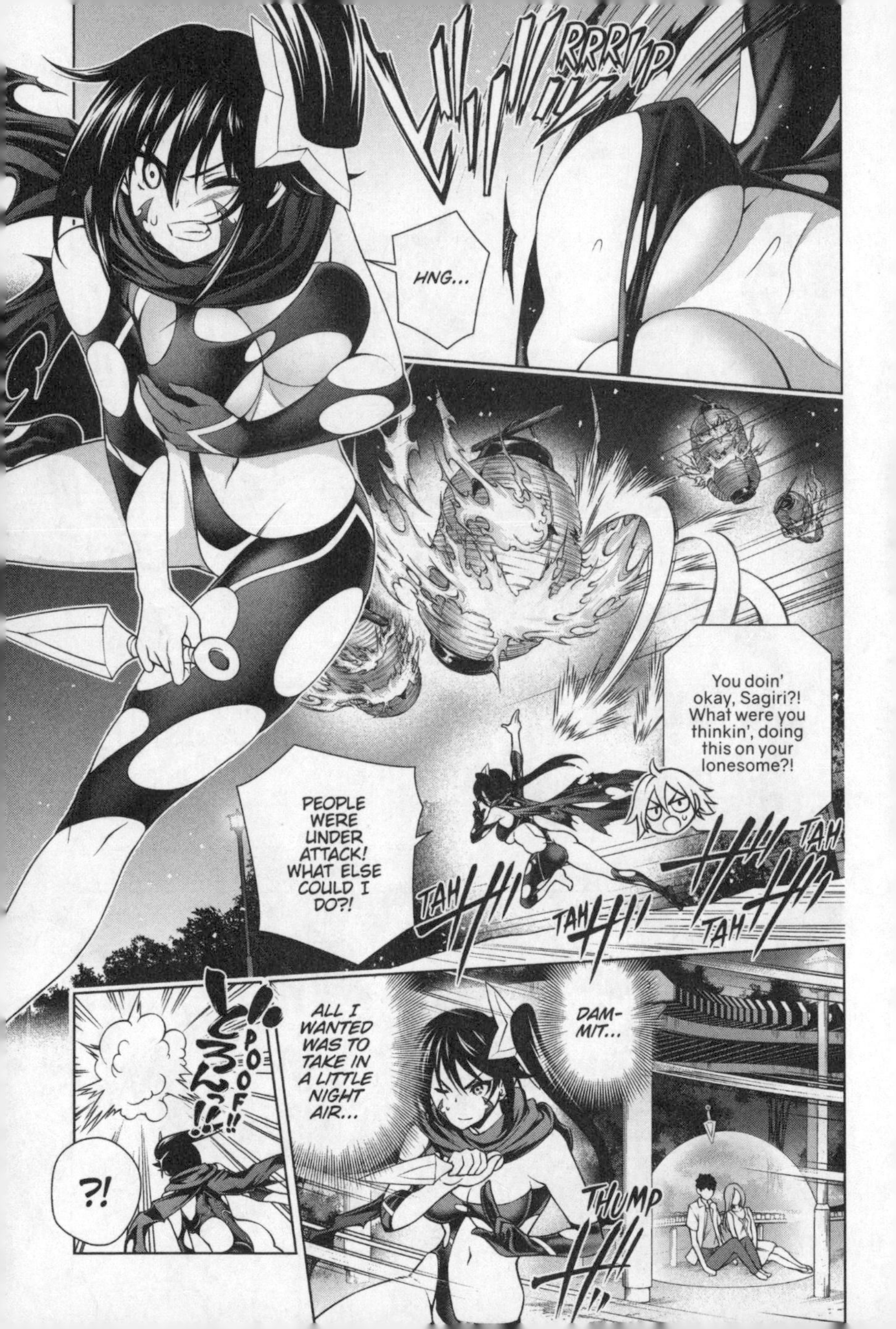
RRRIP
HNG...
You doin' okay, Sagiri?! What were you thinkin', doing this on your lonesome?!
PEOPLE WERE UNDER ATTACK! WHAT ELSE COULD I DO?!
TAH
TAH
TAH
TAH
DAM-MIT...
ALL I WANTED WAS TO TAKE IN A LITTLE NIGHT AIR...
THUMP
POOF!!
?!

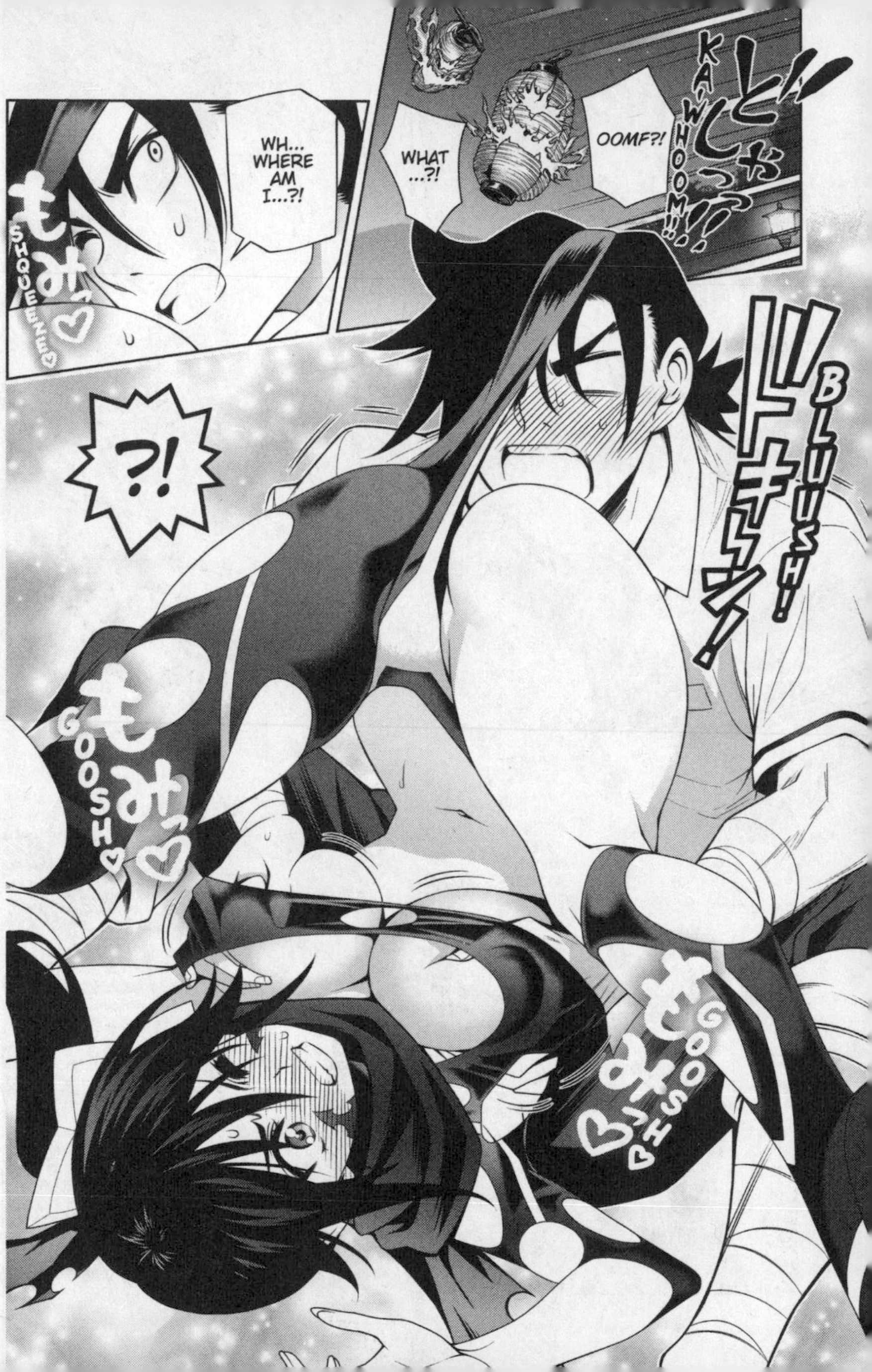
KAWHOOM!!
OOMF?!
WHAT ...?!
WH... WHERE AM I...?!
もみっ♡
SHQUEEZE♡
BLUUSH!
?!
もみっ♡
GOOSH♡
もみっ♡
GOOSH♡

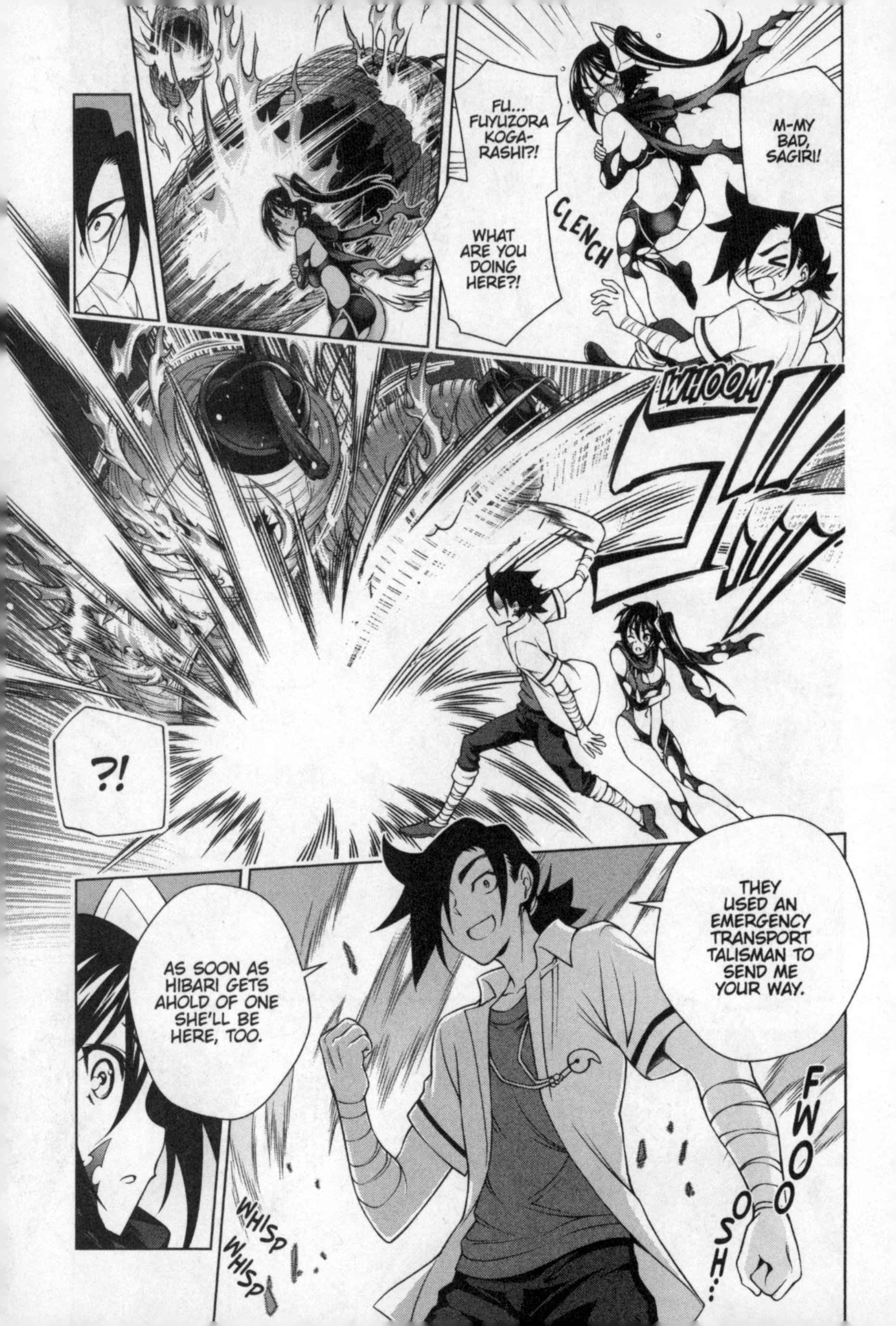
FU... FUYUZORA KOGA-RASHI?!
WHAT ARE YOU DOING HERE?!
CLENCH
M-MY BAD, SAGIRI!
WHOOM
?!
THEY USED AN EMERGENCY TRANSPORT TALISMAN TO SEND ME YOUR WAY.
AS SOON AS HIBARI GETS AHOLD OF ONE SHE'LL BE HERE, TOO.
FWOOOSH...
WHISP WHISP

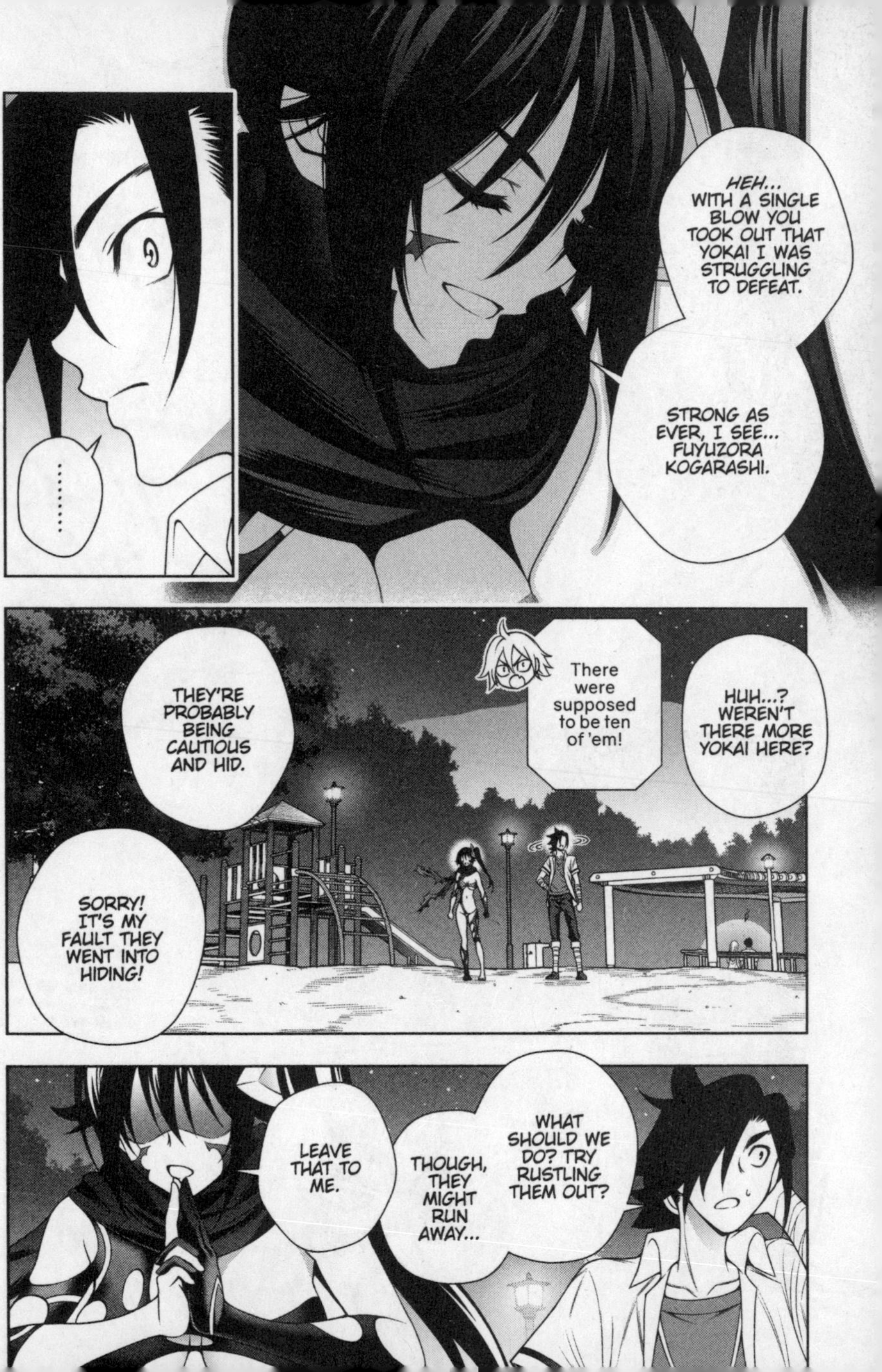
HEH... WITH A SINGLE BLOW YOU TOOK OUT THAT YOKAI I WAS STRUGGLING TO DEFEAT.
STRONG AS EVER, I SEE... FUYUZORA KOGARASHI.
......
HUH...? WEREN'T THERE MORE YOKAI HERE?
There were supposed to be ten of 'em!
THEY'RE PROBABLY BEING CAUTIOUS AND HID.
SORRY! IT'S MY FAULT THEY WENT INTO HIDING!
WHAT SHOULD WE DO? TRY RUSTLING THEM OUT?
THOUGH, THEY MIGHT RUN AWAY...
LEAVE THAT TO ME.

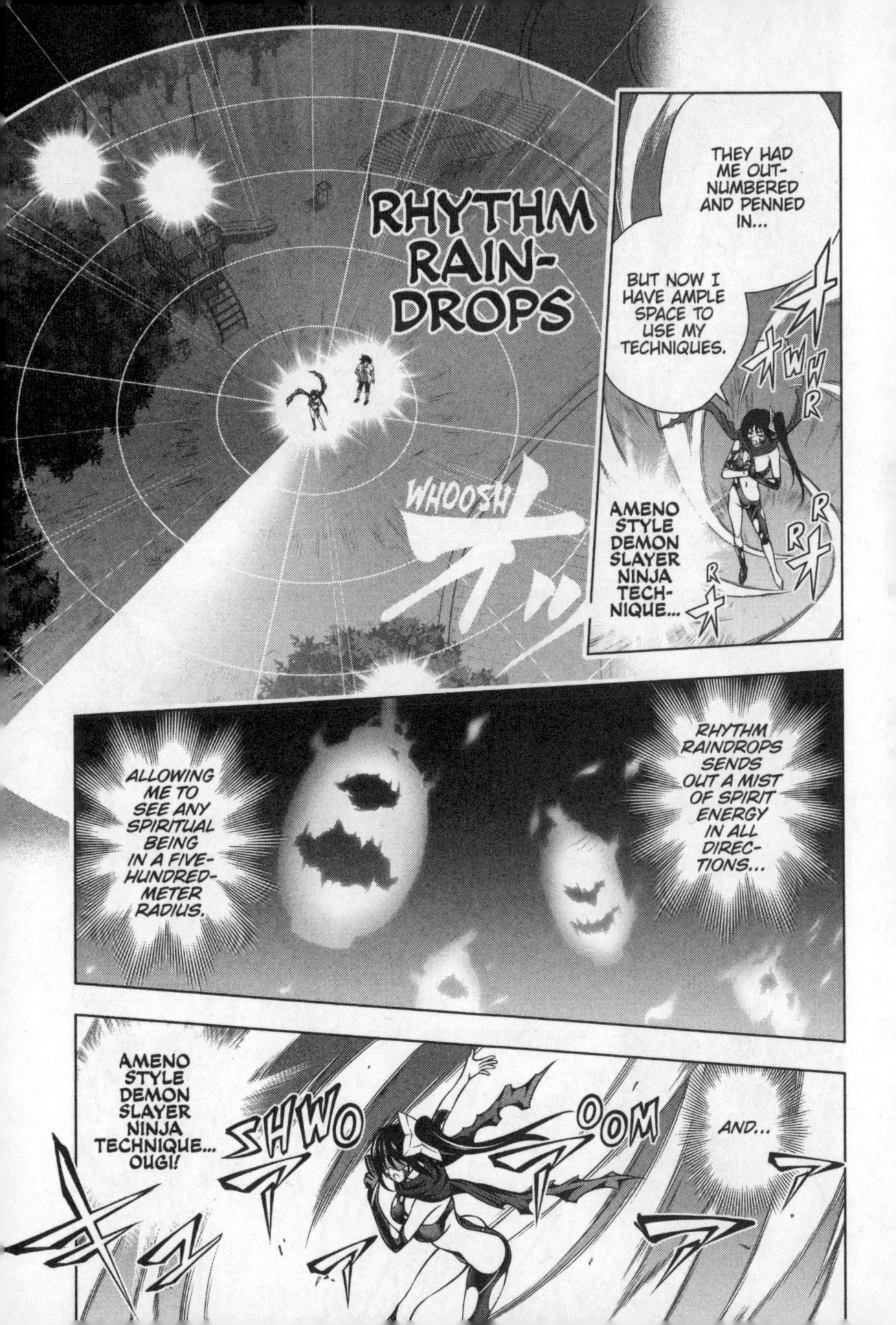
THEY HAD ME OUT-NUMBERED AND PENNED IN...
BUT NOW I HAVE AMPLE SPACE TO USE MY TECHNIQUES.
WHR
R
R
R
AMENO STYLE DEMON SLAYER NINJA TECH-NIQUE...
RHYTHM RAIN-DROPS
WHOOSH
RHYTHM RAINDROPS SENDS OUT A MIST OF SPIRIT ENERGY IN ALL DIREC-TIONS...
ALLOWING ME TO SEE ANY SPIRITUAL BEING IN A FIVE-HUNDRED-METER RADIUS.
AND...
AMENO STYLE DEMON SLAYER NINJA TECHNIQUE... OUGI!
SHWO
OOM

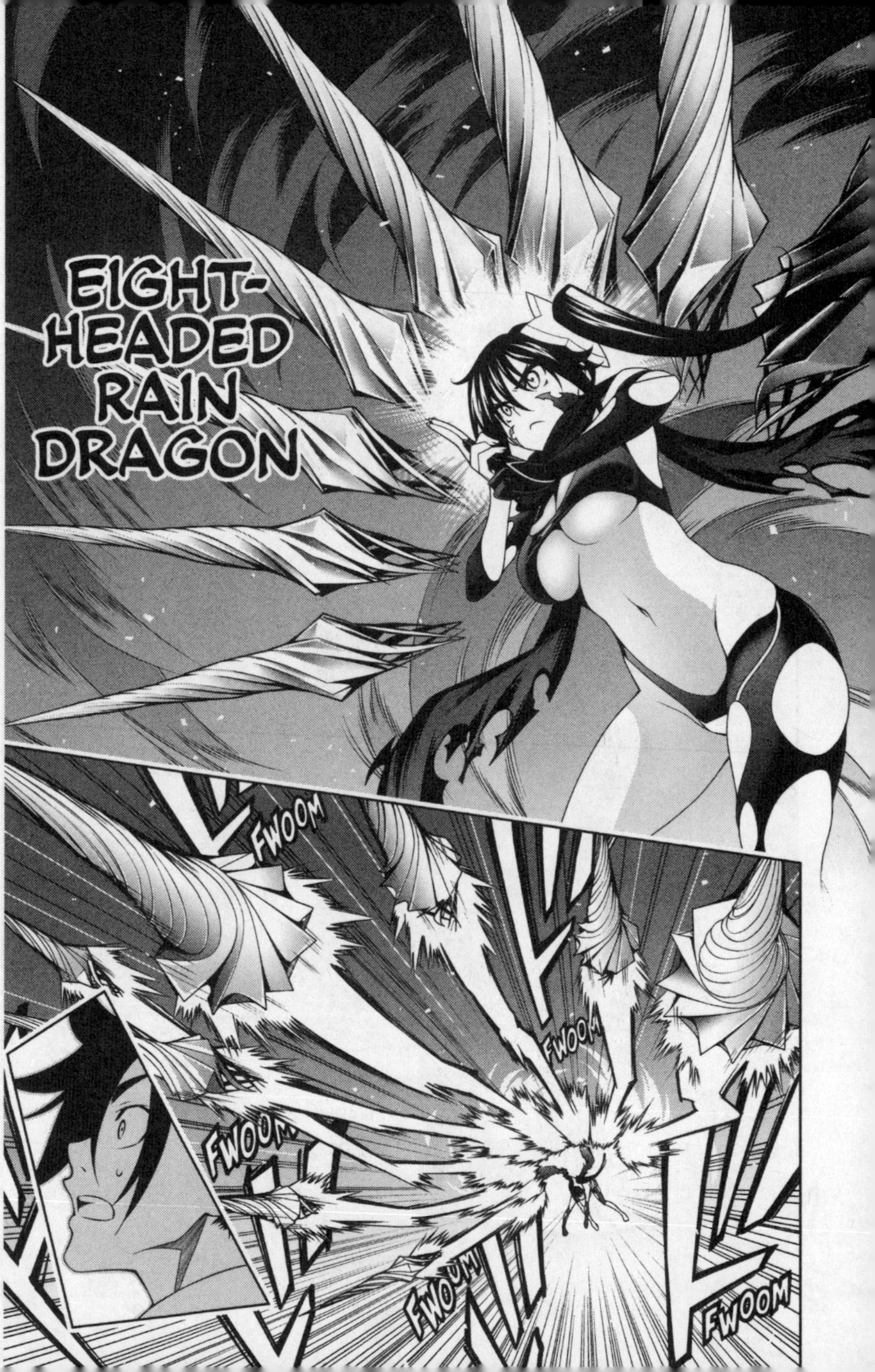
EIGHT-HEADED RAIN DRAGON
FWOOM
FWOOM
FWOOM
FWOOM
FWOOM

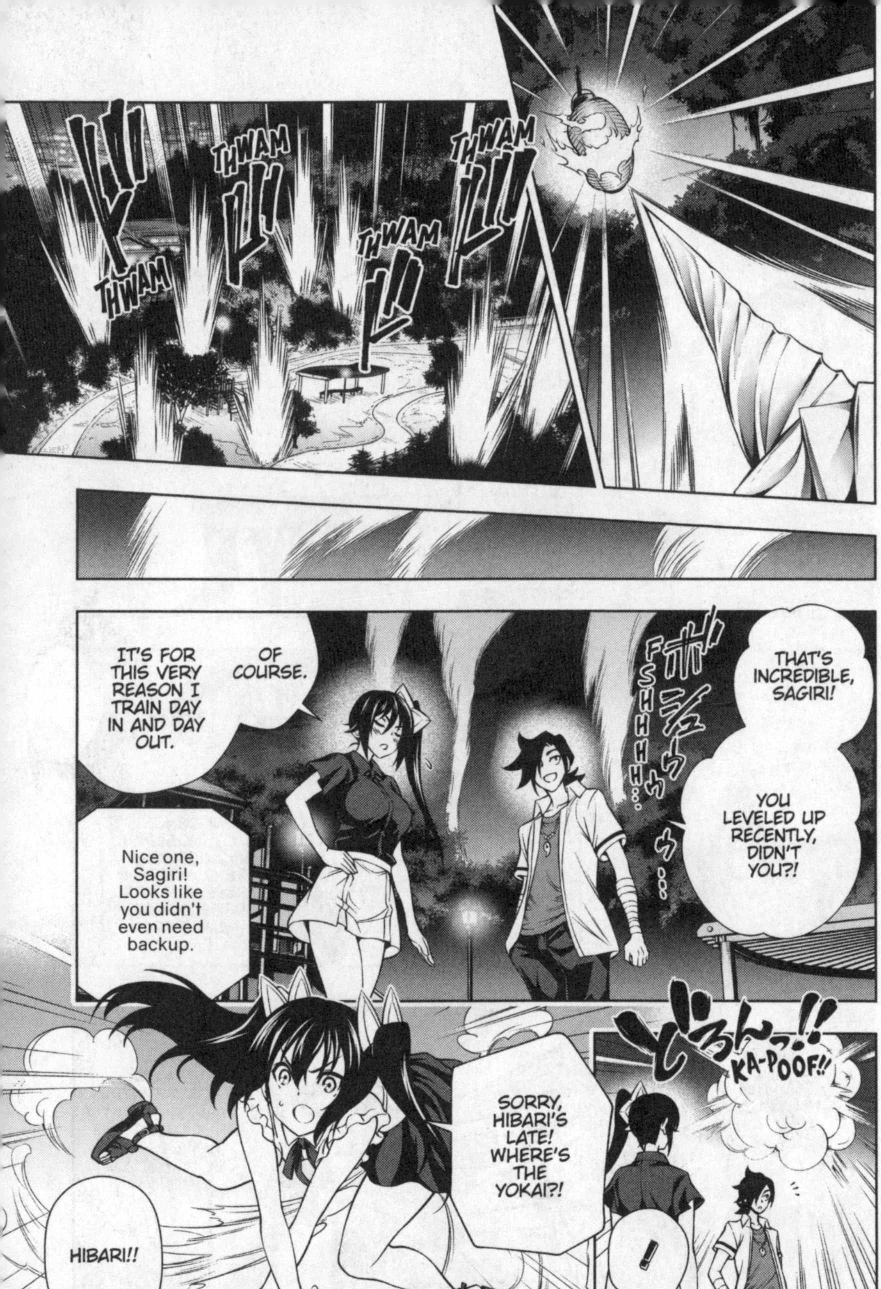
THWAM
THWAM
THWAM
THWAM
THAT'S INCREDIBLE, SAGIRI!
YOU LEVELED UP RECENTLY, DIDN'T YOU?!
FSHHHHH...
OF COURSE.
IT'S FOR THIS VERY REASON I TRAIN DAY IN AND DAY OUT.
Nice one, Sagiri! Looks like you didn't even need backup.
どろんっ!!
KA-POOF!!
!
SORRY, HIBARI'S LATE! WHERE'S THE YOKAI?!
HIBARI!!

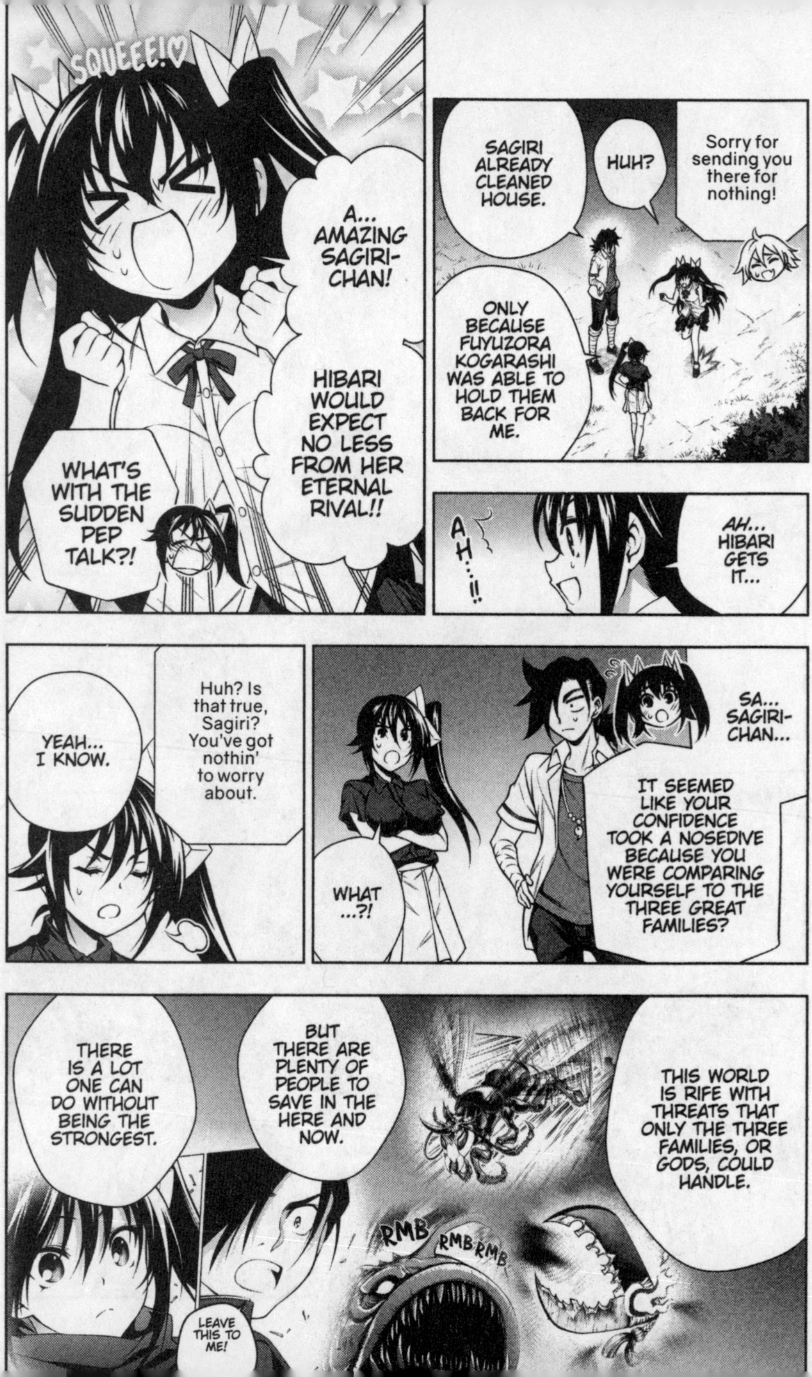
Sorry for sending you there for nothing!
HUH?
SAGIRI ALREADY CLEANED HOUSE.
ONLY BECAUSE FUYUZORA KOGARASHI WAS ABLE TO HOLD THEM BACK FOR ME.
AH... HIBARI GETS IT...
AH...!!
SQUEEE!♡
A... AMAZING SAGIRI-CHAN!
HIBARI WOULD EXPECT NO LESS FROM HER ETERNAL RIVAL!!
WHAT'S WITH THE SUDDEN PEP TALK?!
SA... SAGIRI-CHAN...
IT SEEMED LIKE YOUR CONFIDENCE TOOK A NOSEDIVE BECAUSE YOU WERE COMPARING YOURSELF TO THE THREE GREAT FAMILIES?
WHAT ...?!
Huh? Is that true, Sagiri? You've got nothin' to worry about.
YEAH... I KNOW.
THIS WORLD IS RIFE WITH THREATS THAT ONLY THE THREE FAMILIES, OR GODS, COULD HANDLE.
RMB
RMB RMB
BUT THERE ARE PLENTY OF PEOPLE TO SAVE IN THE HERE AND NOW.
THERE IS A LOT ONE CAN DO WITHOUT BEING THE STRONGEST.
LEAVE THIS TO ME!

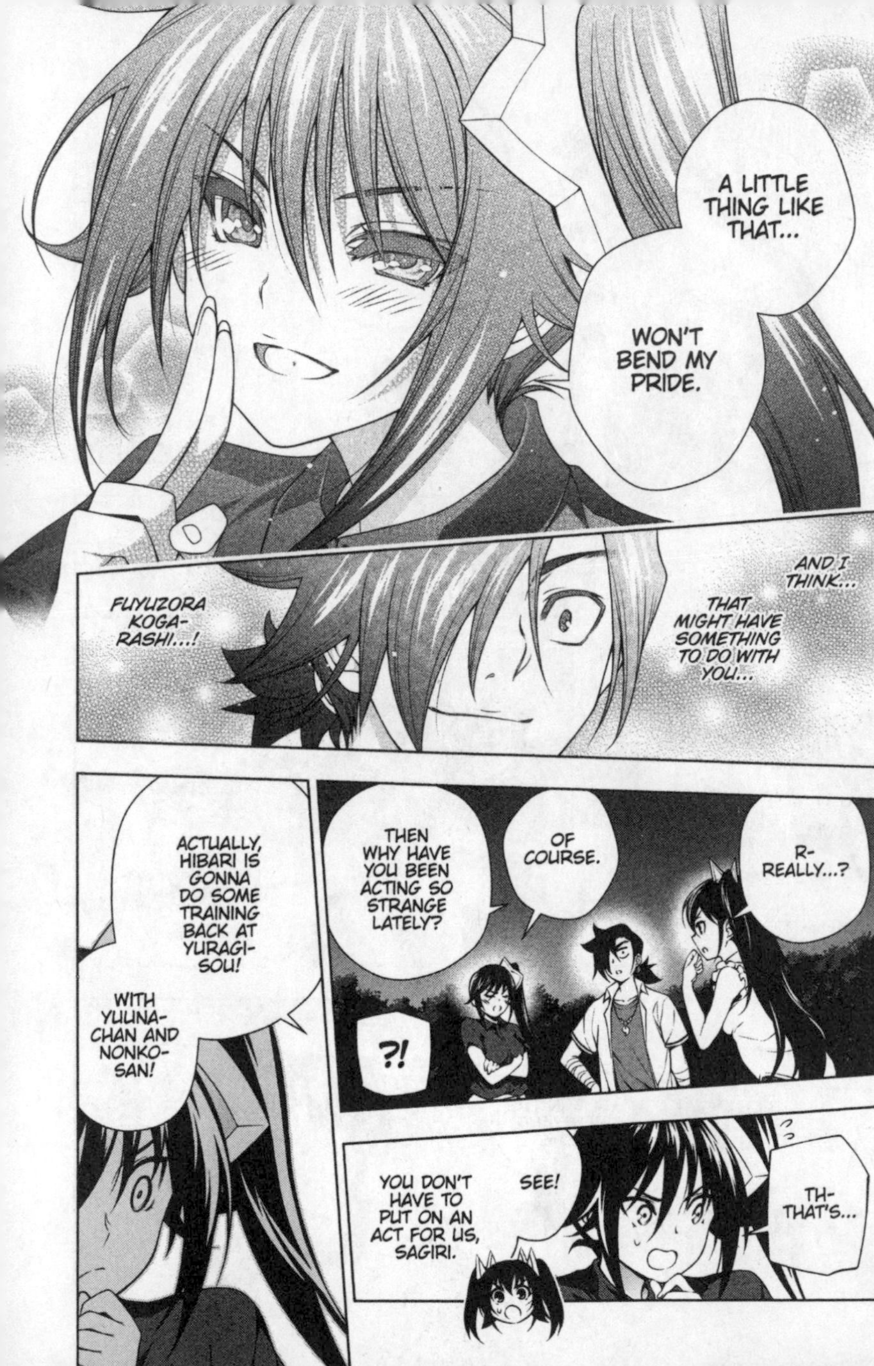
A LITTLE THING LIKE THAT...
WON'T BEND MY PRIDE.
AND I THINK...
THAT MIGHT HAVE SOMETHING TO DO WITH YOU...
FUYUZORA KOGA-RASHI...!
R-REALLY...?
OF COURSE.
THEN WHY HAVE YOU BEEN ACTING SO STRANGE LATELY?
?!
TH-THAT'S...
SEE!
YOU DON'T HAVE TO PUT ON AN ACT FOR US, SAGIRI.
ACTUALLY, HIBARI IS GONNA DO SOME TRAINING BACK AT YURAGI-SOU!
WITH YUUNA-CHAN AND NONKO-SAN!

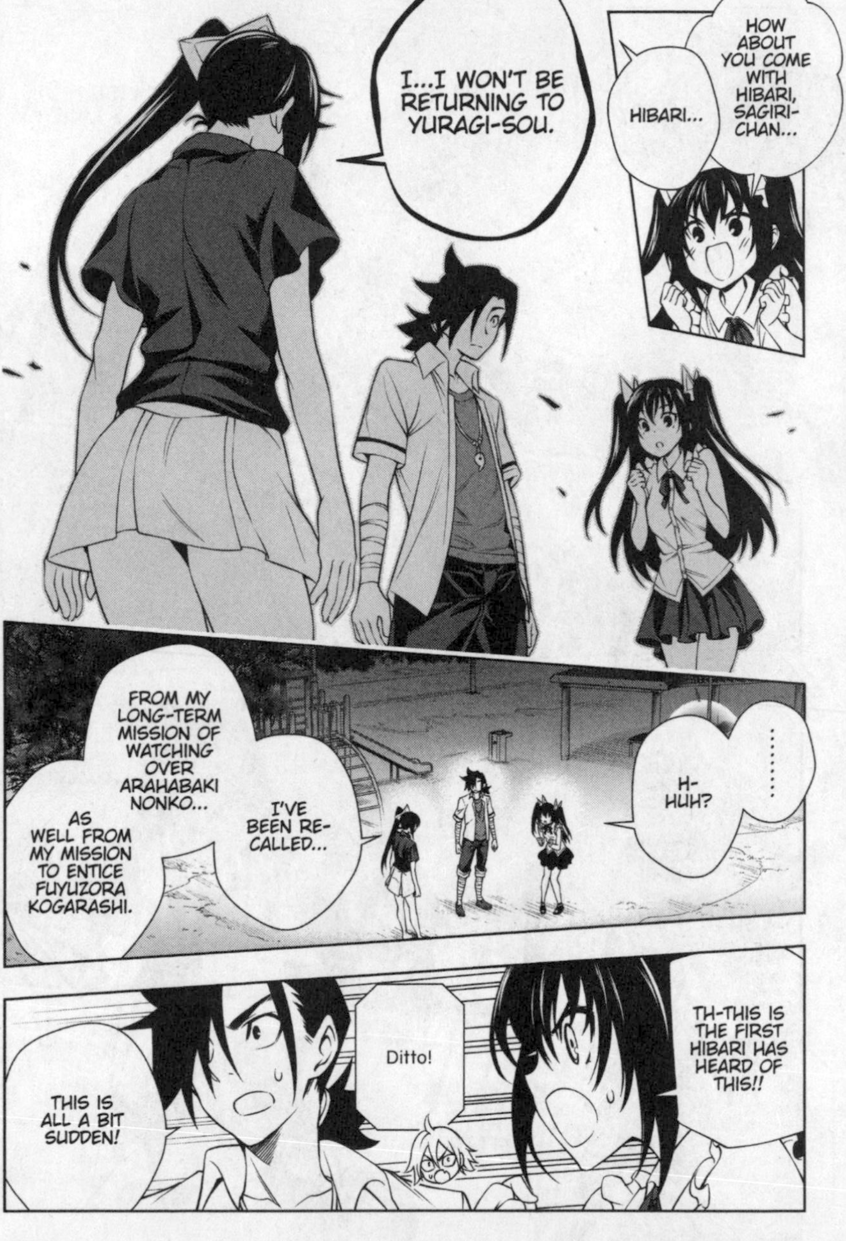
HOW ABOUT YOU COME WITH HIBARI, SAGIRI-CHAN...
HIBARI...
I...I WON'T BE RETURNING TO YURAGI-SOU.
......
H-HUH?
I'VE BEEN RE-CALLED...
FROM MY LONG-TERM MISSION OF WATCHING OVER ARAHABAKI NONKO...
AS WELL FROM MY MISSION TO ENTICE FUYUZORA KOGARASHI.
TH-THIS IS THE FIRST HIBARI HAS HEARD OF THIS!!
Ditto!
THIS IS ALL A BIT SUDDEN!

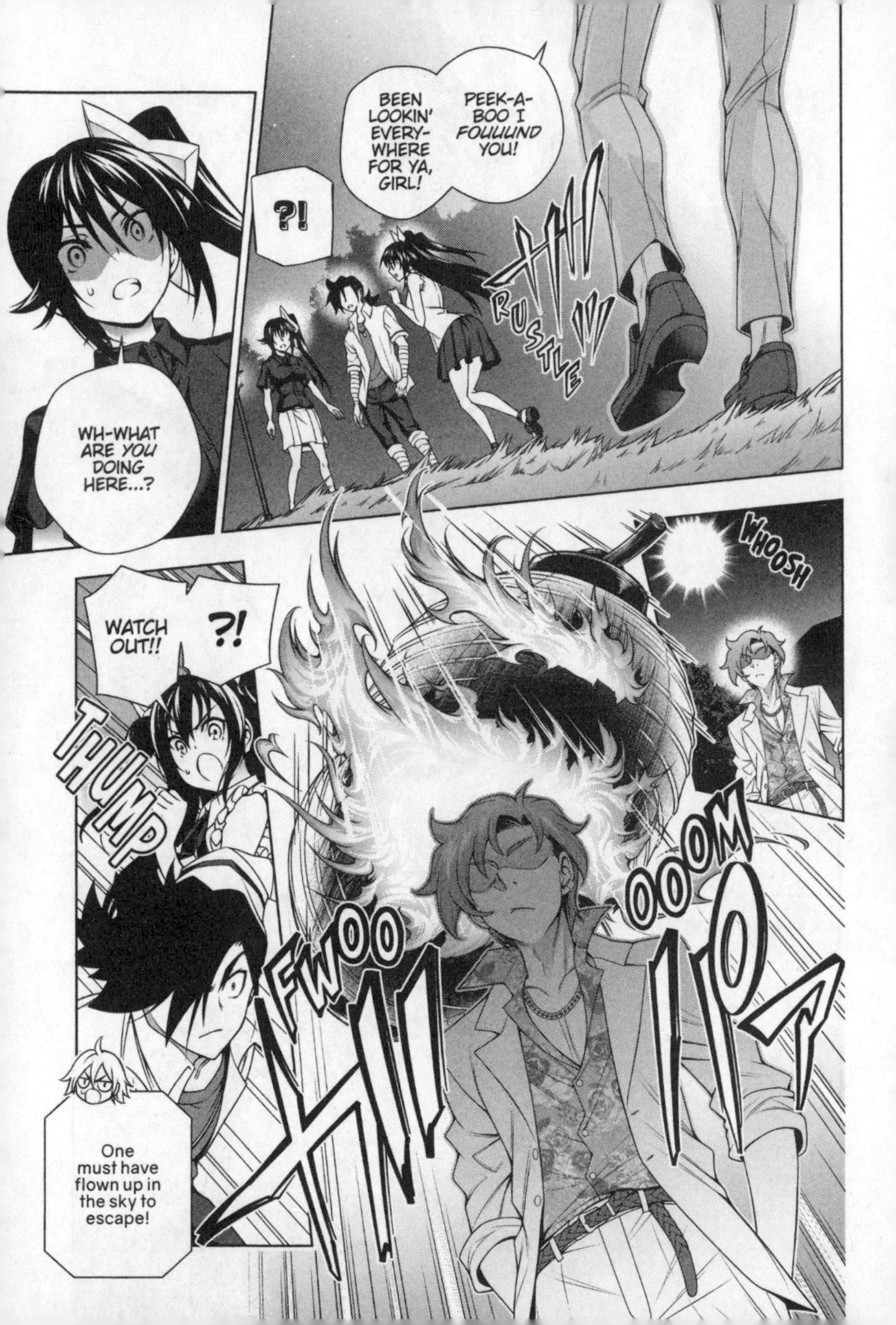
PEEK-A-BOO I FOUUUND YOU!
BEEN LOOKIN' EVERYWHERE FOR YA, GIRL!
?!
RUSTLE
WH-WHAT ARE YOU DOING HERE...?
WHOOSH
?!
WATCH OUT!!
THUMP
FWOOOOOOM
One must have flown up in the sky to escape!

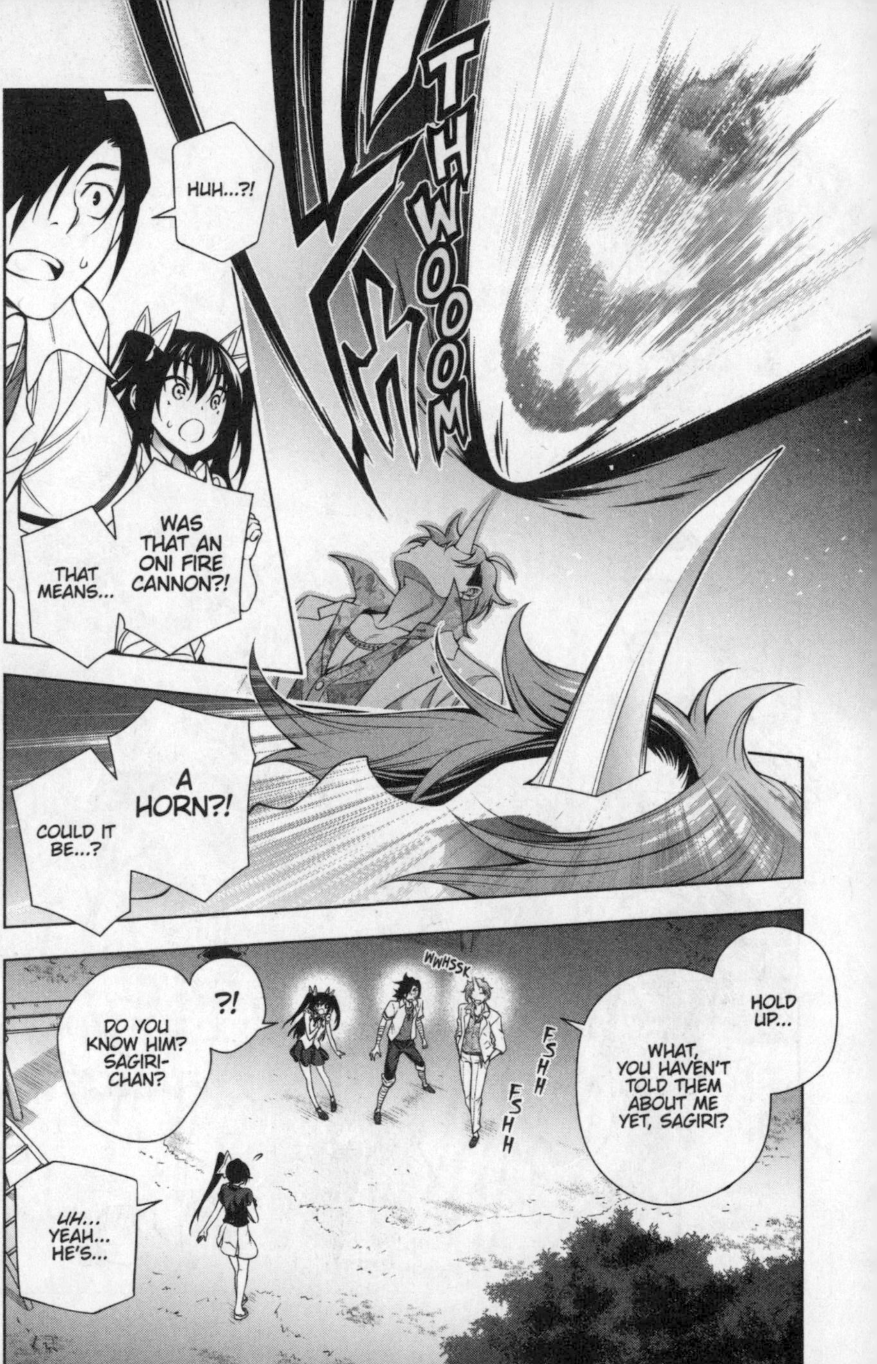
THWOOOOM
HUH...?!
WAS THAT AN ONI FIRE CANNON?!
THAT MEANS...
A HORN?!
COULD IT BE...?
HOLD UP...
WHAT, YOU HAVEN'T TOLD THEM ABOUT ME YET, SAGIRI?
FSHH
FSHH
WWHSSK
?!
DO YOU KNOW HIM? SAGIRI-CHAN?
UH... YEAH... HE'S...

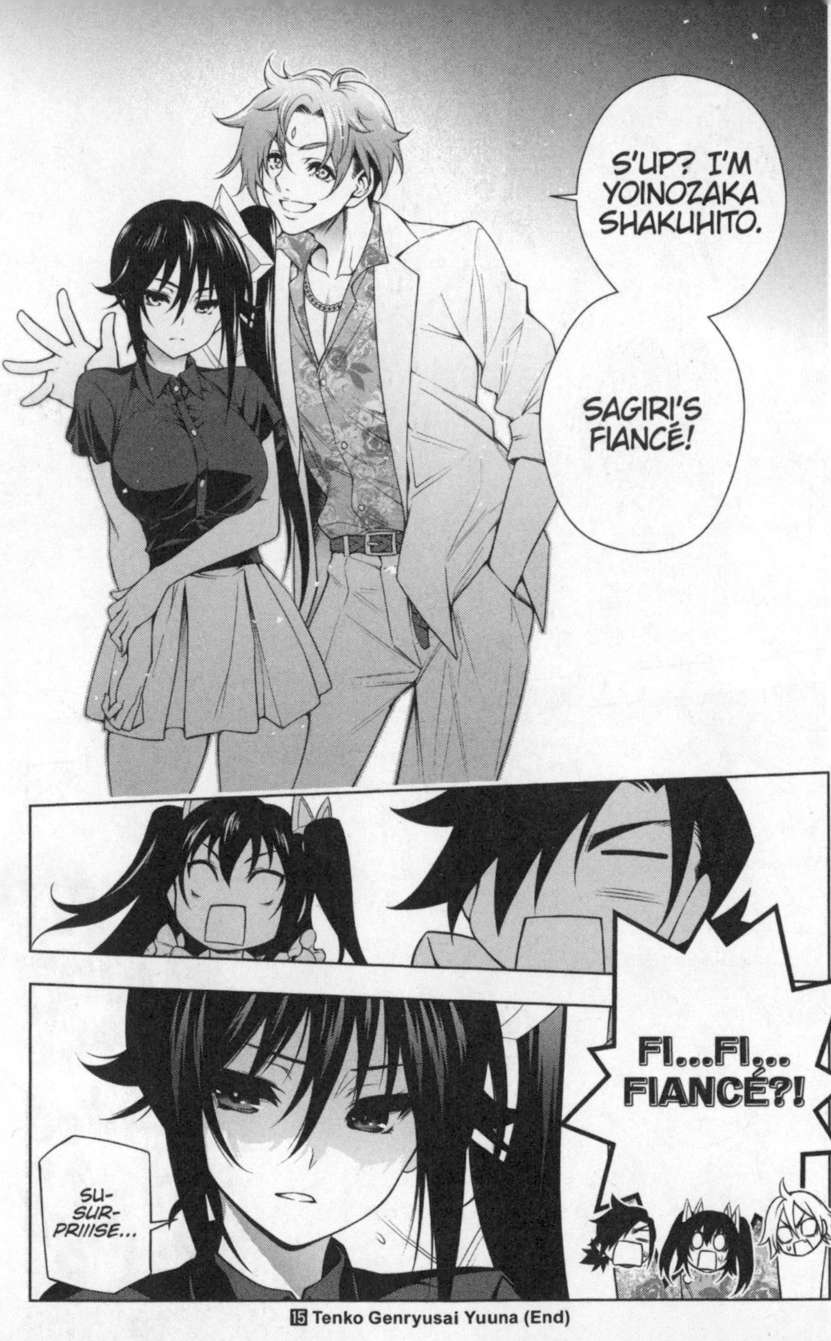
S'UP? I'M YOINOZAKA SHAKUHITO.
SAGIRI'S FIANCÉ!
FI...FI... FIANCÉ?!
SU-SUR-PRIIISE...

15 Tenko Genryusai Yuuna (End)

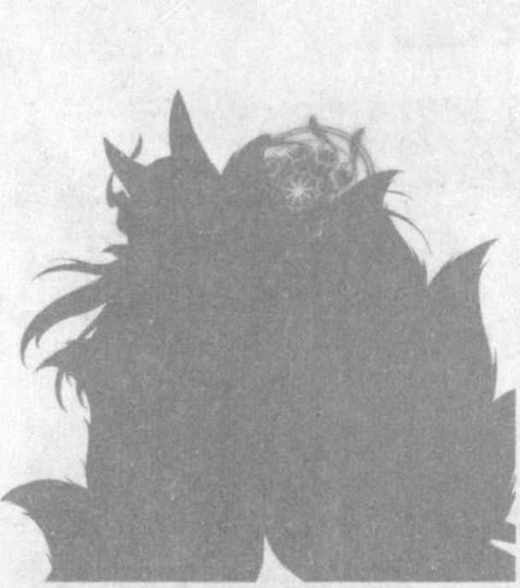

Yuuna and the Haunted Hot Springs

Extra Content Manna-san and the Haunted Hot Springs

Miura Tadahiro x Man ☆ Gatarou

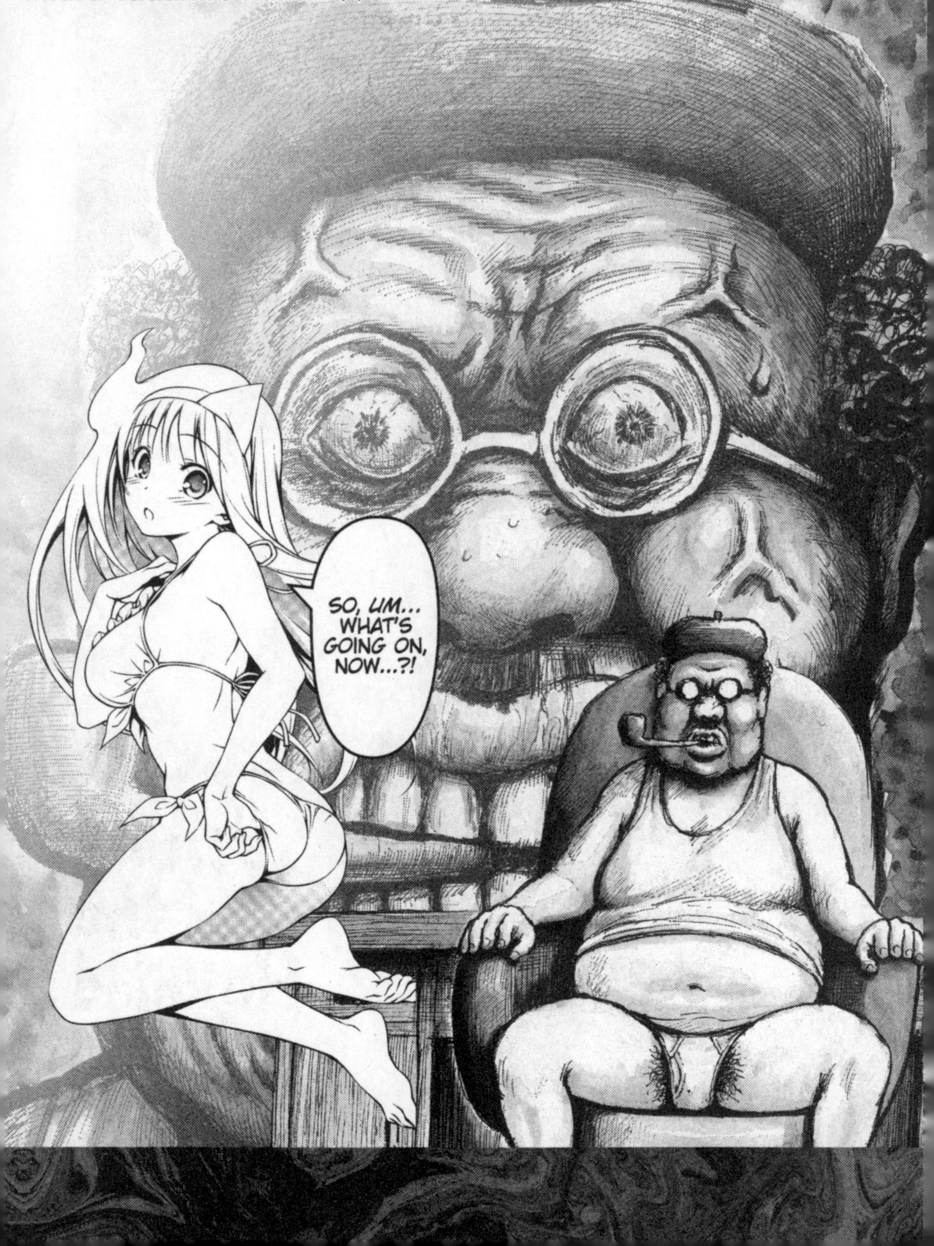
SO, UM... WHAT'S GOING ON, NOW...?!

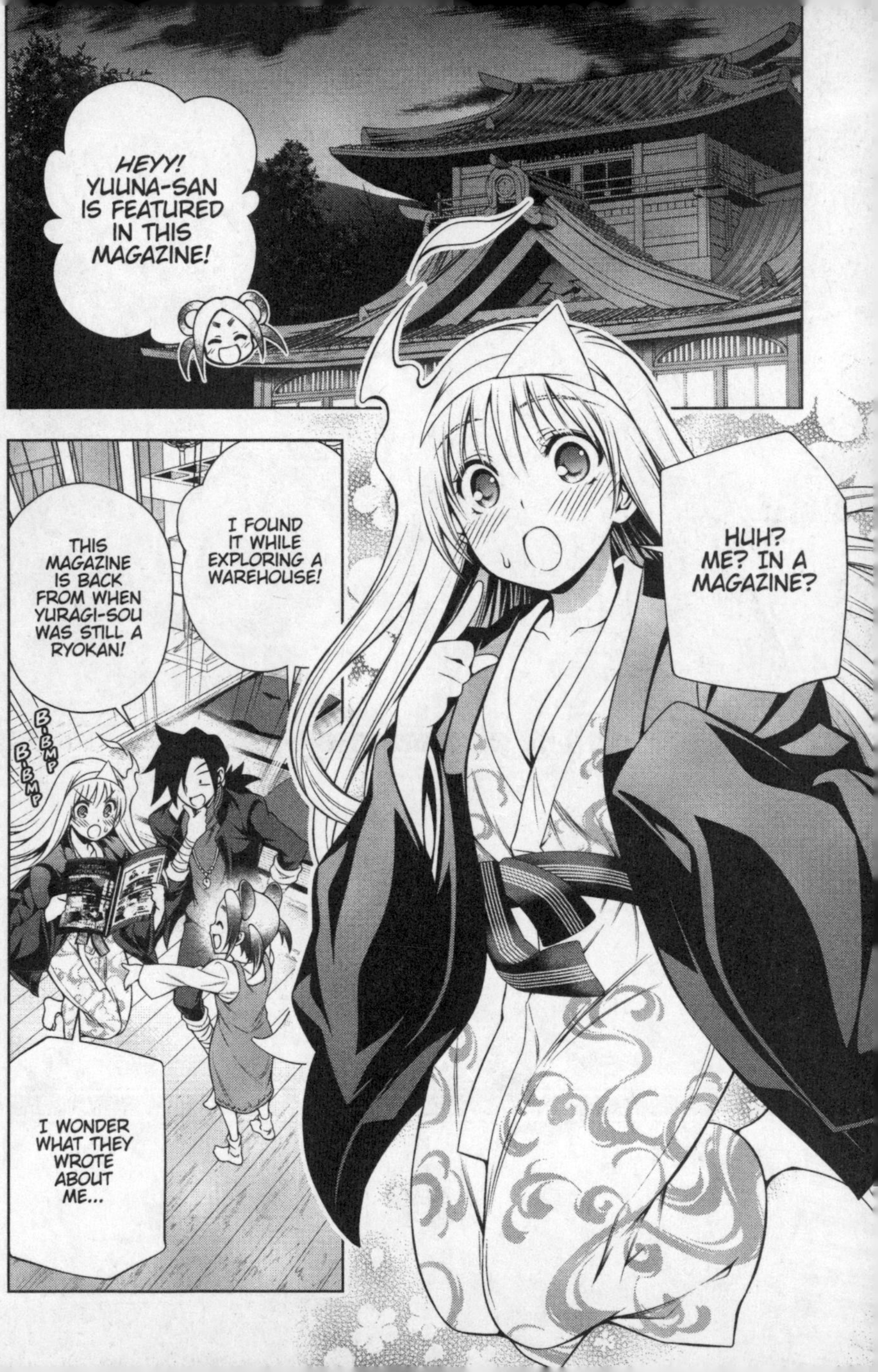
HEYY! YUUNA-SAN IS FEATURED IN THIS MAGAZINE!
HUH? ME? IN A MAGAZINE?
I FOUND IT WHILE EXPLORING A WAREHOUSE!
THIS MAGAZINE IS BACK FROM WHEN YURAGI-SOU WAS STILL A RYOKAN!
B-BMP
B-BMP
I WONDER WHAT THEY WROTE ABOUT ME...

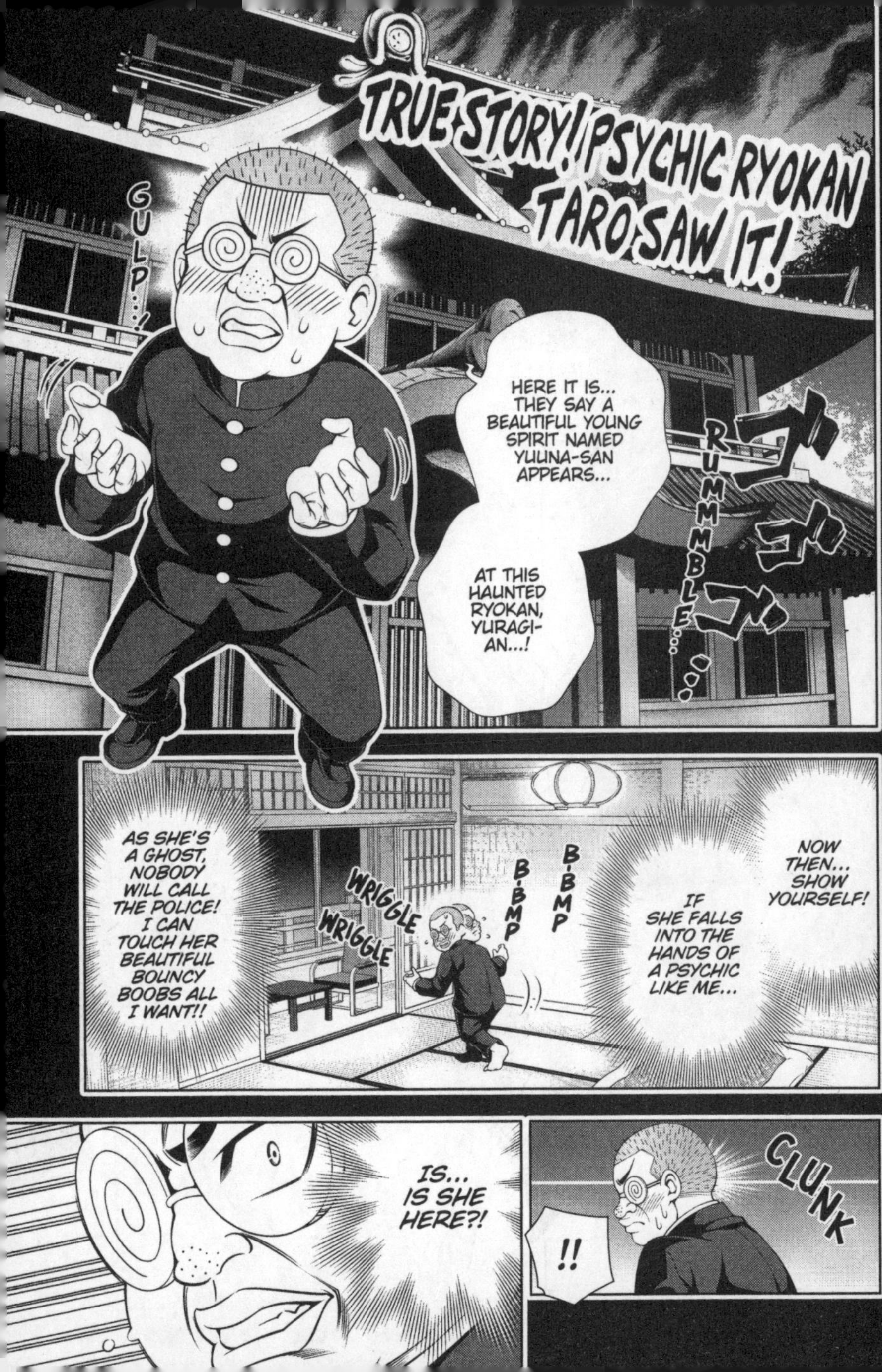
TRUE STORY! PSYCHIC RYOKAN TARO SAW IT!
RUMMMBLE...
HERE IT IS... THEY SAY A BEAUTIFUL YOUNG SPIRIT NAMED YUUNA-SAN APPEARS...
AT THIS HAUNTED RYOKAN, YURAGI-AN...!
GULP...!
NOW THEN... SHOW YOURSELF!
IF SHE FALLS INTO THE HANDS OF A PSYCHIC LIKE ME...
B-BMP
B-BMP
WRIGGLE
WRIGGLE
AS SHE'S A GHOST, NOBODY WILL CALL THE POLICE! I CAN TOUCH HER BEAUTIFUL BOUNCY BOOBS ALL I WANT!!
CLUNK
!!
IS... IS SHE HERE?!

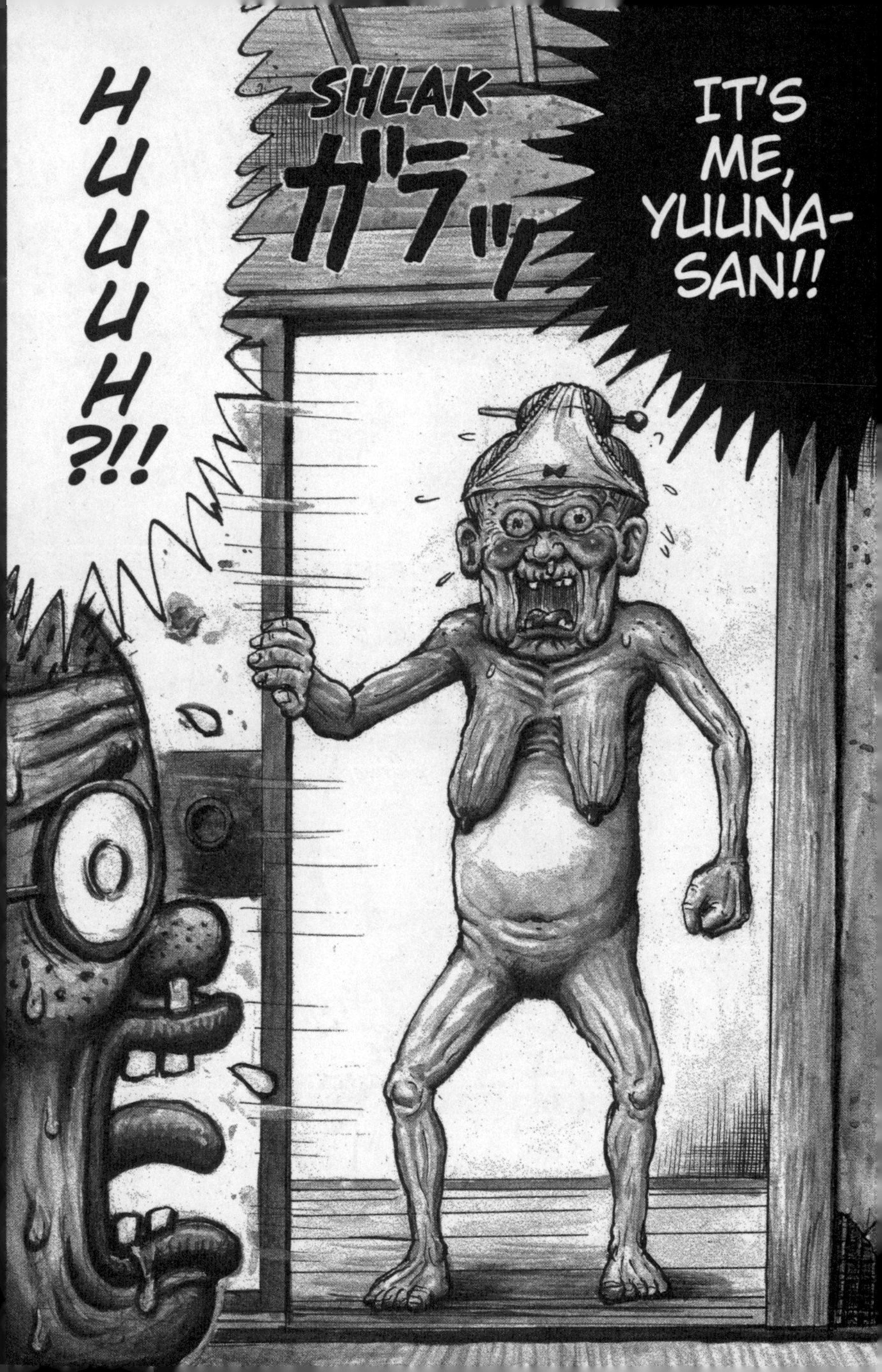
IT'S ME, YUUNA-SAN!!
SHLAK
ガラッ
HUUUUH?!!

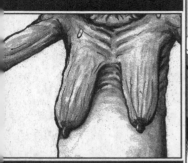

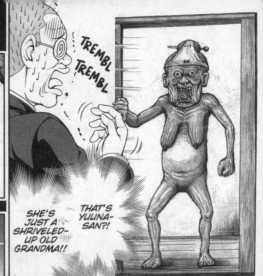

TREMBL
TREMBL
THAT'S YUUNA-SAN?!
SHE'S JUST A SHRIVELED-UP OLD GRANDMA!!
BUT EVEN GRANDMAS... HAVE BOOBS...
GIVEN HOW THEY'RE SAGGING...
THEY MUST'VE BEEN MASSIVE MELONS BACK IN THE DAY.
HM? MAYBE THEY WON'T BE...
SO BAD?!
SHQUEEZE
SHQUEEZE
B-BMP
B-BMP

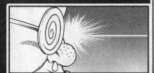

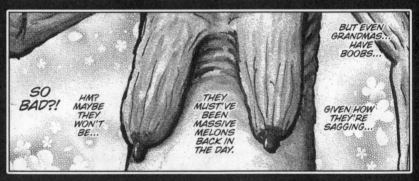

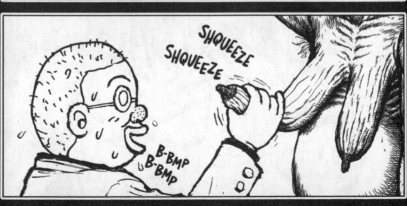

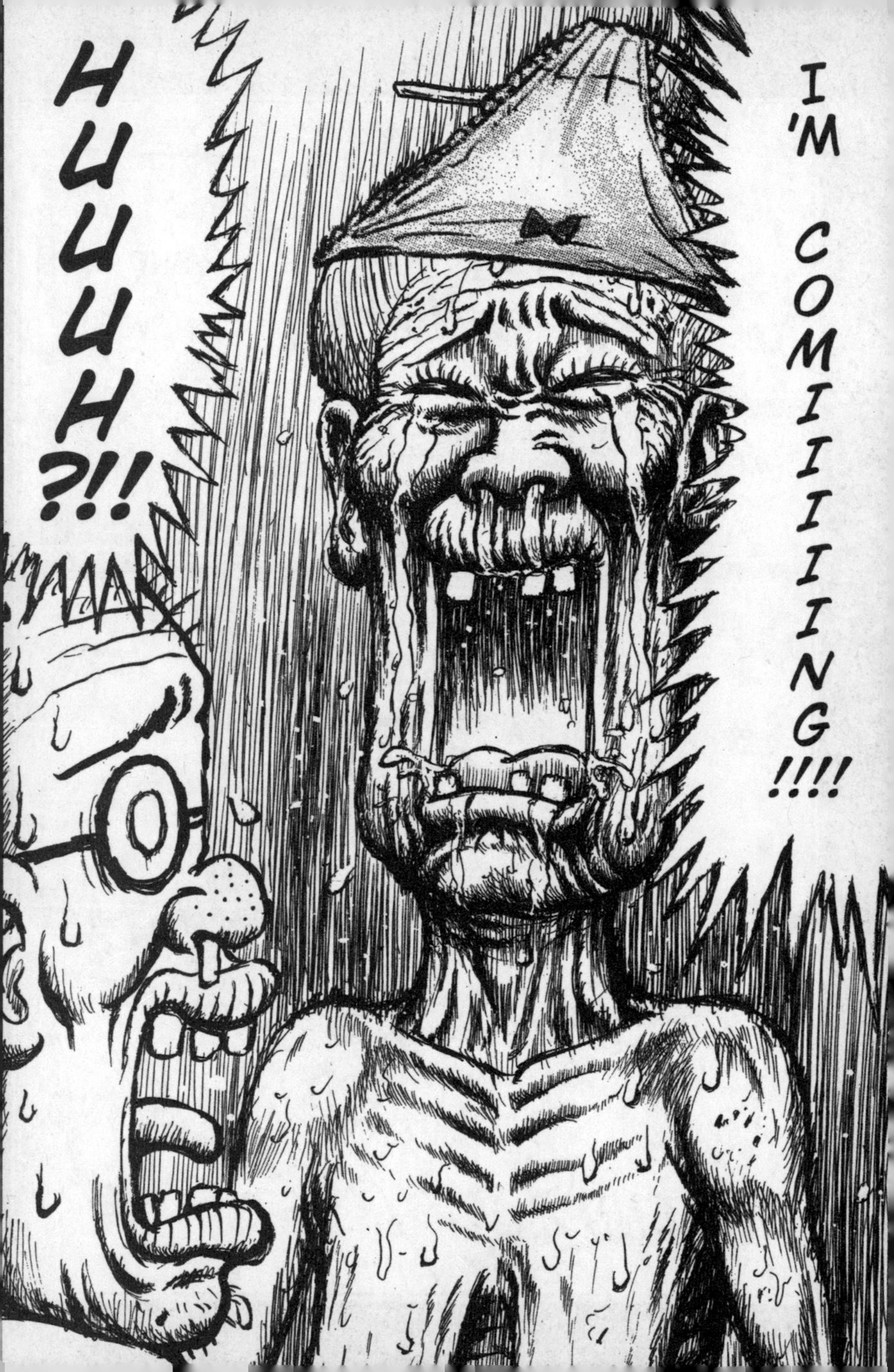

I'M COMIIIIING!!!!
HUUUH?!!

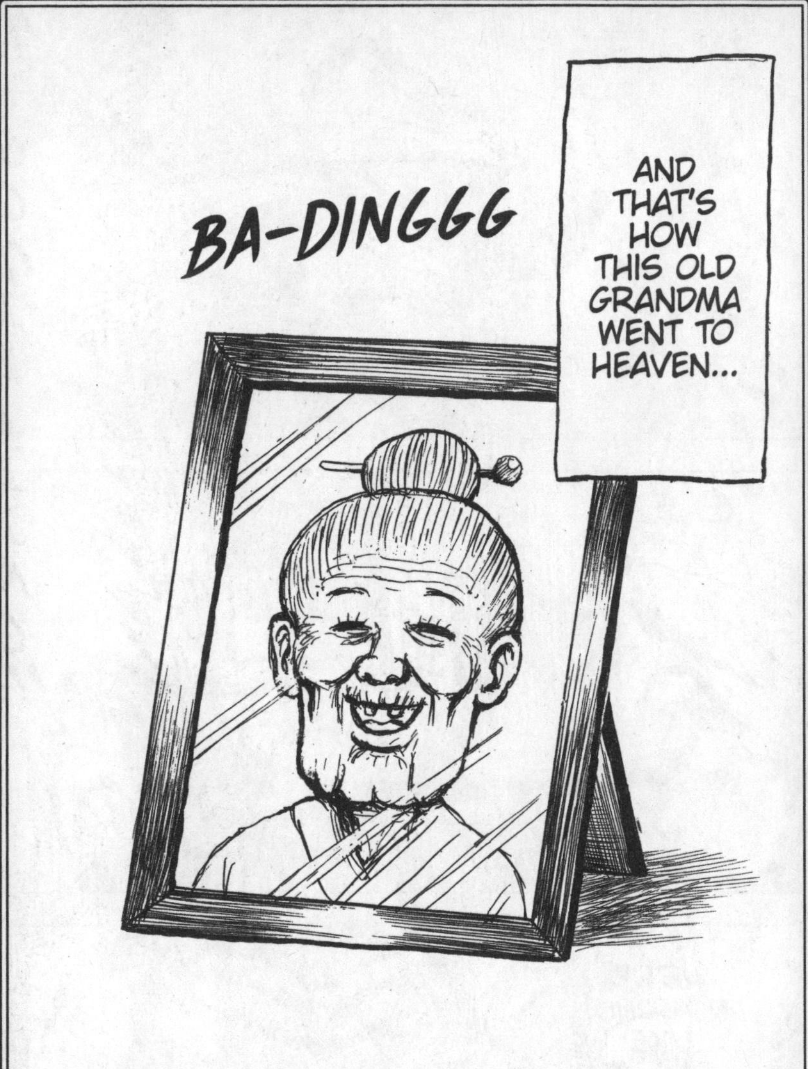
AND THAT'S HOW THIS OLD GRANDMA WENT TO HEAVEN...
BA-DINGGG
THE END

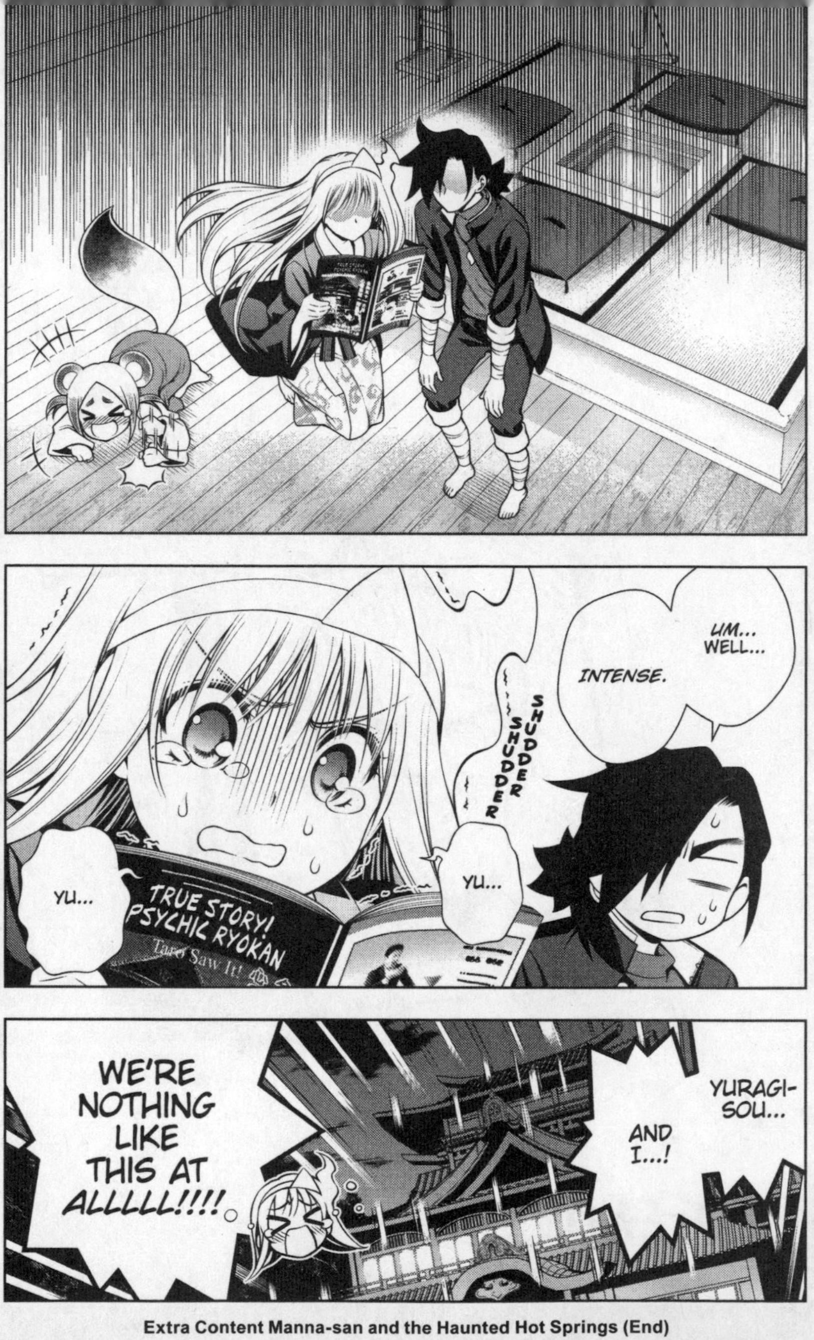
UM... WELL...
INTENSE.
SHUDDER SHUDDER
YU...
YU...
TRUE STORY! PSYCHIC RYOKAN
Taro Saw It!
YURAGI-SOU...
AND I...!
WE'RE NOTHING LIKE THIS AT ALLLLL!!!!

Extra Content Manna-san and the Haunted Hot Springs (End)

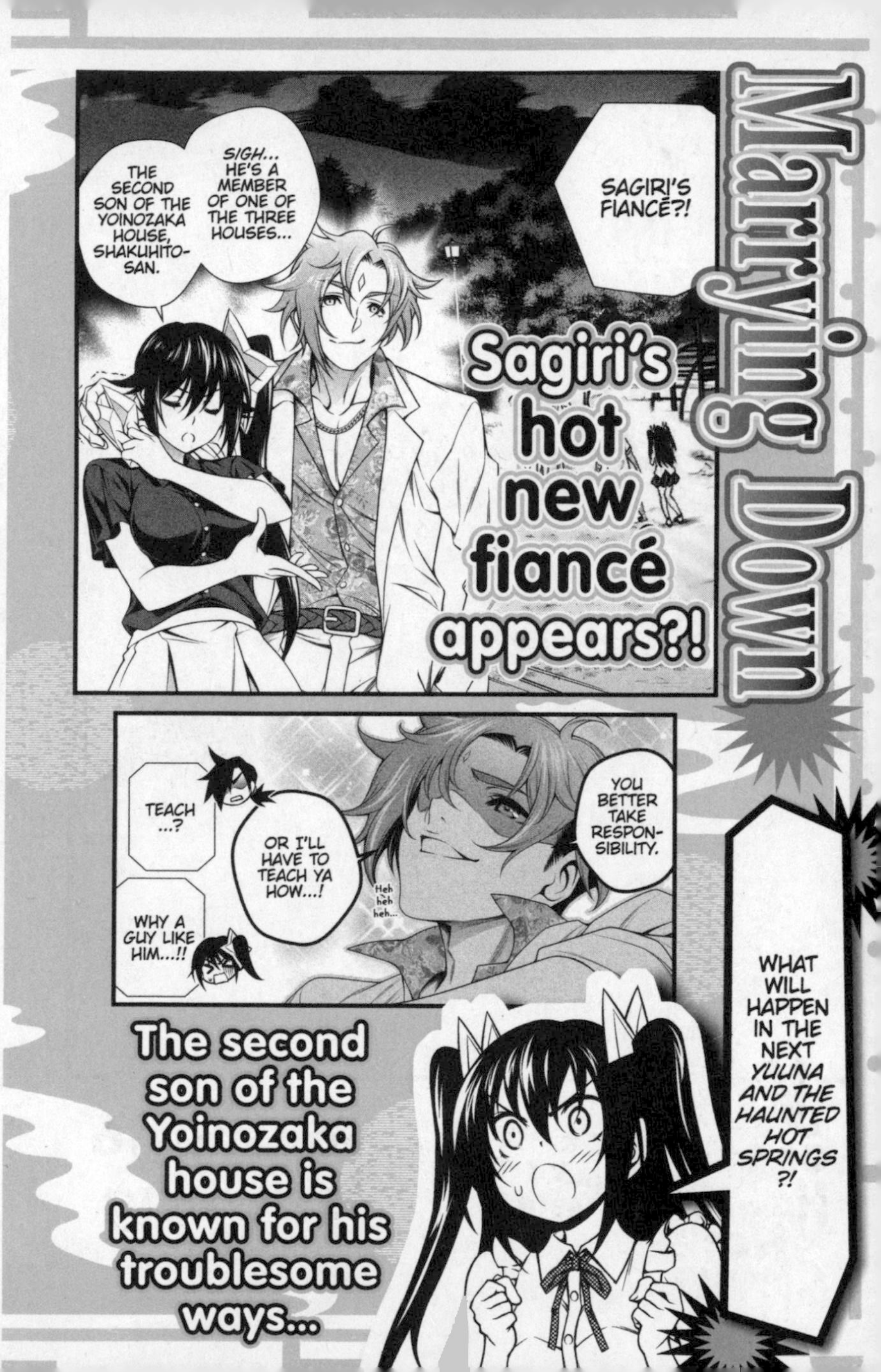
Marrying Down
SAGIRI'S FIANCÉ?!
SIGH... HE'S A MEMBER OF ONE OF THE THREE HOUSES...
THE SECOND SON OF THE YOINOZAKA HOUSE, SHAKUHITO-SAN.
Sagiri's hot new fiancé appears?!
YOU BETTER TAKE RESPON-SIBILITY.
OR I'LL HAVE TO TEACH YA HOW...!
Heh heh heh...
TEACH ...?
WHY A GUY LIKE HIM...!!
WHAT WILL HAPPEN IN THE NEXT *YUUNA AND THE HAUNTED HOT SPRINGS* ?!
The second son of the Yoinozaka house is known for his troublesome ways...

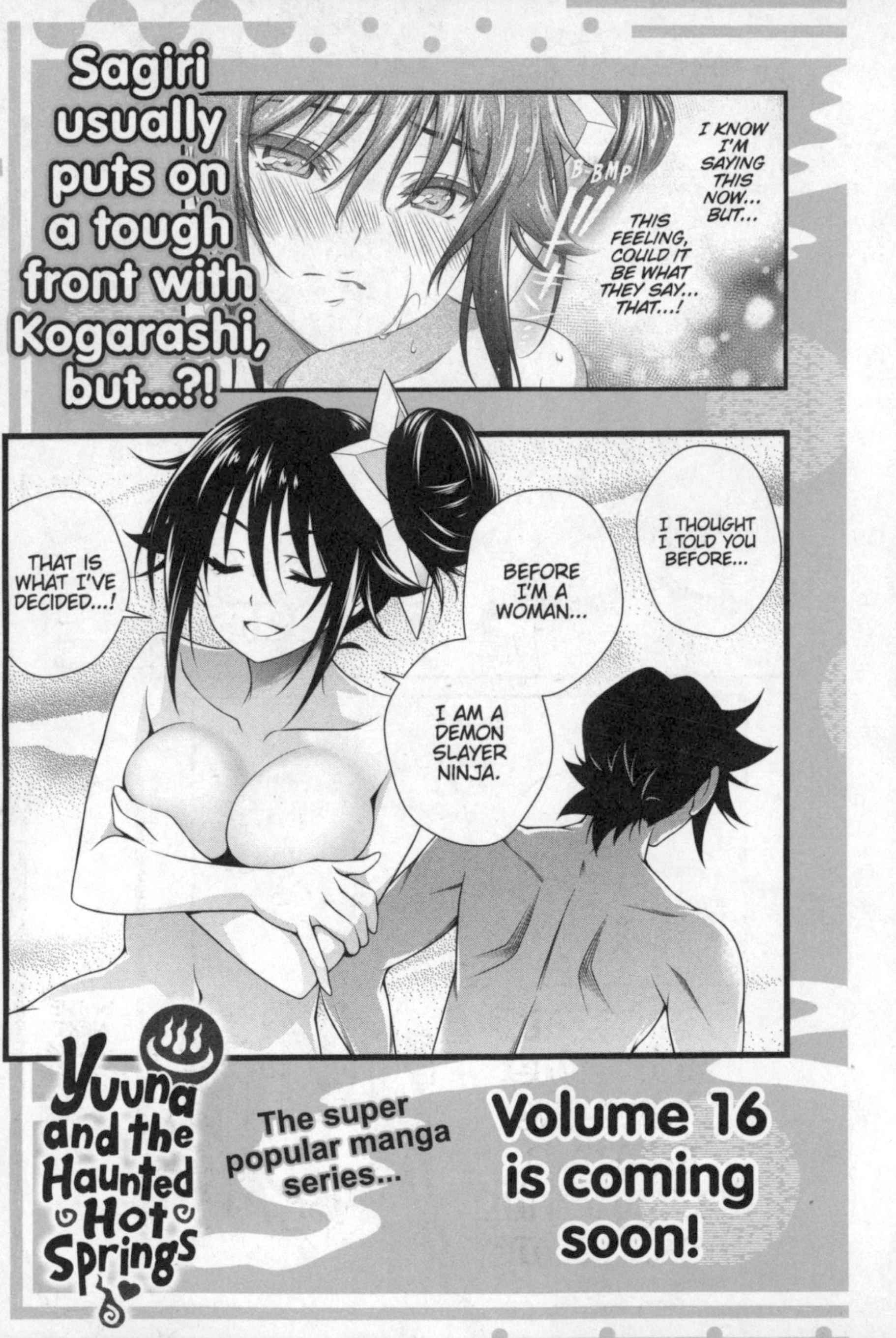
Sagiri usually puts on a tough front with Kogarashi, but...?!
I KNOW I'M SAYING THIS NOW... BUT...
B-BMP
THIS FEELING, COULD IT BE WHAT THEY SAY... THAT...!
I THOUGHT I TOLD YOU BEFORE...
BEFORE I'M A WOMAN...
I AM A DEMON SLAYER NINJA.
THAT IS WHAT I'VE DECIDED...!
Yuuna and the Haunted Hot Springs
The super popular manga series...
Volume 16 is coming soon!

SEVEN SEAS' GHOST SHIP PRESENTS

Yuuna and the Haunted Hot Springs

VOL.15

story and art by TADAHIRO MIURA

TRANSLATION
Thomas Zimmerman

ADAPTATION
David Lumsdon

LETTERING AND RETOUCH
Phil Christie

COVER DESIGN
Nicky Lim
(LOGO) Hanase Qi

PROOFREADER
Kurestin Armada, Dawn Davis

EDITOR
Nick Mamatas

PREPRESS TECHNICIAN
Rhiannon Rasmussen-Silverstein

PRODUCTION MANAGER
Lissa Pattillo, George Panella (GHOST SHIP)

MANAGING EDITOR
Julie Davis

ASSOCIATE PUBLISHER
Adam Arnold

PUBLISHER
Jason DeAngelis

Seven Seas press and purchase enquiries can be sent to Marketing Manager
Lianne Sentar at press@gomanga.com. Information regarding the distribution
and purchase of digital editions is available from Digital Manager CK Russell
at digital@gomanga.com.

Seven Seas, Ghost Ship, and their accompanying logos are trademarks of
Seven Seas Entertainment. All rights reserved.

ISBN: 978-1-64827-489-3

Printed in Canada

First Printing: September 2021

10 9 8 7 6 5 4 3 2 1

FOLLOW US ONLINE: www.ghostshipmanga.com

READING DIRECTIONS

This book reads from *right to left*, Japanese style.
If this is your first time reading manga, you start
reading from the top right panel on each page and
take it from there. If you get lost, just follow the
numbered diagram here. It may seem backwards at
first, but you'll get the hang of it! Have fun!!

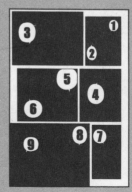